A HANDBOOK TO POLITICAL QUESTIONS OF THE DAY AND THE ARGUMENTS ON EITHER SIDE

A HANDBOOK TO POLITICAL QUESTIONS OF THE DAY AND THE ARGUMENTS ON EITHER SIDE

WITH AN INTRODUCTION

SYDNEY BUXTON

GYAN

Published by

GYAN

Gyan Publishing House
5, Ansari Road
Daryaganj, New Delhi-110002
Phone: 011-47034999, 9811692060
E-mail: books@gyanbooks.com

Distribution Network
gyanbooks.com
India, USA, Canada, UK, Australia

ISBN: 978-93-7447-013-8 (PB)

First Published, 1903

2nd Impression 2026

Printed at: Gyan Press, Delhi.

A HANDBOOK TO POLITICAL QUESTIONS OF THE DAY AND THE ARGUMENTS ON EITHER SIDE
Author: SYDNEY BUXTON

A HANDBOOK TO

POLITICAL QUESTIONS OF THE DAY

AND THE ARGUMENTS ON EITHER SIDE

WITH AN INTRODUCTION

By SYDNEY BUXTON, M.P.

ELEVENTH EDITION

LONDON
JOHN MURRAY, ALBEMARLE STREET
1903

PREFACE TO THE ELEVENTH EDITION.

THIS Handbook has been out of print for some years, but distaste to the unattractiveness of revision has delayed the preparation of a fresh edition.

However, as the demand for the book continues, it seems well that a new edition should be issued.

All the sections which appeared in the last edition have been carefully revised, and in some cases rewritten. Some new subjects have been added, notably the sections on "Preference," "Protection," and "Retaliation," which in former editions were somewhat perfunctorily lumped together into one short section.

In order to find space for new matter, some few subjects which appeared in the last edition, but which seem now to be of less urgency or importance, have been omitted.

The object of this Handbook is to give all the important arguments that can be, or are, advanced on either side on various political questions. In this I have endeavoured to be perfectly impartial. It is probable, however, that I have fallen short of entire impartiality; and no doubt some arguments have been overlooked.

It was in no way the object of this book, as some

seem to have supposed, to point out which arguments are weighty which worthless, which are sound and which unsound, nor to arrange the arguments in the order of their importance. Its existence will, I hope, have been justified, if it has been of any practical use to the public; and if, by showing how much sound argument can usually be urged on the "other side of the question," it has, in any degree, taught toleration.

This book is confined to questions of Home Policy, and it has been often my desire, especially of late, to add a second volume, dealing on the same lines with questions of Foreign, Colonial, and Indian policy. But while an essay might be written on each question, or phase of the question that arises under these three heads, I have not found it practicable to bring them into the compass of numbered arguments on each side.

My cordial thanks are due to friends and critics for the kind way in which they have received this work, and also for valuable suggestions towards its improvement.

I am often asked by my readers to say what is the most useful historical summary of political events. To my mind, Acland's and Ransome's little "*Handbook of the Political History of England*" (Longmans), best fulfils the qualification.

SYDNEY BUXTON.

7 Grosvenor Crescent,
October, 1903.

CONTENTS

INTRODUCTION

We are in this country fortunate enough to possess a system of party government, which, while it divides the political life of Great Britain into two or more parties, and gives rise to angry argument and heated discussion, does not degenerate into animosity. There is, consequently, nothing to prevent men of opposite modes of thought from remaining on amicable and intimate terms, or even from discussing temperately the questions on which they differ.

The reasons for the general absence of personal animosity between the rival political parties are not far to seek. In the first place, there is no diversity of opinion on the general question of the form of government best adapted for the country. Though the various Estates of the Realm, which together make up the body politic, may struggle for power and for influence, and from time to time may vary in constitution, it is taken for granted that a Sovereign who reigns but does not govern, is for us the best Head of the State. The country is thus saved from any agitation and intrigue having for its object a change of Dynasty, or the institution of a Republic; and there is no Pretender caballing against the occupant of the throne. The Sovereign, and the supporters of the existing form of government, have no need, therefore, to be constantly engaged in attempting to crush or paralyse the Opposition in order to preserve their own power, or office; to save themselves from exile, imprisonment, perhaps even death. The Opposition, on their part, are not tempted to engage in secret plotting, to which they would be certain to descend, if the despairing conviction were forced upon them, that their only hope of participating in the government of the country, was by a complete upheaval and reversal of the existing state of things.

Then, again, there is no hopelessness in English politics. Though, from time to time, one of the two great parties in the State has been forced to linger for many a weary year in the cold shade of opposition, while the other has been enjoying the sweets of office and the fruits of victory, a turn of fortune's wheel has always come, sooner or later; the minority has converted itself into a majority, ousted the Government, and taken its seat on the Treasury bench. The party in opposition has the ever-present consciousness that within three or four, or at most six years, it will of necessity have an opportunity of appealing to the intellect, to the interests, or to the passions of the nation. The sanguine expectation of future success which animates politicians, whilst it keeps alive a knowledge of, and an interest in politics, and prevents the defeated party from descending to violence or intrigue, has also, in Parliament and out, a powerful moderating influence on the Opposition. They are aware that, at any moment, they may be called upon to undertake the responsibilities and the cares of office.

Thus party contest, while occasionally effervescing and bubbling over unpleasantly, is honest, sober, and sedate at bottom, and mostly kept within reasonable bounds.

On the other hand, the historic past of the two great Parties, the genuine divergence of opinion and principle, the real interest which is taken in matters of policy and of politics, are sufficient to keep alive a rivalry between them in its best and highest form, and to prevent it from degenerating into a mere conflict between the "ins" and the "outs." Other countries—more especially, perhaps, some of our own Colonies—point the moral for us, that where no traditional or fundamental difference of opinion or principle exists, party politics cannot flourish in an entirely satisfactory form. Without such, politics tend to fall to the low level of personal strife, desire for place, the pitting of class against class—ignoble aims and sordid aspirations.

England is not likely to fall on such evil days. Even when the particular questions which now dominate English politics have been laid to rest, there will yet remain, or there will arise, many great questions of national importance, involving principles and details on which the two parties conscientiously differ. Moreover, we may well believe that, with an Empire such as ours, when the questions of the immediate present, and those looming large in the distance, have been settled, others of equal moment will come to the fore.

Party government, as it exists amongst us, possesses this further incidental advantage, that each side is interested in the orderliness and intelligence of the other, whilst the country itself is almost as vitally concerned in the conduct of the Opposition as in that of the Government.

The stronger and more capable the Opposition—with due regard to the existence of a proper working majority on the Ministerial side—the better, more thorough, and lasting will be the work and legislation of the Government. A weak, lazy, or stupid Opposition cannot exercise half the influence for good, either within or without the House, that will be exercised by one vigilant and strong. A Government which has to bear the brunt of intelligent, searching, and able criticism, will have a great additional inducement to propose well thought-out plans, high principled schemes, and measures which will commend themselves to the nation at large as well as to the Ministerialists.

Moreover, a well commanded, well drilled, and united Opposition will be less of a hindrance to the proper legislation of the Government, than one which is broken up into factions, has little respect for itself, and less regard for the dignity of the House. An Opposition such as this not only unreasonably delays the business of the nation, but brings discredit on itself and on the House of Commons.

In order to obtain an intelligent Opposition as well as a strong Government, the electors must be able to discriminate between the different parties, and to weigh the merits of different candidates. They must examine for themselves, as best they can, each political question as it arises, so that—though they may not perhaps be able to make a very profound study of the situation—they may look at it from an intelligent and common-sense point of view, and cast their votes on the side which seems to them to be most in the right, and which, for the time being, appears to be most likely to promote the welfare of the country.

It cannot be to the interest of either party to veil the truth from the elector, or to keep him in darkness and ignorance. On the one hand, the Liberals may, and doubtless do, imagine that it is to their special interest that light should be shed, intelligence awakened, ignorance dispelled, and knowledge increased. They believe, or ought to believe, so firmly in the truth and vitality of their principles, as to be convinced that, the more these are studied and understood, the wider and more lasting will be their influence. Indeed, if they do not hold this faith, they are either hypocrites, false to their political creed, or meaningless repeaters of parrot cries.

But, on the other hand, the Conservatives must have the same implicit belief in the truth, justice, and eternity of the principles which they profess; and if they are convinced of the righteousness of their cause, they must rejoice to see just intelligence awakened and increased. They also must feel that the more capable a man is of thinking and understanding, the more will the doctrines in which they believe be acceptable and accepted by him.

If, then, it be allowed by the advocates of both parties —as it surely must be—that increased knowledge is an advantage; and if they hold—as they surely must—that the arguments advanced by their own side outweigh those which can be urged by the other, neither can shrink from the test of having these arguments placed fairly side by side, for both must be convinced that the mind of the intelligent and unprejudiced inquirer will incline towards their own creed.

Unfortunately—though the fact may not be without compensatory advantages—men are far too apt to make up their minds that they are in the right in thinking this or that, simply and solely because somebody else thinks it, or has thought it. Such men, no doubt, are not troubled with many qualms of conscience, but wrap themselves up in the impenetrable cloak of unthinking deference to authority of opinion, and, whilst professing to be open to conviction, stubbornly refuse to see that there can possibly be more than one side to a question.

Those, however, who take the trouble to examine both sides carefully, will be ready to admit the force of opposing arguments; and, when they have weighed them well, and after anxious doubt and laborious thought have made up their minds, they will feel that with themselves at least the stronger arguments have prevailed, and that their convictions are founded on truth and justice.

In no case can a man of intelligence allow himself to

remain for ever doubting and hesitating; right or wrong, he finds he must range himself on one side or the other; and the step once taken, his opinions naturally become stronger and stronger, he becomes more and more convinced that his party is in the right. It is well that this should be so, for without an instinctive inclination to believe in the truth of one's opinions, the mind would be enveloped in a mist of doubt, party government would be impossible, and politics would remain a chaos without form and void. "Very few," as Hartley Coleridge said, "can comprehend the whole truth; and it much concerns the general interest that every portion of that truth should have interested and passionate advocates."

There exists, however, a class of men—a very large class—who knowing nothing and caring less about politics, are politically everything by turns and nothing long; and who, unfortunately, make up in many constituencies the margin of voters who turn the scale of the election. These are the men whose wavering conviction opposing candidates must make it their business to arrest, by plying them with every argument that can fairly be urged, with the hope that one at least may strike home.

The spread of education, of newspapers and of literature, the increased means of communication and of locomotion, are gradually decreasing the numbers of this neutral host; and no efforts should be spared on our part in enticing as many as we can of the soldiers composing this body to come over to us, and in ourselves enlisting recruits who would otherwise join its ranks. This army consists of men of all conditions in life, men of all degrees of knowledge, intelligence and capacity; a part of it is distinctly mercenary. The more it can be reduced in numbers the less will be experienced the tremendous reverses of electoral fortune which have been seen of late years. Reverses which have been caused chiefly by a sudden whim, pique, fear, or hope, seizing this usually impassive body of men, and causing them to desert the side which they formerly supported, and to support the side which they had before opposed.

The sin which most besets party politics consists in this, that prejudice and passion too frequently warp the feeling and conduct of politicians.

In order to convince themselves that they are in the right, men are often led to speak ill of opponents in their public capacity, in a way which they would never think of doing, or dare to do, in the private relations of life. It is folly itself to impute to the other side motives which clearly would never actuate them as individuals; and while arrogating to one's own party all virtue, infallibility, and prophetic foresight, to ascribe to his opponents political vice, stupid fallibility, and insane shortsightedness.

The difference between the principles held by Liberals and those held by Conservatives is not, except under the influence of excitement, asserted by either side to be the difference between right and wrong. It is frankly acknowledged to be but a conflicting idea, or a dissimilar point of view; a belief on the one side in the beneficial results of action, on the other a dread of the evil results of great changes—the whole tempered by the personal equation of the individual, by the constitutional difference of feeling and thought. The principles advanced by the two parties cannot be reconciled, and may differ almost fundamentally; but they are, after all, founded on the same basis of supposed right, and the conception and realisation of them is but a matter of degree. Every Englishman, whether he be Whig or Tory, Unionist or Home Ruler, Conservative, Liberal, or Radical, is actuated more or less by the same motives, though the conduct of one man may be governed by feelings and passions which another does not hold and cannot appreciate.

Even where it is evident that a man is personally interested in opposing a reform, we ought, before levelling insinuations against his good faith, to look around, and to see whether those who are supporting the measure are wholly free from personal bias, and are not themselves actuated by personal or sinister interests of their own.

Toleration, indeed, in its largest sense, ought always to actuate public leaders as well as the rank and file, in word, action, and legislation. And the more it is recognised that on the merits of every question a great deal can be honestly urged from the opposite point of view, and that in many cases both opposer and supporter have right on their side, the more widely, one may hope, will political forbearance and consideration prevail.

But, though toleration should always be practised, and mutual recrimination, misrepresentation and abuse always avoided; we ought, at the same time, never to forget that there are cases in which, as Burke once said, "Temper is the state of mind suited to the occasion." Wrong is wrong, and right is right. There are evils that may not be patiently endured; and, in spite of all we nowadays hear of the heat to which political feeling has risen, I am myself inclined to believe that we have among us too much of that lukewarm indifferentism which believes that there is nothing new, and nothing true, and that nothing matters very much.

HAND-BOOK TO POLITICAL QUESTIONS

REFORM

Before the Reform Act of 1832, the number of nomination seats was enormous. It was computed that 175 members were actually returned by 89 peers, while 100 others obtained their seats through the influence of 66 members of the House of Commons, and the Government of the day could itself command 7 seats. In some boroughs there were practically no electors.

The "first" Reform Act, introduced by Lord Grey's Government in 1831, was passed in 1832. Its main provisions: (i.) Simplified and unified the existing franchises, which were so complicated, that in boroughs alone there were no less than twenty-five different qualifications, extending very low down on the one hand, and being very much restricted on the other. This simplification was accomplished (to use general terms) by reducing the franchise in boroughs to an uniform £10 household, and in counties to a £10 freehold and copyhold, and a £50 leasehold qualification. By these means about half a million of electors were added to the register. (ii.) Disfranchised all boroughs containing less than 2000 inhabitants, 56 in number; semi-disfranchised 30 other boroughs of less than 4000 inhabitants, and amalgamated 2 others, making 143 borough seats available for Redistribution, of which 65 were given to the counties. In

England and Wales 43 new boroughs were created, of which 22—including Manchester, Birmingham, Leeds, Sheffield, Tower Hamlets, Finsbury, Greenwich and Lambeth—were to return 2, and the rest 1 member each. Seven counties each received a third member, and 26 were divided, each division to send 2 members; while Yorkshire was given 6 members instead of 4, the Isle of Wight constituency was formed, and in Wales 3 counties had an additional member. In Scotland the representation was completely re-arranged; Edinburgh and Glasgow were given a second member, 5 new single boroughs were created, and 69 towns were formed into 14 "districts of boroughs," each returning 1 member, while 3 additional seats were given to the counties. In Ireland, Belfast, Limerick, Waterford, Galway, and the University of Dublin were given second members. Thus, England was to return 500 members instead of 513, Scotland 53 instead of 45, and Ireland 105 instead of 100, in all 658.

In each of the years 1852, 1854, 1859, 1860, and 1866, Reform Bills were introduced by the Governments of the day, but ultimately withdrawn.

The Reform Acts of 1867-8, introduced by Mr Disraeli—but in their passage through the House greatly extended and altered, both in principle and detail—as passed, provided: (i.) For the reduction of the borough franchise in England and Scotland to the basis of household suffrage, with a £10 lodger qualification; in Ireland to a £4 rating; of the county franchise to a £12 rating qualification, in Scotland £14 valuation. (ii.) For the disfranchisement of 11 boroughs—4 for corrupt practices, and 7 as containing less than 5000 inhabitants—and the semi-disfranchisement of 38 more with populations below 10,000, making in all 52 borough seats available for Redistribution. Seven of these seats were given to Scotland, raising the number of her representatives to 60, and were applied to creating 2 University seats, to giving Glasgow a third seat, to creating the "Border Burghs," and to giving an additional member to Dundee and to 2 counties. In Ireland no change was made. In England, additional members (bringing them up to 3) were given to Manchester, Liverpool, Birmingham, and Leeds; 9 new boroughs, each returning 1 member, were formed, together with Chelsea and Hackney each returning 2; Salford and Merthyr Tydvil had each an additional member; the University of London was created; and 13 counties were divided, and were given 25 additional members. The system of minority voting was applied to the three-cornered constituencies.

The Reform Act of 1884—introduced in the session of that year by Mr Gladstone, was rejected by the House of Lords, and was re-introduced in an autumn session, and passed—was purely a Franchise Bill, the question of Redistribution of Seats being dealt with in a separate and subsequent Act.

The general principle of the Act was to unite the three kingdoms in one and the same "Household" franchise. In order to do this it (i.) assimilated the county franchise to that existing in the boroughs, namely, ratable household suffrage, retaining the £10 lodger franchise; and reduced the £12 county rating to a non-residential qualification of £10 yearly value. (ii.) Included, both in counties and boroughs, by means of the "Service" franchise, those responsible householders who were neither owners nor tenants, but who held their houses as one of the conditions of their service. (iii.) Prevented the manufacture of "faggot" votes, by prohibiting future qualification by rent-charge—except for the whole of a tithe rent-charge—and by forbidding the subdivision of any interest in any land or tenement, unless the owners have derived their interest by will or marriage, or are *bona fide* partners in business.

The Redistribution Act of 1885, introduced in the course of the autumn session of 1884, was a most sweeping measure, which adopted and applied almost universally the system of single member seats, and went far towards the adoption of the principle of equal electoral districts.

The Act disfranchised, by absorption into the county, all boroughs below 15,000 inhabitants, 107 in number with 120 seats; and 2, with 4 seats, for corrupt practices; it semi-disfranchised all boroughs containing between 15,000 and 50,000 inhabitants, 39 in number with 39 seats; and in addition 3 counties each lost a seat.*

This gave a total of 166 seats (of which 163 were borough seats). To these were added 6 seats, then in abeyance for corrupt practices and now revived; while the number of members of the House was increased by 12, thus giving a total of 184 seats available for Redistribution. Of these, 60 were allotted to the counties (an additional representation of 57), and 124 to the boroughs (a diminution of representation of 39). Scotland received 12, and England 6 additional members, Wales and Ireland remaining as before.

Constituencies of 165,000 inhabitants and above received additional members, 1 for about every 54,000 inhabitants, with the exception of London, which was dealt with less liberally. Thus, Yorkshire has now in all 26 members, Lancashire 23, Liverpool 9, Glasgow and Birmingham 7 each, Manchester 6, &c., while London, enlarged in area, returns 60 members, including the University seat, against the 22 previously.

But a further shifting of constituencies took place. For, with the exception of those boroughs of between 50,000 and

* The University seats were exempt from these, as well as from the other provisions of the Act.

165,000 inhabitants, which already returned 2 members, 29 in number, all other constituencies, whether old or new, which returned more than 1 member, were mapped out on the single member system, the counties into divisions, the boroughs into wards or districts, each to return 1 member.* The "three-cornered" constituencies disappeared.

The number of members—in consequence of the disfranchisement of divers corrupt boroughs—amounted in 1884 to 652, of whom England has 489, Scotland 60, and Ireland 103. This number was increased, in 1885, to 670, of whom to England and Wales (population 26,000,000) were assigned 495, to Scotland (population 3,730,000), 72, and to Ireland (population, 1881, 5,100,000), as before, 103.

The Reform Act of 1832 doubled the electorate, increasing it from 440,000, to about 900,000. The number of voters in 1866 amounted to 1,364,000, which was increased by the Reform Acts of 1867-8 to 2,500,000. The number on the register in 1883 was about 3,170,000, of whom England had 2,620,000, Scotland 320,000, and Ireland 227,000. The Reform Act of 1884 enfranchised nearly two million and a half of persons, of whom 1,700,000 were in England, 250,000 in Scotland, and 500,000 in Ireland.† The electors on the register in 1902, with a population of 41,500,000, numbered 6,891,000, of whom 5,464,000 were in England, 705,000 in Scotland, and 722,000 in Ireland.

* The city of London alone, in virtue of its historic associations, remained undivided, but its members were reduced from four to two.

† The number of new electors enfranchised in Ireland, in consequence of the equalisation of the franchise throughout the United Kingdom, was much larger in proportion than in England and Scotland. This was due to the fact that in 1829 Sir Robert Peel raised the freehold qualification from 40s. to £10, thus vastly reducing the Irish electorate; while the Reform Acts of 1832 and 1868 left the Irish franchise almost untouched; on the other hand, the Irish Franchise Act of 1850 reduced the borough franchise to an £8 rating.

PARLIAMENTARY QUALIFICATIONS

In order to vote at a Parliamentary Election a person must possess one or other of the following qualifications:—

1. As a *Householder*, he must have lived in the same Parliamentary Division for twelve months preceding the 15th July. He may have removed more than once, but so long as each house occupied is within the Division, he is entitled to the franchise. Any person who separately occupies *part of a house*, the landlord *not* residing on the premises, is entitled to be registered.

2. As a *Freeholder*, he must have had possession for six months of property producing 40s. per annum clear of all expenses.

3. As a *Leaseholder*, he must have held for twelve months previous to the 15th July a lease of property worth £50 per annum, and originally created for a term of not less than twenty years; or a lease of property worth £5 and upwards per annum, and originally created for a term of not less than sixty years.

4. As a £10 *Occupier*, he must have occupied for twelve months some land or tenement of £10 clear yearly value.

5. As a *Lodger*, he must have occupied rooms in the same house for twelve months. As regards the annual value of the rooms, which is fixed by law at £10, a payment of 4s. a week for unfurnished, or 6s. a week for furnished, rooms, is usually accepted as a sufficient indication of value. A son living at home with his parents may claim, when by agreement with his father he is the sole occupant of a room in the house, and might if he chose lock it up and prevent any other member of the family from entering. Every man over twenty-one who has a right to the exclusive

use of a room or rooms in his parents' house should therefore claim to be put on the register as a lodger.

6. The *Service Franchise.* Bank Managers, Schoolmasters, Caretakers, Servants, and others who occupy rooms or houses rent free on their employers' property, are entitled to this franchise, provided their employers do not reside on the premises.

In Boroughs the Parliamentary Franchise may be exercised by every person qualified :—

1. As a *Householder*, including Bank Managers, Schoolmasters, Servants, Caretakers, and others occupying houses under similar conditions, as in Counties. Any person who separately occupies *part of a house*, the landlord *not* residing on the premises, is entitled to be registered.

2. As a £10 *Occupier*, *i.e.*, any one who occupies an Office, Shop, Warehouse, or other building or land, of £10 clear yearly value.

3. As a *Lodger.* The conditions are exactly the same as previously described under the head of County Qualifications. In all cases lodgers must claim every year.

4. As a *Freeman.* In certain cities and boroughs where such rights are reserved.

The Parliamentary Franchise in no case extends to women.

ELECTORAL REFORM

The chief Electoral Reforms at present advocated are—(1) A Redistribution of seats; (2) The reform of the existing system of Registration; (3) "One man, one vote"; and (4) "Every man a vote"; (5) Shorter Parliaments; (6) Elections to be held on one and the same day; (7) The transference of the Returning Officer's expenses to the taxes or the rates; (8) Second Ballots; (9) Payment of Members.

The general principles propounded by the advocates of Reform are:—

1. (*a*) That the true democratic principle is, not only Government *of* the people, *for* the people, but *by* the people. —(*b*) That to obtain this, there must be complete electoral representation, and complete electoral simplicity and equality; wealth must not enfranchise nor poverty disfranchise.

2. That every man should possess not only the right to vote but the power to be voted for.

3. That all the existing restrictions tell in favour of Property, and against the People.

4. That, in order to improve legislation, the instrument by which legislation is carried out must be perfected. Election Reform is a means to an end.

5. That, without the full power of the people behind, essential and sweeping reforms cannot be carried through.

REGISTRATION REFORM

Under the existing system of Registration, the qualifying period of residence necessary to entitle a man to a vote is twelve months; and the register is made up only once a year. Under this system a man must wait eighteen months, and he may have to wait for two years and a half, before he can be placed on the register.* It is not the duty of any official to see that only qualified persons are placed on the register.

It is proposed that the Electoral Registration Laws should be amended and simplified. That a Responsible Registration Officer should be appointed in each constituency, whose duty it should be to see that every duly qualified person was put on the register, and kept on the register. That the registration should be continuous, all the year round, and made up at least twice a year; that the qualifying period of residence should be reduced from twelve to three months; and that the disqualifications attaching to removals should be abolished.

The Reform of the Registration Laws is supported, on the grounds :—

1. (*a*) That Parliament, in giving the vote, intended that every duly qualified person should be able to exercise the franchise.—(*b*) That, in order to perfect our representa-

* The period of qualification for occupiers and lodgers is twelve months, and the year must be reckoned as the twelve months immediately preceding the 15th of July in any one year; and, for freeholders, full possession of the qualifying property for six months previous to 15th July. The new register does not come into force until the January of each year. Thus, a man who enters into occupation on, say, 16th July, could not even claim to be registered until two years less one day had elapsed, and then a further six months would pass before he would be entitled to vote—in all two and a-half years. At the best—*i.e.* if he entered into occupation on 14th July—it would take him eighteen months of qualification before he would be in a position to exercise the franchise.

tive system, every obstruction in the way of the registration of duly qualified persons should be removed; and registration should be easy, rapid, economical, and automatic.*

2. That the existing system is so replete with technicalities, complications, and anomalies, that every obstacle is put in the way of getting on, and every facility exists for getting struck off, the register.

3. That, at present, a man cannot obtain and cannot retain his vote, without involving himself or others in great expense, trouble, and worry.

4. (*a*) That the present system of registration originated at a time when the franchise was a restricted franchise, and when the vote was treated as a privilege and not as a right. The object chiefly in view then was to prevent persons, not properly qualified, from getting on the register. — (*b*) That, nowadays, with the extended franchise, and with the vote considered in the light of a public trust, a simple, automatic, and efficient, not a complicated, costly, and inefficient system of registration is required.

5. (*a*) That the registration laws have not kept pace with the extension of the franchise, and, being obsolete, are mischievous.—(*b*) That where (as is the case here) a distinct political grievance exists, depending not on principle but merely on mechanism, it should unquestionably be remedied.

6. (*a*) That the obligation of a year's residence, and the general condition precedent to registration, namely, the payment of rates, lead to wholesale disfranchisement; especially of the working classes.—(*b*) That the absurdities

* Some go as far as to argue that each qualified person should be obliged, under penalty, to register himself as a voter; and, further, that every registered voter should be compelled to vote—this proposition need, perhaps, hardly be argued.

and anomalies in connection with "removals" and "successive occupation" result also in wholesale disfranchisement.

7. That the nominal one year's residence, practically involves a two years' residence, and may involve more, before a man becomes entitled to vote.*

8. (*a*) That the only residential qualification required should be just sufficient to enable a correct local register of the voters to be made up at short periodic intervals.—(*b*) That the qualifying period should not depend on an arbitrary date; nor on whether or no a man happened to enter on residence on a particular day.

9. That the electoral qualification should depend on age, not on residence; on citizenship, not on property nor on the payment of rates.†

10. (*a*) That the disqualification attendant on "removals" is anomalous and unjust; ‡ a man, once qualified should be entitled to retain his qualification though he may change his residence.§—(*b*) That change of residence should not stand in the way of qualification for the franchise. (*c*) That, at present, every removal—and removals are constant and habitual—from one constituency to another, destroys the qualification of "successive occupation";

* See note p. 6.

† See *Manhood Suffrage* and *One Man, one Vote.*

‡ Removal from one Parliamentary borough and county division to another disfranchises the voter, and he has to go through the whole qualifying process over again.

§ There is this additional anomaly; that in the case of borough constituencies, which were formerly one, and were divided into two or more single seat divisions by the Redistribution Act of 1885, the qualification for a householder remains good though he may have moved from one Parliamentary division to another. For instance, Birmingham formerly returned three members for the whole undivided borough, it now returns seven members for as many different Parliamentary divisions. Removal from one Parliamentary division in Birmingham to another does not disqualify in the case of a householder, but removal to any other Parliamentary constituency in the kingdom would both disqualify and disfranchise.

See note, p. 12, for London. See also No. 13.

moreover, a lodger must not only occupy lodgings, but lodgings in the same house, during the qualifying period.*

11. (*a*) That a man, who, from the nature of his business and calling, has often to change his residence, becomes a voiceless political vagabond.—(*b*) That, especially is this the case with large numbers of working men, who have to change their dwelling-place according to the location of their work ; and are thus disfranchised simply for following their employment.

12. That every move a man makes may have been a promotion—he may have risen in the world, and from a lodger become a householder—and he may thus have made himself more fitted than before to exercise the franchise ; yet, each move disfranchises him.

13. That the question of disqualification by removal especially affects London, inasmuch as the Metropolis is not, like other boroughs, treated as a whole, but as a series of separate boroughs, those, namely, which existed in 1884.†

14. That the freeholder retains his vote however much he may move about, inasmuch as his qualification remains constant.

15. That the "Overseers," who are supposed to make

* For a householder, or occupier of land or tenement, successive occupation in the same Parliamentary borough and county division during the year of qualification is requisite. For a lodger, occupation of lodgings in the same house. (See p. 6).

† For instance, the old undivided borough of the Tower Hamlets returned two members. In 1885 the old borough was divided into seven Parliamentary divisions, each returning one member. A householder removing from one part of the Tower Hamlets to another, does not prejudice his qualification ; but if he removes over the borders (perhaps only across a street) into Hackney, he disqualifies himself. (See also 10.) How largely removals, &c., disqualify in the poorer parts of London is shown from the very low per centage of electors to population as compared to other large towns. For instance (1902), Birmingham Central with a population of 54,000 has a registered electorate of 11,500 ; while St George's-in-the-East (an extreme case), with a population of 51,000, has a registered electorate of only 3,426.

out the list of voters, are for the most part untrained men, with no particular interest in the work. These lists are, as a rule, most inaccurate; and are not subject to sufficient publicity to enable a man easily to ascertain whether he has been put on the register or no.—(*b*) That the ordinary individual is at a loss to know whether he is duly qualified, and to discover how he ought to proceed to obtain his rights; cost, trouble, and annoyance are involved if he attempts the task.

16. That, thus, the public system of registration has of necessity to be supplemented by private effort and enterprise; with the result, that registration has become part of the necessary duty of the political and party organisation in each constituency; and the voters, in order to obtain their rights, are driven into the hands of political agents.

17. (*a*) That it is manifestly an indefensible anomaly that the registration of a citizen, whose vote is a public trust, should depend on the activity and on the pecuniary position, and be undertaken in the interests, of a political party.—(*b*) That such a system leads to the deliberate and injurious use of technicalities in order to keep off duly qualified persons; and to hard swearing and deception in order to get on persons not properly qualified.

18. That the whole work is done twice over, once by each of the political parties; which involves double expense and great waste of power.

19. (*a*) That the reduction of the qualifying period to three months, the disappearance of disqualification for "removal," and the niceties of "successive occupation," would immensely simplify and greatly reduce the cost, trouble, manipulation, and chicanery of the registration system.—(*b*) That, in connection with Registration Reform,

the costly and troublesome interposition of the revising barristers could be done away with.

20. (*a*) That, with a continuous registration, the register would be as representative and as complete at one period of the year as at another.—(*b*) That at present this is by no means the case; and an election, if taken at one period of the year, might, and probably in many constituencies would, result differently than if it were taken at another.*

21. That a step in the right direction has already been taken in Scotland, by the appointment of a public registration officer—with excellent results.

On the other hand, it is contended :—

"There are no snakes in Iceland." The principle of Registration Reform is not seriously opposed by any persons.

Objecting to particular schemes—pleas of delay—dislike to reopen the Reform question—technical and practical difficulties of carrying out a reform—the possibilties of increased public expense—are sometimes raised, but these do not affect the principle.†

* The register, made up in July, is "new" in January, and becomes ever more "rotten" as the year proceeds.

At the election of 1900, for instance, which took place in October, no voter was able to vote who had not already been on the register for fifteen months; those who had become qualified the previous July were not able to vote, for the new register had not come into force.

† One argument, and one argument only, was raised in the Debate of 1891, directed against the expediency of a shorter period of qualification, namely, that "it would be possible in certain cases, which might easily be imagined, to flood a constituency with new voters in order to win an election."—Mr Chamberlain, 3rd March 1891.

MANHOOD SUFFRAGE

It is proposed to place the franchise on the basis of Manhood Suffrage. so that every male adult—not a criminal, lunatic, or pauper—should be entitled to be placed on the register.

This proposal is advocated on the grounds: *—

1. (*a*) That every adult male who belongs to a Commonwealth has a right to share in the management of its affairs, inasmuch as he is a contributor to the public revenue, by rates and taxes, and to the public wealth, by his labour. He has, therefore, a just claim (and as he can make himself mischievous and burdensome to the nation, it is expedient to allow it) to take part in the passing of its laws, in the healing of its grievances, in the choice of its rulers, in deciding whether it should make war, and what steps it should take for its defence. He cannot rightfully be deprived of all control over matters which touch his well-being so closely; and the only way in which he can legitimately exercise influence on the Government of the country is by the possession of a vote. But that this right is forfeited by lunacy, pauperism or by crime. The man who is either useless or baneful to the Commonwealth has no claim to handle its affairs.—(*b*) That not only every individual, but every class in a Commonwealth, has a claim to share in its counsels, or, at least, to have a spokesman in the National Assembly.—(*c*) That thus alone will a full and fair expression of public opinion be secured.

2. (*a*) That the broader the basis of the Constitution

* See also the arguments in favour of *One Man, one Vote,*

the more firmly will it rest.—(*b*) That were Parliament more under the sway of the whole people, the different classes would be further knit together, legislation would be bolder, more vigorous, and beneficent.—(*c*) That each section of the community has its own way of looking at things, and knows something, and something material to the general weal, which the other sections do not know, and the power of expressing this knowledge will add to the common stock information which else would be wanting. —(*d*) That men understand and manage their own affairs better than others who may perhaps have conflicting interests to serve.

3. That a nation preferring self-government should be self-governed; the basis of the Constitution should be consistent as well as wide; privilege and franchise should not be capricious.

4. (*a*) That there is no intelligible halting-place short of manhood suffrage. It is the logical sequence and completion of Parliamentary Reform.—(*b*) That the principle of any property qualification having been abandoned, the franchise should be based simply a citizenship qualified by age.—(*c*) That, with the introduction of manhood suffrage, we should have got to the rock-bed; and the agitation for electoral changes would cease.

5. (*a*) That manhood suffrage would not enfranchise a fresh "class" of voters, but would admit men earlier to the franchise, and give to the rest of the urban and rural male adults that which has already been granted to most.—(*b*) That, especially in some of the great towns in the Midlands, manhood suffrage is already to a large extent in force.

6. That the men principally excluded under the present system are the younger men—as a class, intelligent, educated, and active members of the community; men who would improve and not lower the standard of the electorate,

7. (*a*) That the unenfranchised man has the same qualification for the franchise as his enfranchised fellow—namely, interest in good government.—(*b*) That as it is to the interest of all to be well governed, there will be no severance of interests between those in question and the nation at large.

8. That the gift of political power strengthens the character, tends to educate, gives greater interest in good government, and furthers the dignity of the receiver.

9. That it is better to give freely than to yield under pressure.

10. That recognised citizenship creates a sense of responsibility; while men denied the privileges are apt to forget the duties of citizenship.

11. (*a*) That the vote should be attached, not to the qualification, but to the individual; electoral rights should be based on manhood, not on property.—(*b*) That electoral qualification should depend on age, not on residence.

12. (*a*) That the increase in the electorate would further diminish the undue influence of wealth and of the aristocracy. —(*b*) But that as property not only gives a plurality of votes, but affects more, the educated and wealthy classes would not really be swamped by the increase in the number of voters, nor find their legitimate influence diminished.

13. That, hitherto, the lowering of the franchise has never been followed by the prophesied evils; the presumption against change has become comparatively weak.

14. (*a*) That the immense simplification of the franchise which would follow on manhood suffrage, would greatly facilitate the registration of voters; doubt and difficulty would be minimised, simplicity would succeed complication. —(*b*) That all branches of the franchise, and more especially the lodger vote, abound in anomalies; manhood suffrage alone would correct these inequalities.

15. That the abolition of plural voting would almost necessarily follow the adoption of manhood suffrage.

16. (*a*) That manhood suffrage is in force in nearly every civilised country. In France, Germany, Italy, &c., as well as in our self-governing Colonies and the United States of America.—(*b*) That the citizens of the United Kingdom are quite as much to be trusted with universal suffrage as those of any other country.

On the other hand, the adoption of Manhood Suffrage is opposed, on the grounds: *—

1. That no one has a "right" to claim the franchise.

2. (*a*) That the object to be arrived at is the best possible government; not that certain persons should be gratified by having a share in ruling. That the claim of individuals, and even of classes, to share in political power is secondary to the paramount claim of the whole people to be ruled by the best rulers, and in the best way. Thus it would be a wrong done to the nation if the better-taught classes, who also have most at stake, and have a greater knowledge of politics, were overwhelmed by mere numbers.

3. That the House of Commons, under the existing extended franchise, fully represents popular feeling.

4. (*a*) That, while dreaming of equality, the greatest inequality would be caused by placing the minority—the rich and educated—at the mercy of the day labourer and the working man.—(*b*) That the enfranchisement of the masses would mean the practical disfranchisement of the rich and educated.—(*c*) That the richer a man is, the greater is his stake in the prosperity of the country, and he should not be altogether swamped, especially in these days of Socialism.

* See also the arguments against *One Man, one Vote.*

5. (*a*) That every person with any stake in the country is already enfranchised.—(*b*) That any one can now, by a minimum of industry and thrift, qualify himself for a vote. —(*c*) That those who have gathered no means, and hence remain on the lowest levels of the working classes, have shown themselves unfit for handling the policy of the kingdom.

6. (*a*) That though previous extensions of the franchise may not have been harmful, a further and lower extension may prove most injurious.—(*b*) That already, though the step cannot now be retraced, too great an element of ignorance has been introduced into the electoral system by the latest extension of the franchise.—(*c*) That the residuum it is now proposed to enfranchise are of necessity, with few exceptions, the most ignorant and the least intelligent body of persons in the kingdom. They cannot improve, and will of necessity lower the electoral standard—already too low.

7. That they will be easily bribed in the concrete, and easily bamboozled in the abstract. Their enfranchisement would tend to electoral corruption, and political dishonesty.

8. (*a*) That the working classes, if the whole of them were endowed with power, would use it to overthrow, or at least to injure, the institutions of the realm.—(*b*) That the voice of the working people would be on the side of extravagance, war, and communism.

9. That those proposed to be enfranchised, having a class interest, would combine against the rest of the community; being ignorant, they would be easily led and swayed by demagogues; and, being numerous, they would obtain whatever they desired.

10. That the extension of the franchise has lowered, and will, if extended, still further lower, the standard of political courage and originality of statesmen, while weakening the

independence of legislation, the vigour of administration, and the capacity of Parliament.

11. That it would give free scope to socialism and ultra-philanthropic tendencies, and result in a great increase of the poor rates.

12. That the extension of the franchise is not really demanded; its concession is not therefore required.

13. (*a*) That the present anomaly does no harm; the extension of the franchise might do untold evil. It is wise to leave well alone.—(*b*) That it is a mistake to be constantly tinkering at the Constitution. It is too soon to begin amending the Reform Act of 1884.

14. That it would increase the costliness of elections.

15. (*a*) (By some.) That manhood suffrage would necessarily involve a considerable redistribution of seats, and probably also equal electoral districts.—(*b*) That a redistribution of seats (especially with equal electoral districts) would necessarily involve the whole question of the proportionate representation of the three kingdoms; thus re-opening the difficult question of the representation of Ireland.

16. That manhood suffrage has, on the whole, not worked satisfactorily in our self-governing Colonies.

"ONE MAN, ONE VOTE."

It is proposed that the system of Plural Voting, under which a man, who possesses a distinct electoral qualification in different constituencies, can claim to be placed on the register of voters, and can vote, in more than one constituency, should cease;* and that, in future, no elector should be entitled to vote in more than one electoral area.†

The abolition of Plural Voting is supported on the grounds:—

1. That it is altogether inconsistent with the principle of representative government, that one man should possess greater statutory electoral powers and privileges than another.

2. (*a*) That each self-supporting and law-abiding citizen is, on the average, as well qualified as another to express an opinion on public affairs.—(*b*) That each one, whatever his position, has a relatively equal stake—life, property, health, happiness, security—in the country, and an equal interest in good government.—(*c*) That the interest of the poorer man in good legislation is in some ways even greater than that of the richer man. Mistaken legislation may reduce the income of the one, it may altogether destroy the subsistence of the other. Social legislation affects the former personally and directly far more than the latter.‡

3. That it is therefore anomalous and unjust that one man should be allowed greater electoral privileges than another.§

* "There does not appear to be any official return of the plural voters. Of the 6,000,000 voters of the United Kingdom (in 1890) 586,000 had duplicate votes; of these, about 400,000 were resident owners, and therefore not plural voters, leaving about 190,000 plural voters."—Mr Ritchie, H. of C., 3rd March 1891. (See also Debate, 3rd May 1892.)

† He would be given the power of electing in which constituency, and on which qualification, he would desire to be registered.

‡ See also the arguments for *Manhood Suffrage*.

§ "I will take my own case. I am a terrible example. I have three votes for as many borough constituencies, and I have three votes for as many county constituencies. That is to say, I have six votes. I use them on the right side, but I know many of my friends who have ten or twelve, and I have heard of one reverend pluralist who has twenty-three."—Mr Chamberlain, Birmingham, 29th January 1885.

4. (*a*) That no part of the electoral privilege should be founded simply on property. The electoral influence of property is already, in other ways, too predominant; and it certainly should not be allowed the additional advantage of plural votes.—(*b*) That brains and character not only ought, but do count for much in politics; yet the qualification for a plural vote depends in no degree on either brains or character, but simply on property.

5. That Parliamentary representation is founded on National, not Local, interests; and a mere multiplication of local qualifications should not entitle to additional electoral privileges.

6. (*a*) That no special privileges, electoral or otherwise, should be given to a particular class or to individuals, and denied to others.—(*b*) That Parliament has decided that each householder has a right to a vote; and, this being so, no one householder should have greater electoral rights than another; or possess the power of multiplying his vote.

7. That the number of plural votes, and their electoral influences, has been largely increased by the division of the kingdom into "single seat" constituencies.

8. That no citizen would be disfranchised by the abolition of the plural vote; it is only proposed to take from a limited number of voters an undue political power which they at present possess.

9. (*a*) That (putting aside faggot votes, and deliberately manufactured plural qualifications, which are absolutely indefensible) the system of plural votes is not founded on any system of justice or equality; it is purely a hap-hazard franchise, uncertain in its operation and full of anomalies.—(*b*) That, for instance, one land owner, the whole of whose estates happen to be in one constituency only, is entitled to but one vote; another, with an equal estate, can claim six votes, because his property happens to lie in six different

constituencies. One manufacturer has his residence and his works in the same constituency; another lives in one constituency, and his business premises are situated elsewhere; the former can have but one vote, the second has two.—(*c*) That the further anomaly exists that, while the boroughs, divided in 1884 into single seats, are still treated as units for electoral purposes, and no elector can vote in more than one division at the same election, the counties, similarly divided, are treated as separate units.—(*d*) That the position of the Metropolis is still more anomalous. For the purposes of voting it is treated not as a single borough, like other large towns, but as a congeries of twenty-seven distinct boroughs, namely, those existing before 1885, divided into fifty-eight electoral divisions. Thus, though an elector may have a voting qualification in each electoral division of any one of the old boroughs, he can only vote once, while if he has a qualification in another borough he can vote also in respect of that.*

10. (*a*) That thus plural voting has no direct connection with wisdom, character, talents, rank, or even wealth. It depends chiefly on whether or no the property the individual possesses happens to be scattered or compact.—(*b*) That, if plural voting be allowed at all, it should be based on some principle of uniformity; and, as in the case of the election of guardians, vary with the amount of property held—a system, nowadays, manifestly absurd.

11. (*a*) That the chief abuse of plural voting lies in the fact that the votes are largely possessed by non-resident

* For instance, the old borough of the Tower Hamlets is divided into seven electoral divisions, St Pancras into four, Westminster into three. (See notes, pp. 11 and 12).

The case of the old county of Middlesex is still more anomalous. Before 1885, the freeholders of London voted in the county of Middlesex. By the Act of 1885 the county was divided into seven divisions, but the freeholders were attached to four of the divisions only.

voters.—(*b*) That these persons, though they possess no active interest in, or special knowledge of the wants and interests of the locality, can come in on the day of poll and over-ride the wishes of the resident voters.*—(*c*) That this is more especially the case in some of the London constituencies.†—(*d*) That the non-resident vote is especially effective, and therefore especially injurious, at by-elections. Further, when the "out-voters" are numerous, the result of the poll may be different at a general and at a by-election; in the former case many out-voters are unable to come and vote, in the latter they can all come.

12. That the existence in any constituency of a large number of non-resident voters tends to destroy public political opinion and to lead to political apathy. The one side depend on the out-voters to keep the seat; the other side are aware that, do what they will locally, they will be out-voted by the non-residents.

13. (*a*) That the "property vote" is to a large extent held by men who do not reside in the constituency.‡—(*b*) That some non-resident "property votes," such as those attaching to the City Livery Companies, depend simply on purchase—a gross anomaly nowadays.§ — (*c*) That the "occupation franchise" enables a man to obtain a vote for business or other premises in which he does not reside.‖

* For instance, in the Wimbledon division of Surrey, out of 15,500 odd electors, about 4000 do not live in the division. It may well happen, therefore, that the wish of the majority of the Wimbledon residents may be defeated by the votes of the 4000 out-voters.

† It is estimated that one-fifth of the non-resident duplicate voters are Metropolitan.

‡ "While there are about 390,000 resident ownership voters, there are 121,000 non-resident ownership voters."—Mr Stansfeld, H. of C., 3rd March 1891.

§ There are some 7000 liverymen voters in the city of London. The non-resident vote in the city far exceeds the resident vote.

‖ "In Central Birmingham (electors 11,000) there are nearly 2000 non-resident voters, in the Exchange division of Liverpool (electors 8000) there

14. That the system of plural qualifications lends itself to the manufacture of votes for party purposes.

15. (*a*) That the "University franchise," attaching to the degree of M.A. at Cambridge and Oxford, is simply a property vote, not given on examination, but purchased for a few pounds by any one who has taken even the ordinary degree.—(*b*) That one advantage of the abolition of plural voting would be the destruction of the University vote.—(*c*) That nearly every University voter is qualified elsewhere, and would not therefore be disfranchised by the abolition of the University franchise.

16. That the abolition of the plural vote would greatly simplify the registration of voters.

17. That the principle of plural property representation does not exist in the case of the election to Town Councils and to County Councils. The principle of "one man, one vote" there strictly prevails; a ratepayer, in the case of a borough, can only vote in one ward, and, in the case of a county, only in one division.* Yet the principle of plural voting is far more defensible in the case of elections for local bodies than in the case of Parliamentary elections.

18. (*a*) That the increased facility of locomotion has accentuated the evil.—(*b*) That to hold elections on one and the same day would be a palliative, but would not get rid of the evil. London would scarcely be affected, and the evils of plural voting are most rampant there.

19. That the question of "one man, one vote" is entirely distinct from that of "one man, one value," *i.e.*, equal electoral

are 1850, in Holborn (electors 9800) there are 1400, in Central Glasgow (electors 13,000) there are 3000 non-resident voters."—Sir George Trevelyan, Newcastle, 3rd October 1891.

* For instance, in London, where there are fifty-eight divisions for Parliamentary and "County Council" purposes, a man could be separately qualified in nearly all of the divisions. At the Parliamentary Election he could vote in each of these divisions, at the County Council Election he could vote in one division only.

districts; the anomaly of plural voting can be and should be dealt with on its merits apart from other anomalies of the representative system.

On the other hand, it is contended :—

1. That the principle on which representative government is founded is due representation of each class and interest, not necessarily pure equality between man and man, or the mere citizenship of the voter.

2. (*a*) That—while "faggot votes" cannot be defended—a man may have a very real and separate interest in more than one constituency, and is entitled to vote separately in each.—(*b*) That, for instance, a man may have a private residence in London, and there pay rates and taxes, employ many persons, support various local institutions, give considerable custom, &c. His business premises may be in the city, where he also pays rates and taxes, employs clerks, &c. Further, he may lease (or own) land and house in the country, reside there part of the year, pay rates and taxes, employ hands, &c. In each of these three constituencies he will have a very considerable, natural, and justifiable interest; and it is neither just nor expedient that he should be deprived of his vote in any of the three.—(*c*) That while the individual with the larger interest would be deprived of a vote, his servants, *employés*, &c., with a lesser interest, would still be entitled to vote.—(*d*) That the proposal ignores the representation of the community and deals with that of the individual only.

3. (*a*) That the theory of the Constitution—emphasised by the adoption of the principle of "single seats"—is that it is the locality that is represented in Parliament.—(*b*) That, therefore, each man who has a substantial interest in a particular constituency, and possesses the proper qualifica-

tion, should, whatever his interest elsewhere, be entitled to vote in the choice of the representative who is elected to watch over the interests of the locality in the House of Commons.—(*c*) That, unless this be so, the interests of the locality would cease to be accurately represented; while an injustice would be done to the individual himself.

4. That, in each separate constituency, the vote of each elector is of equal value and power; there is no local invidiousness or local superiority or inferiority, as between the individual voters in a particular district, caused by plural voting.

5. (*a*) (By some.) That the rich man, as such, has a greater stake in the country; he has more to lose by bad, and more to gain from good government, than the poor man.—(*b*) That the man who has acquired wealth and position ought to possess greater political power than the man who has acquired neither, for he is better qualified to exercise his electoral privileges.

6. (*a*) That the existing system works without any real friction, and with a minimum of injustice or inequality.—(*b*) That the grievance is very minute; the number of plural voters is infinitesimal compared to the whole electorate; and the bulk of those do not exercise their full electoral privileges.*

7. (*a*) That it would involve the abolition of the forty-shilling freeholder; an historical franchise.—(*b*) That it would involve the disfranchisement of the Universities—a system of representation that has many merits.

8. (*a*) That to be continually tinkering at the Constitution is inexpedient.—(*b*) That if the reform of the representative system is going to be taken in hand, other, and far greater anomalies, must be dealt with at the same time.

* See notes, p. 27. Of the 190,000 plural voters, it is estimated that at least 45 per cent. do not vote.

9. (*a*) That, as the chief object aimed at by the introduction of the system of "one man, one vote," is to give to each individual elector equality of voting power; the abolition of plural voting would necessarily have to be coincident with the adoption of the principle of "one vote, one value," that is, a system of equal electoral districts.*—(*b*) That the adoption of the principle of "one vote, one value" would necessitate a sweeping Redistribution Act, both as between the three kingdoms,† and within each of the three kingdoms.—(*c*) That it would, moreover, necessitate a periodical rectification of the electoral areas.—(*d*) That periodical Redistribution Acts would greatly tend to destroy political life and interest in the constituencies.

10. (By some.) That if, as many advocate, elections all took place on the same day,‡ the evils of plural voting would practically disappear.

* For instance, under the present system of unequal electoral districts, the borough of South West Ham, with 22,500 electors, has only the same voting power as St George's-in-the-East, with its 3400 electors. Each St George's elector may be said to possess six times the electoral power and privileges of an elector in West Ham. In the case of several Irish constituencies the inequality is still greater, Galway, for instance, having but 2300 electors.

† According to the Census of 1901 England and Wales had a population of 31,800,000, Scotland 4,470,000, Ireland 4,600,000. The respective number of members is 495, 72, and 103; while according to absolute population, the numbers should be 520, 75, and 75. But against equality of representation founded on present population, there is, as regards Ireland at least, much to be said. (See Debate, 18th May 1892.)

‡ See p. 42.

SHORTER PARLIAMENTS

It is proposed to repeal the Septennial Act and to shorten the legal duration of Parliament. Different terms of years are advocated, five, four, and three—the most popular being perhaps the four years' term.

The existing Septennial Act was passed in 1716, shortly after the accession of George I., superseding the Triennial Act of 1694, which had itself followed on the Revolution of 1688.* During the period of the Triennial Act, the average duration of the Parliaments (exclusive of the six months' Parliament, which was dissolved on the demise of the Crown † in 1702) was two years and five months.

The average duration of the Parliaments between 1796 (the first of George III)., and the Reformed Parliament of 1833, was three and a half years. From the first Reformed Parliament of 1833 until the year 1868, there were nine Parliaments, the

* The first Parliament of Charles II., elected in 1661 (1660), lasted eighteen years. It was dissolved in January 1679 (1678) "in the thirtieth (!) year of Our Reign": "The King's Most Excellent Majesty," ran the Proclamation, "taking into his serious Consideration the many Inconveniences arising by the over-long continuance of one and the same Parliament doth hereby dissolve the same."

† This provision was repealed in 1867.

average duration of which was three years and nine months; two of these Parliaments existed just six years. Including the Reformed Parliament of 1868, until that dissolved in 1900, there have been seven Parliaments averaging four years and six months; the longest term was that of the Parliament elected in 1874, namely six years and twenty days.*

The present Parliament was elected in October 1900, and can legally sit until October 1907.

Shorter Parliaments are advocated on the grounds:—

1. That there exists no constitutional means whereby the nation can express its opinion save at a General Election.

2. (*a*) That under the Septennial Act, the nation is obliged to commit absolutely into the hands of Parliament for a lengthened term enormous powers, that may be used for weal or woe without opportunity of check or change. — (*b*) That "Parliament," in this connection, means, at the best, a majority only, perhaps but a very small majority, of the House of Commons for the time being.

3. That the Parliamentary majority, elected to carry out a particular course of policy, may inaugurate a new policy, may break its election pledges, betray its trust, and forfeit the confidence of the country. Yet it cannot be

* See P. P. 165 of 1892, and *Debrett*, 1902. During the last hundred years there have been 26 Parliaments. Three have been dissolved by the death of the Sovereign, 3 by electoral reform necessitating a new election, 10 in consequence of ministerial crises, and 10 in the natural course.

called to account, and may continue to defy for a lengthened period the evident feeling of the country.

4. (*a*) That in the expiring years of a "long" Parliament questions of moment are decided, which had not even been mooted at the General Election, and thus momentous decisions are taken, or new and grave responsibilities are incurred by Parliament, not only without consultation with the nation, but even, it may be, entirely contrary to their wishes.—(*b*) That public opinion may distinctly change on a particular question; or a hasty and ill-considered verdict on a particular issue may have decided the majority; yet, for seven years, the verdict given at the General Election may remain irrevocable.

5. (*a*) That in these days of quickened communications and increased education, greater knowledge of, and interest in, politics, opinions are formed and change more rapidly than of old, and a length of years formerly not excessive for a Parliament is now far too long.—(*b*) That the condition of the country and the mind of the people goes on changing, and Parliament, remaining unchanged, gradually ceases to reflect the opinion of the constituent bodies.

6. That it is right that the power of election should regularly and at short intervals revert to the people, so that they may have more frequent opportunities of endorsing or reconsidering their choice of rulers, and the policy to be pursued.

7. (*a*) That so long as the franchise was restricted, when elections were costly and corrupt, when the representation was practically confined to the wealthy classes, the question of the frequency of elections was of secondary importance.—(*b*) That, indeed, in days when the poll extended over days or weeks, with open corruption and unchecked

bribery, elections were a positive evil. But successive Reform Bills have purified elections, limited them to one day, and placed the franchise in the hands of the nation at large.

8. (*a*) That every year, under the extended franchise in force, a large number of old voters disappear from, and a large number of new voters come on the register. *—(*b*) That these latter ought to have an early opportunity of expressing their views; for the possession of a vote is of no avail unless associated with the opportunity of recording it.

9. (*a*) That the principle of Parliamentary Government is representation; and a representative system under which the elected do not frequently submit themselves, their acts, and their views to the elector, loses much of its representative character.—(*b*) That in these democratic days it is essential that representatives should be in near touch with their constituents; and more frequent elections would greatly tend towards this consummation.

10. (*a*) That shorter Parliaments, and the more frequent necessity imposed on members of meeting their constituents and justifying their existence as representatives, would quicken their sense of responsibility.—(*b*) That the member goes to Parliament a free man, and becomes a bondsman; and the longer the Parliament the more he tends to become a mere party "item."—(*c*) That the sense of responsibility in members is greater towards the end than at the beginning of a Parliament. The shorter the life of a Parliament the more likely is the member to appreciate his responsibilities.—(*d*) That a member who has decided not to stand again, is likely, during the last year or two of a pro-

* It is estimated that, in the course of five years, some 500,000 of persons cease to be voters, and some 500,000 of new voters are registered; a total change of a million of electors, or one-sixth of the total electorate.

longed Parliament, to become lax in his attendance and interest.

11. That real independence and breadth of character would not suffer, but would be strengthened from more frequent communion between the member and his constituents.

12. That more frequent elections would create a greater general interest in politics; and bring home to the minds of the people the fact that they are a self-governing community, responsible for the action of their rulers.

13. (*a*) That the necessity of more frequently submitting their action to the judgment of the country would, by making them more careful in regard to their measures and policy, have a wholesome effect on the Government of the day.—(*b*) That the knowledge that they would have an early opportunity of appealing to the country against the Government would increase the vigilance of the Opposition; and, at the same time, the possibility of a speedy accession to power would quicken their sense of responsibility.

14. (*a*) That the House of Commons generally would have a better appreciation of the value of time, and business would be more efficiently, adeqnately, and rapidly conducted. —(*b*) That more especially would this be the case, inasmuch as the real and recently expressed will of the nation would be known in reference to the principal questions to be discussed and decided.—(*c*) That the best work is done in the earlier days of a Parliament. The impetus of the General Election alone enables great reforms to be carried through.

15. (By some.) That we should thereby obtain something of an equivalent to the system of the "Referendum" that prevails with much advantage in Switzerland.

16. (*a*) That more frequent elections would tend to diminish the excessive swing of the political pendulum;

would lead to the greater stability of successive Governments, and therefore to greater continuity of policy both at home and abroad.—(*b*) That during the prolonged life of a Parliament, the Government lose touch of the nation; and an earlier appeal for a renewal of confidence would be much more likely to result in the endorsement of their policy and in the attainment of a fresh lease of power.—(*c*) That, thus, while a strong and popular Government would be periodically reinvigorated by a new mandate, a weak and unpopular Government would the sooner disappear.

17. That the fact that a General Election so often goes against the Government shows that more frequent opportunities ought to be given of declaring the popular will.

18. (*a*) That shorter Parliaments would tend to greater continuity of policy in Foreign Affairs; and to increase the influence of the British Government abroad. During the latter years of a prolonged Parliament, the power of the Government of the day to negotiate with foreign nations is largely curtailed in consequence of the uncertainty as to whether their policy will be endorsed at the next General Election.—(*b*) That the tendency is ever more and more towards continuity in foreign policy, and shorter Parliaments would help towards this.

19. That shorter Parliaments and more frequent elections would tend to less sweeping alterations in the *personnel* of the House—"short reckonings make long friends"—and thus each new Parliament would contain a larger porportion of experienced men than is the case at present.

20. That while it is possible that some of those who now enter Parliament would no longer be inclined to stand, their places would be taken by men who would be more interested in politics and be more serious in attempting to remedy abuses.

21. That if elections were more frequent, the tendency would be towards reduced expenditure. The candidate would be less inclined to a large outlay, public opinion would favour reduction, and a further legal limitation of expenditure would take place.

22. (By some.) That the adoption of shorter Parliaments would render irresistible the demand for the payment of members,* for the transfer of the official expenses of elections to the rates or taxes,† and for a reform of registration,‡ and for elections on one and the same day.§

23. (*a*) That, nowadays, with the duration of the poll confined to twelve hours, with expenses limited by law, and with the ballot, elections are conducted in a quiet and orderly way, and a General Election causes but little disturbance to trade.—(*b*) That there would be fewer contested elections, constituencies that had lately unmistakably expressed their preference would not be again fought.

24. That it is better that the country should know in advance approximately when an election will take place.

25. (*a*) That for a period of twenty-two years a Triennial Act was in force and worked satisfactorily.—(*b*) That the Triennial Act was replaced by a Septennial Act chiefly in order to meet a great national emergency, and to secure the Protestant Succession to the Throne.||—(*c*) That the Septennial Act was passed to meet a temporary emergency; and as a political makeshift, its adoption may have been justifiable. The danger has long since passed away, and there is now no dynastic nor constitutional reason for its continuance.

* See p. 62. † See p. 46. ‡ See p. 8. § See p. 42.

|| The Septennial Act was passed in the first year of Geo. I. by the Whig Government of the day, with the object of postponing a General Election until the new dynasty should be more firmly established on the throne. The Act was applied to the then existing, as well as to future Parliaments, and the Parliament of 1715, elected for three years, lasted for over six.

26. That in 1867 the Septennial Act was itself in a degree extended by the abrogation of the provision formerly existing that on the demise of the Crown a dissolution must take place.*

27. (*a*) That the tendency under the Septennial Act is towards a longer average life of Parliament.—(*b*) That the natural inclination of a Government, and of the majority for the time being, is to cling to power, and not to take the risk of a dissolution earlier than they can help.

28. That there would be no real infringement of the prerogative of the Crown; for it is long since the Crown dissolved Parliament of its own initiative.

29. That it would weaken the threat of dissolution by means of which the Government of the day is sometimes enabled to force measures upon its unwilling supporters.

30. That in no other country has the Lower House of Representatives so long a lease of power as in England.†

31. That the term of election in the case of Municipal, School Board, and other local elections is for the most part for three years only.

On the other hand, it is contended :—

1. (*a*) That the "Septennial Act" is septennial only in name; the full legal limit is never reached, hardly ever approached, and the country has a full opportunity at short intervals of re-considering its position, and of recording its verdict.—(*b*) That if the legal period of the life of Parlia-

* For instance, on the death of Geo. III. Parliament was *ipso facto* dissolved, though it had been in existence only eighteen months; on the death of Geo. IV. Parliament was but three years and eight months old, on that of William IV. two years and five months only.

† Germany, Italy, and Spain, and some of the Colonies, five years; France, Belgium, and some of the Colonies, four years; Denmark, Portugal, Sweden, Holland, Switzerland, and some of the Colonies, three years; United States, two years. (See Dickinson's *Procedure Foreign Parliaments.*)

ment were shortened, the maximum period would tend to become a minimum, and, on the whole, the country would have fewer, and not more frequent opportunities of expressing its opinion.

2. That Parliament ought, if the country be in a normal state, to be dissolved at the least a good year before the legal limit, lest it should legally lapse at a moment when an election might be inconvenient or injurious to the country. Thus, if the term were shortened, either the Government would be tempted to go to the extreme legal limit, or else elections would be continually recurring.

3. (*a*) That Parliament, elected on a purely democratic basis, does nowadays faithfully represent the opinion of the country for the time being.—(*b*) That the numerous by-elections that take place tend, by the opportunity they afford of testing public opinion, and of introducing new blood into the House, to keep Parliament ever in touch with the country.—(*c*) That members are far more and increasingly in touch with their constituents, and aware of their feelings and desires.

4. That as a Government depends for its continued existence on the good-will of the electorate, it will always endeavour to propitiate, and not to run counter to the desires of the nation.

5. (*a*) That, as a matter of fact, neither Prime Minister, Government, nor Parliamentary majority can defy the will of the nation, and pass measures or carry out a policy directly contrary to the general feeling of the country. The strongest Governments are forced to yield to the pressure of public opinion.—(*b*) That, short of a General Election, the electors have, through bye-elections, newspapers, and speeches both inside and outside the House, ample and perpetual opportunity of forcibly expressing their views.

6. (*a*) That shorter Parliaments, by involving more

frequent appeals to the country, would impair the independence of the Ministry.—(*b*) That the Government would be tempted to deal with those subjects that were for the moment popular, rather than with those of the greatest permanent benefit; and the measures proposed would be designed with a view to their immediate effect on the public mind, rather than for the solid advantage of the country.

7. That, with shorter Parliaments, the majority would be elected with a "mandate" on some particular question of the moment; and thus legislation would be more likely to be hasty and emotional.

8. (*a*) That the extension of the franchise has tended to political capriciousness on the part of the electors. The decision of one election is often reversed at the next; ministers and Parliaments mostly change together. Political instability and constant change of Government are serious evils, which would be accentuated if elections were more frequent.—(*b*) That the check of the Septennial Act on the capriciousness of the electorate is advantageous to the country.

9. (*a*) That at present there is far too little continuity either in the Home or in the Foreign policy of the country; more frequent elections, implying more frequent changes of Government, would make it still more hap-hazard.—(*b*) That, even now, the Government of the day is much hampered in its relations with Foreign Governments by reason of the possibility of a reversal of policy consequent on its defeat at the next General Election. Increase this possibility, and embarrassment would amount to paralysis.

10. (*a*) That shorter Parliaments, by entailing the more frequent submission of a member to a fresh election, would greatly weaken his independence and impair his political honesty.—(*b*) That good work is not done by men who

"have their eye on the door"; by men who anxiously scrutinise the effect of each vote or speech on their constituents.—(*c*) That the position of the member would be lowered from that of a representative to that of a delegate. He would lose all his individual freedom of thought and action, and be forced to support or oppose measures at the dictation of his constituents.

11. That constant elections would tend to throw political power more and more into the hands of caucuses and wire-pullers, making the members mere machines, and tending to the manufacture of public opinion.

12. That, nowadays, with a very extended franchise, great publicity, and universal political activity, the sense of responsibility of the member and his personal contact with his constituents, extends over the whole of his Parliamentary life, and is not simply quickened by the prospect of a dissolution.

13. (*a*) That each newly elected House of Commons necessarily takes time to acquire experience before it can settle down satisfactorily to the conduct of the business of the nation.—(*b*) That constant elections would involve constant changes in the *personnel* of the House, bringing in at short intervals a large number of inexperienced men, strangers to each other, and new to the work required of them; to the detriment of the public service.

14. That neither the first year nor the last year of a Parliament is devoted to valuable work; in the first the members are learning their business, in the last they are thinking of their constituents.

15. That with elections always in view, the time and attention of the member would be largely devoted to electioneering, and the business of the House would be perforce neglected.

16. (*a*) (By some.) That the result would be to throw

administrative power more and more into the hands of permanent officials, whose irresponsible influence is already too great.—(*b*) That the risk of personal Government from "long" Parliaments is far less serious than the risk of bureaucratic Governments from "short" Parliaments.

17. (*a*) That the additional expense, risk of loss of seat, worry and trouble involved in more frequent elections would deter many good men from becoming candidates.—(*b*) That the best class of candidates would resent the loss of independence involved, and would be loth to stand.—(*c*) That the duties of a member would necessarily become more multifarious, laborious, and irksome, both in the House and in the constituency; and men, whose tastes or whose business prevent them from devoting their whole time to politics, would be deterred from standing.—(*d*) That thus the constituencies would be greatly restricted in their choice of candidates; and the standard of the House would be sensibly lowered.

18. (*a*) That the great additional expense involved in more frequent elections would certainly lead to the transference of the official expenses of elections from the shoulders of the candidate to the rates or taxes, and this would be a mistake.*—(*b*) While it would also render irresistible the demand for the payment of members—a system which would involve many serious evils.†

19. (*a*) That every General Election involves a very considerable disturbance to the trade of the country.—(*b*) That political animosity and party heat engendered by General Elections would be greater if they were more frequent.—(*c*) That with more frequent elections party passion would never have time to cool down, and the country would be kept in a state of perpetual turmoil and in continuous preparation for the next election.

* See p. 46. † See p. 62.

20. (By some.) That, even now, with the Parliamentary, Municipal, School Board, and other elections, there is little enough peace from electioneering turmoil.

21. That too frequent Parliamentary Elections would greatly diminish the general interest taken in them, and this would be a serious evil.

22. That the shortening of the life of a Parliament would greatly diminish the force of the threat of dissolution now often used with salutary effect by the Government of the day.

23. That the prerogative of the Sovereign in the matter of dissolution would be infringed by being greatly curtailed.

24. That the Septennial Act has worked very well for the last one hundred and seventy-four years, and it is unstatesmanlike and dangerous to make a grave constitutional change without adequate cause.

25. That the supporters of shorter Parliaments are not yet agreed among themselves on the best term of years to advocate. To every term proposed grave objection can be taken.

THE BALLOT

The Ballot Act of 1872 was passed experimentally for a limited number of years, and expired in December, 1881, and is only now kept in force by being included each session in the Continuation Act.

The principle of secrecy of voting is, however, so definitely accepted, that it is not worth while to recapitulate the reasons advanced for and against the Ballot.

Illiterate Voters

One point connected with the Ballot was discussed in previous editions; namely, the question whether the illiterate voter, who solicits assistance in recording his vote, should continue to receive the help of the officer presiding at the polling-booth in marking his ballot paper.*

But the spread of education, and increased experience of the system of voting by ballot has so reduced the number of genuine "illiterate" votes, that the question is solving itself, and the arguments need not be repeated.

ELECTIONS ON ONE AND THE SAME DAY

It is proposed that, at a General Election, all the elections should be held on one and the same day; either on a fixed day in the week (Saturday is usually suggested), or within a fixed number of days after the issue of the writs.† At present, the returning officer has a certain amount of discretion,

* In 1886, 4,700,000 electors polled, of whom 186,500 were illiterates. Of these, 98,400 were in Ireland.—P. P. 165 of 1886.

In 1895, 3,860,000 polled, of whom 73,000 only were illiterates. Of these 40,400 were in Ireland.—P. P. 84 of 1896.

† Some suggest that, as a modification, the Borough Elections should be held on one day and the County Elections on another; many propose that, without adopting the system of simultaneous election, the discretion now left to the returning officer should be largely contracted.

after the receipt of the writ, in fixing the day of polling. In boroughs the election must take place within nine days after the writ is received; while in counties the period can be prolonged to seventeen days.*

This proposal is urged, on the grounds:—

1. (*a*) That it is not right that the returning officer, often a partisan, should have any discretion in fixing the day of the poll.—(*b*) That the poll is now often fixed on a particular day because of the anticipated advantage to one party and the disadvantage to the other.—(*c*) Then the poll is often fixed on a particular day merely to suit the personal convenience of the returning officer.

2. That, in many places, certain classes of electors—fishermen, sailors, railway men, &c.—are partially disfranchised by the poll being fixed for one day rather than for another.

3. (*a*) That there is little force in the argument that, with a fixed day in the week, elections would often take place on "market" or other inconvenient days, at present avoided. Elections only come once in several years; and, already, they often, in counties, take place on market days in some places. Nowadays, the disturbance caused by an election is comparatively slight.—(*b*) That the country would soon become habituated to elections on a fixed day in the week; and local circumstances would be arranged accordingly.

4. (*a*) That a fixed period of election would greatly tend to shorten the average period of the contests; and this would

* At the General Election of 1900, the first contested election took place on 28th September, the last (exclusive of Orkney and Shetland) on 16th October.

be an advantage.—(*b*) That it would reduce the expense of elections.

5. That elections are now peaceful and orderly, and no extra force of police is required on the spot.

6. (*a*) That at present the earlier elections exercise an undue influence on the later. The prestige of success of one party at the earlier elections often helps to turn the scale in some of the later.—(*b*) That each elector ought to exercise his franchise independently, and unbiassed by the result of the poll elsewhere—this can only be obtained by means of simultaneous elections.

7. That elections being spread over a considerable period, canvassers, helpers, carriages, can perambulate from one constituency to another, exercising an undue influence.

8. (*a*) That it would do much to minimise the evils of plural voting; time would not permit of separate votes being recorded in different constituencies.—(*b*) That thus plural voting would be got rid of without the necessity of restricting the franchise.

9. That by diminishing the period over which the elections are now spread, the disturbance to trade and other evils attendant on elections would be minimised.

On the other hand, it is contended:—

1. That the present elastic system is far the most convenient for the locality; and allows the day of the poll to be fixed according to the varying circumstances of borough and county, of constituency and constituency.

2. (*a*) That, with a fixed day, the day of the poll would often necessarily fall on a market, or some other inconvenient day; to the disturbance of trade, and to the annoyance of the locality.—(*b*) That, in nearly every locality, one day in the week is usually more convenient than another; a fixed day,

ignoring local circumstances, would, in many places, often practically disfranchise a considerable number of electors.

3. (*a*) That the only day that would be equally convenient to all is Sunday; and Sunday, in England, is out of the question.—(*b*) That the simultaneous elections abroad usually take place on a Sunday.

4. That, nowadays, the returning officer does not use his power unfairly or corruptly; but fixes a day—usually after consultation with the representatives of the candidates—likely to be most convenient and desirable to all parties.

5. That, if the day of poll were a fixed day in the week, the writ might be issued at a moment that would delay the election by five or six days.

6. That it would be difficult, in the counties at least, to find a sufficiency of competent persons to act as returning officers, polling clerks, &c. This would be especially the case if the number of polling booths was increased; and the tendency is all in that direction.

7. (*a*) That, very often, even with elections as peaceful and orderly as they now usually are, extra police have to be drafted into a constituency on the day of the poll to keep order. That, with simultaneous elections, there would be no means of obtaining these extra police, they would each and all be wanted in their own districts.—(*b*) That the argument applies with great force to Ireland, where elections are not invariably peaceful.

8. (By some.) That it is an advantage that earlier elections should, as they do, influence the later elections. It is better for the country that the party obtaining the majority should obtain a large majority, and be strong in the House of Commons.

9. That plural voting would be but slightly affected by simultaneous elections. If plural voting is an evil it should be abolished on its merits, and not by a side wind.

THE "OFFICIAL" EXPENSES OF ELECTIONS *

It is proposed to relieve Parliamentary candidates of the cost of the machinery of elections—in other words, the returning officers' expenses—at present cast upon them.† This proposal is urged on the grounds :—

1. (*a*) That it is unjust and inexpedient that the candidate, desirous of serving his country, should be called upon to bear the cost of elaborate and expensive machinery, the use of which is enforced by the State for its own purposes, and over the working of which he has no control.—(*b*) That more especially is this the case where the burden is from time to time increased by the popular desire to afford greater facilities for voting, or of encouraging purity—the nation is liberal at the expense of the individual.

2. That, at present, however much a candidate and his supporters may desire to conduct the election without expense, they cannot escape the payment of a large sum enforced by the State.

3. That this compulsory charge constitutes a property qualification; yet Parliament, as long ago as 1858, professed to abolish all property qualifications for Members of Parliament.

4. That the theory of the Constitution is that constituencies will be contested. It is not therefore the candidate

* See also section on *Payment of Members*.

† The returning officers' expenses at the election of 1880 amounted to £134,000 out of a total returned expenditure of £1,650,000 ; in 1886 they were £140,000 out of a total expenditure of £624,000. In 1900 the figures were £150,000 and £777,000 respectively. The amounts vary (for contested elections) from some £80 to £670 in boroughs, and from £270 to £730 in counties,

who is responsible for causing an election; and he should not be penalised for so doing.

5. (*a*) That constituencies ought to have the fullest possible choice of candidates.—(*b*) That the necessity of meeting the cost of conducting the election greatly limits the range of choice.—(*c*) That, more especially is this the case in regard to "labour" candidates.

6. That opinion, not purse, should be represented in Parliament.

7. (*a*) That, as the legitimate cost of elections have gradually been reduced, the official expenses constitute an ever larger proportion of the whole cost.—(*b*) That their transference would encourage still more, because it would make possible cheap and pure elections.

8. (*a*) That the returning officers' expenses constitute but a very small proportion of the whole cost of elections; their transference would not, therefore, encourage frivolous or vexatious candidatures.—(*b*) That the cost of "sitting," and not the cost of "standing," constitutes the real deterrent to the political adventurer.

9. (*a*) That the system of Second Ballots * might be adopted in case of a multiplicity of candidates.—(*b*) That if the system of Second Ballots were not acceptable, there would be no great difficulty in checking frivolous or vexatious candidatures, by requiring a deposit from each candidate to be forfeited unless he polled a certain proportion of the electorate.—(*c*) That, abroad, where the official expenses are borne by the State, frivolous candidatures are almost unknown.

10. That in the case of School Board, Municipal and County Courts Elections the official expenses are a charge on the rates.

* That is to say, that if no candidate polls an absolute majority of the total vote cast at the first election, another election takes place, at which the candidate highest on the poll is elected. (See section on *Second Ballots*.)

11. That the payment by the State of that portion of the expenses of elections which is due to the machinery alone, would in no way interfere with the personal and political independence of members.

12. (*a*) That the amount of these expenses varies in different constituencies;* they constitute therefore a varying burden on different candidates, and a varying charge for the same office.—(*b*) That, in a two-membered constituency, the candidate at a by-election is charged with double the expense that he would have to meet at a General Election.

13. (*a*) That the candidate has no check nor control over this expenditure, and cannot, without incurring political odium, refuse to pay the amount demanded by the returning officer. The charges, nominally scheduled, vary enormously in different constituencies.—(*b*) That, as an Imperial or local charge, the amount of expenditure would be strictly supervised, limited and systematised.

14. That so long as the cost is a personal charge, facilities for voting, more polling places, &c., which should be encouraged, are deprecated.

15. That in the case of all the other European nations, this charge is either an Imperial or local one.

On the other hand, it is contended :—

1. (*a*) That the question is not one of abolishing or diminishing the costs of elections, but affects merely the incidence of a certain portion, a necessary and essential portion, of the cost.—(*b*) That it is just and right that the candidate who aspires to a seat in the House should be called upon to pay the cost of the machinery of the election which his candidature renders necessary.

* See note, p. 46.

2. That the official expenses of elections bear but a small proportion to the whole cost, and no *bonâ fide* or representative candidate is prevented from standing by the necessity of producing the comparatively small sum compulsorily required.

3. That the independence of members would be seriously affected, if they were indebted for their election expenses either to the State or to the locality they represented.

4. That, by diminishing the legitimate cost of elections, the social, commercial, and political standard of the House would be lowered.

5. That no comparison with the system prevailing abroad is possible; there, a Parliamentary seat is neither so honourable nor so greedily sought after as in England; while, as a matter of fact, the candidates (in consequence of the payment of election expenses and the salaries of members) are not of a high class.

6. (*a*) That to relieve the candidate of the cost of the election would be to encourage the candidature of political adventurers.—(*b*) That to relieve the candidate of the cost of his election would be to encourage frivolous and vexatious candidatures.—(*c*) That, even in the case of School Board and Municipal Elections, frivolous candidatures are by no means unknown; and the attraction of a Parliamentary candidature would be much greater.

7. (*a*) That it would become essential to introduce some safeguard against a multiplicity of candidates; and no satisfactory safeguard can be devised.—(*b*) That the system of Second Ballots would in itself introduce many evils; it would increase the number of candidates; it would, as it has done abroad, divide parties up into an infinite number of "groups," and so make party government impossible; it would involve the duplication of the worry, trouble, and

expense of elections.*—(*c*) That any system of deposit, to be forfeited unless certain conditions were fulfilled, would act very unfairly, would be almost impossible to work, and would in itself constitute a form of property qualification.

8. That School Board and Municipal, &c., Elections form no precedent. There are local elections for local purposes; the official expenses form the chief portion of the cost of the election; and, as the duties are not very attractive, it is essential to remove every obstacle to candidature.

9. That, the official expenses being fixed by Act of Parliament, exorbitant charges on the part of the returning officer are not possible.

If the principle of the relief of the candidate be granted, the further question arises whether the burden should be thrown on the Taxes, or on the Rates; on the nation at large, or on the constituency.

Those in favour of placing the burden on the Rates argue:—

1. That as the district chooses the member, and he represents them in Parliament, it should also pay the cost of the election.

2. That, in the case of the School Board and Municipal Election, the burden is borne by the locality.

3. (*a*) That, nowadays, ratepayers and electors are practically identical.—(*b*) That, if the burden were placed on the taxes, non-electors would have to bear a portion of the cost.

4. That contests would be discouraged, to the advantage of continuity of policy and of person.

5. That the local interest in economy would act as a check on the expenditure.

* See section *Second Ballots.*

Those in favour of placing the burden on the Consolidated Fund argue, however :—

1. (*a*) That the expenditure is for National not for Local purposes, thereby differing from the cost of School Board or Municipal Elections, which is rightly met from the rates.—(*b*) That, to place the charge on the rates, would be to confirm the vicious principle that the member represented the petty local interests, instead of the general political and national feeling contained in the constituency.

2. That the member would be more independent and less of a delegate, if he were indebted to the State and not to his constituents for the expenses of his election.

3. That ratepayers and electors are not synonymous: to place the expenses on the rates would be to throw a direct burden on many non-electors—women, peers, &c.

4. (*a*) That the charge, if placed on the taxes, would be an uniform burden over the whole country; if placed on the rates, the charge (which itself varies in different localities) would constitute a proportionately heavier burden on small or straggling than on large or compact constituencies.—(*b*) That the ratepayers in one constituency which should not happen to be contested, would escape all charge.—(*c*) That the ratepayers in a constituency in which, through any cause, a by-election took place, would be put to a double expense.

5. That so long as local taxation remains unreformed, the incidence of local taxation is unfair; and to add to it would be to accentuate the existing injustice.

6. That to throw the burden on the locality would tend to discourage contests, which, from a politico-educational point of view, would be disadvantageous.

7. That there should be greater not less facilities for the recording of votes; public opinion would favour these if the

charge were a national one, local opinion would discourage them if the charge were to come on the rates.

8. That Exchequer control and audit would tend towards economy, by ensuring that those who have a pecuniary interest in the amount of the expenditure should not have the power of increasing it.

SECOND BALLOTS

It is proposed that, along with the transference of the official expenses of elections to the taxes or rates,* and the provision for the payment of members,† a system of "Second Ballots" should be introduced.

That is to say, that, if at the first election the candidate highest on the poll does not obtain a clear majority of the aggregate votes cast, a second election shall take place, at which the candidate then highest on the poll will be duly elected.‡

This proposition is defended on the grounds :—

1. (*a*) That, by this means alone will the other electoral reforms be safeguarded; and the object aimed at by

* See p. 46. † See p. 62.

‡ It is usually proposed that, at the second election, the choice of the electors should be restricted (in single seat constituencies) to the two candidates (among those who had not withdrawn) who stood highest on the poll at the first election. Of course, in no case, would fresh nominations be allowed. The second election would take place either a week or a fortnight after the first.

them—true representation of the majority—be attained.—(*b*) That the system of second ballots is simple and effective, and gives logical completeness to the representative system.

2. (*a*) That one of the principal objects of cheapening elections and paying members, is to give the greatest possible choice of candidates to the electors.—(*b*) That these, and other electoral reforms, would unquestionably lead, in very many instances, to a multiplicity of candidates.—(*c*) That, without a system of second ballots, the majority of the electors, where they divide their votes among two or more candidates,* are often out-voted by a compact minority.†—(*d*) That, thus, the minority, instead of the majority, obtains the representation; and the constituency, during the existence of that Parliament, is misrepresented.‡

3. (*a*) That a necessary corollary to single-seat constituencies is, that a candidate should secure an absolute majority of the votes cast before he can be duly elected.—(*b*) That with "double-barrelled" seats, the different shades of opinion existing in a party, and with "three-cornered" seats the minority also, were represented, or might be represented; neither of these things is possible under the system of

* Throughout, for the sake of simplicity, "single seats" are assumed; the arguments mostly hold good for "double-barrelled" seats as well. There are now no "three-cornered" seats.

† At the election of 1874, no less than 13 Liberal seats were lost in consequence of a multiplicity of Liberal candidates. These 13 seats, representing 26 votes on a division, constituted half the whole Tory majority in that Parliament.

‡ At the election of 1885, for instance, two Liberals stood for Peckham and polled between them 3510 votes, the Conservative candidate, however, securing the seat with a poll of 3362 votes. Similarly, in N. Lambeth, the two Liberals polled together 3038 votes, the successful Conservative but 2542, the electorate numbering nearly 8000. In 1900, in Caithness, the three Liberal candidates polled together 2003 votes, and the one Conservative 1161; the Liberal highest on the poll securing the seat by only 28 votes, polling 1189 votes.

single seats, now almost universal.*—(*c*) That it is essential, therefore, that some means should be found, whereby, without endangering the seat, it may be possible to select the candidate whose views are most in accordance with those of the majority. Second Ballots and Single Seats go together.

4. (*a*) That, at present, there is often great difficulty when selecting a candidate, to discover which person or whose views will meet with most support from the party. The first ballot would give an easy means of accurately testing the opinions of the party.—(*b*) That the noisy, active, extreme section of a party often force on the party, as a whole, candidates distasteful to the majority. At present, the fear of splitting the party enforces acquiescence in the selection; with the result, that the seat is lost, or, if won, a large portion of the party remains practically misrepresented.—(*c*) That a system of second ballots would protect the majority of a party in a constituency from the mistakes, or worse, of wire-pulling dictation.

5. That the constituency, as a whole, should not be punished by being misrepresented, because of local jealousies or blunders.

6. (*a*) That even though under a system of second ballots a section of the party might, in the end, be unsuccessful in returning their candidate, their special views and special grievances—at present necessarily stifled or "squared"—would obtain a public hearing.—(*b*) That a system of second ballots would give the best and readiest means of accurately ascertaining the real extent and importance of particular opinions in current politics.

7. That candidates and members would be more independent if they had not, as at present, to submit to

* There were twenty-nine "double-barrelled" constituencies only left by the Reform Bill of 1884.

pressure, or to compromise on so many different questions, in order to meet the views of the different sections of their party.

8. (*a*) That party organisation would be sufficiently effective to prevent the second ballot from being used as an instrument to ventilate any but substantially supported divergencies of opinion.—(*b*) That it is possible that at the first or second elections after the introduction of the system, there would be, in many constituencies, a multiplicity of candidates belonging to the same party, anxious to test the relative strength of their particular views. But the relative strength of the different sections of the party once satisfactorily tested, the party as a whole would deprecate continual division, and become—because unity would be founded on knowledge—more consolidated than before; and thus, a multiplicity of candidates would in the end be discouraged and not encouraged.

9. (*a*) (By some.) That, along with the introduction of a system of second ballots, it would be just and necessary, in order to prevent mere frivolous candidatures, that a deposit should be made by each candidate, to be forfeited if he did not poll a certain proportion of the electorate, or of the votes actually cast.*—(*b*) That, thus, while no *bonâ fide* candidature would be prevented, the cheap indulgence of human

* Two very different things, especially in London. For instance, in Stepney, the voters numbering 6900, the total votes polled in 1886 only amounted to 3970, little more than half the electorate. Thus—assuming that the requisite percentage to be polled to save forfeit is put at ten per cent.—if the percentage were reckoned on the electorate, the candidate would have had, in this case, to poll 690 votes; if it were reckoned on the votes actually polled, only 397. In the case of (for instance) the Darwin election of 1885, where the poll was a very high one, the difference would have been small; 11,750 votes were polled out of an electorate of 12,600. A concrete instance is that of the Mile End election of 1885, where the total electorate being 5880, and the total votes cast 3053, the lowest unsuccessful candidate polled 420 votes; thus, if the percentage were fixed on the electorate, the deposit would have been forfeited; if on the votes polled, it would have been saved.

vanity, selfishness, or cantankerousness, would be prevented. —(*c*) That such a deposit would in no sense constitute a property qualification—it would only be forfeited if an overwhelming majority of the electorate were unfavourable.*

10. That the system of second ballots almost universally prevails abroad and works without difficulty or friction.†

11. (*a*) (By some.) That the Liberal party, even now, suffer from a plurality of candidates.—(*b*) That the growth of "Labour" and "Socialist" opinions, combined with universal suffrage, the payment of members, and the transference of the official expenses, would greatly encourage the multiplication of "Liberal" candidates.—(*c*) That the introduction of second ballots constitutes the only hope for the Progressive of avoiding the loss of many seats; and of maintaining the homogeneity of their party.—(*d*) That, by this means alone, without endangering the seat, can the opinion of the constituency, in regard to the particular "Liberal" opinion most prevalent, be easily and accurately ascertained.—(*e*) That, at the second ballot, the different sections of the party would sink their differences and loyally support the Progressive candidate highest on the poll. (*f*) That the danger of a loss of seat would be minimised; while a desirable, because safe, opportunity would be given to the various sections within the party of testing their relative strength.—(*g*) That thus a system of second ballots would lead to a greater solidarity in the party than at present exists.

* To meet the objection that the deposit would constitute a property qualification, an alternative suggestion is sometimes made that a requisition, signed by a certain percentage of the electors, should be a necessary antecedent to the legality of a candidature. But to this plan there are obvious objections—practical infringement of the secrecy of the ballot, trouble, expense, difficulty of check and verification, &c.

† See Parliamentary Paper C 2987, 1881; and Parliamentary Paper C 6953, 1893. Unfortunately, the information at the disposal of any one desirous of studying the subject is of the most meagre description.

On the other hand, it is contended :—

1. That the present system of elections works well: and, on the whole, results in an accurate representation of the opinion of the constituencies.

2. (*a*) That a divided majority—often differing more seriously from one another than they do from the minority—cannot be said to constitute a majority of opinion.—(*b*) That, if the minority be greater in numbers than either or any of the sections of the majority, and thus obtains the seat, the largest single section of opinion has carried the day, and the constituency is therefore properly represented.—(*c*) That the candidate returned by the majority at the second election would not be the true choice of the constituency, but only the nominee of a section; not the representative of a party but the representative of one particular shade of opinion in the party, and second ballots would encourage sectional candidates.

3. (*a*) That the whole electoral system should not be dislocated in order artificially to arrange local party disputes.—(*b*) That, if a constituency so mismanages that the minority win the seat, it must suffer for its folly.

4. (*a*) That one great advantage of the present system is, that all sections, classes, and opinions in the party combine, and work heartily, loyally, and unitedly for the common cause.—(*b*) That a system of second ballots would encourage divisions, and accentuate differences; would lead to suspicion, intrigue, and jealousy; to the setting of class against class, wealth against poverty, labour against capital.

5. (*a*) That, often, at the second ballot, the party as a whole would not coalesce nor give their united support to the nominee of a section; and thus the minority would still gain the seat.—(*b*) That this is all the more probable, inas-

much as the real contest at the first ballot would have been not between the two opposing parties, but between the different sections of one party. The primary object of each section would have been to place its candidate higher on the poll than the candidate of the other section or sections, so that, at the second ballot, he might become the selected candidate.

6. (*a*) That consequently friction, heat, and ill-feeling would have been engendered, which would prevent subsequent co-operation, and would lead to wholesale abstention at the second ballot on the part of the partisans of the less successful candidate.—(*b*) That unless coalition takes place at the third ballot there is no virtue and no advantage in it —the minority would still obtain the seat.—(*c*) That if the minority of the majority abstain, and the majority of the majority are nevertheless successful in returning their candidate at the second ballot, the member, so returned, will sit, not as a representative and supporter of the party at large, but only and specially of a section.

7. (*a*) That, apart from any divisions in the party, the second election, where it takes place, would not fairly reflect the opinion of the constituency.—(*b*) That it would be impossible to keep up for the second election the excitement and interest that prevailed at the first election; or to get the bulk of the electors to record their votes twice within a few days.—(*c*) That, as it is, many electors are with difficulty persuaded to vote; while to many others, especially to working men, voting involves sacrifice of time or money. Thus a large number, who had voted at the first ballot, would be forced to, or would abstain at the second; while some who abstained at the first, would vote at the second.*

* It appears from the Parliamentary Return, C 6953, 1893, which reports the operation of the second ballot in Germany, that the number of votes cast at the second ballot is, as a rule, substantially less, to the extent of 10 to

—(*d*) (By some.) That this would be more especially the case with the Liberal electors. The Liberal party does not possess the same means and facilities as their opponents of inducing voters to vote, or of bringing them to the poll; it depends more on zeal and enthusiasm. The enthusiasm would have evaporated, the defeated section of the party would be sullen, and largely abstain, with the result that the Liberal votes cast on the second occasion would be considerably less than those cast on the first occasion.—(*e*) That, thus, the opinion of the constituency recorded at the first might be reversed at the second ballot.

8. That the system of voting prevailing abroad is very different to that prevailing here, though even there the votes cast at the two elections vary greatly.* Moreover, the elections are greatly facilitated by being held on a Sunday† —impossible in England.

9. (*a*) That the additional cost involved would be very serious. Every candidate would have to run the risk of, and in a large number of cases would be involved in, the cost, trouble, and annoyance of a second election.—(*b*) That the financial strain on the party and on the individual would thus be very great.—(*c*) That many, otherwise most eligible candidates, would thus be prevented from standing. —(*d*) That the additional risk and the actual expense involved would greatly handicap "Labour" candidates, in whose interests the second ballot system is especially demanded.

20 per cent., than those cast at the first ballot. On the other hand the votes given at the second ballot, occasionally, though very seldom, exceed those given on the first ballot. In one constituency, for instance, they rose from 19,000 to 23,900. In another they fell from 15,300 to 12,400, with a total electorate of 20,000; and in another case from 58,200 to 49,200, the total electorate being 75,000.

* See previous note.

† Not so, however, in Germany.

10. That the country would not stand the worry, trouble, and expense of double elections.*

11. That, in consequence of the unpleasantness of internecine warfare, of the additional worry and trouble involved, while pushing, obstinate, ill-conditioned men would force themselves on the constituencies, moderate, fair-minded, and public-spirited men would be forced aside, or deterred from becoming candidates. Thus the *personnel* of the House would seriously suffer.

12. (*a*) That a system of second ballots would greatly encourage frivolous and vexatious candidatures. A crotchety or notoriety-seeking individual would be enabled, without loss to himself, and without endangering the seat, to air his crotchets, and to obtain the notoriety he sought.†—(*b*) That any compulsory deposit with forfeit, in the event of a failure to poll more than a certain proportion of the electorate, would constitute a property qualification—for no man can tell beforehand what proportion of the electorate he will poll.‡

13. (*a*) (By some). That it would totally destroy all cohesion, already somewhat attenuated, in the Liberal party.—(*b*) That there would be nothing to prevent, and everything to encourage, a multiplicity of "Liberal" candidates of various shades of opinion.—(*c*) That the supporters of those different candidates would be, before

* In Germany there are constantly four or five *bonâ fide* candidates for the single seat. At the election of 1893, second ballots were necessary in nearly half the constituencies, *i.e.* in 180 out of the 397 constituencies.

† The Parliamentary Paper C 6953 already quoted shows that what are practically frivolous candidatures largely prevail in Germany under the system of second ballots. In one instance quoted there were seven candidates, of whom the highest polled 5270 votes and the two lowest 249 and 38 respectively. In another case there were nine candidates; the highest polled 26,700 votes, while the four lowest candidates only polled 249 votes between them.

‡ See note, p. 55.

and during the election, working strenuously against one another; and, whatever the result of the election—and many seats would be lost by abstentions at the second ballots *—the local "Liberal" party would be permanently split up into rival and hostile camps.—(*d*) That the various candidates would stand, and would be labelled as belonging to a particular section of the party; and the member, when returned, would sit and vote with the particular section of the party in the House to which he belonged. Thus, the party, both inside and outside the House, instead of being homogeneous, would be split up into different and distinct sections; and the Liberal party, and especially a Liberal Government, would be completely paralysed.

14. That the effect of second ballots on the system of party Government is seen in France as well as in Germany. In France the Republican (the Liberal) party, though in an enormous majority in the country, is so split up into multifarious and diverse groups, each with its own leader and its own organ in the press, that the Government of the day is merely a Government on sufferance; is constantly being changed, and is almost impotent for action. In Germany there are innumerable parties in the Reichstag.†

* See Nos. 6, 7, p. 58.

† In the German Reichstag elected in 1893, under a system of second ballots, there were thirteen acknowledged parties, and six independent members!

PAYMENT OF MEMBERS

It is proposed that all members of Parliament should be paid a State Salary for their Parliamentary services.*

This proposal is advocated on the grounds :—

1. That sitting and voting are not a privilege enjoyed by the individual, but a duty performed towards the community —and, as such, should be paid for.

2. (*a*) That, in a democratic country, no obstacle ought to stand in the way of a man, otherwise qualified, from serving his country in Parliament.—(*b*) That it is not only the election expenses that prevent men from standing; but still more the cost of maintaining themselves afterwards as members of Parliament.—(*c*) That practically, therefore, the non-payment of a salary constitutes a "property qualification" for members of Parliament.

3. That, so long as constituencies are in any degree restricted in the choice of candidates, the representative system lacks completeness.

4. That the greater the choice of candidates, the better will the electors be represented; the keener will be the

* The salary usually proposed is £365 a year. There are 670 members, but of these about 30 already receive salaries, leaving 640 to be paid. At £365 an annual outlay of £230,000 a year would be entailed; at £500 the cost would be £320,000. It is universally admitted now, that the salaries should be a charge on the Consolidated Fund (*i.e.* the taxes), and not on the rates. It is somewhat curious to note, however, that, in 1885, Mr Chamberlain favoured the latter principle. "Mr Chamberlain proposes to do nothing of the sort" (*i.e.* charge the amount on the Consolidated Fund). "Whatever sum may be paid to the representatives of the people, it would be a charge, not as the *Quarterly* reviewer finds it convenient to assume, upon the Imperial Exchequer, but upon the constituencies."—*The Radical Programme*, p. 27.

interest taken in the elections; and the greater will be the confidence felt in the Legislature.

5. (*a*) That, at present, the choice of candidates is almost exclusively restricted to one class; the well-to-do and leisured; who represent but limited interests.*—(*b*) That except as representatives paid by their fellows, poor men and working men are almost entirely excluded from the House.—(*c*) That the sacrifices entailed on the Labour candidates and on those who send them, are out of all proportion to the sacrifices entailed on other members of Parliament and their constituents.

6. (*a*) That thus the limitation of choice especially affects the working classes.—(*b*) That the working-men delegates are an honourable addition to the House; and it would be very advantageous, for the sake of all classes, that their numbers should be increased.

7. (*a*) That, apart from the "Labour" question, payment of members would greatly and favourably enlarge the choice of candidates. Local men especially, of the best stamp; young men of energy and with fresh ideas, young men from the Universities, and others, who cannot now afford to be in the House, would be encouraged to stand.—(*b*) That the opportunities for the "carpet-baggers" and the briefless lawyer, too often now the only candidates available, would be diminished, not increased.

8. (*a*) That the men excluded from the House by lack of means would be as capable of serving the State as those who, under existing circumstances, are able to stand.—(*b*) That it is a misfortune to the State to be deprived for any reason of the services of any able citizens; and in this case, the disqualification—want of means—can be easily removed.

* The House of Commons of 1892 consisted of 209 members representing the landed interest, 128 representing the services, 24 the liquor interest, business men 33, trading and manufacturing interest 186, railway interest 62, official interest 91, lawyers 135, literary and professional 27, labour 8.

9. That the demands on the time of members have so much increased as to make it ever more difficult for a man to do his duty as a member of Parliament, and, at the same time, to earn his own living.

10. (*a*) That, nowadays, we do not want members of Parliament to play at politics, but to work at politics; we want, not *dilettante* politicians, but practical hard-working men.—(*b*) That, if the members were paid, they would feel a higher responsibility towards those who employed them, and the work of the nation would be less neglected. Parliamentary work would be better and more rapidly done; economy and efficiency would prevail, and the cost to the State would be saved many times over.

11. (*a*) That the salary would not be of a sufficient amount to be an object of desire to the political adventurer; while it would be enough to enable earnest and able men to serve their country without starving their families.—(*b*) That the prophecies made at every stage of electoral reform, that the spouter and the demagogue would become omnipotent, have always been falsified by the instinctive common-sense of English constituencies.—(*c*) That, after all, it is the constituency that returns the member; and they can be trusted, and should be trusted, to distinguish between the political adventurer and the honest politician.

12. (*a*) That the position of the member would be enhanced, inasmuch as his election would be due to a process of selection from the many, not exclusion of all but a few.—(*b*) That payment would lead to greater political purity; a needy member would not have the same temptation to become a "guinea pig," &c.

13. (*a*) That ministers are already paid, and well paid, for devoting themselves to the public service. Doubtless it would be easy to obtain the gratuitous services of good men for these duties, but the nation prefers to pay them, in order

to secure a wider range of selection, and to ensure that no man shall be pecuniarily a loser by devoting himself to the public service. Similarly, the private member, who also has to sacrifice a very large amount of time, should receive some proportionate remuneration. The difference between the Minister and the Member is one of degree, not of principle. —(*b*) That the salaries paid to ministers in no way sap their independence or integrity.

14. (*a*) That the principle of payment for political services is already practically admitted. On personal application, and on proof that the pension is necessary to enable the recipient befittingly to maintain his position, a certain number of political pensions are granted to ex-cabinet ministers.—(*b*) That these pensions are given to men who have already, as ministers, received considerable payment from the nation; and who, when not in office, are charged with duties practically no heavier than those which fall to the lot of private members.

15. (*a*) That, as no stigma attaches to the possession of these pensions, so no stigma would attach to the possession of a salary, granted in order to enable the holder properly to maintain his position as a member of Parliament.—(*b*) That a State salary, if paid to all members, would in no way interfere with the independence of the individual. At present, the poorer member is obliged directly to depend on his friends or his constituents.—(*c*) That the salaries paid to ministers enhance their dignity and in no way sap their independence.—(*d*) That receipt of a national salary would in no way tend to make members more of delegates, or more dependent on their constituencies, than they are at present. —(*e*) That, at present, the Labour members, owing their seats and their salaries to their fellow-workmen, are necessarily more delegates than representatives.

16. That the superior character of the British House of

Commons over similar institutions abroad, arises from constitutional and national causes, not from the mere fact of the non-payment of members.

17. That the system of gratuitous public service elsewhere would not be adversely affected by the payment to members of a small salary.

18. That the total cost would not exceed some £200,000 to £300,000 a year; * a very small sum in comparison with the many advantages that would accrue.

19. (By some.) That payment of members would ultimately lead to a reduction in the number of members of the House; which in many ways would be advantageous.†

20. That it was the ancient practice in England to pay members of Parliament. The unpopularity of that system arose from the fact that it was founded on a wrong principle,—payment by the constituency instead of by the State.

21. (*a*) That in England, almost alone among States possessing a representative system of government, members are not paid.‡—(*b*) That in nearly all the self-governing Colonies the representatives are paid.

22. (By some.) That payment of members is essential to the future existence of the Liberal party; it lacks money and it lacks wealthy candidates.

* See note, p. 62.

† See note, p. 5.

‡ Each American Senator and Representative receives $5000 (£1000) a year, plus 10d. per mile for travelling expenses to and from Washington, and £25 a year for stationary. The cost to the Republic amounts to some £400,000 a year. The payment in the Australian Colonies is at the rate of between £200 and £300 a year. In France the Deputies receive £360 a year. In Russia they receive £1 a day; in Austria 16s. 8d. a day, in Russia 15s. a day, and in Switzerland 16s. a day during the session, or for actual attendance. In most of these cases there are, moreover, travelling or other allowances. Neither the members of the Italian Chamber, nor of the German Imperial Parliament are paid.—(See Dickinson's *Procedure of Foreign Parliaments*, P. P. C 2753 (1881) and C 6975 (1893).)

On the other hand, it is contended :—

1. (*a*) That one source of England's greatness, and of her international position, is that her citizens generally have always been ready to devote themselves gratuitously to the public service.—(*b*) That the payment of members would strike a fatal blow at the system of gratuitous public service prevailing in England, under which men are ready to make private sacrifices for public duty.—(*c*) That if members were paid, payment for municipal work would follow, at great cost and great loss of public service.

2. That one chief reason why the people have so much confidence in the House of Commons is that, with scarcely an exception, men do not enter the House for the sake of gain or reward; but, on the contrary, make some personal sacrifice in order to serve their country.

3. (*a*) That there are an increasing number of men of leisure and ability ready to serve their country gratuitously and efficiently; and it would, under those circumstances, be foolish and wasteful to supersede them by salaried others, probably less worthy.—(*b*) That it would be absurd, in order that a few deserving representatives should be paid, to compel the bulk of the constituencies against their will to pay, and the bulk of the members against their will to receive, salaries.

4. (*a*) That, while it is an excellent thing that an association desiring to be represented in Parliament should pecuniarily support its representative, there is no reason why the whole nation should be taxed in order to give to a few trades or classes special facilities for representation.—(*b*) That it is not advantageous that the representation of a particular class of persons, whether "labour" or otherwise, should be especially encouraged.—(*c*) That the working classes hold the voting power, and can insist on the proper representation of their views.

5. (*a*) That payment of members elsewhere has not resulted in the return of "labour" members; or, where it has, the result has not been satisfactory.—(*b*) That the system of payment of members abroad has produced evil results; in no country are politics on so high a level, are politicians so honest, independent, and patriotic as in England.

6. That to pay them a salary as such, would degrade the office and position of members of Parliament.

7. (*a*) That the independence of the member would be seriously endangered if he were State-paid.—(*b*) That a paid member would be considered, not as a representative but as a delegate; and his freedom of action and power for good would be greatly curtailed.

8. That the whole relation between a member and his constituents would be vitally altered. At present the constituencies can confer honour and position, but not money. With payment of members, the constituency would become the patron and the member the paid servant.

9. That an undesirable class of candidates, needy adventurers and professional politicians would be multiplied; men who would look to membership as a means of livelihood. Thus the whole tone of the House would be fatally lowered.

10. (*a*) That the payment of a salary would tend still farther to attract lawyers; the salary would be sufficient to maintain them while they were trying to pick up a livelihood at the bar; and there are already too many lawyers in the House of Commons—(*b*) That it would tend to the return of a larger number of mere local representatives; men with narrow views and limited aims.—(*c*) That it would tend to increase the number of "carpet-baggers" in the House; men who have no interest in the locality they represent.

11. That, as in the case of the members of the House of

Representatives in the United States, payment of members would lead to more constant changes in the *personnel* of the House; the electors would be inclined to give each candidate a turn at the loaves and fishes.

12. That the individual salary would of necessity be so small, and not as a rule sufficient decently to maintain a needy member; he would be more than ever obliged to make something out of his "M.P.-ship."

13. That the attraction of the salary would lead to such a multiplication of candidates, as to necessitate the introduction of the pernicious system of Second Ballots.*

14. (*a*) That, even under present circumstances, the anxiety of members to keep themselves *en evidence* tends to delay in the transaction of Parliamentary business, and this evil would be enormously accentuated were members paid.—(*b*) That the only way of diminishing this evil would be by a great reduction in the number of members; in itself a disadvantage. †—(*c*) That any reduction of members would entail a fresh redistribution of seats throughout the kingdom; and involve the difficult question of the proportionate representation of the three Kingdoms.

15. That the cost of the election rather than membership afterwards constitutes the bar, and so long as there remain any pecuniary obstacles to their entrance into Parliament,‡ the payment of a salary to members would be an anomaly.

16. That the cost to the country would be very great; while the payment of members of Parliament would

* See section on *Second Ballots*.

† There are 670 members of the House of Commons. The Chamber of Deputies in France consists of 576 members, in Italy of 508, the Imperial Reichstag in Germany of 397, in Austria of 353 members. The House of Representatives in the States numbers 330 members.—(See Dickinson's *Foreign Parliament*, 1890.)

‡ See section on the *Official Expenses of Elections*.

certainly be followed by that of members of County Councils, Town Councils, Town Boards, &c.

17. That the ancient system of payment of members forms no precedent. It was carried on under totally different conditions; and, moreover, it worked so badly that it gradually fell into disuse.

WOMAN'S SUFFRAGE *

It is proposed to extend the franchise to women, so that every woman holding (in her own right) a sufficient property qualification, would be entitled to vote at the Parliamentary elections. Some propose to confine the privilege to spinsters and widows; others would extend it to married women as well.

This proposal is upheld on the grounds:—

1. (*a*) That the electoral system should be founded on a complete representation of the whole people.—(*b*) That as women of property bear the burdens, they should not be deprived of the rights of citizenship; that as women have to obey the laws, they should be allowed a voice in making them. It is property, not sex, which gives the right to vote.—(*c*) That, though certain other persons (minors, men who are not householders, paupers, &c.) share with women electoral disability, women alone retain their disability throughout life and under every condition.—(*d*) That, thus, in the case of women, "the very principle and system of representation based on property is set aside, and an exceptionally personal disqualification is created for the mere purpose of excluding her."—(*e*) That, consequently, just

* The reader is especially referred to *Women Suffrage*, by Mrs Ashton Dilke and the late Mr W. Woodall, M.P. (Imperial Parliament Series), and to *Reasons for Opposing Women Suffrage*, by the late Vice-Admiral Maxse (Ridgway).

that result ensues which it is especially desirable to avoid, that women should be treated as, and become a "class."

2. (*a*) That women have just as much interest in good government as men; and if there be any difference, women being physically the weaker, require protection more than men.—(*b*) That the interests of women are either identical with those of men, and in that case their votes would not affect the ultimate result; or their interests are divergent, and in that case they should be fairly and directly represented.—(*c*) That where the interests of men and women are divergent, the latter, being unrepresented, suffer—witness the laws respecting women's property, divorce, custody of children, contagious diseases, child murder, &c.; while if directly represented, the anomalies and inequalities of the laws as affecting them would be modified or swept away. —(*d*) That even if women are to be subject to men's authority, they require the protection of the Suffrage to secure them from an abuse of that authority; they do not need political rights in order that they may govern, but in order that they may not be misgoverned.

3. (*a*) That the argument that the male vote, on some special occasion, would be swamped by the female, cannot be seriously entertained. Moreover, women would never vote all one way, any more than men do.—(*b*) That women would be much more likely to vote under the influence of the men, than contrary to it.

4. (*a*) That though there may be truth in the assertion that a married woman is represented through her husband, a widow or spinster is entirely unrepresented.—(*b*) That, as a matter of fact, the grievances of women are as much the grievances of wives and mothers as of the unmarried.

5. (*a*) That it is an anomaly for women to be allowed the School Board and Municipal, and to be excluded from the Parliamentary franchise; if they are fit for the one they are

qualified for the other; they pay taxes as well as rates. —(*b*) That as the highest post in the realm has more than once been worthily filled by a woman, it is an anomaly to refuse to women the lesser privilege of a vote.

6. (*a*) That mentally and physically there is no sufficient difference between men and women to justify withholding from the one that which is given to the other; the idea that women are the inferiors of men, and that they should be "subject" to them, is merely a relic of semi-barbarism. —(*b*) That the inferior position which women now hold is due not to natural causes, but to the laws made by men. Repeal these laws, and women would soon take their proper position.—(*c*) That as the question is one of voting and not of being elected, the physical inferiority of women is of no account in the matter.—(*d*) That whenever women have had the opportunity they have shown themselves competent to exercise power and responsibility.

7. (*a*) That the possession of the Suffrage would have a salutary effect on women, by increasing their intelligence and interest, and extending their range of vision, and by removing the idea that they are necessarily inferior; while to withhold it injures their self-respect, and keeps them ignorant and indifferent.—(*b*) That more especially is this latter the case now that the servant and labourer are enfranchised, while the female employer or farmer is refused a vote.—(*c*) That, naturally, so long as women are denied political power, they cannot see the proper sense of responsibility in using their political influence.—(*d*) (By some.) That the enfranchisement of a small minority of women (for the numbers who would be enfranchised would not be overwhelming) would have little effect one way or the other on the character of the whole sex.

8. (*a*) That women being more deeply imbued with religious feeling, and with respect for law and order, than

men, their possession of a vote would be an additional bulwark against Socialism and Anarchy.—(*b*) That the extension of the franchise to women, necessarily women of property, would tend to check the democratic tendencies of the age, and would thus be a Conservative measure. —(*c*) That as the women enfranchised would be chiefly those of education, their opinions (as expressed by their votes) would be of value.—(*d*) That women are more free from party politics and party bias than men, and would therefore judge a political question more on its own merits. —(*e*) That the education of women has made such rapid strides, that to-day they are fitted to exercise a power of which yesterday they were incapable.—(*f*) That the more political women become, the less priest-ridden will they be, and the greater will be their sympathy with the other sex.

9. That the question of enfranchisement ought not to depend at all on the possible way in which the vote will be afterwards cast.

10. That the possession of the franchise would not cause family friction and ill-feeling; for it would be chiefly widows and spinsters of property who would possess votes, and they would be independent.

11. (*a*) That the distinction between voting at Parliamentary elections and being eligible for Parliament, is so absolutely clear, that to concede the one would not be in any way to admit the principle of the other.—(*b*) That the distinction is already clearly drawn in the case of County and Borough Councils—women can vote but are not eligible to sit.

12. That the ballot has so entirely extinguished all rioting and roughness on the day of election, that women could vote in perfect safety and without fear of intimidation or rudeness; just as now they vote at School Board and Municipal elections without any personal unpleasantness ensuing.

13. (*a*) That the assertion that the majority of women

are not desirous of the franchise, proves in what subjection to "custom" they are still bound—"slaves never wish to be free"—and demonstrates the need of further freedom. (*b*) That no woman need exercise the franchise unless she likes. The indifference or aversion of some, should not be a bar to the possession of their rights by others.

14. That though women do not themselves serve in the army, through their fathers, brothers, husbands, they are vitally interested in the preservation of peace; and themselves really suffer more from the horrors of war than men.

15. That to argue that because women are not physically strong they should not be allowed votes is to deny also the right of weaker men to possess the franchise, and is an endorsement of the principle that "might is right."

16. (By some.) That if the franchise be extended to the single women and the widows, it will ultimately be extended to married women as well.

On the other hand, it is urged :—

1. (*a*) That the principle that representation and taxation should go together is by no means fully carried out in the Constitution; all minors, and many men, as well as women, are excluded from the franchise.—(*b*) (By some.) That the change would be opposed to the fundamental principle of democratic government, namely, that persons, and not property, constitute the basis of representation, and that property, and not persons, is the basis of taxation.

2. (*a*) That the existing electoral law was framed merely with a view to the representation of men. It chooses out the head of the family, and gives the vote to him as a man and not as the representative of property. The adoption of "woman suffrage" would entirely reverse this principle.—

(*b*) That to grant the suffrage to women on the ground that, as they are bound to obey the laws, they ought to have a hand in making them, would logically oblige us to concede the suffrage to every man, woman, and child in the kingdom.

3. (*a*) That women are properly represented, in that they can and do exercise immense and legitimate influence over the male voters.—(*b*) That the married woman is much better represented through her husband than she would be through the vote of some spinster or widow; while the two last are directly represented by other male relatives.

4. (*a*) That men and women are, both mentally and physically, in every way different, and it is a mistake to endeavour to break down any of the natural differences—implied in sex—which exist between them.—(*b*) That the female mind lacks the quality of judgment, and mentally, morally, and physically women are unfitted by nature to exercise a calm discretion, more especially on exciting political questions; they cannot, therefore, claim the suffrage on equal terms with men.

5. (*a*) That women are not a "class," their rights and interests harmonise with those of men, and are therefore duly protected.—(*b*) That, of late years especially, very much has been done to redress any legal inequalities which may have formerly existed between the two sexes.—(*c*) That such delays as occur in adopting reform in favour of women are due, not to indifference on the part of men, but to the difficulties which nowadays beset all legislation.

6. (*a*) That if, however, women obtained the suffrage, class distinctions would be set up, "women's questions" would be manufactured, and men and women would be thrown into antagonism.—(*b*) That, thus, not only would the whole nation suffer, but beneficent legislation in favour of women would be retarded instead of being advanced.

7. (*a*) That though at first the women enfranchised

would be those possessing some property, as manhood suffrage will eventually be adopted, the suffrage will ultimately have to be extended to all women.—(*b*) That adult suffrage is only a matter of time; and as the women outnumber the men, they would ultimately predominate in voting power. Such a condition of affairs would be, however, purely artificial, and must disappear when any real strain came. At some moment of national excitement, a preponderance of the women vote would carry some measure which was unpopular with the majority of men, but the physical strength being on the side of the men, they would re-assert their relative position in the midst of confusion, perhaps of revolution and bloodshed.

8. That as the men have practically to put the law into execution, and women would be powerless without them, they should also make the laws. The voting power should correspond with the real strength of the nation.

9. (*a*) That it would be contrary to the natural position of women to be entrusted with power. That women's duties are at home and not in the polling-booth.—(*b*) That men's respect and reverence for women would be fatally undermined if they were allowed to mingle in political strife; while the finer edge of women's nature would be blunted, and they would become unsexed.—(*c*) That if women were enfranchised, the disposal of their votes would lead to family jealousies, ill-feeling, and greater political friction.—(*d*) That the subjection of women by men is a less serious evil than would be the domination of women over men.

10. (*a*) That educational and municipal questions stand on an entirely different footing from matters political; while, as regards the first, women are especially qualified to give advice.—(*b*) That a School Board or Municipal Election is less impassioned than a Parliamentary contest.

11. That as women are not liable to bear arms, and as

they are by nature averse to war, it would be inexpedient to give them the power of voting on questions of peace and war.

12. (*a*) That the majority of women do not want and would rather be without the suffrage.—(*b*) That those alone who would take an active part in politics would be the "strong-minded" women, who are not really representative of the sex, and who are, politically, not advantageous.

13. (By some.) That women are conservative in habit and tendency; while the disposal of their votes would be very much subjected to clerical influence.

14. (*a*) That to demand the suffrage for the spinster and widow and not for the married woman, is illogical, and is not genuine "woman suffrage."—(*b*) That it would be impossible, without great disadvantages, to give the suffrage to married women; and to allow spinsters and widows a privilege which they would lose on marriage would be an anomaly which could not long endure.

15. That the concession of the vote would enfranchise amongst others, a very undesirable class of women.

16. That the evidence of Municipal Elections goes to show that female electors are more open to bribery, intimidation, and undue influence, than male, and thus electoral purity would suffer.

17. (*a*) (By some). That it is illogical and unjust to refuse to allow women to sit where they are allowed to vote; and no one desires that women should be eligible for the House of Commons.—(*b*) (By others.) That the concession of the suffrage would inevitably be followed by the demand, which could not logically be refused, that women should be qualified to sit in the House of Commons themselves; no other electors, except clergymen, being ineligible.

18. (A latent fear in the minds of some.) That women, if given the opportunity, would oust men from many occu-

pations which the latter now monopolise, and would thus diminish their earnings.

[Apart from reasons which can be categorically stated, there is against the proposal a strong feeling, which can best be expressed in the phrase that "women *are* women."]

THE "ENDING OR MENDING" OF THE HOUSE OF LORDS

It is urged that the House of Lords, on its present basis, has become a constitutional anomaly, and that it must either be swept away altogether, leaving the House of Commons to stand alone; or its right of veto must be very strictly limited; or (by some) that its constitution must be so radically altered, that it shall become a more popular and representative body—somewhat on the lines of most "Second Chambers" abroad, and in the Colonies.

The Peers of the United Kingdom (exclusive of 14 minors) number 511.* The Peer-Bishops number 26; the elected Scotch Peers number 16, and the elected Irish Peers 28, but of these representative Peers three are Peers of the United Kingdom. The total voting strength of the House of Lords is thus 578.

The reform or abolition of the House of Lords is supported on the grounds:—

1. That an institution, to be allowed to exist, must satisfy the requirements of general national utility—and this condition the House of Lords has ceased to fulfil.

* Composed as follows:—Princes of the Blood—Archbishops—Dukes—Marquises—Earls—Viscounts—Bishops—Barons. About 350 of the existing peerages have been created since 1830.

2. That the existence, as one of the estates of the realm, of an oligarchical, irresponsible, and unrepresentative body of hereditary legislators, is out of harmony with the spirit of the age. England alone among nations possesses such a legislative body.

3. That the existence of the House of Lords, on its present basis, is contrary to the true principle of representative government. The nation has neither voice in the selection, nor control over the proceedings of the Upper House.

4. (*a*) That, alone among the institutions of the country, the House of Lords has undergone neither renewal nor reform.—(*b*) That while the Lower House has been gradually placed on an increasingly democratic basis, and now rests on the votes of over six million of electors, the Upper House has become in no way more representative.

5. (*a*) That it is a constitutional absurdity that a number of irresponsible individuals should have the power of overriding, or thwarting, the popular will, as expressed by the House of Commons.—(*b*) That more especially is this the case, when the vast majority of these persons are legislators not on account of their own merits, but merely through an accident of birth.—(*c*) That their ancestors were not necessarily nor usually ennobled because of any special fitness for legislative work; while, even where such fitness existed, it is not necessarily nor usually hereditary.

6. That, under the present system, a Peer, however unfit or unwilling to serve, cannot be relieved of his legislative functions.

7. (*a*) That decade by decade the House of Lords has in every way become less and less representative.—(*b*) That in former days, the House of Lords was not a party assembly. It has gradually, during the last half century, and more especially of late years, been converted into a wholly Con-

servative party instrument.—(*c*) That in consequence of the mode of election (election by simple majority), the forty-four co-optatively elected Irish and Scotch Peers are invariably Conservatives, though a singularly small proportion of the parliamentary electors in those countries are Conservative.

8. (*a*) That the Lords are representative of but one class, the landlords, and one interest, the land; which thus obtains an undue influence in legislation.—(*b*) That the legislation which the Lords chiefly obstruct, is that which they imagine affects themselves, more especially as regards lands; their own personal or class interests are allowed to stand in the way of national progress.

9. That while the country has become increasingly Liberal, the House of Lords has become increasingly Conservative.

10. (*a*) That the relative positions of the majority and minority do not change with those of the Lower House; an anomaly which makes itself increasingly felt as successive Liberal Governments come into office.—(*b*) That when a Conservative Government is in office, the Upper House is useless, for it always concurs in that which is done; when a Liberal Government is in office, it is mischievous, for it always opposes everything they do.

11. (*a*) That with a Liberal Ministry in office, the relative and natural positions of the Government and the Opposition are reversed in the Lords. The Leader of the Opposition is practically the Leader of the House, and the Government are always in a minority.—(*b*) That all Liberal legislation suffers in thoroughness from the existence of an irresponsible Upper House. Every Government measure proposed has to be drawn with a view of passing that House, amendments are introduced in the Commons with the same object, and the Bill is still further amended and emasculated in the Lords.—(*c*) Then when a retrograde

measure has been passed by the Conservative Government, the Liberals are impotent to repeal or to amend it; the House of Lords rejects their Bill.

12. That the natural conservatism of the country obtains its proper share of power and representation at the polls; or should not be supplemented by the artificial (though very real) conservatism of the House of Lords.

13. (*a*) That the Lords can, and often do, override the judgment of the Government, the decision of the House of Commons, and the will of the country which sustains both.—(*b*) That often when the Commons, after anxious thought and laborious care, have passed an important measure, the Lords—often with only the semblance of debate—throw out or mutilate the Bill, and thus render barren the Session.—(*c*) That powerful Governments, with the nation at their back, have to appeal to the Lords as suppliants—an undignified position, and one in which no Government should be placed.

14. (*a*) That the only limit which exists to the destructive and damaging power of the Lords, is the expediency of using it—their authority is tempered by necessity alone. Within the limits of supposed danger to themselves they act as they will.—(*b*) That, more than once, when the Lords have overstepped this limit, it has become necessary for the Ministry of the day to create, or threaten to create, a sufficient number of Peers to constitute a Government majority; thereby reducing the constitutional action of the Lords to an absurdity.—(*c*) But that, nowadays, in consequence of the greatly increased numbers of the Peerage, and the increasing disproportion between Liberal and Conservative Peers, it would be impossible to force through a Liberal measure by means of a creation of Peers.*

* It is estimated that out of the 500 odd Peers, only some 30 to 40 are Liberals.

15. That an unrepresentative, irresponsible, and avowedly Conservative body is thus almost omnipotent, and continually comes into conflict with the national will; questions which the country is bent on closing are kept open, and discord and irritation are created and continued; while, when submission is at last made to public pressure, all the grace of concession has evaporated.

16. (*a*) That this body has systematically and obstinately opposed every great reform of the last hundred years, especially in the matter of civil and religious liberty and electoral reform.—(*b*) That as the House of Lords is out of harmony with the progressive spirit of the age, even when it accepts a reform, it mars and mutilates it, and prevents it from being thorough and lasting.—(*c*) That more especially has this been the case with Irish legislation; much of the disquiet state of Ireland is due to the irritation caused by the persistent refusal of the Lords to pass measures of justice and to the mutilated form in which Irish Bills are unwillingly allowed to pass.—(*d*) That not only do measures of importance suffer at its hands, but very many small and necessary measures are delayed; emasculated, or rejected.—(*e*) That thus, while its existence is defended on the ground that it educates public opinion, prevents precipitancy, modifies extremes, and perfects legislation, it really obstructs, mars, and irritates.—(*f*) Instead, therefore, of the House of Lords being an element of stability and permanence, it is a source of obstruction, disturbance, and irritation. It is powerful for evil, and useless for good.

17. (*a*) That it is no real check on the House of Commons, nor useful in revising hurried or imperfect legislation.—(*b*) That the nation is far from requiring an extraneous check on the precipitancy of the Lower House: the difficulty nowadays is to legislate at all.—(*c*) That the

"revision" of the Upper House is mutilation; its "improvements" are usually fatal to effectiveness.

18. (*a*) That the ordinary attendance of the Peers in the House of Lords is small and perfunctory. Three constitutes a quorum.—(*b*) That the Parliamentary work of the Upper House is done in a most perfunctory manner.*

19. (*a*) That the attendance of Peers is only decently good where some important Liberal measure has to be mutilated or rejected.—(*b*) That the important votes of the House of Lords are not decided by the professed politicians, but by the whipping up, as occasion requires, of Peers who take no part in, care nothing, and know less about politics.

20. That the House of Lords has, of necessity, less and less work given it to do, and is becoming, therefore, of diminished practical value as a legislative body.

21. (*a*) That the existence of the Upper House is becoming more and more of a paradox. It has no control over the Government of the day; if it adopts a motion of non-confidence in a Liberal Government the vote is treated with silent contempt. It is obliged to accept measures of which it disapproves; while its amendments are often summarily rejected and reversed by the Commons—and each time it is thus forced to give way its influence is diminished.—(*b*) That every time it strongly resists a Liberal Government it loses somewhat of its power, by raising up a feeling adverse to its action and existence.—(*c*) That, thus, at one period it is treated with contempt, and at another it is assailed with menace and reproach. In either case its prestige and power suffer.

22. That the anomalous position in which the Lords are

* In 1890, for instance, the House of Lords sat 91 times during the Session, covering a period of 129 hours. The longest sitting was 8 hours, the shortest 5 minutes. Only 7 of the sittings exceeded two hours.

placed is their misfortune, and not their fault; they can hardly be blamed if they act on the authority committed to them, and prefer to lose their existence as a corporate body —and be allowed to take their part in politics in other ways—rather than consent to submit to a gradual diminution of their influence and power.

23. (*a*) That the existence of the House of Lords deprives the country of the best services of many able and useful politicians, inasmuch as their powers, energy, and ability are hampered and emasculated by being confined to the Upper House; reform or abolition would enable such men to take a more effective part in politics.—(*b*) That the politician who succeeds to a peerage before he comes of age can never sit in the House of Commons and learn its ways.—(*c*) That those members of the House of Commons who are heirs to peerages may, at any moment, find themselves deprived of the right of sitting in the Commons.—(*d*) That, on many occasions, the accession to a peerage of a leading member of the House of Commons, has retired a prominent politician into virtual political obscurity, and occasionally has seriously affected current politics.* This compulsory translation is hard on the individual, and may be disadvantageous to the country.

24. (*a*) That the fact that a certain number of offices in the Government have to be allotted to Peers, occasionally necessitates an inferior man being preferred, because he is a Peer, to some Commoner of great ability.—(*b*) That the

* For instance, Lord Althorp in 1835; and many less prominent politicians. Both Fox and Pitt, curiously enough, very nearly also "went up"; Lord Chatham and Lord Holland both being at one time at death's door, and without issue. "Lord Chatham's death," says Lord Rosebery, "by the grim humour of our Constitution, would have removed Pitt from the Commons to the Peers. In the prime of life and intellect, he would have been plucked from the governing body of the country, in which he was incomparably the most important personage, and set down as a pauper peer in the House of Lords."—*Pitt*, p. 93.

Ministers in the Upper House are not as accessible to public interrogation, nor so amenable to public opinion, as they would be if they were in the Commons.

25. That the pressure on the Prime Minister to create Peers, and the number of admissions to the Peerage, is ever increasing, and is gradually swelling the House of Lords to unmanageable proportions.

26. That the hereditary principle, as applied in the case of the Crown, is totally different from that applied in the case of the House of Lords. The Crown has no legislative or executive responsibility, and has not exercised its power of veto for nearly two hundred years.

27. (*a*) (By some.) That by limiting the number of legislative Peers, by selection and election from amongst their body, and by the creation of Life Peers, much might be done to render the Upper House more representative, and an efficient and necessary estate of the Realm.*—(*b*) (By others.) That a limitation might be placed on the right of veto.†—(*c*) Or that some system of "referendum," to be applied when the two Houses were at a deadlock, should be introduced.

28. (*a*) (By some.) That the House of Lords, if reformed, would contain admirable materials for a Second Chamber, and might easily be made a powerful and popular authority. —(*b*) That the increased respect and efficiency that would accrue to the Upper House from its reformation on some representative system, would not detract from the power of the House of Commons.

29. (By others.) That the position of the House of Lords

* That is to say, that the House of Lords should have power, if it chose, to throw out, once or twice in succession, a Bill sent up from the Commons; but that, if after that, the Commons again sent up the Bill, the Lords should be obliged to pass it.

† That is to say, that the particular question at issue should be submitted to the electorate, and that their decision should be final.

is so anomalous that it will not stand remodelling, and the sooner it is altogether swept away the better.

30. That the position of the Scotch Peers at least requires alteration. A certain number of them are elected by the whole body of Scotch Peers, from amongst themselves, to sit in the House of Lords; but, as there is a Conservative majority, none except Conservatives are ever chosen. A Scotch Liberal Lord has therefore no prospect of being elected a representative Peer, and as he is ineligible for the House of Commons, he is practically ostracised from politics.*

On the other hand, any radical alteration in the existing Constitution of the House of Lords is opposed on the grounds:—

1. That a constitutional institution which has grown up with the nation's growth, and which is founded on tradition and descent, should not be destroyed unless it can be shown that great advantage would follow its destruction.

2. (*a*) That though the existence and constitution of the House of Lords cannot be defended on theoretical and logical grounds, it has held its position for centuries, and played a great part in history, while its continued existence is of great practical advantage to the State. The Constitution works very well as it stands.—(*b*) That the Constitution of the House of Lords is not by any means perfect or ideal, but the country desires a Second Chamber, and the existing Chamber is better than would be one artificially constructed

3. (*a*) That it is a great advantage to the country that the aristocracy should be drawn into taking an active part in politics. That the House of Lords taps a different

* An Irish Peer, if not elected as a representative Peer, is eligible for the House of Commons. For instance, Lord Palmerston was an Irish Peer.

stratum to the House of Commons.—(*b*) That the English nobility have hitherto deserved and retained their hold over the respect, confidence, and affection of the people; and—to the advantage of equality—are a less distinct class than the aristocracy of any other nation.

4. (*a*) That, in consequence of its ranks being continually recruited from the People, the Upper House becomes ever more and more truly representative. It represents education, intelligence, leisure, wealth, and influence.—(*b*) That a very considerable number of the Peers have had a legislative training as members of the Lower House.*—(*c*) That, moreover, a considerable number in addition have held administrative, judicial, or other high offices, and bring to the House the experience they have thus acquired.—(*d*) That debates in the Lords are dignified, unfettered and useful.

5. (*a*) That the argument urged for reforming the House of Lords—that it has not always gone so far or so quickly as the Commons—is reason rather for desiring to leave it alone.—(*b*) That by preventing, modifying, or delaying the hasty, impulsive, ill-digested, or unjust measures adopted by the Commons, or in case of real need forcing a dissolution, it puts a proper and constitutional check on precipitancy and Radicalism; allows time for popular opinion to mature itself; and thus prevents the Government from acting on first impulses, or under the influence of some sudden popular passion or excitement, or in obedience to a chance majority. Often and often the country has exclaimed, "Thank Heavens for the House of Lords!"—(*c*) That legislative precipitancy will tend to occur more often under the new Democracy; while the

* In 1886, for instance (after the General Election of the year), no less than 182 of the sitting Peers had, at some time or other, sat in the House of Commons.

last check on hasty legislation has disappeared with the reform of the procedure of the Lower House.

6. That when the Upper House has delayed legislation, it has always had the sympathy of a large proportion of the House of Commons, and of the Country.

7. That there is no force in the objection that the House of Lords accepts Conservative and delays Liberal legislation. The former is not radical and drastic, the latter does not in the end suffer from delay and reconsideration; while a legislative step once taken cannot be retraced.

8. (*a*) That though perhaps the House of Commons may not very often be over hasty or rash in legislation, its moderation is greatly due to the latent knowledge that the House of Lords will have a voice in the matter, and that its opinions must be consulted. Remove this check, and legislation would immediately become more impulsive and precipitate.—(*b*) That the result of this influence has been, that while in certain cases legislation may have been somewhat delayed; when an important Bill is ultimately passed, it represents the deliberate and final will of the People. Thus progress, though slow, is sure, and revolutionary swings of the pendulum are avoided.—(*c*) That in ordinary legislation the Upper House smoothes down the rough legislative excrescences of the Lower.

9. (*a*) That having no fear of constituencies, the Peers are independent, and speak boldly their own minds.—(*b*) That their debates on great occasions surpass in interest and intellect those of the House of Commons.

10. That even if it were true, that the legislation which the Lords chiefly prevent or amend is that which mostly affects themselves, they must be acknowledged to be intimate with the subject; while those who press forward such legislation have, as a rule, "sinister interests" of their own.

11. (*a*) That though, theoretically, the power of the Lords is unlimited, practically it is kept within very reasonable and moderate bounds.—(*b*) That, if necessary, the Government can override the majority of the Lords by the creation of fresh Peers, by Royal Warrant, or by tacking a clause on to the "Appropriation Bill," which the Lords must pass, or reject, in its entirety.

12. (*a*) That when popular feeling has been definitely expressed, the House of Lords, if at variance with the national will, gracefully subordinates its own opinions, and gives way.—(*b*) That within the last fifty years especially, the Lords have assented to a vast number of most useful reforms.

13. (*a*) That it is easy to talk loosely of uniting the power of, or of reforming the House of Lords, but practically, unless the Upper House will reform itself, this cannot be accomplished without a dangerous revolution.—(*b*) (By some.) That the ultimate extinction of the House of Lords is certain. It is better, therefore, to leave it gradually to die a natural death, than to hasten its end at the risk of conflict and agitation.—(*c*) That year by year it is becoming weaker, and more impotent to do harm; while an unsuccessful crusade against it might revive and invigorate its vitality.

14. (*a*) That if the Constitution of the House of Lords were once touched, its end would soon follow. It survives chiefly through the existence of a feeling of veneration and sentiment; this feeling once disturbed, the anomalies of its existence would become apparent, and it would be doomed. —(*b*) That no mere creation of Life Peers, or a simple change in the hereditary system, would be effective in strengthening the Upper House.

15. (*a*) That some Second Chamber is essential to the Progress, Prosperity, and Peace of the nation. Without it, every check and every safeguard of the Constitution

would be swept away; and the majority in the single Chamber would be absolutely omnipotent.—(*b*) That no brand-new Second Chamber could ever take the place now occupied by the House of Lords. It would not command the respect of the Country or of the House of Commons.—(*c*) That it would either be powerless, and therefore useless, or powerful, and therefore mischievous. —(*d*) That the House of Lords once pulled down, could never be replaced in any permanent, useful, or satisfactory form.

16. (*a*) That if the House of Lords were abolished, the House of Commons would be swamped with Peers—the fact of a man being a Peer having great influence in many constituencies—and would become more aristocratic and conservative, to the hindrance of progress and reform. —(*b*) That consequently an agitation would spring up for the creation of a Second Chamber, in order to rid the House of Commons of its Peers.

17. That if the hereditary principle were abolished in the case of the House of Lords, that principle would be in jeopardy as applied in the case of the Crown.

18. (*a*) (By some.) That to "mend" and not to "end" the House of Lords would be a fatal mistake. To reform would be to strengthen. The present House of Lords is powerful for evil; a reformed Upper House would be far more powerful, and just as Conservative.—(*b*) That a reformed, non-hereditary, and representative Upper House would be entitled to and would freely exercise its power; and would constitute a formidable rival to the Lower House.—(*c*) That an Upper House, however constituted, would always mainly consist of Conservatives, wealthy men, land-owners, and Churchmen.—(*d*) That a Second Chamber, however constituted, is always reactionary.

19. (By some.) That a mere limitation on the power

of veto would do more harm than good; not only would the technical difficulty of applying it be great, but it would be a distinct encouragement to the Upper House, on every occasion, to throw out Liberal Bills until their right of veto was exhausted.

20. (By some.) That if it be necessary to introduce a check over a Single Chamber—the House of Lords being abolished—the best and most popular safeguard would be the introduction of the "Referendum."

THE EXCLUSION OF BISHOPS FROM THE HOUSE OF LORDS

At present the 2 Archbishops and 24 Bishops, sit and vote in the House of Lords as Life Peers in virtue of their office. It is proposed to deprive them of their legislative powers and of their seats in the House.

This proposal is supported on the most diverse, and sometimes diametrically opposite grounds, namely :—

1. (*a*) That it is neither right nor just that one section of religious belief—a minority, or at most a bare majority —should alone be *ex officio* represented in Parliament. —(*b*) That the exclusion of the bishops from the House of Lords would remove a great cause of sectarian irritation. —(*c*) That thus one strong argument for Disestablishment would disappear.

2. That to remove the bishops from the Upper House would be further to sever the connection between Church and State, and be a great step towards Disestablishment.

3. That the Church would still be amply represented in Parliament by laymen of the Church of England.

4. (*a*) That the bishops lose in popular sympathy, from the possession by them of exceptional and anomalous political privileges, especially as these are tinged with political partisanship.—(*b*) That this is more especially the case, inasmuch as the bishops have mostly shown themselves by their votes and speeches to be opposed to progress; and have never used their political power to the real advantage of the Church or of the community at large.—(*c*) That thus the Church, and the Christian religion suffer in the general estimation.—(*d*) That the withdrawal of these exceptional privileges would strengthen and not impair the influence and position of the bishops; and the Church itself would gain from their exclusion from the House of Lords.

5. (*a*) That the legislative functions of a bishop interfere greatly with his diocesan work and Episcopal functions—already so manifold as to be nearly overwhelming.—(*b*) That either he must neglect his legislative work, or he must partially withdraw his presence and influence from his diocese; in trying to perform both functions, he probably does neither well.—(*c*) That more especially the presence in London of the youngest legislative bishop—as *ex officio* chaplain to the House of Lords—is undesirable: he is called away from his diocese just at the time when it is most necessary that he should devote his undivided attention to his Episcopal functions.

6. (*a*) (By some.) That the inclusion of the bishops amongst the peers weakens rather than strengthens the House of Lords. The bishops have not the freedom of

action of life peers, for they speak as delegates, while they are not really representative, owe their creation as bishops to the Prime Minister, and are responsible to no one.—(*b*) (By others.) That to exclude the bishops from the House of Lords would be a democratic step, tending to weaken the Upper House, by depriving it of men of acknowledged ability, life peers, and men more or less representative.

7. That if it be inexpedient to prohibit the clergy of the Church of England from being elected to the Lower House, it is inexpedient to allow the bishops to sit in the Upper House.

8. That the possession of legislative functions by some bishops, and not by all, is an anomaly.

On the other hand, it is urged :—

1. (*a*) That so long as the Church is joined with the State she ought to have, and is entitled to have, a representative voice in framing laws which she will have to obey, and in deciding on matters affecting the people.—(*b*) That more especially as "Turks, Jews, Infidels, and Heretics" have full liberty to speak and vote in Parliament on matters affecting the Church, she should not be left entirely at their mercy, and alone be deprived of a voice in the councils of the realm.—(*c*) That while it is inexpedient, and out of harmony with their spiritual functions, to allow the clergy personally to involve themselves in party contests, there is nothing undignified or prejudicial in allowing bishops to sit in the House of Lords.—(*d*) That to exclude bishops from the House of Lords would be to strengthen the feeling that politics are merely a party game —(*e*) That as ministers of other denominations can, and sometimes do, sit in the House of Commons, these sects

obtain as full a representation in Parliament as the Church of England does through her bishops in the Peers.

2. That the position of the Church would be lowered in the eyes of the people and much harm be done to religion, if her bishops were publicly degraded by being excluded from the Upper House.

3. (*a*) That it is a principle, not only of the Protestant religion, but of the British nation, that the clergy should in no way be a "caste" by themselves, but should be ordinary members of the community.—(*b*) That while, as already stated, it is inexpedient to allow the clergy to be eligible for Parliament, it is greatly to the interests of the people and of the bishops themselves, that the latter should be brought into contact with the world through their position in the Constitution, and thus be enabled to carry out their work with greater knowledge and more discretion.

4. (*a*) That the attendance of the bishops to their legislative work in the House of Lords need not, and does not, interfere with a due regard to their Episcopal and diocesan functions.—(*b*) That matters affecting the Church seldom arise in the House of Lords; while the sittings of the Upper House are so infrequent, and so short, as to absorb but little time or attention.—(*c*) That large numbers of business men find time, without neglecting their own work, to attend the House of Commons with its more numerous sittings and longer hours.—(*d*) That if the Church were disestablished, the bishops, as necessarily members of the governing body of the Church, would still have to be in London for a considerable part of the year.

5. That, as the bishops are men of ability, and bring special views and a representative element into the Upper House, to exclude them would be to lower the character and position of the House of Lords.

6. That as the "Lords Spiritual" are a recognised part

of the Constitution, to permit any tampering with their position would be to play into the hands of the democratic party; and to weaken the position of the House of Lords against attack.

7. (*a*) That to permit the bishops to be excluded would be to surrender an important outwork of the Establishment, and to render more easy the accomplishment of Disestablishment.—(*b*) That to allow the exclusion would be to confess that the Church of England was not truly representative of the nation.

CHURCH AND STATE

THE fundamental doctrines of the Church of England—which is Protestant Episcopal—were agreed upon in Convocation in 1562, and revised, and finally settled, in 1571 in the form of the Thirty-nine Articles. The King is the supreme Head of the Church, and possesses the right of nominating to vacant Archbishoprics and Bishoprics.

There is no official record of the numbers of the members of the Church of England, or of the other religious bodies.

The Church Enquiry Commission, appointed in 1831 to enquire into the revenues and patronage of the Established Church in England and Wales, gave the number of incumbents as 10,718, and of curates 5230, total say, 16,000; the glebe houses numbered 7675, the benefices without glebe houses 2878, total benefices 10,553.

The total net incomes of Bishops and Archbishops was put at	£160,300
,, ,, cathedral establishments . .	157,500
,, ,, beneficed clergy, and curates .	3,480,000

showing a total revenue of, say £3,800,000.

According to *Crockford*, the total number of working clergy in England and Wales, in 1901, was 22,617. Of these, 13,526 were incumbents, and 7228 curates, the balance being made up of Church dignitaries, chaplains, inspectors, schoolmasters, University officers, &c.

A return of the revenues of the Church of England

made in 1891,* summarised the annual revenues as follows:—

(i.)	Archiepiscopal and Episcopal sees	£87,827
(ii.)	Cathedral and Collegiate Churches	192,460
(iii.)	Ecclesiastical Benefices	3,941,057
(iv.)	Ecclesiastical Commissioners	1,247,827
(v.)	Queen Anne's Bounty (rent)	700
		£5,469,171

Of this total, £284,386 was stated to be derived from "Private Benefactures since 1703."

The values of the benefices were, in 1880, estimated as follows:—

	Number.	Total revenue.	Average revenue.
Benefices under £50	167	£5,747	£34
,, from £50 to £100	854	71,265	83
,, ,, £100 to £200	3,034	450,991	148
,, ,, £200 to £500	7,289	2,298,598	315
,, ,, £500 to £1,000	1913	1,238,766	647
,, of £1,000 and upwards	268	329,824	1,230
,, not valued	334	114,194	—
Totals	13,525	£4,395,251	£325†

The ecclesiastical census of 1851 gives the latest official information respecting the number of religious edifices belonging to the Church of England, as follows:—

	Number
Churches existing at census of 1801	9,667
,, built between 1801 and 1811	55
,, ,, ,, 1811 and 1821	97
,, ,, ,, 1821 and 1831	276
,, ,, ,, 1831 and 1841	667
,, ,, ,, 1841 and 1851	4,197
,, ,, at dates not mentioned	2,118

The number existing now is estimated at about 16,000 ‡ Various statutes have from time to time been promulgated

* P. P. 287 of 1891.

† *Financial Reform Almanac*, 1881; Analysis of "Clergy List," p. 69.

‡ Martin, *Church Revenues*, &c., ed. 1878, p. 98.

with the view of assisting the erection or repair of churches from the public funds. In 1679 a rate was ordered to be levied to rebuild the churches of the City of London destroyed during the fire of 1666. Three years later it was followed by an Act imposing a tax on coals for the re-building of St Paul's Cathedral and fifty other churches. Other Acts, with like intent, were passed during the reigns of James II., William III., Anne, and George I.; and in 1818 an Act was passed "to raise the sum of one million sterling for building and promoting the building of additional churches in populous parishes." The census report of 1851 gave the following as the proportionate grants from public funds and private benefaction during the period from 1801-1851:—

	Grants from Public Funds.	Private Benefaction.	Total.
Period 1801-1831 .	£1,152,000	£1,848,000	£3,000,000
,, 1831-1851 .	511,400	5,575,600	6,087,000
Total .	£1,663,400	£7,423,600	£9,087,000

The Church Building Commission, established by the statute of 1818, during the thirty-eight years of its existence ending 1856, aided in the completion of 615 churches, with sittings for 600,000 people. This Commission was in 1856 merged into the Ecclesiastical Commission, and from 1818 to 1879 the power entrusted to these bodies of forming new benefices and districts, was exercised to the extent of constituting 2963 new districts. During the seventeen years, 1856 to 1874, the amount of benefactions offered by private individuals to the Commissioners, for the benefit of the church, amounted to £5,000,000.

In 1876 an official return was issued of churches built or restored at a cost exceeding £500 since the year 1840. The return (which was very imperfect) showed that, during these thirty-five years, 1727 churches had been built, and

7144 restored, at a cost of £25,500,000, or about £700,000 a year; and this sum was derived from voluntary offerings.

The revenues which the Church derives from pew rents, offertories, and gifts cannot be estimated; they are of course purely voluntary offerings. It is estimated by the editor of the *Official Year Book* of the Church of England, that between 1860 and 1884 the voluntary contributions for sectarian purposes of members of the Church (including elementary education £21,360,000 and foreign missions £10,100,000) amounted to £81,573,000; while between 1884 and 1889 the amount spent on Church buildings, restorations, &c., is estimated by him at £20,700,000.*

The summary of Church Property as given by Mr Martin, in his carefully prepared *Property and Revenues of the Church of England*, was as follows, in round numbers:—

Landed Property (from the "New Domesday Book"):—

Of Archbishops and Bishops	30,200 acres
,, Deans and chapters	68,900 ,,
,, Ecclesiastical Commissioners	149,900 ,,
Under-valuation, omission of Metropolis, &c.	250,000 ,,

say 500,000 acres.

Revenues:—

Annual income of 2 Archbishops and 28 Bishops .	£163,300
,, ,, 27 Chapters of Deans and Canons . .	123,200
,, incomes of Parochial Clergy ministering in 16,000 churches or chapels, chiefly derived from tithes	4,277,000
	£4,563,500
Annual value of 33 episcopal palaces	13,200
,, ,, deaneries, etc.	56,800
,, ,, glebe houses and of parochial clergy .	750,000
	£5,383,500

This total is exclusive of extra-cathedral revenues, of dis-

* Pp. 19 and 600, edition 1902.

bursements of Queen Anne's Bounty, of surplus income of Ecclesiastical Commissioners, estimated together at about £750,000. The total annual revenue was thus estimated at about £6,000,000, and the capital value at not less than £100,000,000.*

There exists no basis of any kind on which to define, to distinguish between, or to estimate, the "old" and the "new" endowments of the Church.

DISESTABLISHMENT OF THE IRISH CHURCH

It may be of interest to recapitulate the principal features of the Disestablishment and Disendowment of the Irish Church, so far as these would be likely to form legislative precedents in the case of the Church of England.

The Irish Church Act of 1869 provided that—(1) The Church of Ireland should cease to be established by law. (2) That no appointment to any preferment should in future be made by the Crown or the Ecclesiastical Corporation. (3) That every Ecclesiastical Corporation should be dissolved, and that the Bishops should no longer have the right of sitting in the House of Lords. (4) That the jurisdiction of the Ecclesiastical Courts should cease. (5) That the Church should be permitted to hold Synods and conventions for framing regulations for the general management and government of the Church. But no alterations thus made in the ritual of the Church were to be binding on the existing incumbents.

A commission was appointed, with full powers to carry out the Act, and in them was vested—(1) All the property of the

* Edition 1878. On the same basis Mr Arthur Arnold, in his *Business of Disestablishment* (1878), elaborately estimates the total revenues of the Church (irrespective of voluntary contributions) at £6,500,000 a year, and the capitalised value at £158,500,000.

Ecclesiastical Commissioners of Ireland. (2) All the property, real and personal, of the Church, subject to the life interest of the present holders. (3) The net incomes of the existing holders were to be ascertained, and to be annually paid to them so long as they performed their duties. (4) The net income of each curate was to be paid him; or the life interest, subject to the consent of the incumbent, could be commuted and paid to him in a lump sum at the ordinary rate of life annuities. (5) The net income of each schoolmaster, clerk, sexton, &c., was to be ascertained, paid him, or commuted. (6) Tithe rent-charges could be commuted, on easy terms, at twenty-two and a half years' purchase. (7) The land vested in the Commissioners could be sold, and the existing tenants were to be offered the refusal of purchase on easy terms. (8) Any person feeling aggrieved by the action of the Commissioners, could refer the question to arbitration.

A representative "Church Body" was incorporated by Law, and the Commissioners were empowered to deal directly with this Body, and to commute through them the annuities and life interests in ecclesiastical property created by the Act; the Church Body being bound to undertake the payment of the full annuity, so long as the annuitant required such payment to be made, though they could make any private arrangements they liked with him. Where three-fourths of the whole number of annuitants in a Diocese agreed to commute, the Commissioners were to pay to the Church Body a bonus of 12 per cent. on, and in addition to, the commutation money. The commutation moneys to be calculated at the rate of 3½ per cent.

As an equivalent for the private endowments of the Church, the Church Body received £500,000. All the plate, furniture, &c., belonging to any church or chapel, was left for the life enjoyment of existing incumbents, but was vested in the Church Body. All trusts for the poor were also vested in this Body, and were to continue unaffected.

As regard the ecclesiastical Buildings :—

(1) All old churches in the nature of national monuments were to be maintained by the Commissioners. (2) Churches in actual use, and required for religious purposes, were, together with the schoolhouse and burial-ground, to be vested in the

Church Body. (3) Any church erected since 1800 at the expense of a private person, if not taken over by the Church Body, and if applied for by the donor or his representative, was to be vested in him. (4) All other churches were to be disposed of by the Commissioners as they thought best. (5) Any burial-ground, not vested in the Church Body, was to be vested in the Poor Law Guardians, and be kept in repair by them. (6) Any ecclesiastical residence and with garden "curtilage" could be purchased by the Church Body at ten years' purchase; in addition they could buy, at a price to be settled by arbitration, an additional 30 acres.

The capital sum, representing the commutation of annuities, paid over to the Church Body, amounted to £7,560,000, the number of annuitants being 2060; the annuities, for which the Church Body thus made itself responsible, amounted to £591,000; the number of years' purchase averaged 12·8; the age of annuitants averaged 56.

The annuities for which the Church Body were liable thus amounted to an equivalent of 8 per cent. on the capital received. The Church Body were enabled to invest the money at 4 per cent., and the laity, responding to their call, subscribed the remaining 4 per cent., required in order that, while the annuities should be paid, the capital should be kept intact.

Subsequently, when it appeared that many of the clergy were superfluous, the Church Body further commuted directly with these persons, but on terms less favourable than that of the general commutation. Thus, by 1877, the number of annuitants was reduced to 1052, and the composition balance acquired by the Church amounted to £10,300,00.

DISESTABLISHMENT *

The proposal to sever all connection between Church and State, both in Scotland, Wales, and England, is upheld on the grounds:—

1. That as all men are not religious, while all are equally desirous to be protected by the State, it should not mix up its Civil with its Religious functions; but should be purely secular.

2. That when the King was supreme governor over both Church and State, their connection was a natural consequence. But now that the Sovereign is no longer ruler by Divine Right, and Parliament is omnipotent, the connection has become an anomaly.

3. (*a*) That the National Church was in former times founded on the idea that all citizens were of the same creed; no one could be a citizen unless he were a Churchman. She thus expressed a National Faith, and aimed at national unity of belief, and uniformity of worship.—(*b*) That there is now no obligation to belong to the Church of England; and she can no longer claim to be a National Church; but, at the best, the Church only of a majority, and that a diminishing one.†—(*c*) "Establishment" means now merely the exclusive

* The arguments for and against Disendowment must be taken along with those for and against Disestablishment.

† There are no official figures on which can be founded any calculation of the relative numbers of the Church and of Dissent. "The Public Worship Census" report of 1851 (the last taken) can hardly be relied upon as sufficient evidence, and is now entirely out of date. It showed, however, that while

alliance of the State with one religious denomination amongst many, together with a State assertion that that particular form of religion is the only true one.

4. (*a*) That religious equality does not mean equality of sects, but equal treatment of all sects by the State; and this principle is violated in the case of the Established Church. —(*b*) That while the State should be tolerant of all religious sects, it ought not to choose out for support any special Denomination. In so doing, the State outstrips its true field of work, and trespasses on freedom of religious thought and on the principle of religious equality, if not directly, at all events, indirectly. For State recognition of a special Church, by taking her under protection, by ensuring her the possession of vast property, by placing her ministers in a position of superiority,* places those who do not belong to her communion, or who desire to leave her fold, in a position of exceptional pecuniary and social disadvantage. —(*c*) That this direct and indirect pressure to remain in, or

in 1801 the provision of sittings in places of worship in England and Wales was

Church of England	4,069,281
Other places of worship	963,169
	5,032,450

In 1851 the relative numbers were—

Church of England	5,317,915
Other places of worship	4,894,648
	10,212,563

The population being then 18,000,000.

* For instance, the Bishops sit in the House of Lords, "the Church dignitaries and the Clergy exercise authority vested in them by the State. They alone can conduct religious services of a national character, and can occupy the pulpits of cathedrals. and other national ecclesiastical edifices. They are the chairmen of parish vestries, trustees of parochial charities, and custodians of the ancient parochial burial places. They hold the greater part of the chaplaincies, the masterships of public schools, and school inspectorships, and largely control the educational machinery of the country." —*Disestablishment* (Imperial Parliament Series), by Henry Richard and Carvell Williams, p. 73.

to join the State Church, is an injustice to other churches; and all State institutions should be founded on the principle of impartial justice.

5. (*a*) That the State recognition of one Denomination injures those whom it favours, and depresses and angers those whom it wrongs; whereby religious strife is perpetuated.—(*b*) That a State-privileged Church divides the community and accentuates religious differences.—(*c*) That if Dissenters were relieved from an irritating injustice, and Churchmen were deprived of a position of superiority, religious differences would lose much of their sting, social exclusiveness would be diminished, and the artificial barriers which now keep good men apart would be broken down.

6. That it is contrary to religion that the secular power should have any voice at all in religious matters; a Church ought in no way to be placed under the control of the State, which is, thereby, as likely to be fostering error as to be upholding the true form of religion.

7. That the Church, if disestablished, will either hold her own, and no harm will be done; or else the State is artificially supporting a religious system which could not otherwise exist (and which should not exist), because out of harmony with the wants and spirit of the age.

8. (*a*) That the connection of Church and State causes, not the spiritualisation of the State, but simply the secularisation of the Church.—(*b*) That as long as the Church is bound up with the State it must be controlled in every particular by the State, *i.e.* by Parliament; and Parliament, being increasingly composed of members of divers sects and creeds, many of them hostile to the Establishment, or even to religion, is a body eminently unfit to govern the Church, or to legislate on religious questions.—(*c*) That so long as the Church is connected with the State, its higher ecclesiastical rulers must be appointed on the advice of the Prime

Minister, who is not necessarily a member of the Church of England, is possibly not even a Christian; while many "livings" will remain in the gift of the Crown, of the Lord Chancellor, or of the Chancellor of the Duchy.

9. (*a*) That the connection of the State with the Church renders her impotent to initiate and carry out necessary internal reform.—(*b*) That the congregation have no power of choice in their minister, nor control over those who appoint him. Once appointed, unless he commit an illegal action, neither they, nor the bishops, have power to free themselves from him, however inefficient he may be, or however objectionable either in doctrine or habit.—(*c*) That thus, in many parishes, there are incumbents utterly unfitted for their duties, to the great detriment of the Church and of religion.

10. (*a*) That, under the present system, presentations to Church livings are bought and sold, quite irrespective of the fitness of the clergyman or the wishes of the congregation. —(*b*) That the presentation to livings is in very many cases in the hands of unfit patrons.—(*c*) That insubordination is increasing in the Church; while the Bishops themselves have little control over the clergy; and only with great difficulty, and at great expense, can attempt to enforce, and that ineffectually, discipline or doctrine.

11. (*a*) That, if the Church were a Voluntary Church, it would be governed by a Church Body, constituted with a majority of its members laymen. Such a Body would exercise complete control; and, while keeping the clergy in check, would be able to initiate reforms where thought expedient, both in doctrine, discipline, and administration.—(*b*) That in a Disestablished Voluntary Church the laity would obtain the influence and the voice in Church matters to which they are entitled, and of which they are at present deprived. —(*c*) That the form of worship would be made more elastic,

and the ritual would be better adapted to the times.—(*d*) That promotion would be more according to merit. Patrons would disappear, and congregations, having a voice in selection, would seek out efficient men; while the Central Body would be in a position to compare the merits of individual clergy.

12. (*a*) That, at present, in consequence of her connection with the State, the Church is not a real Church of the people—it is not founded on popular sympathy and esteem.—(*b*) That she is ceasing more and more to attract to her ministry able and broad-minded men. Thus, on the one hand apathy, and on the other narrow-mindedness and sacerdotalism are increasing in the Church.

13. (*a*) That while there is great force in the "priest in the parish" argument as affecting the country districts,* the clergy, as a matter of fact, have on the whole neglected the agricultural labourer and the poorer classes, have taken but little interest in their temporal welfare or social improvement, and have kept them in a state of political ignorance and darkness.—(*b*) That the so-called "civilising agency" does not civilise, as witness the ignorance, the apathy, and social stagnation of very many country districts.—(*c*) That instead of taking up a catholic position, and welcoming help in spiritual improvement, the spiritual influence and energy of these clergy is chiefly directed against Dissent. —(*d*) That they have, as a rule, used the charities and funds placed at their disposal as "fetters to bind in slavery and serfdom the poor mendicants to whom they administer the charities"; while these are too often so administered as to have a most demoralising effect.—(*e*) That where, as in so many cases, the clergy have been benevolent and civilising, their influence for good has arisen from their being good men, and ministers of religion, not from their being State servants. The good results that have ensued

* See No. 4 against Disestablishment.

have come about, not in consequence of the connection between Church and State, but in spite of its narrowing and numbing influence.

14. (*a*). That far from weakening her influence for good, the Church, if a Voluntary Church, would be more powerful for good in each parish, because more energetic and with greater vitality.—(*b*) That if the Church were liberated from the shackles now laid upon her by the State, she would be freer to do good, would be able to organise and consolidate her forces, and to distribute them more according to the needs of the people. At present she too often squanders her strength in places where it is out of all proportion to local requirements.—(*c*) That under a voluntary system, if a clergyman did not work, neither would he be paid: at present much money, which should be devoted to religious purposes, is absorbed by *fainéants* or worse.—(*d*) That the withdrawal of State recognition from the Church, by placing her on a more even footing with her competitors, would increase friendly rivalry and competition, would tend to make each and all bestir themselves; and religious life would be quickened and extended. The less the State does, the more will voluntary effort accomplish: ease weakens, hardship strengthens religious zeal.—(*e*) That there would be less religious bickerings and more hearty co-operation between the different sects.—(*f*) That the members of the Church, who now have comparatively few calls upon them, would be induced (emulating the example of the Dissenters) to subscribe liberally to her funds.—(*g*) That, thus, instead of the neglect of the poor anticipated by some, there would be active competition to enlist their sympathies, and not, as now, an assumption that they belonged to the State Church.

15. (*a*) That the real sources of the power of the Church of England lie in her doctrines, her modes of worship, her

organisation, her self-sacrificing ministry, her zealous and generous laity, not in the fact of the Headship of the Crown, the Bishops in the House of Lords, the legal privileges of the clergy, Acts of Parliament, &c.—(*b*) That Disestablishment would not destroy the machinery of the Church; or tend to make her abandon her work. If the country continues religious, Disestablishment will not tend to make her irreligious.

16. That there is much more vitality in a religion voluntarily supported, than in one largely endowed. The Church, as a State Church, has failed to do the good which from her position, privileges, and wealth, she ought to have done.

17. That the fear some express lest the sacred buildings should be put to unseemly uses is preposterous. The natural religious and reverential feeling of Englishmen is totally opposed to any such desecration; and, as it would rest with Parliament to determine the ultimate disposal of these buildings, Parliament may be trusted to act in accordance with public feeling. Moreover, the churches would as a rule still remain the property of the Church of England.

18. (By some.) That, at present, instead of the Church being a bulwark against Papal aggression, she has become a nursery for Roman Catholicism.

19. That the question of the Protestant succession is in these days a matter of small moment.

20. (*a*) That the influence of the Church of England, as an Establishment, has always been in opposition to the fuller and freer development of national life.—(*b*) That the State-paid clergy form a compact and powerful force always opposed to progress.

21. That it would be a great relief to the overworked Parliament to be entirely free from all ecclesiastical questions.

22. That the disestablishment and disendowment of the Irish Church has proved in every way a satisfactory precedent.

23. That the non-existence of an Established Church in America and the Colonies has been attended by many advantages.

The connection between Church and State is upheld on the grounds:—

1. That the State, as a State, while practising absolute toleration, must be religious, and must therefore profess and uphold some religious faith.

2. That whether the connection be strictly defensible or not, to break it would be a very dangerous step. Such action would constitute a profound discouragement to religion, and a great encouragement to all the enemies of religion and of the Church.

3. That as an Established Church is a vital part of our institutions, and bestows great blessings on the whole people, the advantages of its existence more than counterweigh the consequent disadvantages of alleged religious inequality.

4. (*a*) That so long as there is an Established Church, every individual in the kingdom, whether he belong to any denomination or no, who may be suffering from spiritual distress, has an official spiritual councillor to whom he has a right to apply; and a Church accessible to him for all purposes of worship.—(*b*) That not only in religious matters, but in every-day life, the existence of a State-paid clergyman to whom every parishioner can apply, is an enormous advantage, especially to the poorer classes; and a guarantee of social progress.—(*c*) That the poor gain greatly from the parochial system; under it the clergyman is the recognised

and impartial dispenser of the gifts and philanthropy of the rich for the benefit of the poor.

5. That the vast majority of the people are directly or indirectly attached by some tie to the Church. The tie being less binding than it would be in the case of a Voluntary Church, many persons, to their spiritual advantage, can belong to the Established Church so long as it is in connection with the State.

6. That under a purely voluntary system the clergy would be only really accessible to the members, or possible members, of their flocks; their public functions would disappear.

7. That under every voluntary system the clergy tend to become more and more mere servants of their congregations, and much freedom of thought, liberty of ideas, and elevation of mind, are thus suppressed and lost. Union with the State is the only way of securing real freedom of jurisdiction to the Church as a whole, and of preventing intolerance and narrow-mindedness.

8. (*a*) And, that, as the different churches would have to be sustained by voluntary subscriptions, the clergy would have to bid for the support of those with means. This "begging system" would degrade the character of the clergy; and their time and attention being thus largely absorbed, the poor, the indifferent, those who cannot or will not contribute, those in short who are especially in need of spiritual aid or seasonable advice, would be perforce neglected.—(*b*) That a clergyman would have to devote himself to making himself popular, and to the preaching of popular sermons; and would perforce cease to be a minister and servant of the poor.

9. (*a*) That the Church would be impoverished, and only able to offer small stipends, and would therefore attract a lower and less educated class of men to her ministry, and

religion would grievously suffer in consequence.—(*b*) And that she would, through lack of means, be obliged to a considerable extent to contract her operations, both religious and educational, with the same disastrous results.—(*c*) That in many parishes the clergyman is the sole centre of civilising influence; disestablishment, by contracting the operations of the Church, and by attracting a less educated class of men, would injuriously diminish this invaluable influence.

10. (*a*) (On the other hand, many are possessed with the idea) That the disestablished Church Body being left, as it would be, with large and uncontrolled powers, and having at its disposal a very considerable capital,* would inevitably tend to become an exclusively, or predominantly, clerical body; the control of the State over the clergy can alone uphold the interests and influence of the laity.—(*b*) That those who differed from the dictum of the Church Body would be driven out of the fold, and the Church would split up into innumerable fragments; intolerance and strife would be increased and perpetuated.—(*c*) That the connection of Church and State is the best guarantee that the religion of the country will be kept broad and comprehensive; while it secures a certain amount of liberty and freedom from ecclesiastical tyranny and dogmatism.

11. (By some.) That the existence of such a wealthy, powerful, and independent body as the Church would become if disestablished, might be dangerous to the Commonwealth itself.

12. That as all religious disabilities are now removed, and as every one is free to remain in the Church, or free to leave, and as her ordinances are not enforced on any person, the presence of an Established Church in no way affects

* Mr Gladstone (16th May 1873) made a computation that, if the disendowment of the Church of England were carried out with the same liberality as that of the Irish Church, she would be left with a capital of £90,000,000.

the question of religious liberty or equality. The supposed hardship is, therefore, no more than a sentimental grievance largely founded on social feeling.

13. (*a*) That the Church of England, established or disestablished, will always be superior, educationally, socially, pecuniarily, to other sects by reason of the culture of her clergy, and the better social position of her members.—(*b*) That, disestablished, the clergy of the Church would tend to become still more of a caste than they are at present; "social exclusiveness" would not be diminished.

14. That if the Church obtained perfect independence of action, her conflict with Dissent would be sharpened and embittered.

15. (*a*) That the best likelihood of reform in the Church, so far as reforms are required, are in its connection with the State. Admitted scandals or anomalies, or anachronisms in Church doctrine, discipline or administration, can be remedied, and are more likely thus to be remedied.—(*b*) That Disestablishment would enormously increase the power of the clergy and diminish that of the laity.—(*c*) That many of the clergy desire to be "each his own Pope"; and only the restraining influence of public opinion and the power of the State-Bishops restrains them. Disestablished, they could be their own masters. The Church would fall into a state of ecclesiastical anarchy.—(*d*) It is better that religious worship should be regulated by the law, than that it should be left altogether to individual clergy.—(*e*) That Establishment is the best security for religious freedom.

16. That the Church may, in the past, have been apathetic, but her members are now active, devoted, zealous, and liberal.

17. That with the question of Disestablishment is necessarily connected the question of Disendowment; and the difficulties attending the possession of the Church

buildings, the commutation of endowments, &c., are insuperable.

18. (By some.) (*a*) That it is intended by the Liberationists to drive all the clergy out of their parsonages, and to put the sacred buildings to unseemly uses.—(*b*) That those who clamour for Disestablishment are simply actuated by a desire to rob the Church of her possessions.

19. (*a*) (The argument which is urged against every reform is also used in this case)—That other institutions are threatened and weakened if one is pulled down.—(*b*) That Disestablishment would dangerously touch even the tenure of the Throne; the Establishment and the Monarchy are necessarily linked, while Voluntaryism is Republican and Democratic.

20. (By some.) That if the Church of England is weakened at all, the Roman Catholic Church will gradually become the most powerful denomination, and will obtain supreme sway in religious matters; while the Protestant succession, being necessarily abrogated, the State might also fall under that sway.

21. (*a*) (By some few.) That each man is bound to yield up his mind to the teaching of the Church, and has no right to choose out another faith for himself; or, at any rate, has no claim to have his dissent recognised by the State, which, being in union with the Church, professes her faith and none other.—(*b*) (By others.) That though the State may tolerate, it must in no way recognise dissent from the Established Church.

22. (*a*) That the position of the Church of Ireland—a very small Protestant minority and an enormous Catholic majority—was in no way analogous to that of the Church in England; its disestablishment forms therefore no precedent.—(*b*) That the Church in England holds a totally different position, and is the Church of the majority.

23. Many, while not defending the principle of an Established Church, refrain from seeking to sunder the Church from the State, on the ground that the Constitution is full of anomalies, and that institutions that have grown with the nation's growth, ought not to be unrooted simply for the sake of theoretical perfection.

24. And others, while equally denying the principle of the union of Church and State, are in favour of retaining the existing state of things, on the ground that any attempt to sever the connection would cause endless confusion, strife, and heart-burnings, especially in the matter of Disendowment. It is better to leave bad alone than run the risk of making it worse.

[There is a large class who—not wishing for Disestablishment if the Church can be reformed, or will reform herself—desire to see her remodelled on a more popular basis, that she may be made wide enough to include all English Christians; holding the principle, that the Established Church was made for the people, and not the people for the Established Church.*

On the other hand, it is contended that, though undoubtedly, and with advantage, the foundations of the Church might be broadened, mere reform would never enable her to comprehend within one fold the different religious sects.]

* See *Church Reform* (Imperial Parliament Series), by Albert Grey, Canon Freemantle, and Geo. Harwood, Revs. S. Barnett, C. W. Stubbs, G. L. Reaney, and L. Davies.

DISENDOWMENT.*

Together with Disestablishment is raised the question of Disendowment: namely, to what extent the Church, if Disestablished, should be allowed to retain her present possessions; or how far they ought to be appropriated by the State and applied to other purposes.

Those in favour of a certain measure of Disendowment uphold their proposals on the grounds:—

1. That the Church being a State Church, all her possessions are national property; and that, strictly speaking, the State would be justified in appropriating the whole, subject to existing life interests.

2. (*a*) That most of the Churches, and all the Cathedrals and Abbeys, are distinctly national property.—(*b*) That the present Church has no prescriptive right to her old endowments. They originally belonged to the Roman Catholics, and were appropriated by the State; if therefore they belong of right to any Church, it is to the Roman Catholic Church.—(*c*) That the Church has equally no private right to her more modern endowments, which were presented to her—as the Protestant Church—when she included all or most Protestants. These endowments were intended for the use of the nation, and not for that of a particular denomination; they belong therefore to the nation.—(*d*) That tithes, which constitute the chief support

* See also the arguments for and against Disestablishment.

of the Church, were in no way voluntary offerings, but were imposed by the State for the support of a National Church; and should therefore revert to the State in case of Disestablishment.—(*e*) That, moreover, the poor are legally entitled to share in the tithes.

3. (*a*) That the endowments of the Church represent to a large extent merely the appropriation of public property to certain ecclesiastical purposes.—(*b*) That the proof that the endowments of the Church are national property is shown from the fact that no part of them can be appropriated or applied to any fresh purpose except by Act of Parliament. The recipients of the annual revenues are, moreover, simply public functionaries; their number, the mode of their appointment, the creed they shall hold, the services they still conduct, the allocation of their incomes, are determined by the State.

4. (*a*) That the property of the Church of England is in the nature of a public trust; the State is, therefore, justified in treating it as national property, and in applying it to national purposes.—(*b*) That the property of the dissenting bodies is held under private trusts, and the State (except in so far as the ordinary law is concerned) has no voice in, nor control over, their disposal.

5. That the action of the Ecclesiastical Commissioners (created by Parliament) in throwing much ecclesiastical property into a common fund, has entirely subverted the theory that Church property is simply the property of the several local Churches, &c.

6. That the endowments given to the Established Church, either by public or private liberality, should not be applied for the benefit of one religious body within the nation only, but should be applied for the benefit of the whole community.

7. That the action of Parliament in regard to the endow-

ments of the Church of Ireland, and the application of the Surplus Fund to secular purposes, is a precedent which proves that the State may, and can with advantage, apply Church endowments to such purposes as it thinks fit.

8. That the congregations of the Church constitute the richest part of the nation; yet they are under no obligation to contribute to her support. If the Church were partially disendowed, they would (as the Dissenters in their own case do) gladly contribute to maintain or extend her present scale of operations; while Disestablishment would tend to economise the resources.

9. (*a*) That the question of the future of the Churches and Cathedrals is only a detail, and should not stand in the way of the acceptance of the principle of Disendowment. Details can always be settled on a just basis afterwards; while, in the case of the Irish Church, similar difficulties were successfully surmounted.—(*b*) That there would be no devastation of the Churches, nor hardship to individual incumbents. Disendowment would be only gradual; all life interests would be scrupulously respected, and the Church would be allowed to retain her recent endowments.

[It is generally allowed that the Church, if disestablished, must be dealt with generously in the matter of her endowments; and that she (or the individuals interested) can fairly claim to receive a certain number of years' purchase of her revenues, the State appropriating only the balance. It is usually contended, however, that the terms given in the case of the Irish Church were too liberal.*; and that the greatest care must be taken to prevent abuse of the powers of "commuting, compounding, and cutting."]

On the other hand, it is contended that, if dis-

* See p. 102.

established, the Church must be allowed to retain all her present possessions, without deduction, on the grounds :—

1. That the State is bound to secure all property to its owners; and the emoluments of the Established Church are strictly and legally her own property.

2. (*a*) That all endowments have been given to the Church as such, while most have been given to her as a Protestant Church, and are therefore her absolute property, and to dispossess her would be robbery and sacrilege.—(*b*) That practically, with the exception of some trifling sums, none of the endowments of the Church have come from the State; the Church costs nothing to the Nation as such.

3. That if the Church of England be disendowed, there must be concurrent disendowment of all other religious sects: they all hold their property practically on the same tenure.

4. (*a*) That whatever may be the advantages of Disestablishment, it cannot be right to divert any of the funds now applied to religious purposes, to other uses.—(*b*) That any diversion of the Church endowments or revenue to secular purposes would be a blow to religion, and a serious curtailment of the good work of the Church.

5. That enormous difficulties, especially in connection with the sacred buildings, would arise in endeavouring to carry out any scheme of partial Disendowment.

SCOTCH DISESTABLISHMENT

In addition to the arguments already mentioned, most of which apply equally to the question of the English, Scotch, and Welsh Churches, it is contended by those in favour of the Disestablishment of the Scotch Church:—

1. (*a*) That the vast majority of church-going Scotchmen are not members of the Established Church.*—(*b*) That, in many parishes, the congregation attending the Established Church is grotesquely small.

2. That the Established Church is simply one section of the Presbyterian Church of Scotland; and her recognition by the State is the chief bar to the reunion of the several branches of that Church—a reunion which would result in great economy of power and resources.

3. That, more especially in Scotland, this sectional Church has possession of national funds which were never intended to be used in providing religious ministrations for one portion of the people only.

4. That the Church of Scotland was established for the purpose of looking after the poor and promoting education, as well as for religious purposes; and she has now been relieved from the two first duties.

5. That the Scotch Established Church is constituted on an entirely different basis to the English Church—being "spiritually and ecclesiastically autonomic." That, therefore, Disestablishment in Scotland could be accomplished without diffi-

* It was estimated a few years ago, that, in Scotland, out of a population of 3,400,000, only 1,063,000 were members of the Established Church. On the other hand, it is asserted that the Church, since the Disruption of 1843, has added and endowed 340 Parish Churches (usually with manses), at a cost of £2,200,000, and that it has shown greater vitality, and increased in numbers and influence in a greater degree than the other churches.

culty, and would not affect the question of Disestablishment in England.

6. That Scotland is ripe for, and desirous of, Disestablishment.

WELSH DISESTABLISHMENT

As regards Wales, it is also contended:—

1. (*a*) That an Ecclesiastical Establishment like other establishments must rest upon the deliberate will of the people.—(*b*) That the voice of the Welsh, as expressed through their representatives, is overwhelmingly in favour of Disestablishment.

2. (*a*) That the Established Church in Wales is neither a National Church, nor the Church of a Nation. It is an alien Church, which has never taken root, nor succeeded in winning the love and loyalty of the people.—(*b*) That it is not the natural organ nor vehicle of the religious sentiment of the whole or of the majority of the people of Wales.—(*c*) That it is an alien Church that alienates everybody; a missionary Church, that converts nobody.

3. (*a*) That the Church in Wales was a spontaneous and native growth, and was only, in later years, incorporated into the Anglican Church.—(*b*) That it has been treated as a sort of annexe to the English Church; and the bulk (especially in earlier days) of the benefices and offices have been given to men who were not Welsh, who could not understand Welsh, and who had no sympathy with the genius of the Welsh people.

4. (*a*) That the Establishment constitutes, therefore, a grievous and glaring injustice.—(*b*) That it has altogether failed to fulfil its professed object as a means of promoting the religious interests of the Welsh people.—(*c*) That it is not, therefore, for the public benefit that it should continue.

5. (*a*) That the Church in Wales ministers only to a small minority of the population, and a Church is not a National

Church unless it contains within its fold the bulk of the people of the country within which it is established.*—(*b*) That even, if in England, the Established Church can claim to be called a National Church, it has no claim to be so designated in Wales; dissent, if local in England, is national in Wales.

6. (*a*) That not only do the Dissenters vastly outnumber the members of the Established Church, but the growth of dissent has been most strongly marked.—(*b*) That, while dissent has made enormous headway, and has been the chief means of fostering and extending religion and education in Wales, the Established Church has carried out its duties in a perfunctory and slovenly manner, and has been a hindrance, rather than a help, to the evangelisation of the Principality.—(*c*) That, freed of the enervating privileges, disabilities, and influence of Establishment, the Church would discharge with greater effect its spiritual mission.

7. That the Church of England in Wales is a proselytising Church, and thus greatly tends to embitter religious feeling.

8. That in Wales, the Episcopalian minority comprises the richer classes, the Nonconformist majority the poorer classes. The Church, which alone receives public aid, is the Church of the rich, not of the poor.

9. That whatever might be the case in England, the Church in Wales could be uprooted without any wrench to the moral or spiritual life of the people.

10. That, therefore, whatever may be the case in England, the arguments are overwhelming in favour of Disestablishment in Wales.

11. (*a*) That the people of Wales differ from the people in England in thought, habits, manners, temperament, language and traditions, and can claim to be treated, and should be treated, separately and distinctly.—(*b*) That the best way of recognising and consolidating the true union of the kingdom as

* In 1676 the population of Wales was 402,250, of whom 391,350 were Church of England, and 11,000 belonged to other churches. In 1851 it appeared that for a population of a little over 1,000,000, the Church of England had accommodation for 269,000 persons, and other churches for 600,000 persons. It was estimated in 1881, that out of a population of 1,574,000, about 300,000 belonged to the Church of England and about 1,000,000 were Nonconformists.

a whole, is to recognise, and within limits of Imperial unity to defer, to the separate national sentiments of the different parts of the United Kingdom.—(*c*) That the question of Church Establishment should be a question of National Option.—(*d*) That as separate legislation has been instituted for Wales on educational and temperance questions, there is good precedent for dealing separately also with the religious question.

On the other hand, it is contended:—

1. That the Church of Wales is of greater antiquity than that of England; while Nonconformity is of modern growth.

2. (*a*) That between the Church of England and the Church of Wales there is a complete ecclesiastical, constitutional, and historical identity.—(*b*) That the Church of Wales is an integral part of the Church of England; the one cannot be Disestablished without the other. Dioceses cannot be separated from the Province of which it forms a part. The question of Disestablishment cannot be limited to the Principality; it must be settled as a whole, not as a part.—(*c*) That Disestablishment must be a National not a Local concern; if not, who is to define the locality?

3. That the cry for Welsh Disestablishment is merely a veiled attack on the Church of England.

4. (*a*) That the Established Church of Wales is no alien Church; and whatever may have been her faults in the past, of late years she has been in sympathy with Welsh feeling, has made vast progress, and is rapidly overtaking dissent, and will before long become, even if she is not so already, the Church of the majority.—(*b*) That while the Church is waxing, Nonconformity is waning. The Church is solvent, Dissent is bankrupt. The Churches are filling, the Chapels are emptying.

5. (*a*) That it is because of this great Establishment revival, and the fear of the loss of the Nonconformist influence, that the cry for the Disestablishment of the Church is raised by its rivals.—(*b*) That the feeling against the Church, if it exists, is one of envy and jealousy. The grievance, if it exists, is a social and sentimental grievance merely.

6. (*a*) That the bulk of the philanthropic and benevolent

work of the Principality is done by the ministers and members of the Church, and not by the Dissenting denominations.—(*b*) That in Wales, even more than in England, the Established Church is the Church of the very poor, and to disestablish and disendow her is to deprive the poor of their religious birthright.

7. (*a*) That, as has been the case in Ireland, Disestablishment would encourage "nationalism" and "separatism"; and lead to a demand for Home Rule for Wales.—(*b*) That it is a fatal mistake to recognise that there are separate nationalities in the United Kingdom.

HOME RULE

It is proposed to create an Irish Parliament to sit in Dublin, which should have power to legislate on, and to regulate Irish Home affairs, leaving "Imperial" questions to be dealt with by the Imperial Parliament, sitting at Westminster. The Irish Executive is to be responsible to the Irish Parliament alone.

The Home Rule Bill of 1893 established a Legislature and Executive in Ireland for the control and management of Irish affairs, subject to the Supremacy of the Imperial Parliament. This supreme authority was to be neither impaired nor restricted, and any statute of the Imperial Parliament expressly extended to Ireland, would over-ride any enactments of the Irish Parliament; while any Irish Act was to be void if repugnant to an enactment of Parliament.

The Legislature was to consist of two Chambers. The Upper Chamber, or Legislative Council, was to consist of forty-eight members, elected by thirty-five constituents. The Councillors were to be elected for eight years; half to go out at the end of each fourth year. The franchise was restricted to owners and occupiers of land and tenements of more than £20 a year. The Lower Chamber, or Legislative Assembly, was to consist of a hundred and three members, elected by the present Parliamentary electors, and representing the existing constituencies. Its duration was to be limited to five years; but it could be earlier dissolved by the Lord Lieutenant acting for the Queen. The Irish Parliament was prohibited for six years from enacting any alterations in the Parliamentary constitution.

The consent of both Chambers was to be necessary to the passing of Bills. In the event of a rejection by the Council of a Bill passed by the Assembly, provision was to be made to avoid a dead-lock. Such a Bill might be sent up a second time by the Assembly to the Council immediately after a dissolution, or in any case after two years, and if it were not adopted by the Council within three months, the two Houses were to deliberate and vote as one body, and the Bill was to be adopted or rejected according to the decision of the majority of the members present and voting on the question.

Peers were to be eligible for election as members either of the Legislative Council or of the Legislative Assembly; but no person, peer or commoner, could be a member of both Assemblies. It is, however, permissible for a member of one of these bodies to be also elected as a representative to the House of Commons.

Subject to certain exceptions and restrictions, the Irish Legislature was to have full power to make laws for the peace, order, and good government of Ireland, in respect of matters exclusively relating to Ireland, or some parts thereof.

They were prohibited for three years from dealing with the Land Question.

The matters reserved for the Imperial Parliament were: —(1) The Crown or the Succession. (2) The making of Peace or War; or matters arising from a state of war. (3) Naval and Military Forces and the defence of the Realm. (4) Authority to use or to carry arms for military purposes. (5) Treaties and other relations with foreign States. (6)

Dignities or titles of honour. (7) Treason, treason-felony, alienage, or naturalisation. (8) Trade with any place out of Ireland. (9) Lighthouses, bueys, or beacons. (10) Coinage; legal tender; or the standard of weights and measures. (11) Trade-marks, merchandise-marks, copyright, or patent rights. (12) The election laws and the laws relating to the qualification of electors of members of the House of Commons. (13) Any change in the Home Rule Act, except in so far as it was expressly authorised in the Act itself.

The Irish Legislature would have no power to make any law:—(1) Respecting the establishment or endowment of religion, or prohibiting the free exercise thereof. (2) Imposing any disability, or conferring any privilege, advantage, or benefit on account of religious belief; or raising or appropriating any public revenue for any religious purpose. (3) Diverting the property; or, without its consent, altering the constitution of any religious body. (4) Abrogating or prejudicially affecting the right to establish or maintain any place of denominational education (or the right of the child to attend it) or any denominational Institution or charity. (5) To interfere with Habeas Corpus. (6) To impose any disability or to confer any privilege on account of parentage or birth.

The Lord Lieutenant, as representing the Crown, retained the right of veto.

The Executive was to be a Committee of the Privy Council of Ireland (the members holding certain specific offices), and which, for the time being, was supported by a majority of the Legislative Assembly—in other words, an Irish Cabinet, depending on the Irish Lower House.

Ireland was to contribute to the Imperial Expenditure in proportion to her population and resources. The proportion was to be fixed for six years, and to be then reconsidered,

One-third of the general revenue of Ireland was to be paid into the Imperial Exchequer; the remaining two-thirds were to form a part of the special revenue of Ireland, which could be enlarged by such taxes in Ireland as the Legislature might impose.

The Imperial Exchequer was to bear one-third (estimated at a million a year) of the cost of the Constabulary until it was replaced by a police force.

Home Rule is supported on the grounds :—

1. (*a*) That each country is best able to manage her own domestic concerns; each has the right, and should have the liberty to do so. To force a detested system of government on an unwilling people is contrary to the principle of constitutional freedom.—(*b*) That it is undesirable for one country virtually to control the domestic affairs of another.—(*c*) And this is more especially undesirable when the two countries differ radically in sentiment, character, and religion.

2. (*a*) That the Union between England and Ireland has brought neither loyalty, peace, nor strength. The attempt on the part of England to govern Ireland according to English ideas has been a disastrous failure; and this, in spite of the fact that some of our best men have applied themselves to the task.—(*b*) That the present state of things, by leading to continued agitation in Ireland, drives away capital, and distracts and impoverishes the country; thousands of Irishmen are in consequence annually driven from home, to carry abroad with them hatred and disaffection to England.

3. (*a*) That, though the Act of Union, fraudulently obtained, united the Legislatures, the nations were thereby divided. After ninety years of a "united Parliament" the integrity of the Empire is little more than a name.—(*b*) That

the Union, as now established, is merely a "Paper Union," and has been only maintained by means of Coercion Acts repeatedly passed by Parliament against the will of the Irish people; and without coercion the Union could not be maintained.

4. (*a*) That in the past—for centuries past—England did vast and irreparable injury to Ireland; first, by wholesale confiscation, plantation of the English, transplantation of the Irish; then by fiscal legislation directed against her trade and commerce, and by penal legislation directed against religious liberty and equality; and, finally, by depriving her, through "means the most base and shameless," of her legislative independence. For all this England owes reparation —(*b*) That England was right first to attempt by the removal of material grievances—Land Laws, Church, Education, &c. —to win over the Irish people to English rule; but these reforms have totally failed in their object.—(*c*) That the fact that the "Irish Question" is further from settlement now than it was before "remedial legislation" was begun, shows that we have not yet gone to the root of the matter. In fact, by the removal of other material grievances, the field for Home Rule agitation has been left clear.

5. That, the "Union" having thus proved to be a failure, the Irish people are entitled to demand the restitution of their Parliament.

6. (*a*) That the Irish people have never ceased to protest against the legislative Union; and, at no previous period, has the feeling in Ireland been so unanimously adverse to the present system of English rule, and in favour of Irish legislative independence.—(*b*) That this is conclusively proved by the result of each general election since 1885. In the year in which the Irish people had, for the first time, an opportunity of constitutionally expressing their opinions; and by an overwhelming majority,

eighty-five members to eighteen, they declared in favour of Home Rule.—(*c*) That there never was in Parliament an Irish party so united on the question of Home Rule; and so little open to corrupt or party influences.—(*d*) That the position of affairs has thus materially altered of late; and it is impossible any longer to shut our eyes to the fact that we are face to face with a national feeling constitutionally expressed.—(*e*) That it is the duty of Parliament carefully to consider a question thus powerfully and constitutionally raised, and, if possible, to comply with the demands of such a large portion of the citizens of the United Kingdom.

7. That it is a mockery to have greatly extended the franchise in Ireland, and then to pay no regard to the voice of the people constitutionally expressed.

8. (*a*) That the Irish people have a passionate aspiration for self-government; and until this be conceded, they will never be content nor loyal to the Crown.—(*b*) That the existence of such a wide-spread feeling of nationality leads the Irish to regard English domination as "Foreign" rule; and to consider it in the light of a tyranny and a burden.

9. That constitutional government implies the government of a country in harmony with the feelings, the wants, and the wishes of the people; and this is not the case in Ireland.

10. (*a*) That, in order to obtain willing obedience to the laws, they must be not only good laws, but laws made by the people themselves, and in conformity with their feeling and sentiment.—(*b*) That the Irish detest our laws, not because they are bad laws, nor because they are made by England, but because they are not made by Ireland.—(*c*) That, in consequence of the "foreign garb" in which the laws appear, and the idea that they are mostly dictated by an unpopular class or faction in Ireland, the Irish people, as a whole, have, to a large extent, refused to obey them, and

have preferred to bow to the behests of popular leaders or secret societies, and to obey their mandates.

11. (*a*) That the presumption that "we can legislate better for the Irish than they can for themselves is," as Fox said, "a principle founded on the most arrogant despotism and tyranny."—(*b*) That Great Britain, in her Irish legislation, has persistently ignored the existence of those differences of race, religion, habits, character, and sentiment which exist between Irishmen and Englishmen. —(*c*) That, by our Irish legislation, which, when conciliatory, has been given grudgingly, has usually been accompanied by coercion, and has not been by any means in accord with Irish opinion, and which, when coercive, has been absolutely antagonistic to Irish feeling, we have fomented the feeling of antagonism between the two nations.—(*d*) That, similarly, by our system of centralised government for Ireland, by consistently disregarding the voice of the Irish representatives, by our administration of the law, by "Castle Rule," by the refusal, until quite lately, of municipal privileges and power, and (until recently) of an equal Parliamentary franchise, we have accentuated the feeling that the government of Ireland is English and not Irish.

12. (*a*) That, under the existing system of Castle Rule, every Irishman who has the confidence of the Irish people is practically excluded from all share in the administration of Ireland.*—(*b*) That in Parliament itself those who are least consulted in Irish legislation are the representatives of the Irish people.

13. That the primary purpose of government is the maintenance of social order. Social order can only be main-

* "An Irishman at this moment cannot move a step, he cannot lift a finger, in any parochial, municipal, or educational work, without being confronted with, interfered with, controlled by, an English official, appointed by a foreign Government, and without a shade or shadow of representative authority."—Mr Chamberlain at Holloway, June 1885.

tained by force or by contentment; and, as in Ireland, there is no contentment, it has to be maintained by force. The only alternative to Home Rule is Coercion.

14. (*a*) That the English Government, being responsible for law and order, have been obliged to enact constant strict coercive criminal legislation, with suspension of constitutional freedom, and of liberty of person, speech, and press —legislation which, though nominally directed against criminals, is really, under the peculiar condition of things existing in Ireland, directed against the people in general and their political leaders in particular.*—(*b*) That this has been more peculiarly the case of late. The latest Coercion Act, that made perpetual in 1887, was especially directed to the suppression of the National League—*i.e.* the suppression of an association representative of, and supported by, the bulk of the Irish people at home and abroad.—(*c*) That most of those who have suffered under Coercion Acts have been, not ordinary criminals, but "political offenders"; men of otherwise blameless character, but whom the Government of the day, responsible for the peace of Ireland, has found it necessary to prosecute and imprison; with the sole result of making them more dangerously popular, and more bitterly hostile.†—(*d*) That political and ordinary crime are thus confounded. The whole law is discredited, and the "village

* Such laws as the curfew law, the Arms Act, the power of search, the levy of a special police rate in a district in which a crime has been committed, the power of dispensing with juries—to quote from a few of the recent Coercion Acts — are clearly weapons directed, not against individual offenders, but against the bulk of the people. Innocent and guilty alike suffer, and bitterness against the law is produced. Between 1800, the date of the Union, and 1892, there has scarcely been a year free from exceptional criminal legislation.

† Of the sitting Nationalist members, a large number have been either prosecuted or imprisoned, many more than once. Such men, too, as the late Daniel O'Connell, Charles Parnell, John Martin, John Mitchell, A. M. Sullivan, and hundreds of others of the same calibre aud character, suffered under different coercive laws.

ruffian" finds his opportunity in the unhealthy state of society; with the result, that the law has diminished in efficiency as it has increased in stringency.—(*e*) That the policy of coercion has been worse than a failure. It moves in a vicious circle. Coercion leads to the necessity of further coercion. That which should be exceptional becomes habitual. Force has been conclusively shown to be not only no remedy, but positively an aggravation of the disease.

15. That, the alternative to Home Rule, the policy of "twenty years of resolute government," has had full scope, yet the Irish Question is no nearer solution than before.

16. (*a*) That, even if, for the moment, by coercion, the Government of the day are successful in maintaining the apparent supremacy of the law, it is, at the best, simply success in driving discontent beneath the surface, with the result of fomenting disloyalty and of encouraging the formation of secret societies.—(*b*) That such a state of things is most injurious to the character of the ruler, as well as of the ruled; and to it is largely due the "moral laxity" of the Irish people, so far as this exists.—(*c*) That a continuation of the system which has worked so disastrously can only lead to further deterioration of character on both sides.

17. (*a*) That, in order to carry out these coercive laws, England has to keep a large military garrison in Ireland; and, at a cost of a million and a half a year, to maintain there some 13,000 constabulary, armed, not as in England merely with a truncheon, but with rifle, bayonet, and revolver.—(*b*) That, thus, the majesty of the law is represented to the ordinary Irishman by an English force, to which he gives unwilling obedience.

18. (*a*) That the present state of affairs constitutes a grave military danger. Even when England is at peace, a large force is needed to keep Ireland in order, and England's

danger would be Ireland's opportunity. In time of war Ireland would welcome a descent of the enemy on her coasts, and allow herself to be made a base for offensive operations. —(*b*) That we have now to reckon, not only with the four millions of disaffected Irish in Ireland, but with double that number of Irish sympathisers in America and the Colonies; and who, in the event of renewed hostility between England and Ireland, would prove a formidable force antagonistic to England.

19. (*a*) That the present state of things constitutes a grave political danger. Under existing circumstances, the presence of the Irish "Nationalist" members exercises a baneful influence on the efficiency, repute, and popularity of the House of Commons.—(*b*) That the Nationalist members are elected, not to assist, but to hinder legislation; not to administer, but to prevent administration. They have largely succeeded in paralysing legislation, and in rendering the party system unworkable.—(*c*) That "Ireland stops the way." Until Ireland has a Parliament of her own, the Imperial Parliament will never be master of itself. If England insists upon governing Ireland, Ireland will at least prevent England from governing herself.

20. That a policy of Home Rule alone gives any prospect of finality and peace; and the grant of complete self-government to Ireland in Irish matters is the only possible alternative to a policy of coercion.

21. (*a*) That the concession of Home Rule will necessarily be attended with some risks. But it is a cardinal principle of the Liberal creed that liberty, self-government, and responsibility are eminently educating, elevating, and sobering.—(*b*) That by going to the root of the grievances of which the Irish complain; by giving them what they do want, instead of forcing on them what they do not want; by allowing them to have a government responsible to, and

representing the Irish people; by stripping the law of its foreign garb and by giving it a domestic character; by treating them with confidence instead of with irritating suspicion and ill-concealed dislike: their disloyalty would be disarmed, discontent would be appeased, real social order would be attained, and satisfactory and harmonious relations would be established between Great Britain and Ireland.—(*c*) That already the change from a policy of despair to a policy of hope, and the expressed sympathy of a large portion of the English people, have had an extraordinary effect in calming agitation, in diminishing agrarian crime, and in promoting good-will between the two peoples.

22. That the Irish people have always been singularly free from ordinary crime; and that, when they were themselves responsible for the peace and order of the country, they would be very strict in the enforcement of the law, and social order will be at once evolved.

23. (*a*) That until the experiment has been tried, it is absurd to say that the Irish people are incapable of self-government. The centralised system of English rule has so far made any experiment of the kind impossible.—(*b*) That while no doubt the control of the domestic affairs of Ireland by England tended to emasculate her strength and stunt her growth, liberty and self-government would foster intelligence, knowledge, self-reliance, and sobriety of mind.—(*c*) That to say the Irish shall not have self-government till they prove themselves capable of it, is to say that a man shall not go into the water until he can swim.—(*d*) That the system of centralised government has sapped the self-reliance and independence of the Irish people, and no time should be lost in altering the system before further harm be done.—(*e*) That there is plenty of good material in Ireland if properly utilised. Ireland has produced many of our greatest statesmen, soldiers, and administrators.

24. That an Irish Parliament sitting in Dublin would naturally be better informed as to the wants and wishes of the Irish people than is the Imperial Parliament sitting at Westminster.

25. (*a*) That it will be very much to the interest of the Irish themselves, who have clamoured for Home Rule, to prove, by making their Parliament a success, that they had good reason for their demand.—(*b*) That, as the constituencies would be interested in good legislation and administration, they would elect men of legislative and administrative capacity.—(*c*) That the responsibilities of office, and the necessity of initiating and carrying through legislation, the existence of a vigilant and active opposition, would have a moderating and sobering effect on the Irish representatives themselves.

26. That the grant, in 1898, of county and district municipal rights and local self-government has worked very well. The County Councils, on the whole, have done their work in a business-like way and proved that the Irish when allowed can conduct their local affairs with sense and moderation.

27. (*a*) That the association in public work of men of different classes and religions would tend to diminish existing class and religious hatreds and jealousies.—(*b*) That the existing antagonism and proportionate numbers of the minority and majority, as now represented in the House of Commons, is certain not to continue in the Irish House. It is the demand for Home Rule, and that alone, which now unites different classes and interests—farmers, labourers, shopkeepers, &c.,—in one common bond. This conceded, the existing majority would lose its cohesion, and would fall naturally into groups and sections, with different interests and different desires; and no one section would be strong enough—even if it so wished—to oppress the others.

28. (*a*) That the different sects in Ireland, if left to themselves, would be perfectly willing and able to live together on terms of amity.* At present there is a temptation to quarrel; for the English Government, and not they, are responsible for public order.—(*b*) That, moreover, the position of the "loyal" minority is one of offensive privileged superiority. Remove the cause, and the antagonism between them and the majority disappears.—(*c*) That in the districts where the Catholics are in a majority, they have shown themselves in local matters tolerant and generous to the Protestant minority.—(*d*) That in the past, since 1798, the leader of the Irish party for the time being has often or usually been a Protestant; a proof that religious animosity and intolerance is not a dominant factor in the Irish question.

29. That, at present, if we are to believe what the "Loyalists" tell us, the condition of the minority could hardly be more pitiable, protected though they are by English force.

30. (*a*) That, while more than half the population of Ulster is Protestant, more than half of its members are "Nationalists," showing that a considerable proportion, even of Ulster Protestants, support Home Rule. Thus Ulster is not in antagonism to the rest of Ireland.—(*b*) That twenty years ago the Orangemen of Ulster declared that they would fight to the death to resist the disestablishment of the Irish Church, and their threats came to nothing; it will be the same in the case of an Irish Parliament.

31. (*a*) That, though the desire for Home Rule is independent of the land question, this latter is, and will continue to be used as a powerful lever for Home Rule. Remove the cause of agitation, and the land question would

* The population of Ireland amounts to about 4,400,000, of whom some 3,500,000 are Catholics.

be settled by an Irish Parliament, representative of the different classes, on a basis just to all.—(*b*) That, at present, the Irish leaders have power without responsibility; give them responsibility as well, and they will find that the land question must be settled, and settled on a broad and just basis.

32. That, the Crown retaining the right of veto, England would be in a position to prevent the enactment of unjust laws.

33. (*a*) That experience elsewhere shows that the concession of legislative self-government is the best cure for disloyalty and discontent.—(*b*) That fifty years ago Canada, as a Crown Colony, was eminently disloyal; she is now, as a self-governing Colony, eminently loyal and content.* The prophecies freely made of the evils which would spring from the concession to Canada of Home Rule have been signally falsified.—(*c*) That the concession of self-government to our other Colonies has been followed by equally satisfactory results.—(*d*) That the only portion of the British Empire which during the late South African war was not warmly and actively loyal, was Ireland. Elsewhere, the possession of self-government brought all our great Colonies to our aid; Ireland, refused self-government, alone wished our enemies well.

34. That Home Rule, by making Ireland more contented and prosperous, would again attract capital into the country; absenteeism, with its attendant evils, would be diminished; and emigration would be discouraged.

35. (*a*) That while it is essential, it is also quite possible, in conceding Home Rule, to guarantee the maintenance of

* Canada "did not get Home Rule because she was loyal and friendly"—she had, indeed, only just before risen in arms—"but she is loyal and friendly because she got Home Rule."—Sir C. Gavin Duffy, *Contemporary Review*, June 1886.

the integrity of the Empire and the supremacy of the Crown. Full legislative freedom to an Irish Parliament in Irish matters can be combined with full and complete Imperial control and autonomy.—(*b*) That, as the limits and extent of the powers of the Irish Parliament would be strictly defined, there would be no danger of their being overstepped; and there need be no collision with the Imperial Parliament.—(*c*) That the fear of losing their Constitution would, even if no other reason existed, cause the Irish people loyally to observe its conditions.

36. (*a*) That, by going to the root of the evil—and it is an essential part of the proposal that the scheme should be acceptable to the Irish people, and be accepted by them as a final solution—separation would be made not more, but less, likely; the Union would become a reality, and not a sham; and the Irish people would be more prosperous and more contented.—(*b*) That the pecuniary,* personal, and political interests of Ireland are so much bound up with those of England, that, if self-government were granted, all interests would be opposed to a separatist agitation.—(*c*) That, even if the concession of Home Rule did not entirely extinguish all the fanatics, rebels, and agitators, it would win over to the side of England vast numbers who are now opposed to English rule. With their support, Great Britain herself, united on the question, would be in a much stronger position to resist a separatist agitation than she is at present.

37. (*a*) That Ireland could not afford to maintain herself as a separate and independent State.—(*b*) That her dream is to govern herself, and she would never consent to place herself under the power or protection of any other nation.

38. That if Ireland still remained turbulent, discontented and disloyal, Great Britain, retaining the ultimate power in

* It is estimated that out of the thirty millions of Irish exports, thirty-nine-fortieths are either consumed in England or pass through England.

her hands, could always resume her gift and return to the *status quo ante.*

39. (*a*) That the transaction of Irish business at Dublin instead of at Westminster would immensely expedite and cheapen such business.—(*b*) While such devolution would, at the same time, relieve the over-burdened Imperial Parliament.

40. (*a*) That the political, social, economical and geographical position of Ireland has been, and is, so essentially different from that of Scotland and Wales, that no analogy is possible between them.—(*b*) That, as a matter of fact, Scotland has not suffered materially from the lack of Home Rule, inasmuch as Scotch affairs, in the House of Commons, are practically settled by the Scotch members alone.

41. (By some.) That Home Rule would be a step towards "Home Rule all round," *i.e.*, separate Parliaments for England, Scotland, Ireland, and Wales, which is the only way whereby sufficient, efficient, and satisfactory legislation for each portion of the United Kingdom can be obtained.

42. (By some.) That Home Rule would be a great step towards "Imperial Federation"—the knitting together of all parts of the Empire by means of an Imperial Parliament: the best, perhaps the only, hope in the future of keeping this great Empire together.

43. That Great Britain has always sympathised with the aspirations of other nations, or races, for liberty and free institutions; she cannot consistently refuse to listen to the appeal when it proceeds from a portion of her own dominions; to practise what she has so often preached elsewhere.

On the other hand, the grant of Home Rule to Ireland is opposed, on the grounds :—

1. (*a*) That Ireland is not, and never has been in any

sense, a nation.—(*b*) That if the question of nationality be raised at all, it cannot be denied that Ireland consists of two nations, and not one. If Home Rule be given to Ireland, Ulster, also, must have a separate Parliament.

2. That no one portion of a kingdom has any absolute right to self-government, without regard to the welfare and security of the rest of the community. Four millions have no right to dictate to forty. Great Britain has maturely and emphatically declared against Home Rule.

3. (*a*) That the principle of federation is to knit the confederated communities more closely together, whilst Home Rule is intended to relax a pre-existing bond; the one is consolidation, the other disintegration.—(*b*) That between countries so widely differing in sentiment, character, and religion as England and Ireland, Federalism is impossible.—(*c*) That the various forms of Federalism existing in foreign countries differ radically from that proposed for Ireland, and there is no analogy between them; while most of these Federations have passed through phases of internal agitation, which, if the federated kingdoms had been in the relative positions of England and Ireland, would have ended in civil war.

4. (*a*) That the Colonies stand in an entirely different relation to England, geographically and socially, from that of Ireland; the Home Rule they possess bears no analogy to that demanded for Ireland. Not being represented in Parliament, the Colonies must necessarily possess a large measure of self-government; while Ireland, being vitally interested in all Imperial questions, would never consent to be placed on the footing of a Colony, which governs itself but which is not represented in Imperial matters.—(*b*) That if, at any time, separation were to follow from the concession of Home Rule to a particular Colony, it would be a misfortune, but the immediate advantages derived from the

grant of self-government outweigh the possible risks; in the case of Ireland, the risk is too great to be run. Geographical considerations cannot be subordinated to national sentiment. Until Ireland can be towed out into the middle of the Atlantic she must remain an integral part of the United Kingdom.

5. (*a*) That the Irish Union and the Scotch Union were wise and statesmanlike measures, inasmuch as they welded together the different parts of the now United Kingdom. Take it all round, the Irish Act of Union (as well as the Scotch) has been a success.—(*b*) (By some). That the Irish Act of Union may have been fraudulently obtained and a mistaken policy: but it exists, and to weaken or to dissolve it now would be feeble and foolish.

6. (*a*) That to grant Home Rule would involve a strictly defined and written constitution for Great Britain as well as for Ireland, while the merit of our constitution is that it is not a written constitution at all, and therefore eminently elastic, strong, and workable.—(*b*) That Home Rule would break the united Parliament into two distinct bodies, the Imperial Executive into two separate executives, and sever the whole sphere of legislative government into two separate domains.

7. (*a*) That it would not be possible, under any system of Home Rule, to guarantee the integrity of the Empire and the supremacy of Parliament.—(*b*) That, until it can be satisfactorily shown that the concession of Home Rule would in no way menace the integrity of the Empire, the question is not one that ought to be considered.

8. (*a*) That the difficulty which has arisen with reference to the exclusion or retention of the Irish members in the Imperial Parliament, shows the absolute impossibility of reconciling the creation of an Irish Parliament with the maintenance of the unity of the Empire and the supremacy

of the Imperial Parliament.—(*b*) That the futility of all the so-called guarantees—provided in order to attain this object—would be proved on the first occasion of collision between Irish and English opinion.

9. (*a*) That the often avowed, and real aim and object of the Nationalist Party in Ireland is Separation; Home Rule is to them only a step towards the accomplishment of that object.—(*b*) That, in any case, nothing short of Separation will satisfy the American Irish, who are the paymasters of the movement.—(*c*) That the fact that Ireland is in no way more loyal, and in no way grateful for the benefits and concessions already showered upon her, shows that she is incurably antagonistic to England.

10. That if, as is argued, Ireland is to have Home Rule because she demands Home Rule, logically Separation cannot be refused if she demands Separation.

11. (*a*) That the existence of a powerful Central Body in Ireland would create a rallying-point for disaffection; and make any agitation or outbreak more formidable than at present.—(*b*) That in the event of war, a disaffected Irish Parliament would constitute a far more serious danger than could an unarmed and unorganised people.—(*c*) That our experience at the time of the South African war was conclusive; the Irish members and their constituents sympathised with and desired the victory of the enemy.—(*d*) That even if, under ordinary circumstances, the English and Irish pulled together; in time of some great European excitement or contest, England being Protestant and Ireland being Roman Catholic, their aims and desires would come into active collision.

12. That as Ireland would not be strong enough to maintain herself as an independent kingdom, she would endeavour to place herself under the protection of France or of the United States—and this could never be permitted,

or, if permitted, would constitute a most serious menace to Great Britain.

13. That, as a matter of fact, England could never permit separation, but the attempt to prevent it would lead to much bloodshed, and to increased enmity between the two countries.

14. That the principle of Home Rule cannot be considered apart from its details; and the details of the only scheme of the Home Rule so far offered to the public are impracticable.

15. (*a*) That it is impossible strictly to define the limits and powers of an Irish Parliament.—(*b*) That it is impossible to draw the line between local, domestic, private, and Imperial matters; and constant disputes would arise on the subject.

16. That any scheme of Home Rule involves either the retention at, or the exclusion from Westminster of the Irish members; and to either alternative there are insuperable objections.*

17. (*a*) That, by the nature of things, Ireland would have to pay an annual sum to the Imperial Exchequer. The difficulties of apportioning the National Debt and of fixing the amount of the Irish Contribution would be very great. The amount that might be just one year would not be so the next; while, in years of distress, abatement might be demanded, coupled with a refusal to pay.—(*b*) That, in any case, the contribution would come to be looked upon as a "tribute," and an agitation against its payment would soon arise.

18. That demands for further privileges and powers would constantly be made by the Irish Parliament. If these were refused, the friction between the two countries would ever tend to increase, and there would be imminent danger

* See p. 154.

of civil war; while, if the demands were conceded, Ireland would gradually obtain complete independence.

19. That among the first demands of the Irish Parliament would be the power to create a volunteer force, and to control the militia, demands which of necessity would be refused, and an irritating dead-lock would ensue.

20. (*a*) That the Imperial Parliament never would nor could allow either the land question, or any question affecting religious equality, to be decided in accordance with Irish ideas; and English interference in these matters, and the necessary exercise of the veto would create intense bitterness against England.—(*b*) That in fact any exercise of the veto would cause irritation and a sense of injustice in Ireland; and would soon lead to demands for entire independence.

21. That either the Imperial Parliament would overshadow the Irish Parliament, and make it of little account, or constant conflicts would arise between the two rival bodies.

22. That the Imperial Parliament would have no means of compelling Ireland to adhere to the terms of the federal compact, except, in the very last resort, by levying war.

23. (*a*) That to constitute an Irish Parliament in Dublin, with full powers over all Irish matter, would be to hand over to the party of violence and disorder, the lives, property, and religious liberty of the loyal and law-abiding minority.—(*b*) That it would be treacherous and cowardly of Great Britain to desert the minority, the Protestants, of Ireland, who have always been the loyal and industrious portion of the community, and who still desire to remain under English rule.—(*c*) That an Irish Parliament would unquestionably confiscate the property of the landlords.—(*d*) That, even if protection and compensation could be afforded to the landlords, England would be abandoning to the tender mercies

of their bitterest enemies, a number of loyal persons scattered over the country, who, during the last few years, have been concerned, under English orders—as judges, jurors, witnesses, or officials—in carrying out the administration of the law.—(*e*) That even now—even under the protection which the English Government can extend to them—the minority are persecuted by the "Nationalists."—(*f*) That already—to judge from speech and newspaper—the majority are reckoning on the time when they will have the power of harrying the persons, confiscating the property, and harassing the trade of the minority.

24. That the concession of mere local self-government has emphasized these fears. The Nationalists have utilised the powers, obtained under the County Government Act of 1898, to ostracise the minority, to monopolise all the power, and to utilise it for party or personal purposes or gain.

25. That, once constituted, it would be practically impossible for the Imperial Parliament to interfere with the proceedings of the Irish Parliament, however unjust they might be to the minority.

26. (*a*) That religious antagonism in Ireland is so bitter, that if Imperial control were withdrawn, strife would ensue; the Roman Catholics, being the majority, would swamp and oppress the Protestants, and religious hatred and jealousies would be intensified.—(*b*) That Home Rule would be Rome Rule.

27. (*a*) That Ulster would resist, and rightly resist, to the death, the domination of a Dublin Parliament, and thus civil war would ensue, or we should be obliged to use force to put down that party in Ireland which alone has been loyal to this country.—(*b*) That, in any case, the majority of the people of Ulster would refuse to have any part or lot in the Dublin Parliament. Their abstention would either bring matters in Ireland to a deadlock, or they (the Loyalists)

would have to be coerced by England into the acceptance of a constitution that they abhorred.

28. (*a*) That the Irish are, and have everywhere shown themselves to be by temperament, thriftless, improvident, and incapable of self-control and of self-government.—(*b*) That where they now have power over local matters, they job, mismanage, and spend extravagantly.—(*c*) That their Parliament, when they had one, was a disastrous failure.—(*d*) That the action and language of the Irish members in the House of Commons show that Ireland is unfit for Parliamentary institutions, and that the Irish leaders are unfit to govern.

29. (*a*) That neither the Irish people nor their leaders have sufficient regard for life, order, and property to fit them for self-government—witness Fenianism, agrarian crime, refusal to pay rent, persistent acquittal of criminals, dynamite outrages, &c. — (*b*) That an Irish Government would entirely ignore that which is the paramount duty of every Government—the maintenance of law and order.

30. (*a*) That an Irish Parliament would weaken the self-reliance and self-help of the Irish nation by paternal and pauperising legislation.—(*b*) That the Irish Parliament—following the example of all young communities—would be protectionist, and differentially protectionist against England.

31. That there would be no security that the lighthouses, buoys, &c.—of vital importance to British commerce—would be kept in a state of efficiency.

32. That Home Rule would create a feeling of commercial insecurity, and thus capital would be still further repelled from Ireland.

33. That Ireland is so much impoverished, and her credit would be so bad, that she could never raise enough money or revenue to meet her wants; she would therefore soon

become bankrupt, disorder and distress would ensue, and England would have to come to her assistance.

34. That Home Rule would lead to the bitter disappointment of sanguine expectations; the failure would be attributed to England; and, instead of contentment, there would be greater discontent, and the demand for separation would be strengthened.

35. (*a*) That, though it is true that we have, in times past, oppressed and misgoverned Ireland, this is no reason for now handing her over to what would be certain misgovernment.—(*b*) That England long ago expiated any wrongs she may have done to Ireland; she has conferred on her exceptional benefits, and is anxious fully to remedy any real or material grievances from which Ireland can be shown to be suffering.

36. That the right policy to be pursued towards the Irish is "that Parliament should enable the Government of England to govern Ireland. Apply that recipe honestly, consistently, and resolutely for twenty years, and at the end of that time you will find that Ireland will be fit to accept any gifts in the way of local government or repeal of coercion laws that you may wish to give her. What she wants is government—government that does not flinch, that does not vary—government that she cannot hope to beat down by agitations at Westminster—government that does not alter in its resolutions or its temperature by the party changes which take place at Westminster." *

37. (*a*) That Ireland is surely, though very slowly, improving in quiet and prosperity.—(*b*) That, if we have patience, and carry out a resolute policy, combining with it a plan of "equal laws, equally applied" to all parts of the United Kingdom, and the remedy of proved grievances, Irish disaffection will gradually disappear.

* Lord Salisbury at St James's Hall, 17th May 1886.

38. (*a*) That Scotland and Wales are contented and prosperous without Home Rule, yet they at one time were eminently disaffected.—(*b*) That it would be suicidal to risk the integrity of the Empire, the strength of England, and the happiness of the people of Ireland, on the mere chance of contenting a handful of professional agitators at home and abroad.

39. (*a*) That the Irish Question is economic, and not political.—(*b*) That if Ireland were fairly prosperous, and the discontent purely political, the remedy would be political too; but when, as is the case, the discontent is mainly due to economical causes, we cannot look with any reasonable hope to a purely political remedy.

40. (*a*) That nobody really wants Home Rule; the desire for Home Rule is merely a sentimental grievance; while the Irish delight in political agitations, and manufacture grievances where none exist. Nothing will really content them.—(*b*) That the movement is not a national one, but depends for its vitality on the land question; were the land question settled, the Home Rule movement would speedily collapse.—(*c*) That the Irish people are coerced into supporting Home Rule by the action of agitators, whose power rests on boycotting and violence.

41. (*a*) That it is the first duty of any civilised government to enforce the law, and to maintain social order.—(*b*) That so-called "coercion" is merely special criminal legislation, directed to the repression of exceptional crime or outrage, with which the ordinary law has proved itself unable to cope.—(*c*) That exceptional legislation is required in the case of Ireland to prevent the unlawful coercion of individuals and classes.—(*d*) That in no case is the liberty of a law-abiding citizen curtailed by coercion.—(*e*) That if the Irish "will abandon the habit of mutilating, murdering, robbing, and of preventing honest persons who are attached to

England from earning their livelihood," there would be no need for coercion; but meanwhile coercion must be resolutely applied.

42. (*a*) That to yield Home Rule because of the difficulties of the present situation would be pusillanimous.—(*b*) That the concession of Home Rule would be a capitulation to sedition, violence, and crime—cowardly in itself, and creating a disastrous precedent.

43. (*a*) That as a matter of fact, Ireland does not "stop the way." It has of late been conclusively proved that Parliament can legislate, though Home Rule be refused. Parliament has shown itself to be quite capable of coping with the constitutional difficulties which have in the past been thrown in the way of legislation by the Nationalist members.—(*b*) That even with Home Rule, the Imperial Parliament would not be free of the Irish element, which would have to be represented, at least in Imperial matters; that, thus, the Irish would have more than their fair share of political power, while one of the chief arguments for Home Rule—that the Imperial Parliament would be quit of the Irish members—would not be fulfilled.*

44. That the Nationalist Party has no power and no authority to accept any measure as a final settlement. It is impossible, therefore, that there could be any guarantee of finality about any Home Rule measure.

45. That both the position and influence of the Empire among nations would be greatly weakened by the concession of Home Rule to agitation; and her international position, her commercial supremacy, and her influence for good, depend upon her strength and prestige being unimpaired.

46. That if Home Rule be conceded in the case of Ireland, the fever of disintegration would not stop there. Scotland and Wales would also be induced to demand Home

* See p. 154.

Rule, and the bonds between the different portions of the United Kingdom would be disastrously weakened.

47. That the constitution of the old Irish Protestant Parliament was so entirely different from that proposed for the Irish Parliament of to-day, that no precedent for restoration can be founded on it.

[Some contend that while an Irish Parliament may well be the ultimate aim, it is best attained by a "step by step" policy, *i.e.* that the grant of local self-government might gradually be extended if it proved itself a success, and thus County Councils might become absorbed in National Councils, and ultimately a National Council for the whole country could be created.

On the other hand, it is contended that the further extension of the principle of mere local self-government as a substitute for Home Rule would do more harm than good. It would not satisfy Irish aspirations, nor make Ireland more loyal. To give Ireland district self-government, and to give her nothing more, would in no way abate the discontent, but would merely supply further opportunities for its expression and indulgence. Under extended powers of local government, the majority, who would still be discontented and disloyal, would (if so disposed) have very considerable powers of oppressing the minority, without let or hindrance, and without the responsibility which would accrue from the creation of a Parliament.]

IRISH MEMBERS IN IMPERIAL PARLIAMENT

Under any measure of Home Rule the question will arise as to whether or no Ireland should retain her representation in the Imperial Parliament.

The exclusion of the Irish members is urged on the grounds:—

1. (*a*) That it passes the wit of men to distinguish, in Parliament, between Imperial matters, on which the Irish members would be entitled to a voice, and local matters, on which they would not.—(*b*) That, if this distinction were not drawn, the Irish would obtain more than their fair share of representation; they would not only decide their own local affairs, but would practically control those of the rest of the kingdom as well.—(*c*) That such a position would be unjust, intolerable, and degrading to Great Britain.

2. (*a*) That, even if a distinction could be drawn between local and Imperial matters, the presence of the Irish members would be an element of disturbance in the constitution. The Government might be in a majority on local matters, where the Irish members could not vote, and in a minority on Imperial matters where they could vote, and *vice versâ*.

3. That it is possible to devise a plan whereby Ireland could maintain for her representatives a title to be heard on Imperial and reserved matters.

4. That the supremacy of Parliament, and the unity of the Empire, would be fully maintained by the restrictions which would be placed on the power and discretion of the Irish Parliament.

5. That as the Irish contribution to the National Exchequer would probably be in the nature of a fixed sum, which could not be increased without the Irish assent; as the Irish members would be excluded with their assent and at their desire; as the arrangement with reference to the collection of Customs and

Excise would be a matter of mutual convenience; and as the Irish members would be recalled when any proposals were made affecting the taxation of Ireland, the question of taxation without representation would not arise.

6. (*a*) That to retain the Irish members in the House of Commons would keep up a feeling of irritation between the two countries. The temptation to the Irish to use their Imperial representation as a means of obtaining further concessions for Ireland would be extreme.—(*b*) That the Irish members would come to Westminster to fight out Irish, local, and personal quarrels.—(*c*) That, thus, one of the chief objects of the concession of an Irish Parliament—namely, to enable the Imperial Parliament undisturbed to apply itself to British legislation and Imperial policy, would be defeated.

7. That their presence would necessarily involve the revision by the Imperial Parliament of all the Acts passed by the Irish Parliament, a proceeding that would inevitably lead to endless confusion and dispute.

8. That the essential condition of the problem of Home Rule is that the proposal should be accepted by, and be acceptable to the Irish people; and they do not wish to be represented in the Imperial Parliament.

9. That Ireland will require the services of all her best men in her own Legislature, especially at first—to restore order, to re-establish credit, to attract capital, to develop trade and industry, to smooth over religious and educational difficulties, to settle the land question. It is better that Ireland should "keep her cream at home, and not only the skim milk."

10. That questions in dispute could always be settled by reviving the latent power of summoning back the Irish members to Westminster.

On the other hand, the exclusion of Irish representation is objected to on the grounds:—

1. (*a*) That to exclude the Irish members from the Imperial Parliament would cast a doubt on its supremacy, and would impair the unity of the Empire.—(*b*) That their presence at

Westminster is an outward and visible sign of the supremacy of the Imperial Parliament, and the reality of the Union.

2. (*a*) That with the Irish members included, the veto of the Imperial Parliament would be effective; excluded, it could never be effectively enforced; or, if attempted, the action would be considered as tyrannical.—(*b*) That, included, subjects of dispute would be amicably decided; excluded, they would cause dangerous irritation and agitation.

3. (*a*) That to call upon Ireland to contribute towards the Imperial revenue (which she will have to do), without allowing her Parliamentary representation, would be an abrogation of the constitutional doctrine that taxation and representation should go together.—(*b*) That, without representation, the contribution would soon be looked upon as a "tribute," and an agitation against its payment would arise.—(*c*) That exclusion complicates, while inclusion would simplify, any fiscal arrangements with reference to the levying of Customs and Excise duties, &c.

4. That exclusion, by depriving her of all concern in Imperial affairs, degrades Ireland to the position merely of a tributary province; that, though the present Irish representatives apparently do not object to this degradation, they cannot bind the constituencies either now or in the future. Sooner or later the degradation would be felt, and resented, and the Irish, in order to remove the reproach, would clamour for separation.

5. (*a*) That we have no right to strip Ireland of her Imperial titles, and to deprive her of all share in Imperial traditions or Imperial aims. The Empire belongs to the people of Ireland as well as to ourselves.—(*b*) That Great Britain cannot afford, in Imperial matters, to lose the assistance and advice of such a large proportion of her citizens.

6. (*a*) That there would be no real difficulty in distinguishing between, and defining local and Imperial matters; Imperial matters would, in any case, have to be defined when the limits of the powers of the Irish Parliament were fixed.—(*b*) (By some.) That it would be possible to have different Sittings or Sessions for Domestic, and for Imperial matters; the Irish representatives attending the one and not the other.—(*c*) (By others.) That no attempt should be made to reserve certain questions; the Irish

members, if included at all, should be on the same footing as the other members.

7. That the duty of legislation is not a privilege but a responsibility, and there would be no unfairness to the English, Scotch, and Welsh members in increasing the duties of the Irish members.

8. That included, the concession of Home Rule would be a step towards Imperial Federation; excluded, real Federation would be rendered impossible.

[There is a feeling on the part of many that the difficulty might be overcome by excluding the Irish members for a few years only, until their Parliament was in satisfactory working order.]

LEGAL LIMITATION OF HOURS

It is proposed that Parliament should intervene in the question of the hours of work of the adult male; and should fix the maximum number of hours during which one man might employ another in manual labour, where men work together or under like conditions; "overtime" to be allowed only under special and exceptional circumstances.*

Some propose that a uniform "eight hours' day" (or forty-eight hours a week) should be applied to all trades and industries alike. Others, a larger number, while in favour of the principle of legal limitation, would desire, both that the maximum number of hours to be fixed should vary with different trades, and that the principle of "Trade Option,"† in respect to the introduction of a legal limit at all, should find a place in the Act.‡

The legal limitation of hours is supported on the grounds:—

1. (*a*) That morally, physically, and intellectually, the present long hours of labour are injurious. They allow no

* See No. 29, p. 169.

† See section *Trade Option*, p. 185.

‡ For discussion of *Miners' Eight Hours' Bill*, see p. 191.

leisure for the duties or pleasures of home life, of fatherhood and of citizenship; no opportunity for rational recreation or enjoyment, for education, for self-improvement. They tend to crush out all individuality, and to degrade human beings into mere machines.—(*b*) That the health of the nation is being sapped by overwork. That, consequently, not only is the physique and health of the present generation being undermined: but the seeds of weakness and debility are being sown for the future. Yet the very existence of the nation depends on the moral and physical soundness of its working classes.

2. (*a*) That (eight) hours' continuous hard work is enough for any man. That especially is this the case when the worker has no personal interest in the results of his labour.—(*b*) That the processes under which work, especially factory work, is now carried on, with its minute sub-division of labour, monotonous and uninteresting, but yet requiring perpetual attention; with its incessant noise and unhealthy atmospheric conditions, involve an ever-increasing strain on the nervous system.

3. That in very few industries are the hours limited to eight, and even, where so limited, the space of time occupied by the workman and his work considerably exceeds eight hours: while "overtime" is habitually worked.

4. (*a*) That there is a growing and healthy desire on the part of the working classes, not only to participate more fairly in the wealth produced by their labour; but that, together with greater means of enjoyment, they should have greater leisure to enjoy.—(*b*) That reasonable and rational recreation cannot be enjoyed when body and mind are overwrought; hence the usual demoralising "pleasures" resorted to after the day's work.—(*c*) That, without reasonable leisure for study, thought, and discussion, men are not capable of acting useful citizens, or of giving an intelligent vote.

5. That the long hours could, with advantage to everybody concerned and with injury to none, be greatly curtailed.

6. (*a*) That, practically, no one denies that overwork exists and that it ought to be minimised, or that unrestricted liberty of working causes excessive hours. Yet without compulsory legislation, it is hopeless to expect that substantially shorter hours of labour will ever be introduced into the great majority of our national industries.—(*b*) That legislation constitutes the best, speediest, least costly, and most practicable way of attaining the end in view.—(*c*) That the object in view is to obtain the legal recognition of the principle that (eight) hours a day (or forty-eight hours a week) of hard manual labour is, in the view of the community at large, the maximum consistent with a healthy, profitable, and civilised life.

7. (*a*) That the only way in which an individual, either employer or worker, can secure a sufficient and satisfactory guarantee that his competitors will follow the same course as himself in regard to the hours of labour, is through legislation applied equally to them as to himself.—(*b*) That the legal endorsement of the will of the majority of the masters or of the men in a particular trade, is the only way of protecting them from having practically to submit to the will of the minority in the matter of the hours of labour.—(*c*) That this is especially the case in regard to "overtime."

8. (*a*) That, at present, a few employers greedy of profit, a few workmen willing to overwork, render nugatory all the efforts of the others, of humane employers or intelligent workmen, to curtail the hours of labour. The many should be allowed to coerce the few to the advantage of all, instead of, as at present, the few being allowed to coerce the many to the disadvantage of all.—(*b*) That, indeed, except by the aid of the law, individuals cannot

secure shorter hours though they may be all agreed in desiring it, the immediate interest of each individual is to work longer hours.

9. That a law limiting hours would be equal and impartial.

10. (*a*) That "freedom of contract" between capital and labour does not really exist. The individual working man is, for the most part, not in a position to protect himself, nor to negotiate on anything like equal terms with his employer.—(*b*) That, as a unit in a vast industrial army, he has practically no freedom in regard to, nor control over, his hours of labour.—(*c*) That a legal limitation of hours would really increase, not diminish, the personal liberty of the worker.

11. (*a*) That the best mode by which "independence" and "self-reliance" can be developed among working men, is by the formation of Trades Union; and the essence of a successful Trades Union is that each worker, for the common advantage and for the sake of collective freedom, shall sink his own "independence" and his individual freedom of action.—(*b*) That legislative interference has certainly not undermined the independence or self-reliance of the workers in the industries where it has been chiefly applied. The workers in these trades—cotton trade, mines, &c.—are probably the most independent of any in the kingdom.

12. (*a*) That the old *laissez-faire* argument in regard to labour has long since been exploded.—(*b*) That modern statesmanship has long since realised that "unfettered individual competition is not a principle to which the regulation of industry may be safely entrusted."

13. (*a*) That human labour cannot be regarded simply as a marketable commodity. It affects interests greater than mere pecuniary gains, and must be dealt with on

grounds higher than those of commerce and economics.—(*b*) That it is quite consistent to support the removal of all restrictions on trade, and, at the same time, to advocate restrictions on labour. The one is traffic in merchandise, with freedom of contract; in the other, no freedom of contract exists, and the traffic is in human beings.

14. (*a*) That no real distinction, moral, physical, or economic, can be drawn between interference with the hours of labour of adult males and interference with those of women.—(*b*) That, as a matter of fact, the adult male, if married and a father, is as a rule less independent in his negotiations with an employer than is the "young person" whose protection as a worker the law already recognises as a necessity. The latter can far more easily than the former transfer his labour to other districts or to other occupations.

15. (*a*) That, as a matter of fact, Parliament has already interfered, both directly and indirectly, in the hours of work of adult workers, *i.e.* by the prohibition of Sunday Labour, by Bank Holiday Acts, and in other ways.—(*b*) That the Railway Servants (Hours of Labour) Act specifically interferes with the hours of railway servants.—(*c*) That, whatever may have been the original intention of the Factory Acts, the legal limitation of the hours of labour of women and young persons in factories and workshops, indirectly limits the labour of the men employed in those industries; and in some cases directly limits it.—(*d*) That the acceptance by the House of Commons of the Fair Wages Resolution of 1891,* which declared it to be the duty of the Government, in all Government contracts, to make every effort to secure the payment of such wages as are generally accepted as current in each trade for competent workmen, is a Parliamentary admission that the State is entitled to

* See Appendix I,

interfere with the conditions under which adult male labour may be employed.

16. (*a*) That adult male labour is directly and specifically regulated, controlled, and protected by the Factory Acts, Mines Regulation Acts, Merchant Shipping Acts, Employers' Liability Acts, Artisans' Dwellings Acts, Building Acts, Acts affecting particular trades carried on in shops, especially public-houses, &c., &c.—(*b*) That the Truck Acts, which prohibit the master from paying wages in any form but in cash, even should the workman desire it, and the Act for the Prevention of Payment of Wages in Public-houses, constitute direct legislative interference with the conditions of adult male labour.—(*c*) That the Artisans' Dwellings Acts empower the Local Authority to build and let lodgings to artisans. There is no difference in principle between providing the working man with lodgings at a rent fixed by a Public Authority, and State regulation of the hours of labour.—(*d*) That "a costermonger may not wallop his donkey, nor a knife-grinder harness his dog, nor a publican sell a glass of ale, nor a milkman sell a pint of milk, nor an apothecary sell opium, nor a cyclist ride without a lamp, nor a *lion comique* sing a broad song, nor a *lionne comique* wear a short dress nor dance a particular jig, without finding the law at hand, the policeman alert, and the magistrate inexorable."

17. (*a*) That, thus, there already exists a comprehensive code of regulations which restricts, modifies, and controls adult labour, directly or indirectly, introduced for the general advantage of the community, which has proved eminently beneficial, and the repeal of which none are found to advocate.—(*b*) That the proposal made is simply to extend the already existing principle of State interference with the conditions of labour. Labour, in the matter of hours, requires further protection on the grounds of the health and of the well-being of the community.

18. That the alleged difficulties in the way of a further extension of the Factory and other operative Acts, so as to deal directly with the hours of adult male labour, are very much exaggerated. These Acts, minute and complicated as they are, deal successfully and without friction with hundreds of divers trades and interests. It would be far less difficult to extend them than it was originally to apply them.

19. That no one of repute seriously proposes to enforce at one sweep a rigid Eight Hours' Law, with entire prohibition of any "overtime," to be applied indiscriminately to all industries alike. It is recognised that there must be much elasticity of working, and that different trades require different treatment; that, in certain industries, from natural or artificial causes, there exists a greater pressure of work at one period of the year than at another; that, in others, the maximum number of hours (which might for certain workers be fixed at a higher average than eight a day) must be reckoned not by the day, but by the week, or even by the month; that provision must be made for accidents and cases of emergency. Moreover, it is generally conceded that the limitation of hours must not be applied to any particular trade or industry except at the express desire of those engaged in it.*

20. That in regard to the difficult question of the cessation of work at a fixed moment, and to the question of "overtime," the existing Factory Acts form a useful and satisfactory precedent. The hours during which women and young persons may work are strictly limited, but, without infringement of the principle of fixed maximum hours, considerable elasticity of administration exists where elasticity is required.† Moreover, it has been found, by ex-

* See section on *Trade Option.*

† Under the Factory Acts, "overtime" in certain trades, and under certain conditions, may be worked by women and young persons.

perience, that as the legal "overtime" has been gradually curtailed under successive Factory Acts, to that extent the employer has been able so to arrange his work as to comply with the law, and to avoid habitual overtime.

21. (*a*) That the Act would, as in the case of the Factory Acts, &c., be enforced by inspectors. The penalty (when incurred) would, as now, fall on the employer.—(*b*) That there would be no "class" legislation involved in thus penalising the employer. All labour legislation has been conducted on those lines, and the object of limiting hours is not to prevent a man from working as long as he chooses, but to prevent his being employed (to the detriment of his fellows) in one occupation beyond a certain number of hours a day.

22. That the "impossibility" argument was even more strongly urged against the Factory Acts and other labour regulating Acts, than it is used against an Eight Hours' Law, yet they have all worked well and smoothly.

23. That a well-marked distinction can be drawn between State interference in the matter of hours, and State interference in the matter of wages. Hours can, if thought advisable, be regulated, wages cannot.*

24. (*a*) That, under existing conditions, while many men are injuring themselves, mentally and bodily, by overwork, many others are suffering from inability to obtain work at all.—(*b*) That the reduction of hours, and the abolition of systematic "overtime" by leading to the employment of a larger number of persons, would greatly diminish the numbers of the "unemployed"; and reduce their competition with those in work.—(*c*) That the "unemployed" are by no means wholly unskilled; a large number of the skilled workers in each trade are on the average habitually un-

* See, however, Nos. 15 and 16.

employed, and most of these would be advantageously employed if there were a limitation of hours.

25. That the existence of those "unemployed" is a source of danger and detriment to the State; while their competition with those in work tends to keep down wages.

26. (*a*) That shorter hours would not necessarily nor probably lead to a reduction in the rate of wages.—(*b*) That the rate of remuneration given for piece-work, or for work by the hour, depends on, and varies with that for day-work, and would rise or fall accordingly.—(*c*) That wages would not fall, but would actually rise. The cause of low wages is over-competition for employment. A reduction of hours would increase the demand for labour, and labour would be in a better position to command higher wages.—(*d*) That this has already been the case in industries, such as that of gas production, in which the eight hours' system has been adopted.—(*e*) That long hours and low wages, short hours and high pay, almost invariably go together.

27. (*a*). That shorter hours, even though not followed by any, or a proportionate reduction of wages, would not in the end affect profits.—(*b*) That during the last thirty or forty years, the hours of labour have been shortened, and wages have largely risen, yet profits have increased. —(*c*) That the restrictions imposed by the Factory Acts, the Mines Acts, &c., have not injured but have improved the condition of the industries to which they have been applied.—(*d*) That the prophecies of the ruin that would result from the limitation of hours in factories have all been falsified. While the condition of the workers has been greatly bettered, the commercial position has been improved, not impaired.

28. (*a*) That a shortening of the hours of labour is compatible with the maintenance of the present aggregate product of labour—(*b*) That each reduction or curtailment

of hours, whether brought about by Factory Acts, or by agreement in a particular industry or business, has been followed by an actual increase in the productiveness of individual workers.*—(*c*) That experience has shown that shorter hours mean more profitable labour and more ecomonical working. The speed and efficiency of work diminishes as the day advances, and the great majority of accidents occur near the close of the day's work;† weariness makes a man less apt and less careful.—(*d*) That an individual worker might, and very likely would, produce more in a single day of ten or twelve hours, than another would do working eight hours only; but, by the end of the year, the latter would have produced more and better work.

29. (*a*) That there would be a considerable saving in the extra payments now made for "overtime"; a system of work uneconomical to employer and hurtful to employed. —(*b*) That the workers would begin work more punctually. —(*c*) That with an eight hours' day there need be but one break for meals; and each break adds to the cost of working.—(*d*) That work done before breakfast is usually inefficient and wasteful.—(*e*) (By some.) That where the system of "shifts" could be introduced or extended, the output would be materially increased, at a reduced proportionate cost.

30. (*a*) That the adoption of shorter hours would tend still more towards the disappearance of the smaller industrial establishments, and their replacement by larger concerns: with the result that the work would be carried on under more favourable physical and economic conditions. —(*b*) That attention would be turned towards the improve-

* It is asserted that an average factory hand produces far more at a lesser cost, working 56½ hours a week, than was the case when the working hours amounted to 72 a week.

† This, however, is denied as far as regards mines.

ment of machinery, and production would be more rapid and less costly than before.

31. That thus, while the probable economic effect cannot be accurately ascertained, on the whole it is probable that the amount of production would not be diminished, nor its cost increased.

32. That where the "eight hours' day" has been adopted by individual employers, it has worked satisfactorily, and to the advantage both of the employers and the men.

33. That the question of cheapness of production as affecting foreign competition is no doubt a grave one. But it is only in certain branches of our industries and trades that profits are in any way affected by foreign competition. The railways, tramways, gasworks, shops, building trades, engineering trades, &c., &c., are not dominated by it, and here at least a legislative beginning might be made.

34. (*a*) That, even where the question of foreign competition does come in, its dangers are greatly exaggerated. —(*b*) That long hours and low wages do not give a real advantage in international competition. High wages, short hours, and the resulting improved metal and physical development, facilitate the introduction of more effective methods, and thus reduce the cost of production.—(*c*) That, as a matter of fact, the severest competition comes from those trades and those countries in which the hours of labour are the shortest. The nation that possesses the most energetic, intelligent, and capable workmen will win in the end.

35. That labour movements in this country are and will be ever more and more imitated abroad. Other nations are rapidly approaching our standard of wages and hours; and the more they have done so, the more formidable rivals they have become.

36. (*a*) That the manifold restrictive legislation already in existence, has in no way tended to drive capital abroad; and further restrictive legislation need not cause alarm.—(*b*) That, indeed, capital is not really volatile. Capital cannot be easily withdrawn from business, nor can a trade or industry be easily transplanted. Many forms of "capital," land, mines, railways, buildings, &c., could not, in fact, be removed from the country.

37. (*a*) That the limitation of hours would lead to a more uniform output year by year, and thus tend to diminish the great fluctuations in trade: inflations and depressions so injurious to all classes.—(*b*) That the limitation of hours, and especially the prohibition of "overtime," would lead to a more steady and equal production over the year; and thus tend to diminish over-pressure at one period of the year, and the under-pressure at another.

38. That the abolition of systematic "overtime" would tend to make work and wages more regular and less spasmodic. The existence of "overtime" is largely due to the irregularity and uncertainty of employment.

39. That as legislative restrictions on hours would be introduced gradually, and with considerable elasticity of working, trade would be able to adapt itself to the changed economic conditions.

40. (*a*) That while a few minor industries might suffer somewhat from the enforced limitation of hours, they would soon recover; while, if they disappeared, their places would be taken by more indigenous, and consequently more robust, industries.—(*b*) That in regard to some industries, worked under degrading conditions, their extinction would be the social price, and one worth paying for the sake of the improvement in the general condition of the workers.

41. (By some.) That if the extra outlay on labour, due to limitation of hours, were not covered by increased and

profitable production, the loss would fall mainly on profits. In other words, there would be a somewhat fairer distribution of wealth, a larger aggregate payment in wages, a smaller aggregate receipt for interest, in itself an advantageous result.

42. (*a*) That the chief argument of those who declare themselves in favour of shorter hours of work, but against legislative interference, is that the desired result can be, and should be, obtained by voluntary means, by arrangement and negotiation between employers and employed, and especially by means of Trades Unions.—(*b*) That by whatever means, voluntary or legislative, a limitation of hours be obtained, the same economic results would ensue. The amount, and the cost of production would be equally affected. If it is right, proper, and advantageous to secure a maximum day by organisation, it cannot be mischievous and disadvantageous if the same result is brought about by legislation.

43. (*a*) That it may be fully admitted that, if the question of hours could be settled by voluntary agreement, legislation would be inexpedient because unnecessary. But, under existing conditions, any such voluntary arrangement, if possible in a few, is impossible in the vast majority of trades.—(*b*) That nothing approaching a universal limitation of hours can ever be obtained by the action of Trades Unions alone. At the best, success would be within the bounds of possibility only in those particular trades which were wholly and strongly organised, and these are very few in number. The Trades Unions have failed to regulate trade matters of less difficulty, *i.e.* overtime, piecework, &c.—(*c*) That the object in view is to obtain reasonable hours of labour for all. Those who work the longest and under the worst conditions, require the first attention yet it is just these trades in which the organisation of the

workers is, as a rule, weak or non-existent, and in which it is hopeless to expect that greatly reduced hours can be obtained by voluntary means alone.—(*d*) That to leave the question of hours solely to the actions of Trades Unions is to favour the strong at the expense of the weak.

44. That the bulk of the Trades Unions have confessed their inability to deal with the question, by asking for legislative interference.

45. (By some.) That, if Trades Unions could impose their own terms upon industry, it would be inexpedient (at any rate in some industries, such as railways, gasworks, &c.), that they should be able to do so without some limitation by law on their unrestrained dictation.

46. (*a*) That where restrictions of hours have been obtained, they have been conceded by the employers only under pressure and protest.—(*b*) That the only effective method by which Trades Unions can obtain or retain shorter hours, is by the threat of, and, if necessary, recourse to a strike.—(*c*) That industrial warfare—a strike with its retaliatory lock-out — involves widespread suffering, loss and demoralisation to the men, great loss to the employer, and immense injury, not only to the immediate trade concerned, but generally, and to the community at large. It leads to violence and intimidation, to antagonism between one section of the workers, the strikers, and another, the "blacklegs," and to the embitterment of the future relations between capital and labour.—(*d*) That the public deprecate strikes, and will not tolerate the intimidation without which a strike cannot be successful; yet, short of legislation, a strike is the only leverage by means of which shorter hours can be obtained. Action by "voluntary effort" implies the advice, "Unite and strike."—(*e*) That the strike, after all, may not be successful, and all its attendant evils will have been undergone for no advantage, present or prospective.

47. (*a*) That advantages won by Trades Unions, in good times, at great cost and with great difficulty, are often lost when bad times come; and the whole battle has to be fought over again.—(*b*) That in either case, the struggle to fix a standard rate of hours is certain to lead to constantly recurring fights between labour and capital.—(*c*) That it would be very expedient, looking to the future relations between capital and labour, if one fruitful cause of dispute could be removed.

48. That, if the desired results could be obtained by legislation, the gain, economically, commercially, and individually, would be great.

49. (*a*) That the legislative enactment of a maximum period of work would not weaken the general position or prospects of Trades Unions; but, on the contrary, would leave them free to devote their energies to the question of wages, and to the settlement of the other conditions of employment.—(*b*) That legislative interference in the conditions of labour has in no way weakened the position of the Trades Unions in those trades to which it has been applied.

50. (*a*) That the proposal is no more socialistic than much of our social legislation.—(*b*) That "we are all socialists now."

51. That the argument that a legislative nine or eight hours' day would soon be reduced to six, four, or even three, need not be considered, inasmuch as it is not proposed to abrogate, by Act of Parliament, the common-sense of the nation.

52. (*a*) That, in the Australian Colonies, the eight hours' day prevails, and is all but universal.—(*b*) That, though it is not statutory, it has the force of law, and works admirably, to the advantage of the whole community.—(*c*) That "in Australia the effect of the Eight Hour, and in the Cape the

Nine Hour day, is socially conservative—that is to say, the comfort conferred by it upon the working classes prevents agitation for revolutionary change." *

On the other hand, it is contended :—

1. (*a*) That while a reduction in the hours of labour is no doubt expedient and desirable, this object can only be satisfactorily and advantageously attained by voluntary effort.—(*b*) That public opinion is becoming less patient of social inequalities, and more sensitive to social evils. It is ever more earnestly in favour of shorter hours, and is ever making itself felt in that direction.—(*c*) That education, co-operation, Trades Unions, Boards of Conciliation, &c., are all factors making in the same direction.—(*d*) That, as a matter of fact, the hours of labour on the average are being gradually shortened.

2. That it is not possible to say what should be the ultimate maximum hours of labour in any particular industry, and it is unreasonable to allege that all trades could or should be treated alike, in respect of the hours of work; the elasticity of voluntaryism can alone work out the solution.

3. (*a*) That while no one advocates a policy of unrestricted *laissez faire*, it is not to be expected that Parliament should or could provide a remedy for all the ills which arise from the struggle for existence.—(*b*) That freedom of contract, and the individual liberty of the adult male, should, as far as possible, be left unfettered by law.—(*c*) That Parliament ought not to be called upon to interfere in matters in which the people are, or reasonably ought to be, able to protect themselves.—(*d*) That Parliament should not attempt to regulate the relations between employer and employed,

* Dilke's *Problems of Greater Britain*.

except for the purpose of preventing fraud, preserving health or securing safety to life and limb.

4. (*a*) That Parliament is not competent to deal with the delicate and complex machinery of British industry; the relations of labour, capital, trade, and commerce: ignorant interference is certain to work mischief.—(*b*) That the State, in former days, attempted to fix wages, to regulate hours, to limit the price of commodities: attempts altogether futile or disastrous.

5. (*a*) That each man has an absolute ownership in his own muscles and his own brain, which should not be infringed.—(*b*) That his labour is to a working man his only capital; and to interfere with his right to use this capital to the best advantage amounts to confiscation.—(*c*) That many workers would rather work twelve hours a day than eight, preferring the higher wages to the reduced hours; and it would be tyranny to compel them against their will to reduce their hours.

6. That to treat grown-up men as incapable of protecting their own interests would be an aspersion on the working classes; would disastrously weaken their self-reliance and manly independence, and would seriously react on the national character.

7. (*a*) That the question of legislative interference is one of degree, interference is justified only for the prevention of widespread misuse or mischief.—(*b*) That the Factory and similar Acts have been dictated by motives of health, humanity, and protection of the weak; not with a view to interfere with freedom of contract and with individual liberty.—(*c*) That the Factory Acts apply directly only to women, young persons, and children, to those persons, namely, who are not in a position to protect themselves.—(*d*) That the Truck Act is directed against fraud, and is in no way an attempt to regulate the ordinary relations of labour and

capital.—(*e*) That the Merchant Shipping Act, the Railway Servants Act, and other similar Acts are dictated by the desire to protect the public from the danger of overwork, &c., in peculiar industries, not by the desire to interfere with the hours of labour as such.—(*f*) That the question of Sunday Labour, and of Bank Holiday Acts are not analogous to the question of limiting the hours of labour.

8. (*a*) That it is probable that no legal limitation of hours could be enforced in regard to any particular trade, and it is certain that it could not be universally applied.—(*b*) That it would be absurd and unfa·· to attempt to apply one uniform standard of hours to different industries; or, under varying circumstances, at different places, and at different times, to the same industries.—(*c*) That, unless the Act were universally applied, it would be grossly inequitable.

9. That, as yet, we have no authoritative definition as to what is meant by a legal limitation of hours, or how it is to be carried out.—(i.) Is the limit of work to be eight hours each day, or forty-eight hours each week? If the latter, is the worker or the employer free to apportion the time over the week? (ii.) Are the number of hours fixed to constitute an absolute maximum; or is "overtime" to be allowed; and, if so, under what conditions? (iii.) Is the fixed limit of hours to include the time of actual work only, or the intervals when the men may be going to their work or "standing by"? (iv.) Are the hours necessarily to be consecutive? (v.) Are meal-times to be included? (vi.) Are "shifts" to be allowed? (vii.) What arrangements will be made, and how, for overtime in case of accidents, emergency, or exceptional pressure? (viii.) How is it going to be applied in the case of those trades in which the pressure of work is greater at some periods of the year than at others? (ix.) Is the Act to be applied to those working at home, as well as to those working in factories and workshops? (x.)

Is it to apply equally to those employed in arduous, trying, and dangerous work, and to those employed in light and healthy work? (xi.) Is it to be confined to manual workers; and if so, why are brain-workers to be excluded from the benefits of the Act? These essential queries show the impracticability of the proposal.

10. (*a*) That to make the Act operative at all, so many exceptions and exemptions, and so much elasticity of working would have to be introduced, that the principle would be destroyed, and the supposed advantages rendered nugatory.—(*b*) (By some.) That no amount of elasticity would render such an Act practicably workable in any trade.

11. That there is no particular virtue in "eight hours"; some manual labour is light, other arduous; some occupations are healthy, others unhealthy; some labour is purely mechanical, other involves the continual application of thought and attention. An eight hours' day might be too long in one industry, and too short in another.

12. (*a*) That in many industries, indeed in most, there is necessarily and unavoidably much greater activity at certain periods of the year than at others. The application of a rigid limitation of hours over the whole year would cripple or destroy such trades.—(*b*) That, similarly, in other industries, trade is busiest on certain days in the week or month, and a uniform eight hours' day could not be applied. (*c*) That other industries—such as farming, &c.,—depend largely on the weather and the seasons; a fixed daily limitation of hours would be disastrous.—(*d*) That in some industries (mines especially) it is not possible to continue output in anticipation of a demand. Thus work is often at a standstill, in consequence of a temporary or accidental falling-off in the demand. Under a legal limitation of hours, neither the employer nor the worker would be able,

when the orders came, to make up the deficiency of output, and the loss in profits and wages would be permanent.—(e) That in the case of many classes of workers—for instance, sailors, engine-drivers, &c.—a fixed limitation of hours could not possibly be applied.

13.—That, in the nature of things, the workers in many trades have, after reporting themselves, to go some distance to their work; while in others, through no fault of their own or of their employer, they have constantly to "stand by" for considerable periods in the day. Not to allow them to make up the time thus lost would involve great hardship and inequality.

14. (a) That public opinion would never permit such an extension of the criminal law as to make it a penal offence for an adult man to work after the clock had struck a certain hour.—(b) That humanity would revolt from the idea of a man's being punished because he attempted to work additional hours in order to earn something extra to make up the deficiency caused by sickness, accident, or previous slackness of work.

15. That, even in those trades in which, under ordinary circumstances, a fixed number of hours a day might constitute a proper limit, a legal restriction would, in times of depression or in times of activity, be totally at variance with the interests both of men and masters.

16. (a) That such an exasperating law would be constantly evaded by collusion between masters and men. It would either become a dead letter; or, in order to meet the constant efforts at evasion that would be made, have to be made ever stricter and more penal.—(b) That the existing Factory and other similar Acts are not easily administered, yet they apply chiefly to females, young persons, and children; and to these only where congregated together and easily supervised and inspected. The difficulties of enforcing

a still more stringent law, of applying it to adult male labour, and of extending it to all classes of workers, would be insuperable.

17. (*a*) That much of the "overtime" is worked simply in order to make up "undertime."—(*b*) That as "overtime" is always paid at a higher rate, there is no inducement, save necessity, to the employer to encourage it, and in many trades it is an absolute necessity.

18. (*a*) That the employer alone is made liable under existing Factory Acts, because, in the case of women and children—to which they apply—the assumption is that the employer is the stronger party, and should therefore be made liable for any breach of law.—(*b*) That to make the employer only, and not the employed, liable in the case of the hours of his adult male workmen, would be class legislation of the worst description; yet it would be impracticable to penalise the workmen.

19. (*a*) That, if Parliament once interfered with the hours of adult male labour, it would be called upon to interfere with wages and prices. It could not leave a man to a starvation wage while it protected him from over-exertion. It could not logically prohibit an employer from giving nine hours' employment one day, yet allow him to give only four the next.—(*b*) That thus, logically and inevitably, interference with the hours of work would lead to the adoption and application of the socialistic idea that the state should nationalise the materials of production, and control the industrial and commercial interest of the country.

20. That the position of England as a manufacturing nation, and her commercial supremacy, is due to the fact that Parliament has refrained from meddling with the relations of trade or commerce, and has left private enterprise unfettered.

21. (*a*) That any attempt radically to interfere with the relations between employer and employed, and to introduce a cast-iron limitation of hours, would be economically disastrous. It would involve diminution in profits and an increase in the cost of production, and would constitute a serious and paralysing blow to trade and commerce. (*b*)—That the first to suffer would be the working classes themselves. Existing industries would be crippled or ruined, no new industries would be started; capital would be driven away, manufacturers would transfer their business and plant abroad. The workers, nevertheless, would have to remain in the country. State interference would increase the distress it was intended to relieve.

22. (*a*) That foreign competition dominates all labour questions. Our industrial supremacy is being seriously challenged both in the home and in foreign markets, and we cannot afford to run any risks of losing our hold over those foreign markets which we still supply with goods.—(*b*) That England is not a self-supporting and self-supplying nation. She depends largely for her existence on her foreign and shipping trade;* and that trade depends for its existence on the cheapness and quality of production, on the enterprise of traders, and on a large available supply of capital.—(*c*) That a legal limitation of the hours of labour would increase the cost of production, impede the course of trade, hamper the manufacturer and trader, and discourage the investment of capital at home.

23. (*a*) That competition, both at home and abroad, has already cut down profits on the average to the lowest possible point; there is no margin for a further reduction. —(*b*) That capital is very sensitive and easily driven from one industry into another, or transferred from one country to another.—(*c*) That, from national and patriotic motives,

* See Appendix III., Nos. 1, 2, 8, &c.

many capitalists and traders are content to receive a lesser interest on their money invested at home than they could obtain with equal security if it were invested abroad; a further reduction in profits would counteract their tendency and drive capital abroad.—(*d*) That, thus, while industries at home would be starved or ruined, competing industries abroad would be stimulated and encouraged; and English trade would be doubly affected.

24. That, already, British labour has to compete with foreign labour working a larger average number of hours at a lesser average wage; the inequality cannot safely be increased.

25. (*a*) That to cut down hours is to cut down wages; and wages are too low already.—(*b*) That reduced hours would mean a proportionate reduction in wages. In many cases, where the reduction of hours brought about was very great—*i.e.* from twelve or fourteen to eight—the wages earned would not be sufficient to keep body and soul together.—(*c*) That as labour is to a large extent paid, not by the week or by the day, but by the hour or under a system of piecework, a reduction of hours would, in these cases, be directly equivalent to a reduction of wages.—(*d*) That the abolition of "overtime," which is usually paid at a higher rate, would mean a considerable reduction in the wages of many workers, especially affecting the best and most skilled.—(*e*) That, in one industry, a sufficient wage might be earned with the working day limited to eight or nine hours; while, in many others, the worker would find it impossible, under such a restriction, to earn even a bare subsistence wage.

26. (*a*) That it would be a gross injustice to forbid a man from doing his best to earn all he could for himself, his wife and family, because his neighbour had less energy or fewer wants.—(*b*) That the weaker and less experienced

worker, who now by working longer hours is able to earn a decent wage, would be prevented from so doing.

27. That, if the present wage fund were merely to be spread over a larger number of persons, the workers, as a whole, would be worse off than before. There would be a larger number working at starvation wages; and a general lowering of the standard of living of the working classes.

28. (*a*) That, if individual wages are not to be proportionately diminished, and if a greater number of persons are to be employed, the output must be proportionately enlarged, or else the cost of production would be largely increased.—(*b*) That it is impossible that the output could be increased proportionately to the increased cost. In certain arduous, unhealthy, or trying industries, the productive power of labour is doubtless not diminished and may be even increased by the shortening of hours; but this profitable point has already, for the most part or altogether, been reached; there is little scope for a further economical reduction of hours.—(*c*) That, if it were true, that shortened hours of labour were not inconsistent with, or would even bring about increased production, such an economic result would have been attained by mutual agreement.—(*d*) That many industries are of such a nature, or the sub-division of labour in them has been carried so far, that long hours of labour do not seriously affect the efficiency of the worker.—(*e*) That, in the past, much of the cost resulting from the gradual reduction of hours and increase of wages, has been met by improvement in machinery, better organisation, a system of shifts, greater sub-division of labour, greater combination of capital, &c. These reforms have been carried to such perfection that there is little scope for further economy in that direction.

29. That the probabilities are that there would be an

actual diminution of output in consequence of the interference with trade and the increased cost of production.

30. That the increase in the cost of production, besides injuring the foreign trade of the country, would raise the price of all articles of consumption at home. Thus, the purchasing power of income and of wages would be reduced, consumption would be checked, and the demand for goods diminished; a lessened demand for labour would ensue, and would be followed by a fall in wages.

31. (*a*) That production being diminished, there would be fewer, not more, openings for the "unemployed."—(*b*) That a forced limitation of hours would tend to the invention and adoption of still more efficient labour-saving machines; and thus, in the end, less, not more, labour would be employed. —(*c*) That a limitation of hours would tempt, or even oblige, many persons to carry on "home work" of different sorts, besides their ordinary work; work for which other persons have been hitherto employed and paid. Thus the numbers of the unemployed would be increased, not diminished.—(*d*) That, in any case, there would be but little opening for the "unemployed." So far as these are workers at all, they consist mostly of unskilled labourers; whereas it is in the skilled industries especially that a limitation of hours would tend to increase the demand for labour.

32. (*a*) That limitation of hours would not tend to regularise output; but, on the contrary, by the employment of a larger number of persons, would tend to increase production in times of activity; and the necessary dismissal of these persons in bad times would intensify the depression and distress. Instead of trade being steadied, fluctuations would be increased.—(*b*) That, when trade is exceptionally brisk or exceptionally depressed, the hours of labour require to be modified by, and adapted to, the varying conditions of trade—in some cases almost day by day.

33. That pressure of work at certain periods of the year would involve, with limited hours, the influx of additional population into certain centres at the busy times. When the slack period came, these families would have again either to migrate, or to be maintained from the rates. In either case, distress and destitution would ensue.

34. (*a*) That the demand for a legal limitation of hours is simply at bottom a demand for further and increased pay for "overtime." The working classes do not object to, but, as a rule favour, overtime work if they are paid extra for it. —(*b*) That, if overtime were prohibited, the employer and employed would continue to evade the Act; if it were allowed, the State would then have to decide at what additional rate "overtime" should be paid, otherwise the proposed limitation of hours would be rendered nugatory.

35. (*a*) That all questions of hours should be left to be settled by voluntary effort and private arrangement. Thus, alone, can proper elasticity of working be assured, labour obtain its proper reward, capital its fair profit, and trade continue in its natural course. Thus, alone, will the advantages arising from shortened hours be secured, and the evils arising from an artificial system be avoided.— (*b*) That there is all the difference in the world between the economic effect of a change in the relations of labour and capital brought about by voluntary agreement, and that brought about by legislation.—(*c*) That, in the former case, if experience showed that the action taken was injurious, the step could be easily retraced. To repeal an Act is always difficult; and while commercially necessary, it might be politically impossible.

36. (*a*) That all impediments in the way of the combination of labour have been removed. The working classes, by means of their Trades Unions, have already done much to improve the conditions of labour. Trades

Unions are rapidly increasing in numbers and in influence, and the question of a reduction of hours of labour is best left in their hands, to be obtained by negotiation with the employers.—(*b*) That strikes and lock-outs would not be averted. The wages question would become still more acute if the hours were fixed by law—and most strikes are due to questions concerning wages.

37. That Trades Unions are of great advantage to the workmen and to the cause of labour generally, and anything that would tend to weaken their position, extension, and influence, would be disadvantageous, but an Act limiting hours, one of the principal incentives to their formation and support would disappear.

38. (By some.) That the maximum tends to become a minimum, and it would be unfair to the working men—miners for instance—who had already, by their own exertions, obtained a reduction of hours below eight, to enact an eight hours' day.

39. (*a*) That it would establish the right of Parliament to interfere with the ordinary relations between employer and employed.—(*b*) That if the State interfered to curtail the hours of labour, an irresistible demand would be advanced by the employer and the capitalist for protection against his foreign rivals.

40. (*a*) That the eight hours' day in Australia, where alone it prevails, is founded on custom, not on law.—(*b*) That, even there, "overtime" to a large extent prevails.—(*c*) That the conditions under which an eight hours' day is worked are wholly different to those existing in England. Labour is not abundant, protection for the most part prevails, trade and competition, especially foreign competition, are limited.—(*d*) That, even in Australia, the problem of the "unemployed" has in no way been solved by the introduction of au eight hours' day.

41. (By some.) That is a socialistic idea, and on that ground should be resisted.

42. That the reduction of hours of labour is not a panacea ; but, at the best, a palliative. The real problem to be faced is the problem of over-population.

[Some urge that at least the legal limitation of hours should be tried experimentally in the case of all Government factories and of municipal workshops. The Government and the Municipality ought to set a good example as employers of labour; while, if the system be proved to be unworkable or disadvantageous, the step could be retraced, and no economic injury would have been done; if successful, the experience gained would be of great value, and the principle could be gradually applied to other trades and industries.

On the other hand, it is urged that it is not the business of the State or of the Municipality, at the expense of the taxpayer or ratepayer, to try experiments as an employer; or to pay more than the market-rate for labour.

"TRADE OPTION"

The principle involved in so-called "Trade Option," as applied to the question of a legal limitation of hours, is, that those employed in a particular trade, both workmen and employers, should be enabled, if they so desired, to call in the aid of the law to fix the maximum working day or week.

Some propose, that the legal limitation should be enforced in all manual trades and occupations, save where a majority of those engaged in that trade or occupation dissent by vote against the same. This may be called *Trade Exemption.*

Others propose, that the law limiting the hours should come into operation only with the express assent by vote of a large (a two-thirds) majority of those engaged in the particular trade or occupation. This may be designated *Trade Option.*

As regards the principle of Trade Exemption, it is supported, practically, on the grounds already given in favour of a legal limitation of hours; with the additional argument, that it would enable a particular trade, if it so desired, to contract itself out of the Act. On the other hand, the arguments already given against any legal limitation of hours apply almost equally against this proposal; and it is further argued that, as such a law could take no account of the varying conditions of different trades, for, by implication, a uniform fixed limit of hours would be necessitated, it would involve all the disadvantages of a "universal eight hours' law"; that it would be forced on those who had not asked for it; and, in the absence of organisation, a particular trade might, however desirous, be unable to obtain exemption; that it would cause dislocation and disturbance in every trade, whether ultimately affected or no; and, in the end, would practically become a dead letter.

The principle of Trade Option is supported, not only on the general grounds urged in favour of a legal limitation of hours, but also on the further grounds:—

1. That it is a moderate and middle course between leaving everything to voluntary effort, and the introduction of a universal limitation law.

2. (*a*) That, in the matter of statutory interference with

hours, each trade must be dealt with separately. It is inexpedient and impossible to apply a uniform and arbitrary standard of hours to different trades, working under varying conditions. —(*b*) That by a system of Trade Option, the varying circumstances of differing trades would be separately met; and the needful elasticity of working would be obtained.

3. That it is not just, that because some trades do not desire legal interference, or because a legal limitation of hours would be in their case disadvantageous or difficult of application, that other trades, desiring it, and believing its application to be possible and advantageous, should be debarred from appealing to the law.

4. (*a*) That it would involve the smallest amount of legislative interference compatible with the object in view.—(*b*) That it would be on the lines of least resistance; would be extremely elastic, and would cause a minimum of disturbance and friction; while the experience gained in each particular case, would enable other trades to decide whether they would or would not be wise to resort to the law themselves.

5. (*a*) That there is no particular virtue in "eight hours," or in any other fixed number of hours. Trade Option would, of necessity, imply, not only Trade Option in the question of whether or no there should be legislative interference at all, but also Trade Option in the question of the actual number of hours to be fixed.—(*b*) That thus the legal reduction of hours in each trade would, under the system proposed, be not an arbitrary reduction, but that best adapted to the peculiar circumstances of the particular trade.

6. That, while most trades are ripe for some reduction of hours, few are in a position to stand, without injury, a great and immediate reduction.

7. (*a*) That under the system of Trade Option proposed, the reduction of hours could and would take place gradually, step by step; no great or disturbing reduction would be enforced at any particular moment.—(*b*) That each reduction effected would be secured by law; and would thus form a firm foothold from which, after an interval, a further step could be taken at a practicable and convenient time.

8. (*a*) That no legal limitation of hours would be forced on

any trade against its will. If the workers desired, or felt obliged, to retain and maintain the existing hours of work, or preferred the elasticity of voluntary arrangement, the law would not interfere with them.—(*b*) That where, however, the large majority in a particular trade desired to invoke the aid of the law, they would be able to do so.—(*c*) That by this means the whole of a trade would be protected from the coercion of a small minority; or even against themselves.

9. (*a*) That the chief difficulty in shortening the hours of labour by law, is the difficulty of dealing with any large minority in the trade; who would either have to be coerced, or who would evade the law and render it nugatory.—(*b*) That, under a system of Trade Option, the law would not be applied except after the deliberate declaration of a large majority in its favour. That there would thus be neither coercion, except, at the worst, of a very few; nor evasion, for the vast bulk of the workers would favour the law.—(*c*) That there would thus be no fear of the law becoming a dead letter where it was applied.

10. (*a*) That the fear of disturbance, dislocation, or injury to a particular trade or industry need not be entertained.—(*b*) That no legal limitation of hours would be enforced, except after prolonged discussion, adequate enquiry, and after negotiation and probably agreement between employer and employed.—(*c*) That the opponents of the proposed limitation would have ample opportunity to show, if they could, that the proposal, if adopted, would unduly increase the cost of production, aggravate foreign competition, or in any respect injure or cripple the particular trade or industry.

11. (*a*) That the question of whether, and how far, the shortening of the hours would necessitate a reduction of wages, would be fully discussed, and properly considered in the decision arrived at.—(*b*) That the relative bearing of the question on piece-work and on day-work respectively would be duly considered.

12. That as the reduction of hours would almost certainly be enforced step by step, no great reduction taking place at any one moment, and that only after ample notice, there would be plenty of time and opportunity for each trade to adapt itself to the changed economic conditions.

13. That the system would probably be first and experimentally applied to industries such as railways, tramways, &c., in which the hours of work are very long, and in which the question of injury to trade, &c., would not arise.

14. That the step taken could always be retraced; the law, if found unworkable in a particular trade or industry, would cease to apply.

15. That Trade Option would probably take effect chiefly in those industries—railways, tramways, &c., in which reduced hours would necessarily mean increased employment; and so would lead to the absorption of many of the unemployed.

16. That it would tend to encourage not to discourage voluntary effort; Trade Option pre-supposes voluntary effort to be supplemented only by legal enactment.

17. That it would not discourage, but would greatly stimulate, Trade Union effort. All those *bonâ fide* engaged in the trade would be entitled to a voice in the settlement of the question; but it would be the organised labour that would primarily move in the matter, either for or against the application of the law.

18. That, thus, without the necessity of strikes, with the minimum of friction between capital and labour, the working classes would have a goal before them which they could reach by peaceful and legitimate means.

19. That the indirect—as well as the direct—effects of the adoption of the principle of Trade Option would be very great. The importance of the declaration of Parliament that the present hours of labour were as a rule too long, and ought to be reduced, would be enormous. Public opinion would be strengthened on the subject; and the sense of responsibility in the employer would be stimulated. Thus, in many trades, reduction of hours would voluntarily be granted on the passing of the law, which would not otherwise have taken place.

20. That there would be little difficulty—the principle once accepted—of deciding who should constitute the electorate, how the voters should be registered, and the method of giving expression to the will of the majority of those engaged in the trade or industry.

On the other hand, in addition to the general arguments already given, it is urged:—

1. (*a*) That the evil effects to trade and industry would be equally great and inevitable, whether a legal limitation of hours were introduced by means of Trade Option or of a "universal eight hours' day."—(*b*) That the possibilities of the introduction of a limitation of hours at any time by means of Trade Option would be a perpetually paralysing danger hanging over trade and industry.

2. (*a*) (By some.) That Trade Option contains all the evils of legislative interference, and would produce none of the good.—(*b*) (By others.) That the system of Trade Option would never be enforced; and would "simply damn the whole thing." That a prohibitory, not a permissive Bill, is the only means by which the long hours of work can be effectively reduced.

3. That Trade Option would be absurdly unjust as between trade and trade. The only trades in which it could be possibly enforced, would be those strongly organised; and these are just the trades in which the hours are already the shortest, and in which legislative interference is least required.

4. That in the particular trade itself, Trade Option would work unequally and unjustly. In one district, the workers in a trade might be organised, educated, ripe for, and desirous of the application of the law; in another district, they might be unfit for and not desirous of shorter hours. The former would either have to wait indefinitely for the improvement in their condition, or the latter would have to be coerced into an operation that would be disadvantageous to them.*

5. (*a*) That no practicable means exist, or could be discovered, of ascertaining the real views of a majority in a trade, on the subject of legislative interference.—(*b*) That it would be grossly unfair if the "option" were enforced merely by the votes of the workers, and yet it would be impossible to fix any proportionate vote for the employer.—(*c*) That the workers in a trade are not a fixed quantity; a man may be working at one trade to-day and at another to-morrow.

* To meet this difficulty, some propose "Local Option" as well as "Trade Option" in the matter of legislative interference.

6. That the length of hours worked in one branch of a trade are often governed by the number of hours worked by the men employed in another and distinct branch of the trade; yet, under a system of Trade Option, the former might be altogether debarred from any voice in deciding the number of hours they should work.

7. That Trade Option would tend to increase the power and influence of agitators and Trades Unionists; a power and influence that would be used by them for their own selfish ends.

AN EIGHT HOURS' LAW FOR MINERS *

The Eight Hours' Bill for Miners † is also specifically supported on the grounds:—

1. That miners work under exceptionally unfavourable conditions, and coal-mining forms a class of work apart by itself. ‡

2. (*a*) That eight hours of such arduous, disagreeable, perilous, and unhealthy work as that of coal-mining underground is quite enough, if not too much, for any man.—(*b*) That the miners have to work in a close and unhealthy atmosphere without natural light or pure air.—(*c*) That the sickness and mortality among miners is higher than that in other trades.—(*d*) That the bulk of the accidents in mines occur in the latter

* See, in addition, most of the arguments already given on the question of a general Eight Hours' Bill, which, mostly, will not be repeated.

† The Bill of 1902 contained two operative clauses only, as follows:—

"A person shall not in any one day of twenty-four hours be employed underground in any mine for a period exceeding eight hours, from the time of his leaving the surface of the ground to the time of his ascent thereto, except in case of accident.

Any employer, or the agent of any employer, employing or permitting to be employed any workman in contravention of this enactment, shall be liable to a penalty not exceeding forty shillings for each offence."

‡ There are some 600,000 men and boys working in connection with mines in the United Kingdom, with some 3,000,000 persons dependent on them.

part of the day. Shorter hours would be conducive to health and safety.

3. (*a*) That though in a considerable number of cases the miners work less, the bulk of them work more than eight hours a day;* and the average time away from home is longer than in any other organised industry in the kingdom.—(*b*) That the short day is only enjoyed by some of the workers underground—by the hewers, not by the drawers.†

4. That the miners desire, and are entitled to demand and obtain, greater leisure.

5. That most of the arguments effective against a general Eight Hours' Law, are entirely beside the mark in regard to miners; the bulk of them already work on the average but little more than eight hours a day.‡

6. That as a very large proportion of miners already work but little more than eight hours, and many of them less, a legal limitation of hours would in their case involve the minimum of disturbance.

7. (*a*) That the principle of legislative interference with the working of mines is already admitted, inasmuch as the mining

* An elaborate Parliamentary Return (No. 284 of 1890) gives the number of hours and days worked by all classes of workers employed in mines, stated by counties and groups of counties. The return cannot be properly analysed in a short note. Taking the number of hours worked at the face in coal-mines, it appears that the longest average number of hours per day actually worked was 8.40 in Leicestershire, and the shortest 5.66 in Durham. The average number of hours per day from bank to bank were respectively 9.58 and 7.23, and this on 4.87 days per week in the former case, and 5.40 in the latter.

An interesting return issued by the Miners' Federation (November 1890) gives particulars of 679 collieries, with the following results, as obtained by the check-weighers and lodge secretaries:—

Colliers' hours at face	8 h. 25½ m.
Boys' ,, ,,	8 h. 48 m.
Labourers' ,, ,,	8 h. 49 m.

In addition, the average time spent in travelling underground was 39 minutes. On these figures the net average reduction in the length of the working day, if the Eight Hours' Bill for Miners became law, would be 65 minutes, or 12¾ per cent.

† A boy of sixteen may be working underground some hours per day longer than his father in the same mine.

‡ See note to 3 (*a*).

industry is regulated in every detail. To extend these regulations so as to include the question of hours, would be to carry interference but one step further.—(*b*) That the Coal Mines Regulation Acts, limiting the hours of boys, has limited also the hours of the hewers who depend on the boys.

8. That mines can with facility be inspected and supervised; regulations affecting them can therefore be easily and effectively carried out.

9. (*a*) That the reduction of output (if any) would be very slight, seeing that the average hours of work are in fact already but little over eight.—(*b*) That there would be no difference in the effect on the out-put or on the price, whether an eight hours' day were obtained by legislation or by the actions of Trades Unions; yet it is almost universally admitted that an eight hours' day obtained by voluntary means would be advantageous.

10. (*a*) That in the last forty years, there has been a very great reduction in the hours of miners; yet the output has incrëased from 64,000,000 tons in 1845, and 175,000,000 tons in 1889, and to 225,000,000 tons in 1900.—(*b*) That the hours worked per man is only one of the elements affecting output. (*c*) That any tendency to reduction of output effected by legislation, would be more or less counteracted by other natural forces tending to increase output.—(*d*) That the output of existing mines could be much developed, and new mines could be opened.

11. That the legal checks which from time to time have been placed on the free working in mines, have but led to economies of working, and have not increased the cost of production.

12. (*a*) That improvement in "winding" machinery, &c., would meet any reduction in the time available for winding.* —(*b*) That, as a matter of fact, in many collieries the men are raised and lowered down separate shafts.

13.—(*a*) That the output depends largely on the efficiency of the miner; and with shorter and fixed hours he could and would increase his individual output. He would be healthier and

* The "eight hours' day," moreover, it is generally admitted, would count, not from the moment that the first man went down, but for each man individually, from the time he went down.

stronger, would work harder and more regularly.—(*b*) That, with a re-arrangement of hours waste of time would be avoided, most of the time now lost over meals could be saved; and the saving thus effected, would in many cases more than compensate for the nominal reduction of hours.—(*c*) That the short-time miners turn out the most coal per man.*

14. That, thus, neither the output produced, nor the wages earned, would in the end be affected.

15. (By some.) That our supplies of coal are limited, and anything that would tend to limit output, while at the same time improving the condition of the miners, would be advantageous.

16. That experience has already shown that coal-mining would not cease to be profitable under an eight hours' day.

17. That the supposed difficulties of organising the work above ground and below ground, if a legal limitation of hours were applied to those working underground, would disappear if the law were passed. The work would be so arranged (as is already the case in many mines) that the different classes of labour could be fairly and fully employed.

18. That practically coercion would be necessary in the case of very few of the owners; they, would, for the most part, gladly fall in with the limitation, if their competitors were equally affected.

19. (*a*) That, with the exception of those of Durham and Northumberland, the miners of Great Britain are practically unanimous in favour of a legislative eight hours' day.—(*b*) That knowing the conditions under which it is worked, they believe that the mining industry could be everywhere practically and profitably carried on under an eight hours' system.—(*c*) (By some.) That the opposition of the Durham and Northumberland miners is a selfish opposition; while the miners themselves work considerably less than eight hours a day, the boys and youths have to work from ten to ten and a half hours.

20. (*a*) That though the miners' Trades Unions are powerful,

* For instance, in Lancashire, where the men work nine and a half hours, the output is estimated at 350 tons per worker per annum; in Yorkshire, with eight hours, the output is 350 tons; in Durham and Northumberland, with seven and a quarter hours, the output is 420 tons.

they have not been successful in obtaining an eight hours' day.—(*b*) That the short hours, where they prevail, have not been done through Trades Union action, but have been voluntarily instituted by the employers, in order to carry out a system of double shifts, to limit the area of working, and to lessen the cost of production.

21. That the only way, other than by Parliamentary interference, in which miners can obtain a universal eight hours' day, is by a universal strike. Such a strike is already threatened, and would mean the serious dislocation of every industry and trade in the kingdom. Peaceful legislation would be more expedient and more effective than such industrial warfare.

22. That the liberty of the minority, who desire to work longer hours, is interfered with just as effectually whether the proposed, and generally agreed essential, reduction of hours takes place by legislation or by the pressure of the Trades Unions.

23. (*a*) That the legal enactment of a maximum number of hours of labour could not conceivably lead to its adoption also as a minimum where already a lesser number of hours were worked. The tendency would, on the contrary, be still further to reduce the hours all round.—(*b*) That the shorter hours worked in certain mines have not prevented their successful competition with other mines. If the working day elsewhere were compulsorily limited, the reduction of hours in these mines could be carried still further.

24. (By some.) That the peculiar position of the mining industry, and the fact that a legislative restriction of hours could be there applied with the minimum of disturbance, makes it a suitable subject for an experiment, with a view to seeing whether the principle of legislative interference with the hours of adult male labour could be safely and satisfactorily introduced.

On the other hand, it is contended :—

1. (*a*) That, already, the miners actually work on the average but little over eight hours a day; while very many work less than eight hours; and their hours compare favourably with those worked in other trades.—(*b*) That if it be inex-

pedient to put in motion the vast machinery of compulsory legislation for the benefit of those working long hours, still less should it be invoked for the sake of a reduction of but a few minutes of labour a day in a particular industry.

2. That, nowadays, mining work is done under comparatively healthy conditions, and in a well-ventilated atmosphere.

3. That the greater number of accidents occur during the earlier hours of work; proving that they are not due to fatigue of body, but to other causes, mostly entirely beyond the control of the miners.*

4. (*a*) That the miners have already, by voluntary effort, enormously reduced their hours of labour. Reduced them almost to, in some cases below, the limit suggested; the further reduction required would be best effected by their Trades Unions.—(*b*) That the miners' Trades Unions are the most powerful in the kingdom, and if they can show that a universal reduction of hours to eight, in all mines, would benefit the workers, and not seriously injure the owners, they can obtain further reduction by the pressure of their Associations.

5. (*a*) That mines vary enormously in ease of working, depth of shaft, proximity of coal to shaft, thickness of seam; in unhealthiness, danger, heat, &c., and no cast-iron rule of hours could be universally applied.—(*b*) That in one mine the miner will have, in his hours of working, to timber and build up his stalls; in another, these precautions are not necessary. (*c*)—That in the individual mine, the work of some men is easier than that of others, while some are employed much nearer the pit-shaft than others; an Eight Hours' Law reckoned from bank to bank, and applied equally to all underground work, would act most unequally and unjustly.

6. That, under the Mines Regulation Acts, a miner must make his working place safe before he leaves it, and the coal must not be so left that it impedes the air course. If this necessary work is included within the legal limit, the operation of the law will fall very unequally on different workers; if not, there would be great opportunity for, and temptation to evasion of the law.

7. (*a*) That the deeper mines, and those more difficult and

* See Returns of Accidents in Mines, and Reports of Inspectors.

expensive to work, can only be profitably worked by the employment of the men for a longer period than in the case of mines more favourably circumstanced. — (*b*) That the inland coalfields compete at a disadvantage with those on the sea-board. – (*c*) That the short-time mines are, as a rule, those most easily worked.—(*d*) That an Eight Hours' Law would still further handicap those mines that are already at a disadvantage.

8. That limitation of hours would lead to undue, and therefore dangerous, haste in working.

9. (*a*) That the term "miners" does not cover nearly the whole of those employed. Besides the hewers, there are many other workers employed below ground, and many others above ground, whose daily task and wage is dependent on the output of the hewers. All of these would be seriously and adversely affected by any limitation of the hours of the hewers.—(*b*) That in consequence of the diversity and interdependence of the work, the same number of hours cannot be worked by all the different classes of labour employed in mines. A limitation of eight hours, for instance, in the case of the drawers who work underground, would involve a lesser number of hours than eight on the part of the hewers. It would be impossible, under an Eight Hours' Law, so to organise the work of the mine that each class of labour above and below ground should be fully and fairly employed.

10. That if each person employed underground is to be drawn out within eight hours of the time he goes down, the period appropriated to winding the coal will be greatly curtailed; involving a great reduction in output.

11. (*a*) That, in practice, the difficulties of introducing a system of additional shifts would be enormous. The cost, also, would be very great; more men would be required to do a given quantity of work. The system of shifts is in itself undesirable, as involving night work.—(*b*) That, in some places (especially in Durham and Northumberland), the short hours worked by the miners are simply due to the existence of shifts; introduced in order to enable two shifts of hewers to work to one shift of drawers and overhead workers. If shifts were forbidden, or if these men were expected to work longer hours, thousands of

men and boys would be thrown out of work.—(*c*) That the double or treble shift is often worked in mines, in which there is not sufficient pit room for more men; the abolition of shifts would therefore greatly reduce the output.

12. That, in consequence of a temporary and accidental falling-off in the demand, collieries are often for days together laid idle. The best coal cannot, without deterioration, be worked and stacked in contemplation of a demand; and under a legal limitation of hours, neither owners nor men would be able to make up a temporary deficiency of output or loss of wages caused by enforced idleness.

13. That, at present, the deficiency of one day is made up on another. This would be impossible under an eight hours' law; the individual miner would suffer, and the output would be reduced.

14. (*a*) That a system of piece-work generally prevails in mines; and thus, under a legal limitation of hours, the men, being forced to work a shorter time, would be able to earn less wages.—(*b*) That in any case a limitation of hours would lead to a reduction of wages.

15. (*a*) That either the miners working shorter hours would produce less coal, and so increase the cost of production; or it would be necessary to introduce a system of increased shifts, and to bring in additional workers.—(*b*) That, in the former case, the public would suffer by an increase in the price of coal; in the latter, the miners themselves, especially in times of depression, would suffer from the great overstocking of the labour market that would ensue.

16. That the mine-owners, having to pay the same or larger fixed charges on a smaller output, would have their profits greatly curtailed or altogether destroyed, and many mines would be closed.

17. (*a*) That the public at large, and the working classes especially, would suffer greatly from the rise that would take place in the price of coal, caused by the restriction of the output, or the increased cost of working.—(*b*) That coal and coal mining lie at the heart and root of our commercial and industrial supremacy; and the trade and commerce of the country—especially the iron trade, already seriously depressed—

would suffer severely from the general increase that would ensue in the cost of production through any restriction of output.

18. That the competition with Continental and American coal-fields is becoming year by year more severe; and the maintenance of our supremacy in foreign markets is essential for our national existence.

19. That an eight hours' maximum would tend to become an eight hours' minimum; and the hours of those miners who now work less than eight hours a day would tend to increase.

20. That very many miners are opposed to legislative interference in the matter of hours, and it would be unjust to coerce them.

21. That the reduction of hours that has taken place in the case of miners has been due to a desire to limit output and to raise prices, and not from a desire to reduce the hours of work.

22. That legislative interference in the matter of hours, would destroy the miners' Trades Unions by depriving them of their reason for existence and their incentive to action.

23. That the principle of legislative interference with the hours of work of adult male labour once admitted in the case of miners would be extended and applied elsewhere.

LIQUOR LAWS

SINCE 1552, when the first Licensing Act was passed, a vast amount of legislation has from time to time been promulgated, dealing with the different questions connected with the sale of intoxicating liquors. The aim of this legislation has usually been to restrict and safeguard the trade by checking and regulating its dealings, with a view to diminish drunkenness, and to preserve public order and morality, on the principle that the State may interfere with a trade in order to keep people out of harm's way, even though that trade does not itself trespass on any individual rights.

As long ago as 1871, Mr Bruce (Lord Aberdare) introduced a comprehensive measure of reform, which was intended:—To repeal in whole, or in part, forty or fifty Acts of Parliament relating to liquor traffic; to abolish the right of appeal from the decision of the local licensing justices; to enforce greater care in the issue of new licences; to provide that all new licences should be advertised, and submitted to a vote of the ratepayers, a majority of three-fifths to possess the power of vetoing or reducing, but not of increasing, the number proposed; while at the same time it was to be the duty of the licensing justices to prevent the number of public-houses falling below a certain proportion to the population; to cause fresh licences to be disposed of by tender; to determine all existing licences after ten years, when they would come under the regulations applied to new certificates; to diminish the hours of opening; and to increase the severity of punishment for adulteration. This

Bill was withdrawn, but was followed, in 1872, by an Act (introduced by Lord Kimberley in the House of Lords), the main provisions of which, as passed, were :—To improve, by strengthening, the licensing boards, without departing widely from the existing system; to increase and consolidate the police regulations with reference to convictions for illegal acts, and the forfeiture of licences; and to curtail the hours of opening.

In 1874, Mr (now Lord) Cross introduced a Licensing Act, which modified the Act of 1872 by :—Fixing by statute the hours of opening and closing, instead of leaving them to the discretion of the magistrates; by extending for half an hour the authorised hours of opening in some towns; by slight alterations in the police regulations, and the law of adulteration; and by curtailment of the power of search.

The public revenue derived from the liquor trade amounts to about £37,000,000 annually; and it is estimated that the annual national expenditure on intoxicating liquors amounts to some £140,000,000.

The existing forms of licence in England granted by the Excise are :—

1. Wholesale, to sell beer, wines, and spirits. 2. Retail, which include :—

(1) The licences to sell any description of intoxicating liquor, wholesale and retail, for consumption "on" or "off" the premises. (2) Beer-house licences, to sell for consumption "off" the premises. (3) Ditto, for sale "on" the premises. (4) Wine licences to shop-keepers, for consumption "off" and to refreshment-house keepers for consumption "on" the premises. (5) Spirit and liqueurs retail licences, for those who have taken out a wholesale licence. (6) Ditto, retail beer licences. (7) Licences to dealers in table-beer.

"On" licences are granted, in counties, by the local

magistrates in Brewsters' Sessions, their decision to be confirmed by the County Licensing Committee, chosen annually at Quarter Sessions. In boroughs, by the Borough Licensing Committees, to be confirmed by the whole body of Magistrates. Confirmation is not required in the case of "off" licences.

Licences for consumption "on" the premises may be refused by the magistrates at their discretion, without assigning any reason. "Off" licences can only be refused on one of the grounds—that the applicant has failed to produce satisfactory evidence of good character; that the house is a disorderly one; that the applicant has, by his misconduct, forfeited a licence; or that the applicant or the premises are not legally qualified.

In the Metropolis, the week-day hours of closing are from 12.30 to 5 A.M. In towns and populous places, from 11 P.M. to 6 A.M.; and, in rural districts, from 10 P.M. to 6 A.M.

LOCAL OPTION

IN former editions, were discussed, at one time "Local Option"; at another, the "Permissive Bill"; and another, "Local Veto."* The two last proposals

* The Local Veto Bill (of 1894) provided for a direct plebiscite of the parochial electors, by ballot, in a given area. The areas were to be a borough, an urban district, a rural parish, and in London what would now be wards of boroughs. A poll could not be taken oftener than once in three years. It was not proposed to alter the Licensing Authority.

The questions to be put were:—

(1) Whether, after a certain time had elapsed, any ordinary licences at all should be granted? This required a two-thirds majority to enable it to be carried. (2) Whether the number of licences should be reduced by one

may be said to have expired still-born—they were in public opinion too drastic and inequitable.

Any popular reform of the Liquor Laws will probably be in the direction of "Local Option," by which is commonly meant that the whole licensing powers should be taken out of the hands of the Justices,* and placed in the hands of the Town Councils in boroughs, and of the County Councils in counties, as directly representative of the inhabitants of the district.

The principle of this proposal was contained in the Local Government Bill of 1888,† but the com-

quarter of the present number? and (3) Whether the public-houses should be shut on Sundays?

The two last resolutions required only a bare majority to become effective. Any decision could be reversed in three years by a bare majority.

* Neither the Majority nor the Minority of the Royal Commission 1899 found themselves able to report in favour of any form of Local Prohibition, chiefly on the ground that there is no public desire for Local Prohibition by plebiscite, and that under their plan for reconstructing their Licensing Authority, a sufficient popular element would be introduced.

The Majority recommended that the County Councils and the Town Councils should, in their respective areas, nominate, from their own members, one-third of the whole Licensing Body, the other two-thirds to consist of Justices of the Peace nominated by the Justices of the Peace of the petty sessional division. The Committee to be selected triennially. The Court of Appeal to be created, to consist however of selected Justices of the Peace alone.

The Minority recommended that the elective element (elected as above) should constitute one-half of the whole Licensing Committee and also of the Appellate Body which they recommend.

† An Abstract Resolution affirming the principle of "Local Option" was carried in the House of Commons in 1880 by 229 votes to 203; again in 1881; and again in 1883 by 264 to 177. The Resolution ran as follows:—"That this House is of opinion that a legal power of restraining the issue or renewal of licences should be placed in the hands of the persons most deeply interested and affected, namely, the inhabitants themselves, who are entitled to protection from the injurious consequences of the present system, by some efficient measure of Local Option."

pensation provisions were so strongly opposed,* that the licensing clauses of the Bill were withdrawn, though the taxation on the Trade imposed in order to provide for compensation, was retained and applied to a totally different object.

The principle of Local Option is upheld on the grounds:—

1.—That the present licensing system is open to objection, both in its construction and in its working.

2.—(*a*) That it gives to partial and non-representative persons belonging to one class only, powers which ought to belong to the general community, seeing that all suffer or benefit from their exercise.—(*b*) That the existing licensing body, not being amenable to public opinion, is greatly influenced by pressure from the publican interest; the magistrates have issued far too many licences, and have not exercised with sufficient stringency the power of cancelling licences for misconduct.

3. That, even if it be granted that the licensing powers have not been abused, it is not right that such enormous power, affecting so greatly the well-being of the people, should, in these democratic days, be in the hands of a non-representative body.

4. (*a*) That the people themselves, in this, as in other things best understand their own wants and wishes.—(*b*) That as the question of the liquor trade is of vital importance to the inhabitants of each locality, they ought to have full control over the issue and renewal of licences, so that these may be regulated according to their wants, sentiments, and desires.

* See section on *Compensation*.

5. (*a*) That, more especially in the case of a trade so pernicious as the liquor trade, they ought, through their representative local authority, to have full power of protecting themselves if they so desire.—(*b*) That the liquor traffic legally exists for the sake of the people it ought therefore to be under their full control.

6. That there are at present far too many licensed houses in existence, and public opinion, if allowed expression, would be in favour of their reduction.

7. That each representative local authority has already large powers of dealing with matters affecting local interests, and there would be nothing novel nor dangerous in conceding to them the further power of licensing.

8. That the principle of consulting local opinion in the matter in licensing is already conceded, from the fact that the publican, before applying for a licence, has to give public notice in the locality.

9. That, in many parts of England, individual landowners have exercised their authority, derived from the ownership of the soil, to limit the number of, or altogether to prohibit, public-houses on the estate. That which an individual can do for the satisfaction of his own wish, should be in the power of each locality to carry out for the benefit of the general community.

10. (*a*) That this popular control should be exercised by the ordinary representative local authority, the Town Council in boroughs, the County Council in counties, and not by a special body elected *ad hoc*.—(*b*) That the question of licensing would be thus more moderately, judicially, and sensibly considered, the election would be more orderly and less embittered, than if directed to one special object only.—(*c*) That thus progress would be steadily made, and there would be no fear of a reaction in public opinion.

11. That the question of compensation is one for future

discussion, and does not affect the principle of the justice of enforcing local control over the liquor traffic.

On the other hand, the principle of "Local Option" is opposed on the grounds:*—

1. That, on the whole, the existing system works well; the licensing laws have been admirably administered by able and impartial tribunals, sufficiently subject to popular opinion and to popular criticism.

2. That to hand over these powers to a local authority, would lead to the arbitrary extinction of very many public-houses, to the vexation of the legitimate consumer, and to the infringement of public liberty.

3. (*a*) That to hand the licensing powers over to popularly-elected bodies, would be to import into the municipal elections a most undesirable element of contention.—(*b*) That the elections, instead of turning on the merits or demerits of the different candidates in regard to their administrative capabilities, would turn entirely on the liquor question.

4. (*a*) That the transference of the licensing powers to the local authority would give them an interest in a trade which is injurious and demoralising.—(*b*) That, if compensation had to be given on extinction of licence, or if the extra local taxation of the trade were allowed, it would be to the interest of the local authority to allow the drink trade to continue undiminished.

5. That the question of compensation is vital, and, until this is settled on a just basis, it would be grossly unfair to hand over the liquor interest to the uncontrolled authority of the ratepayers.

* See also the section on *Compensation*.

It is further urged by those who favour some system of Local Veto, that Local Option does not go far enough; that what is required is, not only public control, but a direct public vote on the question, and full local power, by means of a plebiscite, arbitrarily to abolish or largely to reduce the number of licences.

This on the grounds:*—

1. That drinking and drunkenness are the great curse of the country, and by stringent means alone can this great evil be mitigated.

2. The local needs are best known and understood by the people of the locality.

3. That as drinking and drunkenness greatly injure the inhabitants of a district (in rates as well as otherwise), it is right and expedient to permit them to interfere for their own protection, by conferring upon them the power to prohibit or to limit the common sale of intoxicating liquors.

4. (*a*) That direct popular veto will alone be effective. Simply to confer on the ratepayers the right of voting in the election of a body which, among its manifold duties, would possess that of controlling the liquor trade, would be either useless or pernicious. Either the liquor question would be sacrificed to other local interests; or, as is more probable, men would be elected on to the Local Body, because of their views on the liquor question, and with no regard to their administrative ability.—(*b*) That it is to the best interests of Municipal Government that the local elections should be free of the heat and passion that would be imported into them if they turned on the question of

* See also the section on *Compensation*—against.

licences.—(*c*) That by a system of local veto (in addition to the possession by the local authority of the other licensing powers), would the end be best secured, with least embarrassment and disturbance to other local interests.

5. (*a*) That the popular will, on a question such as this, which goes to the very root of social life, should be expressed directly, and not at second hand through a representative body, which has to deal with many other questions and interests.—(*b*) That the issue, when raised, should be a direct one, and not be confused or obstructed by the importation of any other question.

6. (*a*) That the representative bodies, especially in counties, control extensive areas, often including many distinct localities; unless each district possessed the power of popular veto, the liquor trade would, in many cases, still be forced on unwilling populations. It is imperative that each separate district, however small, should be able to enforce its wishes in this important matter, and should be defended against the arbitrary domination of even representative licensing bodies.—(*b*) That though the people themselves could administer the licensing laws only through their representatives, they should be enabled to express a distinct opinion on the question of "licence," "no licence," or "number of licences."

7. That the principle of a plebiscite—a direct expression of local opinion on a particular point—is already admitted in the case of free libraries, &c. The special vote would be no reflection on the representative body.

8. (*a*) That no question of tyrannical exercise of authority by a majority arises. Whether the power be exercised by direct veto, or through the Representative Body, the majority rules; but in the latter case, a bare majority could act, while, in the former, a substantial

majority is required.—(*b*) That landowners often exercise a complete and unrestricted power of prohibition on their estates.* A power such as this, possessed and exercised by individuals, should be vested also in the majority of the inhabitants of each district.

9. (*a*) That in the United States and in most of our Colonies, the power of prohibition is practically in the hands of the ratepayers.—(*b*) That in other countries—notably in the State of Maine, U.S.A.—the absolute prohibition of the sale or possession of intoxicating liquors has worked beneficially.—(*c*) That where total prohibition has been tried on certain estates in England, it has been followed by eminently satisfactory results.

On the other hand, any scheme in the nature of prohibition or limitation by means of a direct popular vote, is deprecated, on the grounds :—

1. (*a*) That while it is just and right that public opinion should have a large share and voice in the control of the liquor traffic it would not be just that a majority should, by a vote, be able arbitrarily to deprive the minority of their rights.—(*b*) That it would be neither just nor expedient that the purchase, and moderate use, of liquor by the ordinary citizens should be prevented, because there are some who abuse it to their own hurt, or to that of others.—(*c*) That it would place tyrannical powers in the hands of a majority.—(*d*) That it would be a gross infringement of the liberty of all for the sake of a few; "it is better for the people to be free than sober."—(*e*) That the House of Commons, in the Eastbourne (Salvation) case, established

* It was stated in debate on the Welsh Direct Veto Bill (18th March 1891), that the Duke of Westminster had suppressed thirty-seven out of forty-eight public-houses on his estate.

the principle that no locality can veto a minority, however small, out of their just rights, and the common law of the land.*

2. That though liberty which leads to abuse may fairly be restrained, the abrogation of all liberty in the matter of drink would be followed by a sweeping reaction—and more harm would in the end be done.

3. (*a*) That as the Bill would prohibit the sale only, and not the manufacture, importation, or possession of intoxicating liquors, it is unsound in principle, and likely to prove mischievous or inoperative in practice. It is not consistent for the State to prohibit the sale of an article, while it does not prohibit its manufacture, importation, or possession; either the article is so dangerous to the people that all dealings in it should be prohibited, or it is not sufficiently dangerous for the sale to be forbidden.—(*b*) That, while professing only to be directed against the sale of liquor, the proposal would indirectly affect the use of all alcoholic beverages, and so would affect the manufacture, importation, and possession of them; and the Legislature, while avowedly injuring one trade only, would injuriously affect others also.

4. That it would be illogical for the State to allow a trade to be tolerated in one district and to be prohibited in another; the trade is equally harmful or harmless in both. If it be pernicious, the State should prohibit it altogether; prohibition or toleration should not be left to the chance vote of the ratepayers.

5. That the districts in which restrictions are most needed, would be those least likely to adopt them.

6. (*a*) That where one district in which the sale of alcoholic drink had been prohibited adjoined another where the sale was tolerated, the Act would prove inoperative; there would be no difficulty in obtaining liquor.—(*b*) That

* 10th March 1883, by 269 against 122.

where such escape from the letter of the Act was difficult or impossible, prohibition would lead to the illicit and secret sale and consumption of liquor; abroad, where prohibition has been attempted, the prohibitive laws are largely evaded.—(*c*) That bogus clubs would take the place of public-houses; and clubs are much more difficult to deal with or supervise.

7. That, on the other hand, if the principle of Local Option be adopted, the inhabitants would, through their representative body, possess as full and complete a control of the liquor trade as they can fairly desire; and the best results would follow with the least friction.

8. (*a*) That under the system of a plebiscite *ad hoc*, the popular will would only be able to act by a mass vote; a system entirely subversive of, and contrary to, the principles of representative Government on which the Constitution is based, under which the electors choose out certain trusted persons to look after and protect their interests.—(*b*) That the proper tribunal for carrying out the popular will is a representative body, not the ratepayers individually. Thus alone the question at issue will be properly considered in all its bearings.—(*c*) That it is illogical that the franchise under which prohibition is to be carried out, should be household and not manhood. In America, where prohibition is allowed, the suffrage is manhood.

9. That it would be an improper delegation of the functions of Parliament to give to local bodies the absolute power of toleration or prohibition in this matter. The liquor question is a National not a Local one.

10. That if the principle is conceded, that the ratepayers in a given district have the right to forbid a trade or calling of which they disapprove (though the trade may be perfectly lawful elsewhere), logically they could claim a right to forbid unpopular places of religious or political

resort to be opened—and this could never be conceded. If liberty is sacrificed in the matter of alcohol, it will eventually be sacrificed in more important matters, to the detriment of civil and religious liberty.

11. (*a*) That the institution of a plebiscite would necessarily combine together, in resistance to prohibition, the moderate drinkers and the drunkards, to the moral deterioration of the former.—(*b*) That instead of gradual improvement and diminution of licences, there would be violent fluctuations; a great reaction of public opinion against the temperance cause would take place because of the intemperateness of its advocates.—(*c*) That there would be too much or too little action taken. If the majority voted negatively, nothing in the way of restriction of licences would take place. If the majority voted affirmatively, all the public-houses would be closed. It would be either prohibition or excess.

12. That ceaseless agitation and strife would result from the (absolutely indispensable) provision that the adoption of the law should be periodically subject to revision by the votes of the ratepayers.

13. (*a*) That to be subject to a hasty or passionate vote of the ratepayers would mean absolute ruin to the trade.—(*b*) That, tenure being less secure, and liable to constant fluctuations, through a change in public opinion, the trade would be unsettled, and would be given a more speculative character, and thus respectable men would be deterred from entering the trade.

14. That the restrictions proposed would be especially unfair on the working man, inasmuch as the public-house is his only place of social resort; while he is unable, like the wealthier classes, to lay in any store of intoxicating liquor.

COMPENSATION FOR SUPPRESSION OF PUBLICANS' LICENCES.

In former editions was discussed the general question of whether the owner of a liquor licence was entitled to claim compensation in case the renewal of the licence was refused, not by reason of any misconduct on his part, but because the Licensing Authority desired to reduce the number of public-houses in the district :—

But in consequence of the Report of the Licensing Commission of 1899,* the question of "Compensation" has assumed a somewhat new phase.

The Majority of the Commissioners signed one Report; the Minority signed another. But they are, as regards the question of Compensation, substantially agreed on the following points. Both declare a reduction in the number of public-houses to be essential. They agree that, in the case of new licences, a heavy licence rental should be charged. They agree that any Compensation to be paid must come from the trade itself, and be obtained by additional taxation on the remaining houses in the form of mutual Compensation. They agree that the Compensation should be confined to the licence and goodwill, excluding the value of the premises.

They differ, however, as to the right to Compensation of

* P. P., C. 9379.

existing licence-holders; as to the amount of Compensation that should be given; and as to the method under which it should be assessed and paid.

The Majority assert that the dispossessed licence holder has a right to full compensation. They suggest that the compensation fund should be raised by a special tax on the various licence-holders.* That to obtain a fair value of the licence and goodwill, for the purposes either of taxation or of compensation, the persons interested are to declare their value. As in declaring the value, they will be unable to anticipate whether they will be bought out or whether they will be taxed (for compensation) on the declared value, it is thought that the fair value of the licence and goodwill will be disclosed. In the event of the Licensing Authority being dissatisfied, they will have the right to a judicial valuation under the Land Clauses Act. The scheme of reduction, taxation, and compensation to be worked in septennial periods, and to be subject to revision at the end of each period.

The Minority, on the other hand, recommend that the Licensing Authority should decide what number of licensed houses shall be allowed to exist in the locality, and how these houses shall be distributed. This power is to be safe-guarded by fixing a statutory maximum, not to be exceeded, of one "on"-licensed house to every 750 persons in towns and 400 in country districts. The Minority further state, that, while from the point of view of strict justice, no claim to compensation can be urged by those who lose their licences, some allowance might be made, as a matter of grace and expediency, though not of right. And they recommend that a period of seven years should be fixed as the basis of a time

* The taxation proposed is suggested at the rate of 6s. 8d. per £100 per annum of declared value on public-houses; a like proportion to be raised from other places (including Clubs) where liquor is sold.

notice and compensation arrangement, during which time the number of houses should be reduced to the statutory maximum. In order to allow of this reduction, money compensation—to be provided by a tax on the remaining licence-holders—based on the rateable value of the premises, would be given to those licence-holders whose licences were withdrawn under the special reduction scheme, before the end of the seven years. The compensation would be proportionate to the loss of so much of the seven years' notice of which the licence-holder was deprived. At the end of the period of seven years all question of compensation should cease. The Licensing Authorities would then have full power to reduce the number of licences below the statutory maximum, without any compensation being given; and the field would be clear for such legislation, experimental or otherwise, as Parliament might be disposed to enact.

The total number of fully licensed houses was, in 1896, about 67,000, of beer-houses with "on" licences 30,000, a total of 97,000. There has been, of late years, a considerable diminution in the total number. The total in 1840 was 90,000; in 1860, 102,000; and in 1870, 117,000. At the same time, the population has steadily increased, and if the same proportion of licences to population prevailed now as in 1870, there would be now 162,000 licences instead of but 97,000.

The number of licences refused on the ground of "non-necessity" has averaged about forty-six a year for the last eleven years.*

The general principle of Compensation and the particular proposals of the Majority as against

* See Appendix XXI. Liquor Commission Report.

those of the Minority, are supported on the ground: *—

1. (*a*) That, even assuming that for the last one hundred and fifty years—since 1758—the holder of a licence has been liable to have it terminated at the end of the year at the discretion of the Magistrates; as a matter of fact, and of practice, licences have been almost invariably renewed in favour of persons who have not abused them.—(*b*) That, if the Magistrates have been wrong in so acting, they have been misled by the phraseology and spirit of the licensing laws.—(*c*) That if they have been misled, it is equally true that the public, as a whole, have misconceived the nature of a licence.

2. (*a*) That the licence, though nominally only issued for one year, practically, by long prescription, attaches to the house, and is granted to the individual during good behaviour. —(*b*) That its continuance year after year encourages the legitimate expectation that it will be renewed.

3. That as a matter of fact the summary power with which the Justices are endowed, were given to them for the regulation, not the suppression, of public-houses. For regulation to be twisted into suppression, would be inconsistent with the intentions of the Legislature.

4. That, for the past fifteen or twenty years, the Justices have generally abstained from granting new "on" licences, except where one or more existing licences have been surrendered. Where such a bargain has been made, a confident expectation of renewal legitimately exists.

5. (*a*) That, during the same period, the total number of licences refused solely because they are not required has been infinitesimal.—(*b*) That where licences have been refused, it has been generally the case that either the house

* See also pp. 274-277 of 9th Edition of *Handbook*, section *Compensation.*

had been closed for a considerable period, or the licence was practically dropped by consent.—(*c*) That the case of Sharp *v.* Wakefield loses much of its significance from the fact that the house had been closed for a considerable period, and that police supervision was impracticable.—(*d*) That in populous places, and in permanent houses, the renewal of the licence can be counted on with almost absolute certainty.

6. That, habitually, the licence is granted only on the condition of considerable structural alterations to the premises; an outlay that presupposes a continuous use of the house for the purpose in question.

7. (*a*) That the clear distinction drawn between the procedure necessary in reference to a new licence, and that necessary in regard to the renewal of an old licence, proves, on the part of the State, a manifest expectation of renewal. The existing licence-holder has not to give public notice of renewal; he need not attend the court; if objection is taken to renewal, the evidence must be on oath; if the licence is refused, there is an appeal to Quarter Sessions.—(*b*) That the fact that the licencee need not attend the Court unless he receives notice of opposition, shows that Parliament did not intend that he should be ruined without notice.

8. (*a*) That, even if there be no actual legal estate, the publican has invested his capital, and ordered his whole life, on the strength of a licence in a lawful business; a trade which is under legislative supervision,* and therefore sanction.—(*b*) That, apart from the bricks and mortar, the whole value of the business depends on the licence, which gives to the trade its marketable value, clearly proving that in public opinion the licensed victualler has a right to expect

* Not only is there police and excise supervision, but the Justices can insist on certain structural alterations in the building before granting a licence.

the renewal of his licence.*—(*c*) That no vested interest would be created that does not already exist.

9. That in assessing the value of the public-house for Death Duty in the case of the publican, the brewer, or the distiller, the value of the individual interest is assessed, as stated by the Inland Revenue, on the assumption that "the licence will continue to be renewed"; a proof that a legally recognised vested interest does exist.†

10. That the money of individuals has been expended upon, and invested in houses which have been considered to have additional value, and have actually had increased value in the market, because licences have been granted in respect of them. The expenditure and investment in question has been in consequence of, and based upon, the value thus considered to be conferred by the licence. That value has itself been due to a general notion entertained by the public that a licence, once granted, was renewable during good behaviour, and therefore practically perpetual; and to an expectation, equally general, that the practice followed by the Magistrates for so many years in renewing licences, being in accordance with the law, would be followed in the future.

11. (*a*) That when any legitimate interest which has been brought into existence with the sanction of the Legislature is interfered with on public grounds, it is the duty of the community to compensate those whose interests are disturbed.—(*b*) That where vested interests have been allowed to grow up, Parliament—witness the freeing of the

* Under the Local Taxation Bill of 1890 it was proposed to devote £440,000 a year, part proceeds of an increased duty on spirits and beer, to the purchase of licences. This sum was to be handed over to the County and Borough Councils, and they were to apply the money in buying up public-houses by agreement with the owners. The proposal was withdrawn, but the taxation remained, and the amount produced was allocated to technical education

† See P.P. 176 of 1890.

slaves, the abolition of Army Purchase, the former an immoral, the latter an illegal, traffic—has always fairly and liberally compensated those interests, when, for the general benefit, it has expropriated them.—(*c*) That it is nothing to the point to allege that the liquor traffic is pernicious, and therefore not entitled to compensation. A trade that has been allowed to grow up by the State, and which has hitherto been treated as legitimate, cannot suddenly be treated as criminal.

12. That it is nothing to the point that there are many and various interests in the licence. The different interests cannot be in justice distinguished. If compensation is right in itself, it matters not into whose pockets the money may eventually go.

13. That the estimates given of the probable cost of compensation are absurd. None expect, and few desire, the total extinction of the trade; the extreme temperance party is in a small minority almost everywhere, and would never be able to persuade the majority to such a tyrannical act. Only a small proportion of the public-houses would be closed, and the total amount of money required for compensation would not be great.

The scheme of Compensation proposed by the Minority is further objected to on the grounds:—

1. (*a*) That arbitrarily to deprive the licence-holder of his licence for no fault of his own, and to refuse full compensation, is sheer confiscation.—(*b*) That either the licence-holder is entitled to compensation or he is not. Compensation is generally understood to mean equivalent value. Fractional compensation is a contradiction in terms.

2. (*a*) That the "seven years' grace," as an equivalent for compensation, is farcical.—(*b*) That the market value of

licence and goodwill is twenty, thirty, or forty years' purchase; to offer a maximum of seven years' purchase would be to offer less than 5s. in the pound.—(*c*) That the compensation proposed, and spoken of as "seven years' purchase of the annual rateable value," is nothing of the sort.—(*d*) That, in any case, the cash compensation will be only received by the houses suppressed within the seven years.—(*e*) That, under the maximum fixed, about half, and in some cases nearly the whole, of the existing public-houses will have to be suppressed in the seven years.*—(*f*) That, as the compensation is to be levied solely on the remaining houses, they will be totally unable, in the short period allowed, either to pay the compensation or to put by a sinking fund against their own extinction.†—(*g*) That the whole trade will be completely disorganised during the provisional period; and the houses remaining will be unable to recoup themselves for the burden thrown upon them.

3. That thus the so-called "Compensation" will not represent in the faintest degree the compensation to which the individual licence-holder is entitled if he be arbitrarily suppressed.

4. That rateable value is inadmissible as a basis for compensation: the value of the premises may in no way show the value of the business. The assessment is on the building, for which no compensation is to be given; not on the licence and goodwill, which form the subject of compensation.

* In Norwich, for instance, 7 out of 8, in the City of London 13 out of every 14 public-houses, would have to be closed within the seven years.

† For instance, suppose there are ten public-houses in a town of 4000 inhabitants. These must be reduced by four within the seven years. Assume their rateable value to be £150 each, and the average years' purchase given to be four, the remaining six public-houses will, in the seven years, have to pay a sum of £2400, and at the end of the seven years can be themselves suppressed without a penny of compensation.

5. That the result of inadequate compensation would be invariably to ruin the retailer. There are always secured creditors ahead of him, and they would absorb the limited compensation allowed.

6. (*a*) That the proposed fixed maximum of licences would work most unequally and unsatisfactorily. Different districts have varying circumstances and needs. The density or sparseness of the population; the temporary, periodic, or season influx to which districts are liable; the varying social grade of different districts, make any fixed maximum impracticable.*—(*b*) That a gradual, rather than a sudden reduction of licences, would, in the end, best benefit the temperance cause, as being less likely to cause a reaction in public opinion.

7. (*a*) That without the admission of the principle of proper compensation, there can never be real reduction; public opinion would revolt at the confiscation involved.—(*b*) That, at present, the Justices are practically forced to renew all licences—the invidiousness and injustice of selection for suppression without compensation prevents action. Were compensation admitted, the difficulty would disappear; they would be free to deal with the question of reduction from the point of view solely of the needs of the district.

The Compensation proposals of the Majority are further supported on the grounds :—

1. (*a*) That the Majority proposal, on the other hand, while admitting the right to full compensation on the part of the licence-holder, if arbitrarily suppressed, does not

* *I.e.* a popular seaside resort requires more accommodation for three months in the year than during the other nine months, a market town on one day in the week; a West-end district in London, inhabited chiefly by the "cellar" population, requires far less accommodation than an East-end district populated entirely by the "cellarless."

admit any right to compensation from the public; but only from the trade itself.—(*b*) That there is therefore no question of taxing the public in order to provide compensation for the publican, but only a system of mutual compensation in the trade.—(*c*) That the trade therefore would have no motive to demand an excessive compensation.—(*d*) That as the whole of the compensation is to come out of the trade itself, the admission of the principle could not add to the value of the business.

2. That the scheme of reduction and compensation would work automatically.

3. That the proposal of the Majority for declaration of value, on which either compensation would be given or taxation be imposed, would be eminently fair. The licencee could not know beforehand whether he would be likely to receive compensation or to be taxed for compensation, and would have therefore no inducement to return other than the fair value of his premises. Further, the declared value is subject to the check of a jury.

4. (*a*) That the proposal is just. The suppressed licencee is to receive compensation from the remaining licencees whose business would be improved by his suppression.—(*b*) That to suppress a portion of the licences at a fractional compensation, is to inflict very material loss on one set of licencees arbitrarily selected, and to benefit the remainder.

5. (*a*) That the Majority scheme has the advantage of being provisional and experimental.—(*b*) That it is better, in such a gigantic and novel operation, to work gradually and tentatively, rather than suddenly and arbitrarily.—(*c*) That at the end of seven years, and at each septennial period, the scheme can be revised and improved.

(6). *a* That a too rapid reduction would lead to crowding and disorder in the remaining houses.—(*b*) That it would cause a reaction in public opinion—to the disadvantage of temperance.

7. (*a*) That this system would, while reducing the number of public-houses, improve the status of the licence-holders, and therefore the character of the houses.—(*b*) That the other proposal would, by destroying security, disorganise and demoralise the trade, and drive out the more respectable men.

8. (*a*) That any great reduction in, or restrictions on, public-houses, would infallibly lead to the establishment of innumerable clubs, not under police control, and not subject to limitation of hours.—(*b*) That—as regards sobriety, home life, supervision, public opinion—public-houses are better than drinking clubs.

On the other hand, it is argued that no Compensation should be given for the suppression of licences on the grounds: *—

1. (*a*) That the publican's licence is expressly limited to one year, and has to be annually renewed.—(*b*) That though spoken of as a "renewal of licence," there is really no such thing in law; the licence annually expires, and a new one is issued. The continuance of the licence is specifically not guaranteed by statute, and the strict limitation of the term clearly proves that the State has always reserved to itself the right of withdrawing the permission to sell.

2. (*a*) That the law has always been perfectly clear that a licence ran only for one year, "and no longer," and that, without any claim to compensation arising, renewal could be refused by the licensing Justices (subject to appeal to Quarter Sessions) for any reason which seemed to them to

* See also pp. 278-282 of 9th Edition of *Handbook*.

be sufficient.*—(*b*) That the decision in Sharp *v.* Wakefield was not new, but merely confirmed several previous well-known decisions.—(*c*) That this reading of the law was well-known to and thoroughly understood by the liquor trade, and Sharp *v.* Wakefield merely made it widely known to the general public.

3. (*a*) That, in any case, whatever may have been the doubt as to the law once honestly held, since 1891 the doubt has been entirely dispelled.—(*b*) That, therefore, all transactions that have taken place in the last ten years have taken place with the knowledge that the licence is absolutely annual only.

4. That, even apart from this legal decision, the renewal of some licences are every year refused by the Justices on the sole ground that they are "not required."

5. That the fact that application has to be made every year for renewal, implies that renewal may be refused; while the procedure required is only a matter of convenience, and in no way fetters the discretion of the Magistrates.

6. That it is in the full power of the Licensing Authority at any time, without compensation, to add to the number of licences; and thus to reduce or destroy the profits of existing holders. Similarly, they are entitled to reduce the number without compensation.

7. That the publican thus possesses no vested interest in his licence beyond the one year. To admit any further legal claim to compensation, would be to convert a one year's lease into a freehold, a speculative and artificial value into a State endowment; would be to give a vested interest in that which had already expired; would add largely to the value of all public-houses; would endow and renew

* Case, Sharp *v.* Wakefield, Court of Queen's Bench (on appeal), 30th April 1888. Decision confirmed by the House of Lords, 20th March 1891.

a decaying trade, and place it in a financial position that it never occupied before.

8. (*a*) That the legal liberty to sell intoxicating drink is not a right common to all citizens, but a privilege confined to a few.—(*b*) That the privilege is not a property. It is granted, not for the private benefit of the individual, but in the public interest; and is specifically subject to annual revision in the interests of the community.

9. That the manifold legislation of the past in regard to the liquor trade has been rendered necessary by its dangerous nature. That the origin and object of the licensing laws was the protection of the public. To say that these limiting statutes legalise the trade, is to misconceive the manifest object and intention of the law, which has been to prevent abuse and to limit the sale.

10. (*a*) That, in the past, the trade has enormously benefited from the neglect, ignorance, and lack of moral courage on the part of the Licensing Authorities. This, however, reduces, and does not increase, the claim to compensation.—(*b*) That past leniency has not created—and could not create—a vested interest. The fact that the Licensing Authorities have not freely used their power to refuse renewals, does not diminish their full right to exercise it.

11. (*a*) That the value imparted to a public-house by the licence, over and above its value as so much building and so much accommodation, is purely fictitious, and arises from the monopoly derived from the limitation of licences.* This monopoly, and therefore the fictitious value, could be destroyed by an unlimited issue of licences; without any claim for compensation arising; similarly, no claim for

* A typical case was quoted by Mr Gladstone (Rochdale, 27th May 1888), in which a public-house which cost, to build, but £2,030, on obtaining its licence, was sold for £16,000.

compensation can arise on a further limitation of licence. —(*b*) That monopolies bar all claim to compensation, since, by the advantage they give to the monopolist, they have conferred that which is equivalent to compensation. To demand anything further is to demand that the trader shall have all the profits and take none of the risks of a monopoly.—(*c*) That such pecuniary benefit as is derived from the monopoly which the limitation of licences causes, properly belongs to the public, and not to the trade.

12. That the publican has invested his money with his eyes open, on the strength of a licence the renewal of which he knew might at any time be refused.—(*b*) That it is nothing to the point that an individual may have given an extravagant price for the speculative chance of a continuation of the licence.

13. (*a*) That there is, by law, no property in a licence. It cannot be legally bequeathed, given away, or sold. —(*b*) That the State levies death duties on the existing market value of the licensed premises just as it does in regard to all other property. It does not thereby give any guarantee of the correctness of the valuation, or of the permanence of the value.—(*c*) That where a public body purchases a public-house to enable it to make improvements, &c., it purchases the whole premises as such, and has no power to deal with it except at its existing market value as decided by agreement or arbitration.

14. That the only person who can even assert a claim to compensation is the licence-holder. He is usually the tenant, with but a slight interest in the premises; and the licence he can neither sell nor take away.

15. That, over and over again, Parliament has reduced the hours of opening; and in Scotland, Ireland, and Wales, has altogether closed public-houses on one day out of the seven; and this, without giving a penny of compensation

for the serious loss thereby occasioned to the trade. Limitation can be logically carried up to total prohibition.

16. That the public-houses that the Local Authority would primarily desire to extinguish would be those which were the greatest nuisance to the neighbourhood—just those cases in which the principle of compensation would be the most questionable.

17. That a man who is inflicting an injury on the public has no claim to compensation when he is forced to cease or abate the injury. The respectable publican may have a claim to consideration, but he has nothing more.

18. (*a*) That the twenty millions paid on the emancipation of the slaves was not given by way of compensation, but was a compassionate loan (afterwards turned into a free gift) in relief of the planters. Moreover, the right of the planter in his slaves was permanent, and did not annually expire.—(*b*) That in regard to army purchase, the right purchased (even if of illegal growth) was the right to pay and pension covering a considerable number of years. Moreover, the compensation was given for money already paid away by the officers, and not for a fictitious value created by competition.

The Compensation proposals advocated by the Minority against those of the Majority are further supported, on the grounds :—

1. (*a*) That the adoption of the Majority proposal, by admitting the right to full compensation, would create a vested interest which, up to the present time, has never been acknowledged; and which does not legally or morally exist.—(*b*) That it would definitely and for ever establish the principle of full and permanent compensation in the

case of licences refused renewal on the ground of public interest.—(*c*) That once having recognised this vested interest, and having bought out licences at the trade valuation, it would be impossible to return to the existing conditions and refuse renewals without full compensation.

2. That the first result would be to enormously increase the value of licensed property. A free gift of many millions would be made to the trade.

3. (*a*) That the trade would be entrenched in a stronger position than before; an almost insuperable barrier would be placed in the way of future effective reforms.—(*b*) That if, in every case of non-renewal, the licence had to be bought up at its full value, the power of control and reduction now possessed by the Justices would be most seriously curtailed.

4. (*a*) That without a fixed maximum proportion of public-houses to population, there will never be effective reduction.—(*b*) That without a time limit—after which no claim to compensation can arise—there will never be effective reduction.

5. (*a*) That the reduction which would be brought about by the action of the "Compensation Fund" would be altogether inadequate.—(*b*) That as the trade is to bear the burden of the full compensation, the reduction of licences must necessarily be very gradual, else the additional taxation levied on the remaining houses would be unbearably heavy.—(*c*) That, in any case, the necessity of the provision of compensation would prevent reduction beyond a very limited extent; the remaining houses would not be in a position to bear the burden of further suppression involving compensation.—(*d*) That the complete extinction of public-houses in a particular locality, however much desired by public opinion, would be rendered impossible.

6. That, in many populous centres, the reduction would be less, or certainly no more, than is now taking place without compensation; while the process of natural reduction would cease.

7. That, in such places, the "Compensation" scheme would be altogether unworkable, except by using funds raised from other districts. But this is not possible; nor would it be fair to the publicans in these other districts.

8. That though the compensation is to come from the trade, and not from the taxes, that which otherwise should be a source of revenue is really utilised. The proposed licence rental would be, in itself, a very fair tax to levy. If not used for compensation it would go to the reduction of taxation, as will, indeed, be the case after the seven years are over.

The special proposals of the Minority are further recommended, on the grounds:—

9. That the varying circumstances and needs of localities would be provided for under the Minority scheme because—(1) The number of public-houses and beer-houses fixed is the maximum required. Fewer would suffice in many, if not in most, districts.—(2) Where special accommodation is supposed to be necessary—as, say, in the City of London, in market towns and in pleasure resorts—the accommodation required is of the nature of hotels, restaurants, &c., not of drinking-bars; and these could be treated in a different manner to the public-house.

10. That the difference between the two Reports is that the one recommends full compensation as a right; the other recommends a seven years' notice as a matter of grace, not as compensation for loss of licence.

11. (*a*) That the "Compensation" proposed by the

Minority is not compensation for dismissal; but compensation in commutation of notice. Seven years' notice is given to all as a matter of grace. When this period of notice is shortened, a cash payment is granted in lieu of the unexpired term.—(*b*) That the contribution of the surviving licence-holders would be in proportion to the reduction in competition in their own licensing district. It would be no more than they would gladly pay now to get rid of the competition.

12. (*a*) That, with the question of Compensation finally disposed of at the end of the seven years, schemes for popular control, &c., could be considered on their intrinsic merits, unhampered by the interests of individuals.—(*b*) That, meanwhile, the number of licensed premises would be gradually reduced; and this without friction or injustice.

13. (*a*) That the matter has come to be a struggle for mastery between the State and the Trade.—(*b*) That "the Trade" must be brought definitely, efficiently, and fully under control.

14. That, as regards clubs, it is proposed, by both Majority and Minority, that they should be registered, restricted, and supervised.

[There are some who object to the compensation proposals of the Minority as well as to those of the Majority, on the ground that, if the Temperance Party agree to any kind of monetary compensation whatever, the principle of compensation will have been admitted, and Parliament will concede the full claim of the trade.]

[There are many persons who, while they cannot accept the proposals of the Minority as rational or fair, are disposed to dissent from any scheme which could give a legal right to full compensation at market values; being of opinion that excessive competition has led to an inflation of prices beyond the fair measure of value for which compensation can legitimately be claimed and should be given.]

THE "TIED-HOUSE" SYSTEM

The so-called "Tied-House" system, which largely prevails in the brewing trade, means as a rule (1) in London, that the brewer either holds a mortgage on the premises, or owns the premises; in either case, the tenant of the house—the licencee—is bound to get all his malt liquor from the brewer. The tenant usually has a long lease over which he has absolute control, and usually has a considerable stake in the premises himself. (2) Elsewhere, the brewer may own the freehold or leasehold; and the tenancy of the licencee is often terminable at short notice. The stringency of the tie varies from the simple contract to repay a loan, through many varieties of obligation to purchase beer, or wine, or spirits, or all of them, from the brewer or distiller; up to, in occasional instances, the obligation to purchase from the owner or landlord every article of consumption. (3) There is also a "manager" system, where the licencee is merely a salaried servant.

The Majority and the Minority of the Licensing Commission of 1899,* agree that, under a good and careful brewer, the system may operate very well indeed, and produce excellent results. Both, however, point out that there are brewers and brewers; and, that, unless under careful regulation, the system in many cases works ill.

They do not, therefore, recommend the abolition of the Tied-House system; and they agree that such a proposal would be impracticable. They recommend, however, more careful and

* P.P., C. 9379.

stricter supervision by the Justices over every agreement and arrangement governing the tenure of a licensed house; and that these should also be submitted to the Licensing Authority on each application for a transfer or a new licence.

The Tied-House system is condemned on the grounds:—

1. (*a*) That the Tied-House system has developed very rapidly of late years, and threatens to envelop the whole trade.—(*b*) That fully 75 per cent. of the licensed houses are now "tied" in some way or other.

2. That the system has grown up outside the licensing laws; and is contrary to the spirit of those laws; and has altered for the worse the relations between the licencee and the Licensing Body.

3 (*a*) That the object of the licensing laws was to bring the Justices into direct communication with the licencee, and to give them large powers of control over the premises.—(*b*) That these powers of control are largely diminished when the party substantially interested is not immediately and personally responsible to the Licensing Authority.

4. (*a*) That the ease of transfer under a "tied" system renders it difficult to fix the responsibility for misconduct, or for continuous misconduct. The character of the house is supposed to be purged by a transfer; the tenant of whom complaint is made is dismissed, and another is put in his place.—(*b*) That, thus, by the ease of transfer, facilitated by the agreement between retailer and brewer, the power of supervision is largely withdrawn from the Justices.

5. That the big brewery company, or brewer owning many tied houses in a district, is apt to exercise a perhaps unconscious influence both over the Police and the Justices.

6. That the tenants are under very onerous conditions, both as to notice, and as to what they may sell, &c.

7. That the ostensible licencee is absolutely dependent on the owner; and the ease of transfer puts the former entirely at the mercy of the latter.

8. (*a*) That the tied-licencee having less interest in the

business, and less to lose, is less particular as to the respectability of his house.—(*b*) That anything which tends to make the position of the licence-holder more precarious is prejudicial to good order.

9. (*a*) That the general effect of the system is to push the trade and sale of liquor to the utmost; and thus to increase drinking and drunkenness.—(*b*) That the brewer (and especially the brewery company), having purchased the house, has to justify his purchase by the extension of custom.—(*c*) That, as evidence of this, "six-day" licences (it is alleged) are seldom taken over by tied houses.—(*d*) That the tenant's continued existence depends on the satisfaction he gives to the brewer; and he is therefore under compulsion to use every exertion to increase the sale of the liquor.

10. That excessive prices for the liquor are charged to the tied tenant by the manufacturers; and the licencee cannot deal elsewhere. To make a profit he has to resort to questionable practices.

11. That, as the publican must sell the liquor provided for him, and that only, he cannot guarantee its quality, nor suit the tastes of his customers.

12. That the transfers under the Tied-House system are more frequent than under the free system; proving that the tenant fails to make it answer.

13. (*a*) That men of substance will not take tied houses. —(*b*) That the lesser responsibility involved, and the requirement of but a small capital, tempts those who have saved a little money, but are totally inexperienced, recklessly, to go into the trade to their ultimate ruin.

On the other hand, the system of Tied-Houses is defended on the ground :—

1. (*a*) That the rapid development of the Tied-House system is mainly the result of inevitable competition, and the desire of brewing firms to secure their existing trade in houses which they own or have financed.—(*b*) That this is only in accord with the system adopted in several other trades. For instance, bakers'

shops are largely financed by millers, and those of grocers are promoted and financed by wine-merchants and tea-dealers.

2. That this is especially the case in regard to the Limited Liability Companies which have sprung into existence, and which have large amounts of capital to invest in the trade.

3. That it is a natural business arrangement, advantageous both to the retailer and the brewer; and in no way disadvantageous to the public.

4. (*a*) That the tendency is towards the disappearance of the small house, and the amalgamation of two or more licences into one.—(*b*) That thus it becomes more and more difficult—without the tied system—for men to enter the trade without very substantial capital.—(*c*) That under the tied system, men of small capital can take their share in the trade.

5. (*a*) That the Tied-House system tends to greater respectability of person and premises.—(*b*) That the guarantee for the respectability of the licencee is increased by the fact that he has over him a principal vitally interested in his good conduct.—(*c*) That it is manifestly to the interest of the brewer that the licence should not be endangered.—(*d*) That the facility of transfer enables the owner to have greater control over the publican, and, if necessary, to remove him and to replace him by a more respectable tenant.

6. That thus the applicant for a licence for a Tied-House is more likely to be a selected man than the ordinary applicant; while a watchful supervision over his conduct is guaranteed.

7. That, his livelihood being at stake, the Tied-House tenant is proportionately as much interested in the continuance of his licence as is the licencee of a free house.

8. That the system tends to concentrate the houses more and more into the hands of the big brewers. The larger the firm the higher, as a rule, their standard, and the greater their desire to improve the status and respectability of the trade.—(*a*) That, it is so entirely to the interest of the brewer to retain a satisfactory tenant, that he will not arbitrarily exercise his powers as a landlord to the detriment of the tenant.—(*b*) That, in a large number of cases, the management of a tied-house remains for generations in the same family, thus showing that the trade is constant and profitable to the tenant.

9. (*a*) That there is absolutely no evidence or presumption to show that the Tied-House system leads to more drinking.—(*b*) That the free licencee, who is under no obligation to a brewer, has a greater personal interest in the house, and is therefore under a greater temptation to push his sale.

10. (*a*) That the system is the result of competition; it does not increase competition.—(*b*) That, if anything, it would reduce it in the actual house; for no other malt liquor may be sold in competition with that of the owner.

11. (*a*) That, on ordinary business principles, the brewer provides liquor of good quality and of the description desired by the tenant.—(*b*) That the fact that the tied-houses are mostly owned by the big firms is a guarantee of the quality and purity of the goods supplied and sold. A free tenant is tempted to buy inferior liquor in the cheapest market.—(*c*) That when (as alleged) apparent excessive prices for liquor are charged by the owner to the tenant, the account is balanced by low rent, landlord's repairs, &c.

12. That the power of the Licensing Authority is not really diminished. They retain the fullest power of control over the licence.

13. (*a*) That the Licensing Authority has to deal, and does deal, with the actual holder of the licence, and has full power of control over him; and, through him, over the owner.—(*b*) That there is nothing in the system contrary to either the spirit or the letter of the licensing laws.

14. That as this system of business arrangement entails no proved public disadvantage, there can be no valid reason for interfering with the relations between landlord and tenant.

GROCERS' LICENCES

The actual "Grocers' Licences" apply to Scotland and Ireland only. In England the licences, popularly known as "Grocers' licences," are really "off" licences, or licences to sell beer, spirits, or wine (as the case may be) ***not to be consumed on the premises.***

It is proposed that no trade in intoxicants should be allowed to be carried on in the same premises as the trade in groceries or other articles.

This proposal is supported on the ground:—

1. That the principle applied, as a general rule, to the sale of intoxicants for consumption *on* the premises—*i.e.* that the premises should be exclusively devoted to that purpose—ought to be extended to the sale of intoxicants *off* the premises.

2. That whatever may have been the original intention of the so-called "grocer's licence," the system has been dangerously extended by the multiplication of "off-licences."

3. That the number of the licences in question show an alarming increase.

4. (*a*) That the combination of ordinary trade and trade in liquor on the same premises, renders supervision difficult, and detection of illegal practices well-nigh impossible.—(*b*) That especially is this the case in remote districts.

5. (*a*) That it leads to a great deal of illicit trading in liquor.—(*b*) That it leads to illegal consumption on the premises. —(*c*) That as there are no statutory closing hours for ordinary retail goods, it leads to much sale of liquor—especially on Sundays—during illegal hours.

6. That the liquor sold under these licences is to a large extent delivered in vans and carts with other goods; thus the hawking of liquor in contravention of the law is rendered easier; the purchase of the liquor is greatly facilitated, and temptation is brought to every door.

7. That, though nominally confined to consumption off the premises, there is nothing to prevent a person having his bottle filled, consuming the liquor outside, and repeating the process.

8. That all those entering the shop for ordinary purchases are unnecessarily and unfairly exposed to temptation.

9. (*a*) That much temptation to drink is thrown in the way of women in consequence of the ease of purchase, and the non-necessity of going to the public-house.—(*b*) That it leads to temptation and secrecy combined. The mixture of trades makes

it easy for the "grocer" to co-operate with customers who wish to deceive their husbands, and to book intoxicants as items of groceries.—(*c*) That such a system of deception extends to officials in workhouses, etc., to whom liquor is supplied in lieu of the ostensible groceries.

10. That the facilities thus afforded to procure liquor lead to much secret drinking at home.

11. That thus temptation, fraud, and deception are encouraged; evils that might be avoided by the prohibition of mixed sale.

12. (*a*) That no question of compensation for suppression could arise; for, in the case of wine, spirit, cider, and sweets licences, there is no monopoly value, *i.e.* the licence must be issued if applied for.—(*b*) That these mixed trades deprived of the liquor licences, would have their other business to fall back upon.

On the other hand, it is contended:—

(*a*) 1. That the "off" licence system—commonly called "grocers' licences"—was introduced in the interests of sobriety and respectability, thus making it unnecessary for a person requiring a bottle of wine or spirits to enter a public-house.—(*b*) That it was introduced especially with a view to facilitating and encouraging the sale of light and less intoxicating wines in competition with more intoxicating liquors.—(*c*) That this class of licence has tended to secure moderate prices and improved quality.

2. (*a*) That, since their establishment forty years ago, no single complaint has been made in regard to them to the Board of inland Revenue; not a single prosecution has been rendered necessary.—(*b*) That the police authorities have made no complaint as to any difficulty of supervising the "off" licences in question; nor complained of any illegal practices connected with the trade.

3. (*a*) That even if, in some cases (which is denied) it has led to abuse, the system has certainly, on the whole, tended towards temperance.—(*b*) That undue indulgence is less likely to arise where the article forms part of the ordinary consumption

at meals; and is associated with home surroundings.—(*c*) That the alternative is the public-house, with its temptation to greater consumption on the premises.

4. That there is no evidence to show that the privilege has been abused: or that the system has led to secret drinking or fraudulent working.

5. That the alleged frauds, secret drinking, &c., would not be affected by the mere separation of the premises into two parts.

6. That there is a tendency to confuse drink with drunkenness: the use with the abuse of the article. It is not politic to penalise the moderate drinker in order to protect the drunkard.

7. That the system of "off" licences is an immense convenience and advantage to the ordinary consumer who can thus supply himself with liquor in small quantities and for home consumption; and without having to go to the public-house.

8. (*a*) That the proposal to prohibit the sale on premises where other goods are sold, would practically destroy the "off" trade, and transfer it to the public-house.—(*b*) That, at the best, only in large towns and populous places could the "off" trader obtain sufficient custom from this liquor trade alone to gain a living.—(*c*) That it is especially in the country districts, where there is not sufficient demand to maintain a public house, that the grocer's licence supplies a necessary want.—(*d*) That if this system of licences were abolished, instead of the licence being in the hands of a respectable tradesman, a small and probably badly conducted public-house would be substituted, to the disadvantage of morality and the neighbourhood.

9. That, at present, it is more or less immaterial to the shopkeeper on what goods the customer spends his money. If he had to fall back on the liquor only, he would be obliged to press his sales of liquor to the utmost extent.

GOTHENBURG SYSTEM

Some still believe that the best way of obtaining the ends in view, would be to adopt (in large towns at all events) the plan which is known under the name of the "Gothenburg System"—though the scheme proposed differs somewhat from that which prevails in Sweden.

This scheme would empower Town Councils in boroughs, and County Councils in counties, to acquire by agreement, or failing agreement by compulsion, the freehold of all licensed premises within their respective districts, and to purchase the leases, good-will, stock, and fixtures of the present holders. It would further empower them, if they thought fit, to carry on the liquor trade for the convenience and on behalf of the inhabitants, but so that no individual should have any pecuniary interest in, or derive any profit from, the sale of intoxicating liquors. It would also empower the Town or County Councils to borrow money for these purposes on the security of the rates, and to carry all profits to the alleviation of the rates. The power of the Justices to grant licences would cease on the adoption of the scheme.*

This proposal is supported on the grounds:—

1. That as full compensation would be given for all interests affected, there would be no "confiscation."

2. That as the local authority would possess absolute control over the issue of licences and the district liquor traffic, each locality could please itself as to the number of its public-houses.

3. That while the number of public-houses would be greatly diminished, the remainder would improve in respectability, convenience, and management; as the manager would have no

* See also, for both sides, many of the arguments already given in previous sections.

direct interest in the sale of the intoxicating liquors, and as refreshments, and non-intoxicating, or less intoxicating liquors would be sold, the public-houses would gradually assume the character of eating-houses, and of working men's clubs.

4. That there would therefore be a diminution of intemperance, and a consequent decrease in crime and disorder.

5. That as no one would benefit from the supply of bad liquor, adulteration would cease.

6. (*a*) That the undue influence of the publican at Parliamentary and Municipal elections would be eliminated.—(*b*) That if the public-houses were under the control of the municipality, they could, and probably would, be closed on the day of elections —to the promotion of order, quiet, and purity of election.

7. That the surplus profits would be applied to the relief of the rates; and instead of a few individuals, all the inhabitants of the borough would benefit from the sale of liquor.

8. That the Local Authority would be sufficiently subject to public control and criticism to prevent any undue multiplication of the number of public-houses, and to ensure economy and efficiency.

9. That many local authorities are already traders in gas, water, &c., and to transfer to them also the management of the liquor trade would impose on them no novel obligations.

10. That if a district were willing to take the trouble, and run the risk, of introducing the scheme (since no vested interests would be unfairly dealt with), the State should allow the experiment. If it succeeded, a good example would be given; if it failed, the loss would be local.

11. That a scheme drawn on somewhat similar lines has greatly diminished drunkenness in Sweden.

12. That without some more decided action on the part of the State, or of local bodies, intemperance cannot be effectually checked.

The scheme is objected to on the grounds:—

1. (By the extreme temperance advocates.) That the

trade in liquor is universally pernicious, and no half measures can possibly be effectual—it must be totally suppressed.

2. (By some.) That, as the liquor trade is demoralising to those who conduct it, it would be highly objectionable to hand the management over to the local authority, and to cast the responsibility of the traffic on the ratepayers as a body.

3. (*a*) (By some.) That the fear of burdening the rates would tend greatly against any reduction in the number of public-houses; while the temptation of profit, and consequent relief to the rates, would induce the local authority to increase the number of public-houses.—(*b*) (By others.) That the local authority might largely increase or entirely suppress the trade in a particular district, against the wishes of a large number of citizens.

4. (*a*) That the enormous preliminary outlay attendant on the acquisition of the property, if anything like a fair price be given, would never permit of any profits being made from a trade conducted by a public body.—(*b*) That as one object of the scheme is to diminish drinking, and the temptation to drinking, the profits of necessity will be greatly reduced, and the burden on the rates will be heavy.

5. That a Town or County Council is a body eminently unfit to conduct so vast a business with economy and care.

6. That such an attempt would lead to a great deal of jobbery and waste, and undesirable influence at elections.

7. That the payment for the licences, whether by agreement or arbitration, would still further justify the assertion that the licence was a vested interest.

[There is now in existence a company, the Public-House Trust Company, which is endeavouring to do by private means that which the Gothenburg plan would enable the locality to do by public means, namely, the purchase of public-houses with a view of carrying them on as houses of refreshment, and not only as liquor shops. One can but wish success to this scheme.]

SUNDAY CLOSING *

It is proposed to give to the local authority in England — Town Council or County Council — the power of closing, on Sunday, all public-houses within its jurisdiction.† The law in England limits their opening to certain specified hours,‡ while in Scotland, Ireland, and Wales it closes them altogether on Sundays.

The proposal is upheld on the grounds :—

1.—(*a*) That there is much more drinking, with all its attendant evils, on Sunday than on any other day; and, with the added result, that men often cannot or will not work on the Monday.—(*b*) That the bulk of the wages are paid on Saturday, and practically the only shop open the next day is the public-house; thus a great and special temptation is placed in the way of the working classes.—(*c*) That the working classes are entitled to demand that this special temptation shall be removed.

2. That it is inconsistent and unjust that, while innocent trades are prohibited from being carried on on Sunday, this most pernicious of all trades should be allowed to be carried on.

3. That as the State interferes with, and limits the hours of Sunday opening, it might, with perfect consistency, altogether prohibit opening on Sundays.

* Cf. section on *Local Option*.

† This proposal was contained in the original Local Government Bill of 1888, but the clause was withdrawn, along with the other licensing clauses.

‡ In the Metropolis the hours of opening are fixed from 1 o'clock to 3, and from 6 o'clock to 11 P.M. Elsewhere they are from 12.30 to 2.30 and from 6 to 10 P.M.

4. That those employed in the sale of drink are entitled to be relieved from Sunday labour, the more so that they work a larger number of hours during the week than the law permits in the case of many other trades.

5. That the publicans themselves would welcome a compulsory closing; without compulsion, competition compels them to keep open.

6. That there is no analogy between clubs and public-houses; the latter are distinctly places of drinking resort, which the former are not; nor are clubs more frequented on Sunday than on any other day.

7. That the question of Sunday closing is particularly a matter in which the locality should have a voice through its duly elected representatives; and Local Option would prevent any hardship being done in any particular locality.

8. That the Sunday Closing Acts in Scotland, Wales, and Ireland* have worked well, and have greatly diminished drunkenness on that day.

9. (By the extreme temperance body.) That the closing on Sunday would not only be a good thing in itself, but would also tend towards further limitations of sale.

On the other hand, Sunday closing is opposed, on the grounds:—

1. That the hours of opening on Sunday have already been greatly curtailed; and to close the public-houses altogether would be a gross infringement of the liberty of the subject.

2. That experience shows that total closing leads to illicit sale and surreptitious consumption of liquor—a process that cannot fail to lower the morality of the population.

* See Report of Select Committee on the Irish Sunday Closing Acts, 1888. The Irish Sunday Closing Act was passed in 1878, and applies to the whole of Ireland, with the exception of five large towns.

3. That it would lead to increased purchases of liquor on the Saturday for consumption at home on the Sunday; and to excessive drinking on the Monday.

4. (*a*) That while the closing of public-houses on Sunday would cause no inconvenience to the richer classes, who have their clubs and their cellars, it would be a great hardship on the working classes to deprive them of their only place of resort and refreshment.—(*b*) That to carry out the proposal would create an embittered and indignant feeling among a large majority of the public, whose habits and requirements would be materially interfered with.—(*c*) That it would be class legislation of an objectionable character.

5. That entirely to close the public-houses would cause extreme inconvenience to travellers.

6. That to close the public-houses one day in seven would involve a very serious loss to the publican; and could not justly be permitted without proper compensation.

7. That we already have too much paternal legislation.

8. That the proposal is an embodiment of teetotal tyranny and Sabbatarian severity, and should therefore be rather resisted than conceded.

9. That as the Scotch and Irish chiefly drink whisky, which can be kept without deterioration, they do not suffer much inconvenience by Sunday closing; while, in England, where beer is much drunk, a store cannot be laid in without the fear of it spoiling.

10. (By some.) That Sunday closing in Scotland and Wales, and especially in Ireland, has not diminished drunkenness; has injuriously affected the temperance movement by the reaction it has caused, and has done more harm than good.

CAPITAL PUNISHMENT

THE abolition of Capital Punishment is advocated on the grounds :—

1. That human life is too sacred to be destroyed.

2. That capital punishment has not put an end to murder; while executions familiarise the public with slaughter, and thus rather promote than restrain murder.

3. That the administration of justice being in the nature of things fallible, death, if inflicted at all, will sometimes be inflicted on the innocent.

4. That the existence of the punishment of death for murder increases the difficulty of inducing juries to convict for that crime; while it leads to groundless pleas of insanity being raised and readily accepted, and consequently to the escape of some criminals from justice.

5. That, to the would-be-criminal, the prospect of penal servitude for life would be just as effective a deterrent as hanging.

On the other hand, the total abolition of Capital Punishment is opposed on the grounds :—

1. That the State is justified in taking the most effectual means of preventing murder.

2. (*a*) That punishment is not solely intended for the prevention of crime, but is also a vindication of justice by

society; and death is the just penalty for murder.—(*b*) "Que Messieurs les assassins commencent!"

3. That a murderer has, by his deed, forfeited all his right to mercy from the State.

4. That as a murderer cannot with safety be allowed to work out his punishment and go free, there is no chance of his social reformation, and the State is justified in ridding itself of a pest.

5. (*a*) That if all fear of capital punishment were taken away, many minor offences, such as housebreaking, burglary, aggravated assaults, &c., would be more likely to lead to murders.—(*b*) That it prevents many murders which would otherwise be premeditated.

6. That capital punishment must be retained as a last resource, otherwise there is nothing absolutely to deter a felon, sentenced to penal servitude for life, from attempting over and over again the murder of his gaoler in revenge or with a view to escape.

7. That capital punishment is now rarely inflicted, and only in cases of premeditated or specially brutal murder.

8. That where there is any moral or legal doubt of the actual guilt of the criminal, capital punishment is now never inflicted; it is, therefore, almost certain, that no innocent persons suffer death at the hands of the law.

9. That executions being now conducted in private, the public are not familiarised with a degrading spectacle.

MARRIAGE WITH THE DECEASED WIFE'S SISTER

It is proposed to legalise marriage with a Deceased Wife's Sister, on the grounds :—

1. (*a*) That these marriages are no breach of the law of God, whether written or unwritten.*—(*b*) That they are no trespass on the rights of others.—(*c*) That therefore men should be allowed freedom in this respect. And, in such a matter as this, in which no blood relationship or confusion of succession is involved, it is neither right nor expedient that the State should interfere with the liberty of the citizen in the chief concern of his life.

2. (*a*) That it is an infraction of the principle of religious liberty to make the laws of the Church of England binding on those who do not belong to that Church.—(*b*) That in the Roman Catholic Church, dispensation is often granted for such marriages,† a proof that they are

* The Biblical reference to this matter is contained in Leviticus xviii. verses 16 and 18, from which it is argued that, while the marriage with the deceased husband's brother is prohibited, the marriage with a deceased wife's sister is not actually forbidden.

† "Taking the question with reference to Scripture, is such a marriage (the marriage with two sisters in succession) held by your Church as prohibited?—Certainly not; it is considered as a matter of Ecclesiastical legislation.

"Then the Commissioners are to understand that in your Church the general prohibition of these marriages is a matter of discipline, and permission to contract such marriages is granted or not, according to what you may think most advantageous and proper?—Certainly.

"With respect to marriages of this description, do you find amongst not considered immoral or forbidden by Scripture.—(*c*) That the Jewish Church recognises and, indeed, distinctly encourages such marriages.*

3. (*a*) That even in regard to the Church of England, the prohibitive degrees of affinity were drawn up, in 1563, by Archbishop Parker on his own responsibility, and were never confirmed by the synod of the Church, nor by the authority of Parliament.—(*b*) That the table of prohibited degrees does not form part of the legalised Book of Common Prayer.

4. That the change in the law was made for the sake and benefit of one noble family; and in connection with the change a great injustice has been done to others.

5. That, up to 1835, these marriages were recognised and were not void *ab initio;* but only at the instigation of one of the parties or persons interested.

6. That the original Bill of 1835 (Lord Lyndhurst's Act) proposed to legalise such marriages, future as well as past. To enable the Bill to pass, an amendment, introduced in the House of Lords, prohibiting such marriages in the future, was accepted; but on the understanding that the matter would be dealt with at an early date. This has never been done; and the temporary limitation has become a permanent prohibition.†

Catholics that persons contracting such marriages are received with the same kindness and good feeling as persons who have contracted ordinary marriages?—With a dispensation, perfectly so."—Cardinal Wiseman before the Royal Commission in 1847.

* "The marriage of a widower with his deceased wife's sister is not only not prohibited, but it is distinctly understood to be permitted.

"These marriages are considered proper, and even laudable, when there are children, and the usual time for remaining a widower is abbreviated in such cases."—Dr Alder, the Chief Rabbi, before the Royal Commission in 1847.

† See Debate, 24th April 1901, especially page 1223, &c ; and Debate, 5th February 1902.

7. That there is an essential difference — morally, materially, physically—between affinity and consanguinity.

8. That in the matter of taxation, the State recognises no affinity; but for death duties, treats the sister-in-law as a "stranger" to the husband. It is illogical therefore that in the matter of marriage the State should treat her as a close relation.

9. That kinship by marriage being in no way the same as kinship by blood, this concession would not lead to a demand for further relaxation in the prohibited degrees of affinity.

10. (*a*) That the present state of the law makes it very difficult for the sister-in-law to come and live with the widower and look after the children.—(*b*) That as such a connection cannot lead to marriage, it often (among the working classes) necessarily leads to concubinage.—(*c*) That thus all the disadvantages of prohibition exist, and none of the advantages.

11. That, in spite of the law, these marriages do take place in a large number of cases, yet the children are not recognised as legitimate.

12. That if legal marriage might ensue, the position for all parties would be much more clear and definite.

13. (*a*) That legalisation of these marriages would not break up home life, but would consolidate it.—(*b*) That the sister of the deceased wife is the most natural, and will be the most loving stepmother to the children; yet she is the one person that the State proscribes.

14. That if, in spite of the law, the parties do marry, they become social outcasts; a position which would entirely disappear if such marriages were legal, for there is no public prejudice against them as such.

15. That it is a monstrous thing that the children of

such marriages should be treated as bastards, and suffer the disadvantages of illegitimacy.

16. That the law comes especially hard on the working classes; it is particularly in such homes that the widower requires the assistance of a sister-in-law; and they cannot (like the rich) go abroad in order to go through the form of marriage, or live abroad.

17. (*a*) That these marriages are legal in all our Colonies, and the prohibition here leads to much scandal and inconvenience.—(*b*) That these marriages, if morally right in Sydney or Toronto, cannot be morally wrong in London—morality is not a question of latitude or longitude.

18. (*a*) That none of the alleged difficulties and drawbacks are found to exist in the Colonies and elsewhere, where these marriages are allowed.—(*b*) That before the passing of the Act of 1835, when there was virtually no prohibition, it was not found that the relations of the husband and sister-in-law were adversely affected, caused discord in the home during the life of the wife, or difficulties afterwards.

19. That no one will be compelled to marry his deceased wife's sister.

20. That public opinion has for long been in favour of the reform, and, since 1841, the Bill has passed its second reading in the House of Commons fifteen times, and all its stages seven times.*

* And, in 1896, the Bill, there introduced, passed the House of Lords, but no opportunity occurred of passing it through the Lower House. The House of Commons majorities in 1901, were *401 to 122*; in 1902, *249 to 126*. In 1903 the Bill was read a second time, and referred to the Grand Committee on Law. It passed through the Committee, but did not come back to the House in time to be carried further.

On the other side, the legalisation of such marriages is withstood on the grounds :—

1. (*a*) That the Levitical Law, and the Church, in consequence of her interpretation of the Levitical Law, forbids such marriages, and her prohibition must be binding.—(*b*) That the Levitical Law is equivalent to the Divine command.

2. (*a*) That prohibition has been the unwritten law of all Christian marriages from their inception.—(*b*) That Convocation, in 1571, passed a canon affirming the prohibition.

3. That, as regards the Roman Catholic Church, there is general prohibition of such marriages, and dispensation is only granted for good and weighty reason.

4. (*a*) That in this matter, a distinction cannot be drawn between affinity and blood relationships. Husband and wife *are* one flesh.—(*b*) That marriage is the keystone of the arch of our social prosperity; the sanctity of marriage must not be infringed. To admit this description of marriage would be to break down the idea that marriage is a sacred institution, and to reduce it to the mere civil contract; and would strike at the root of family life.

5. (*a*) That kinship by marriage is equivalent to kinship by blood, and any concession would at once lead to further demands, difficult to resist, for relaxation of the prohibited degrees of affinity.—(*b*) That one relaxation of the marriage laws would certainly lead to others, and the standard of purity and the moral basis of the home would be lowered.

6. That the restrictions on marriage are a mark of civilisation, and to weaken them would be a step backwards towards barbarism.

7. That the social stigma would not be removed, public opinion being opposed to these marriages of affinity.

8. That it is the province of the law to save men from annoyance as well as to secure their rights; and great discomforts would arise from the legalisation of these marriages.

9. (*a*) That the removal of the prohibition would break down that which has become a very convenient, often essential, and most natural arrangement (especially among the working class), *i.e.* that the sister-in-law should immediately take charge of the children and of the home of the widower.—(*b*) That the working man is not in a position to make other arrangements, or to engage assistance. In thousands of cases the widower is entirely dependent on the sister-in-law for timely assistance.—(*c*) That if the two cease to be on the footing of brother and sister, it would be impossible for the sister-in-law to undertake these duties; and the mutual relations of the widower, the sister-in-law, and the children would be placed on an impossible footing.

10. That, at present, in a vast number of cases, the two are living in the same house on relations of perfect purity and without scandal. If the prohibition to marriage were removed, they must choose between marriage and separation, neither of which they desire.

11. (*a*) That thus, on all hands, the loss to the children would be serious and irreparable.—(*b*) That where the sister-in-law ceases to be an aunt, and becomes the stepmother, the marriage might raise up rival claimants to her affections, nearer and dearer.

12. (*a*) That the existing innocent, dispassionate, and happy relationship between brother-in-law and sister-in-law would disappear.—(*b*) That if marriage were allowed, the present unaffected brotherly feelings of a man towards his sister-in-law would be destroyed, especially where she is living with her married sister. It might easily create jealousy between the former and the latter.

13. That the law must be obeyed, and it is no harder on the children of such a marriage, than the law relating to the children of all irregular unions. The fact that people have broken the law, affords no argument for its repeal.

14. That it would create two classes of marriage (for the Church will not recognise these marriages of affinity), *i.e.* a Church marriage and a State marriage; marriage enjoying State recognition, but not Church recognition.

15. That this is not a poor man's question; the bulk of these marriages are made among the richer classes: and they can, if they like, avoid difficulty and scandal by being married abroad and living abroad.

16. That the change in the law is demanded merely by those who, having already broken it, wish to be absolved from the consequences of their illegal action.

17. (*a*) That we must legislate for our own domestic concerns just as the Colonies legislate for theirs—without regard to any anomalies which may arise from Colonial legislation.—(*b*) That, as a matter of fact, difficulties do not arise for a marriage lawful in the Colony and recognised as lawful here for all practical and social purposes.

SUNDAY OPENING OF MUSEUMS, &c.

It is proposed to legalise the opening of all National or Local Museums, Picture Galleries, &c., on Sundays,* on the grounds :—

1. That as all contribute towards the maintenance of these buildings, it is unfair to close them on the only day on which the mass of the people can visit them.

2. (*a*) That the contemplation of works of art and interest, &c., has a refining, elevating, and educating effect on the mind, and would be to the moral, mental, and social advantage of the people.—(*b*) That the superiority which foreign operatives possess over the English in matters of taste and fine workmanship, is largely due to the opportunities the former possess of contemplating and studying works of art, &c.

3. (*a*) That anything which tends to increase the innocent enjoyments of life should be encouraged.—(*b*) That more especially is it to the interests of religion and morality that Sunday should be made brighter and pleasanter—a day of recreation and reasonable enjoyment, not one of gloom and inanity.

4. (*a*) That the opening of these buildings would con-

* It is usually proposed to open them only after 1 o'clock, so as not to interfere with morning service.

stitute for the working classes, who alone are really affected, a powerful counter-attraction to the public-house — at present the only place of resort open to the working man upon his only holiday.—(*b*) That more especially would it tend towards improved family relations, all the members could with advantage visit the galleries, &c., together.

5. (*a*) That the religious scruples of some should not stand in the way of the innocent enjoyment of others; none need frequent these places unless they choose.—(*b*) That the Divine injunction to the Hebrews to rest on the Saturday, can hardly be taken to imply that we may not contemplate works of art on the Sunday.

6. That the opening of these public buildings on Sunday would in no way tend towards the desecration of the Sabbath—there is a vast difference between throwing open public buildings and legalising the opening of specutative places of entertainment.

7. (*a*) That the number of people who would be required to work on Sunday, in consequence of the opening of these buildings, would be insignificant, and would add very few to those who, for the pleasure or convenience of the public, are now obliged to work on that day.—(*b*) That therefore there would be no increased tendency towards Sunday labour.—(*c*) That the gain to the many should outweigh the inconvenience to the few.

8. (*a*) That the so-called "Continental" Sunday is due entirely to the general habits and manners of the people who indulge in them, and would in no way be attained or approached by the opening of Museums, &c., in England.—(*b*) That the working classes, through their Trades Unions and in other ways, are quite able to protect themselves from any imposition of Sunday labour.

9. That in many places Sunday opening has been locally tried, and with great success.

On the other hand, the proposal is opposed on the grounds:—

1. That it is contrary to the Divine injunction that we should rest on the Sabbath. No labour should be undertaken on that day that is not absolutely essential.

2. (*a*) That the proposal is only the thin end of the wedge; if "free" places are thrown open on Sunday, theatres and speculative places of amusement would soon be also opened on that day, and the British Sunday would gradually tend to become "Continental."—(*b*) That consequently the working classes would ultimately be expected to work seven days a week—probably without any increase in wages.—(*c*) That the absolute rest on one day in seven has greatly benefited the nation physically, morally, and mentally.

3. That the argument for a universal half holiday on the Saturday would be weakened, if the Sunday were available for visiting the galleries, &c.; and this would be calamitous.

4. (*a*) That in any case it would involve a large amount of work on Sunday on the part of the custodians of these buildings, and it is unfair to demand such labour from some merely to give pleasure to others.—(*b*) That the tendency of the time is to reduce Sunday labour as far as possible—witness the suspension of the Sunday post in London, &c.—not to increase it.

5. That no educational advantage is gained by uninstructed gazing at pictures and works of art; the opening on Sunday would have to be followed by instruction on Sunday.

6. (*a*) That those who would visit these places are not those who frequent public-houses on Sunday—no counter-attraction to the public-house would therefore be consti-

tuted.—(*b*) That, on the other hand, those who were attracted from a distance to visit the collections, would be perforce constrained to enter the public-houses in order to obtain necessary refreshment.

7. That where Sunday opening has been tried by local bodies, the experiment has been so successful that the Art Collections have usually again been closed.

8. That even if it be in the abstract advisable, such a change should not be undertaken without the manifest wish of the vast majority of the working classes—who alone would be affected—and at present the majority are opposed to the opening.

LONDON GOVERNMENT

In some former editions the question of London Government was discussed from the point of view of the reform of the vestries, and the creation of some Central Representative Authority to take the place of the Metropolitan Board of Works.

Both these reforms have, however, been carried out. The so-called London County Council, directly elected by the ratepayers, has taken the place of the old secondary election Board of Works. Vestries and District Board of Works have been replaced by the so-called Metropolitan Borough Councils, under a system of grouping, and more popular election.

The City of London alone remains un-reformed.

The Metropolis, according to the census of 1901, contained a population of 4,540,000 persons ; its gross rateable annual value amounted to £49,000,000, of which the City, with 27,000 inhabitants, contributed £6,000,000.

The Authorities who, in 1903, between them,

controlled and governed the Metropolis,* were as follows:—

I. The *Corporation of the City of London*, which consists of 206 Common Councilmen and 26 Aldermen, and which has full municipal authority over the City, and levies therein rates and taxes.

II. The *London County Council*.—Previous to 1888, various unsuccessful attempts were from time to time made to confer on London the municipal privileges granted to other large towns by the Act of 1835, from which London was then specifically excluded.

In 1888,† under the Local Government Act of the year, a central representative Body for the whole of the Metropolis, outside the City, was created.‡

The County Councillors, directly elected by the ratepayers and Parliamentary electors, number 118, two for each Parliamentary division, except the City, which returns four; the Aldermen, selected by the Councillors, are not to exceed in number one-sixth of the whole number of Councillors. The Councillors hold office for three years, and all go out together; the Aldermen for six years, half going out every three years. The first Council was elected in November 1888, but the date of the triennial election has now been altered to March.

* The state of the case as regards fires is a good instance of the confusion of authorities which still exists in London. The fire brigade is under the authority of the London County Council, the police obey the Home Office, the salvage corps is under the command of the Fire Insurance Offices, the turncocks are servants of the Water Companies, and the thoroughfares are the property of the Borough Councils.

† 51 and 52 Vict. chap. 41.

‡ The City, though practically outside the authority of the London County Council, elects four members to it, but those Councillors are not entitled to vote on matters affecting expenditure for which the City is not liable to be assessed.

All the powers, duties and responsibilities of the Metropolitan Board of Works were transferred to the London County Council; as well as those of Quarter Sessions, so far as elsewhere transferred under the Act to other County Councils.

III. The 28 *Metropolitan Borough Councils* created in 1899.*

In that year the whole of the duties, powers, and responsibilities, of the 25 Vestries and 14 District Boards disappeared, and their place were taken by 28 Borough Councils.

The number of Councillors in each borough vary between 30 and 60. They are elected under a wide rate-paying and Parliamentary franchise, including women voters. In addition to the Councillors there are Aldermen in a proportion not exceeding one-sixth of the Councillors. The total number of Councillors is 1362, of Aldermen 227. The Chairman of the Borough Council is a Mayor elected by the Councillors. Women are not eligible on the Councils. The Borough Council can decide whether its elections shall be annual or triennial.

The whole of the duties, powers, and responsibilities of the Vestries and District Boards were handed over to the Borough Council. In addition, they are the "overseer" for all purposes relating to rates and rating. They became the authority to deal with Baths, Wash-Houses, Free Libraries, etc. They were given certain further powers in regard to streets, main roads, public health, etc. They can promote Bills in Parliament. They were brought under effective audit. They were given certain concurrent powers over the London County Council in regard to Building Acts, Housing Acts, etc. Power was given for the transference, by agreement, to or from the London County Council of certain other powers.

* 62 and 63 Vict. chap. 14.

The position and powers of the London County Council are scarcely affected by the Act.* The City of London is left unaffected by the Act.

IV. *Educational Authority.*—Between 1871 and 1903 the elementary Education of the Metropolis was entrusted to the directly elected London School Board. In 1890, the "whisky money" was paid to the L.C.C., and devoted to education under the Technical Education Committee.

In 1903 the School Board and the Technical Education Act disappeared; and their places were taken by the London County Council as the Education Authority of London.†

V. The thirty elective *Board of Guardians*—who have charge of the Poor Law administration. There is also an Asylums Board, which consists partly of guardians, partly of nominees of the Local Government Board, to look after the sick poor.

VI. *The Water Board,*‡ created under the Act of 1902,§ which is to purchase, manage, and carry on the undertakings of the eight Metropolitan Water Companies.

The Metropolitan Water Board consists of 67 members, together with a chairman and vice-chairman chosen from outside the Board, if the Board so desire. The L.C.C. appoint fourteen members, the City, and the City of Westminster, two each, each Metropolitan Borough one, West Ham two, the County Councils of Essex, Kent, Hertfordshire, Middlesex and Surrey, one each, various Councils of outer districts, grouped or other, one each.

* This was not quite the case in the Bill as originally introduced, but, in its passage through the House, practically all the provisions adversely affecting the London County Council were struck out or amended.

† See *Elementary Education*, p. 342.

‡ In former editions appeared a section in which was discussed the question of whether or no the L.C.C. be constituted the Water Authority for London and be given full power to buy up the Water Companies.

§ 2 Ed. 7 Ch. 41.

The Thames Conservancy and the Lea Conservancy, one each.

The purchase, failing agreement, is to be by arbitration before a special tribunal, and Water Stock is to be issued to pay for the purchase money, secured on the rates of the whole area of supply.

VII. The *Thames Conservancy Board* non-representative, which has the control of the River Thames, until it may be superseded by the Port of London Board.

VIII. In addition, the *Home Secretary* has control of the Police Force outside the City, while within the City it is under the control of the Corporation.

The Home Secretary also has jurisdiction over the cabs, omnibuses, and tramways.

The Gas and Dock Companies * are at present private concerns.

MUNICIPAL HOME RULE FOR LONDON

It is proposed that the London County Council should be put in possession of full municipal powers. Should have the Police placed under its authority. Should be allowed to acquire the control of its Water † and Lighting supplies; of its Markets,

* A Bill was introduced in 1903 by the Government to create a Board to buy up the Dock Companies, and to control the Port of London, and was carried over until next session.

† This sentence is left as it stood in the last edition; but the water question has now been settled, and the purchase and control has not been given to the L.C.C.

Tramways, and steamboat service; and of the Port of London, and the River Thames. Should be enabled to deal fully with the Housing question; and the Land question as it affects London. Should be empowered to make juster the assessment, burden and incidence of Local Rating and Taxation.

These proposals are defended on the grounds:—

1. (*a*) That, on true democratic principles, the Central Representative Body of the Metropolis should have the fullest possible powers of administering the affairs of London for the benefit of Londoners.—(*b*) That this is more especially the case, inasmuch as London is the most populous town, the greatest manufacturing city, the most important port in the world; and the centre of English commercial and social life.

2. (*a*) That London is not a County but a City; to call the Governing Body of London a "County Council" is a misnomer. It is really a Borough Council like the Governing Body of the large towns, and should be treated accordingly.—(*b*) That while, from its position and importance, the London County Council should be possessed of greater, it has really considerably less powers of managing the affairs of its citizens than other great Municipal Bodies.*—(*c*) That, at present, it is hampered, fettered, and chained in every way; and all sorts of great as well as petty restrictions are placed on its powers of action.

3. (*a*) That, while the London County Council can, in a limited way, as the Representative of the London ratepayer, oppose local and private Bills in the House, it cannot, as such, promote a Bill even for purely local

* There are at present 62 "County Boroughs" in England and Wales. The largest is Liverpool with some half million of inhabitants; the smallest Cambridge, with some 20,000 persons.

purposes.*—(*b*) That its loan transactions necessitate an annual money Bill which has to pass the House of Commons.

4. (*a*) That the London County Council has constantly to apply to Parliament for authority to do this, that, and the other.—(*b*) That a majority in the House of Commons hostile to its views, may (and does) mutilate or destroy its measures.

5. (*a*) That Parliament either declines to devote sufficient time to the due discussion of London questions; or the time of the House is wasted on what are Metropolitan and not Imperial matters.—(*b*) That the Government of the day being, in some matters, partly or wholly responsible for the administration of Metropolitan affairs, questions of purely local concern are elevated into Imperial questions on which the fate of a Ministry may depend.—(*c*) That London's parochial demands have therefore, of necessity, been turned into a political and party programme.

6. That true decentralisation is that which relieves Parliament and the Executive of local affairs; and true centralisation that which hands them over to large Representative Bodies.

7. That, so long as the Central Municipal Body in London was not really representative of the ratepayers, there was some excuse for limiting its powers. This cause or excuse has now disappeared; and the fact that, for fifty years, London has been deprived of those rights of self-government which have been freely granted to other large towns, make it all the more necessary that the grant now should be full and complete.

8. That the persistent refusal of municipal privileges

* The London County Council Bills are introduced as private Bills by individual members of Parliament who happen also to be members of the London County Council.

and powers to the Metropolis, has largely deprived Londoners of any interest in their own affairs. The habit of local co-operation for local purposes, the sense of common life and common interests, that prevails to such a large extent in other self-governed towns, has, to the great disadvantage of London life, been discouraged, instead of being developed.

9. (*a*) That the best security for efficient, economical, and honest administration is vigilant public control.—(*b*) That the greater the powers, the duties, and the responsibilities of the Central Body, the greater will be the desire to obtain good men to serve, and the greater the public interest that will be taken in its work.

10. (*a*) That the London County Council, hampered and harassed though it has been, has done excellent work; has deserved well of the ratepayers, and has fully shown itself worthy to be trusted with extended powers.—(*b*) That, in other large towns, no disadvantages, but great advantages, have arisen from the grant of the fullest possible freedom of action in local affairs.—(*c*) That the ratepayers themselves, through the triennial election of Councillors, would always retain full and direct control over the doings of their Council.

11. (*a*) That no possible national or political danger could arise from granting to the representative Body the fullest possible powers in purely local affairs.—(*b*) That the national danger is more likely to arise from the appalling mass of destitution and discontent existing in the Metropolis; a social evil and danger that can only be adequately dealt with by a powerful Local Body given a free hand.

Further, it is especially urged:—

12. (*a*) That the London County Council should have

full power to deal with the Land question as affecting towns, with the Housing question, the Trading question, and with the question of Local Taxation; in order that by effective collective action, justice may be done, and the convenience and comfort of the community may be improved.—(*b*) That, at present, the individual London ratepayer is helpless in the hands of the Water Companies, the Gas Companies, the Tramway Companies; in that of the ground landlords, of the house farmers, of the vestry jobbers; in that of the market monopolists, and of the river monopolists. No common action is possible, for the Central Body has, as yet, practically no power to deal with these questions.

13. (*a*) That, at present, the few exploit the many—tht community bears the burden, the individuals obtain the benefit.—(*b*) That the advantages and profits that the action, the expenditure, the very existence of the Community have produced, should go to the benefit of the Community and not to that of individuals.

14. (*a*) That collective municipal action is the best hope for the future; by these means alone can be obtained for all those social advantages and conveniences which very few are able to obtain for themselves.—(*b*) That, by collective municipal action mainly, can a greater diffusion of wealth, and the advantages springing from wealth, be brought about without undue pressure or injustice on any class or on any individuals.

15. (*a*) That the municipal provision of water and gas would not only lead to a reduction in price, and a more universal supply of these necessaries of life, but would result also in a profit on working.—(*b*) That the improved incidence of local rating and taxation would render juster and lighter the burdens on the ratepayers; and thus the governing Body of the Metropolis would be enabled more

freely to expend money for the benefit of the Community at large.

On the other hand, it is argued, that largely to increase the powers of the London County Council would be detrimental, on the grounds :—

1. That over-centralization is a mistake, and any tendency in that direction is to be avoided.

2. That, already, the London County Council takes too much upon itself.

3. (*a*) That the London County Council have already as much and more to do than they can properly manage. —(*b*) That what they do they do badly.—(*c*) That to thrust new and responsible duties upon such a Body would necessarily lead to grave mismanagement.

4. That there is not the same cohesion among Londoners as among the citizens of other large towns; hence the public check over the proceedings and actions of public Bodies in London is far less effective than elsewhere.

5. That, already, the *personnel* of the London County Council is tending rapidly to deteriorate; and this tendency would be accentuated if membership involved a still larger sacrifice of time.

6. (By some.) That the late Metropolitan Board of Works, though representative of the ratepayers, was a corrupt and inefficient Body; and the London County Council will soon fall into the hands of a similar class of needy and iucompetent administrators.

7. (*a*) That the London County Council is becoming more and more of a political machine, an engine used for party purposes.—(*b*) That to give considerably greater powers to such a Body would be politically inexpedient, or even dangerous.—(*c*) That though, no doubt, London

would never become like Paris, a source of danger to the rest of the country, a powerful Central Representative Body in the Metropolis, where the seat of government is situated, might become a most undesirable influence in time of grave crisis.

8. That London, being the Metropolis of the country, is not, and cannot be placed, municipally, in the same position as other large towns.

9. (*a*) That a powerful democratic Municipality in London would threaten the principle of the rights of property.—(*b*) That it would alter the incidence of local taxation in an unjust and oppressive way.

10. (*a*) That (as regards the question of water, lighting, tramways, etc.), industrial concerns are far better carried on by private individuals or companies, than by public Bodies.—(*b*) That, as a rule, public management is neither efficient nor economical, and is, too often, corrupt.—(*c*) That, in the end, the consumers and the ratepayers would lose and not gain, both in pocket and in convenience.

TAXATION OF LAND VALUES*

It is proposed to reform the incidence of taxation in the Metropolis and other large towns, by requiring some direct contribution towards local expenditure from the "owners" of the land values.

The owner may be defined as the person or persons (and usually more than one) who derive advantage or profit from real property, other than that derived from mere occupation. The land or ground value † may be defined as that portion of the value of the property which is due to the existence, the industry, and the expenditure of the adjacent population, over and above the actual labour and capital expended on the property itself. In other words, it denotes the unimproved value of the land itself, as distinguished from any

* The question of the Division of Rates between Landlord and Occupier, and the question of a Municipal Death Duty, will be found discussed in the Ninth Edition.

† The "owner," it must be clearly understood, is by no means merely the ultimate reversionist or freeholder. If a freeholder lives in his own house he receives all the emoluments of ownership, and is at once owner and occupier. If the property be let or sublet, there will be two or more owners of it as distinct from the occupier; and the actual freeholder, if the lease be a long one, and the ground rent a low one, may have a very small present interest in the property.

additional value due to the expenditure of labour or capital upon it.

The questions involved are discussed at considerable length and with great ability, in the Reports—both Majority and Minority—of the Royal Commissioners who were appointed in 1896, to enquire into the subject of Local Taxation, and who reported in 1901.

The general principle of the direct taxation of Land Values is supported on the grounds:—

1. *a.* That the existing system of Urban Rating should be placed on a broader basis and a juster foundation. Under it some persons are not taxed, or are insufficiently taxed. If these inequalities were removed, there would be secured for the over-burdened occupier a substantial relief from the pressure of rates.—(*b*) That relief is urgently needed, rates have enormously increased in the last thirty years.*

2. (*a*) That at present the owners of Land Values escape all direct payment of rates.†—(*b*) That, apart from contract, the law throws all rates on the occupier.—(*c*) That the custom as regards contracts is specifically to provide that the whole of the rates shall be paid by the occupier.—(*d*) That the fact that a ground rent is distinguished from the ordinary occupation rent, is a legal liability, though all local taxation may have ceased from the destruction of the

* Between 1869 and 1899, the local rates in England and Wales increased by over 150 per cent., from 16½ millions to 40¾ millions. During the same period, the rates in London increased 200 per cent., from £3,700,000 to £11,000,000.

† Report 1901, P. P. Cd. 638. See especially Minority Report, from which I have freely borrowed.

building, proves that the taxation is put on the building, and is paid by the occupier.

3. (*a*) That when land, from agricultural becomes urban land, and thereby becomes more valuable, it should take its share of the increased liabilities incidental to urban districts. —(*b*) That rural land possesses a creative power, and its value is made and kept by the continual application of labour and capital; urban land requires no application of labour or of capital on the part of the owner to maintain or to increase its value.

4. (*a*) That there is, in urban districts, a large fund of real property which is rapidly increasing in value*; but which owes its increasing value in no way to the exertions of the owner, but entirely, or almost entirely, to the presence, energy, industry, and outlay of those who live on or near the property, and which is greatly benefited by the consequent local expenditure from the rates.—(*b*) That the increase in value, the value itself, the monopoly which enables increased values to be exacted, is also only maintained by the increasing local expenditure.†

5. (*a*) That the annual "unearned increment" on the land in the Metropolis increases at the estimated rate of about £300,000 a year; representing a capital value of at least £6,000,000.—(*b*) That there is thus a constantly increasing tribute by the whole community of the town to the individuals who own the land.

6. (*a*) That taxation (and rating) are grounded on two

* The gross value of property in the Metropolis rose from £25,000,000 in 1871 to £38,500,000 in 1891, and is now £49,000,000.

† A house in Cornhill (to give but one instance) was up to 1862 let at a rack rent of £150, value, say, £3,000. In that year the freehold in possession was sold by public auction and fetched £11,000; in 1882 it was again sold and fetched £25,000, or eight times as much as it was worth forty year before.—Sir S. Montagu, in debate on "Ground Values," H. of C., 13th March 1891.

principles, ability to pay, or benefit received; and the owner of the land value, while contributing nothing directly to the rates, is benefiting from the expenditure.—(*b*) That between rate expenditure and land values there is a direct relationship; the one leads to the other.

7. (*a*) That a very large proportion of the rates go directly to improve the value of the property of the owner, and not that of the occupier.—(*b*) That all rates, in a greater or lesser degree, benefit all the successive interests in the land. Even the most ephemeral (for lighting, cleaning, &c.), and certainly the more permanent rates (for police, poor, education, drainage, &c.), help, not only to create and to increase, but are essential to maintain, the value of the property.

8. (*a*) That, at present, the whole burden of the local expenditure, public and private, falls on the one class of persons who have but a limited interest in the property, while a large part of the benefit goes to another; whereas each interest should bear the burden in proportion to the benefit it receives.—(*b*) That as urban local expenditure is ever tending to increase, the disparity and disproportion of burden and benefit is ever being accentuated and aggravated.

9. (*a*) That, more especially, is this the case in regard to Municipal expenditure on permanent improvements which add to the permanent value of land. The whole of the debt incurred for these purposes is repaid within a limited period, and the reversioner obtains all the ultimate benefit without having liquidated any of the burden.—(*b*) That the larger part of the Metropolitan debt* has been incurred for permanent improvements. The value of these permanent improvements, and their effect in enhancing the value of

* The outstanding London County Council debt is about £50,000,000 sterling. By 1931, three-quarters of the present debt will have been repaid. Nearly the whole of this has been incurred in the years since 1851.

property in London, does not diminish, but tends ever to increase.*—(c) That, thus, in the main, the burden of the communal expenditure falls on the occupier, and the benefits, in the main, go to the owner.

10. That the lease-holding occupier bears all the burden during the currency of the lease, and at the end of the lease all the unexhausted benefit is confiscated and absorbed by the owner.

11. (a) That it is just, that the owners, who benefit so largely by the existence, industry, and outlay of the population, should directly contribute a fair share to the expenditure involved.—(b) That there can be no injustice in apportioning the burden to be borne according to the benefit received.

12. That the class or condition of those who may be owners, has nothing to do with the justice of taxing them; as a matter of fact they are mostly great monopolists.

13. (a) That when the ratepayer, through his local authority, desires to acquire a property for public purposes, he has to pay to the owner a value which has been created by the expenditure of his rates and of his own communal outlay.—(b) That under the present system, an undue burden of taxation is thrown on the processes, products and earnings of trade and industry, to their detriment and to the public disadvantage.

14. (a) That the existing incidence of local taxation encourages and perpetuates the leasehold system,† by making it increasingly to the advantage of owners to retain intact rather than to divide up the property.—(b) That the

* Such improvements, as, for instance, Thames Embankment, Holborn Viaduct, Shaftesbury Avenue, Northumberland Avenue, the Strand improvement, widening streets, freeing bridges, never "waste," but continue to appreciate in value.

† See section *Leasehold Enfranchisement* in the Ninth Edition of this Handbook.

extension of the leasehold system tends to diminish the interest of the inhabitants in their citizenship; the occupier has no real interest in the house he occupies or the land on which he lives, while the owner has none of the enjoyment, responsibility, or advantages of ownership that arise from occupation. He is a mere rent receiver, an absentee in the worst sense of the term, receiving a large income from a district and spending nothing in it.

15. (*a*) That rates have increased faster than rateable value; and it is becoming ever more essential to obtain a new source of revenue. The question is a social as well as a fiscal one. So long as the incidence of taxation remains so unequal, and presses with such severity on the occupier, the Local Authorities are disinclined, and indeed unable, to undertake many important and necessary works of public convenience and utility.—(*b*) That the increased expenditure is not only due to the necessities caused by the current needs of increased population; it is due also to the fact that new communal wants, necessities, and even luxuries, have arisen, for which provision has to be made out of communal expenditure. The tendency of the times is towards increased local expenditure for public (and chiefly permanent) objects —on improvements, housing, sanitation, open spaces, free libraries, baths, wash-houses, education, &c.; much of it actually forced on the locality by Parliament.

16. (*a*) That in view of the importance and urgency of the Housing question, it is especially necessary to obtain additional local revenues in order to enable the question of housing to be undertaken on a large scale without overburdening the rates.—(*b*) That the improved facilities of locomotion induce and enable the working classes and others to live outside the urban centre. This transference of population is greatly and rapidly increasing the value of suburban land, and renders more urgent the taxation of land values,

so that the ratepayer may reap part of the benefit of the unearned increment.

17. (*a*) That land has always been far too much favoured in the matter both of local and Imperial taxation, and it is time to put an end to the anomalies that exist.*—(*b*) That in England land bears far less of the direct burden of taxation than it does on the Continent.

The general principle of the Taxation of Land Values is opposed on the grounds:—

1. (*a*) That it is not possible, in most cases, to distinguish with any precision between the "owner" and the "occupier"; and to adjust the burden fairly between them.—(*b*) That the complete ownership is made up of a series of different interests. Between the "occupier" pure and simple and the freehold reversionist, there are, usually, a large number of intermediate beneficial interests in the property: of which the occupier is probably possessed of a portion and the reversionist of another portion. No man can say whether, and how far, he is an "occupier" or an "owner."

2. That the various "occupiers" and "leaseholders" have acquired their interests on varying terms; the actual rent they pay in no way necessarily represents their beneficial interest in the property. Hence, it would be difficult or impossible to divide the burden according to the benefit received.†

* Speaking of Imperial burdens, Mr Goschen stated, in 1871, that "the amount paid by land alone in England is 5½ per cent.; in Holland, 9½ per cent.; in Austria, 17½ per cent.; in France, 18½ per cent.; in Belgium, 20½ per cent."

† The land may be held on a great variety of tenures. The landlord may build a house and live in it. He may build the house and let it directly to an occupying tenant. He may let it on lease to a tenant who may sublet it. He may let the land to a builder, charging only a ground rent, the

3. That in the case of a long leasehold, the occupier paying a rent fixed, say eighty years ago, and enjoying to the full the entire of the increased value of the property for a long period, is not merely occupier but temporary owner, and it is partly in that capacity that he bears the increased rates.

4. (*a*) That ground rents in no way represent the real interest of the owner in a particular plot of land. The ground rent is usually a certain annual payment spread over a considerable number of plots of land, and arbitrarily apportioned between those plots irregularly and unequally. —(*b*) That to tax ground rents and not the other interests in the ground value, would be grossly unfair; and yet they are the only visible interest that can be directly and easily taxed.—(*c*) That, if ground rents are to be rated, "fines," which are merely anticipated ground rents, and "reversions," which are practically deferred ground rents, should be rated too—and this is practically impossible.

5. That ground values are but one form of investment which is appreciated by the "unearned increment"; it is unjust to pick them out for special taxation.

6. That the owners of fixed interests in the property—*i.e.* rent charges without reversion, &c.—who receive no advantage from, and have no control over, the communal expenditure, would be additionally taxed without receiving any additional benefit.

7. That the reversionary portion of the interest in "improved ground values" is practically capital, and to tax capital during life is opposed to the first principles of our system of taxation.

builder to erect houses on it; the builder may build and sub-lease to another, who may again sub-lease, creating several interests in the property, &c. On the expiry of the lease, the owner may either take over the structure, or he may increase the ground rent, or take a part of the increased rent out in the form of a fine or a premium, or insist on certain expenditure by the leaseholder, &c.

8. (*a*) That the benefit accruing from the "unearned increment" goes in a far larger degree to the advantage of the occupiers and leaseholders, than of the ground landlord.—(*b*) That the continual increase in the rateable value of London is an alleviation, not an aggravation, of the position as regards the occupier. The value of his beneficial interest is largely increased, and the aggregate increase in value diminishes the amount of the rate that he is called upon to pay.

9. (*a*) That the increase in the aggregate rates, so far as it is due to new buildings or to increased rateable value, does not affect the individual occupier; he is only concerned with the rate in the pound on his own house, and in this respect the increase of late years has been slight.—(*b*) That he has, on this score, no equitable ground for legislative relief; the increased burden of the rate is fully compensated by the increased benefits derived from the expenditure.

10. (*a*) That it is only the rate levied for permanent improvements that can be said to benefit the reversioner. The other rates are for temporary, recurring, and immediate purposes; of these, the occupier and successive owners obtain year by year the full benefit, and should therefore bear the whole burden.—(*b*) That, even as regards so-called permanent improvements, there are few or none the benefits of which are not largely or altogether exhausted (and therefore also enjoyed) during the period over which the loan raised to create them extends.—(*c*) That the immediately resultant value of permanent improvements is usually more than the cost, and the investment is a beneficial one to the occupier and leaseholder.

11. That owners of ground rents, with or without reversions, derive no appreciable benefit from local public expenditure for current purposes. Those who have no reversions (such as superiors in Scotland and the owners

of fee farm rents in England), or no substantial reversions (such as the owners of ground rents on very long leases), derive no appreciable benefit from the expenditure on public improvements. The benefit to other ground rent owners from improvements is sometimes inappreciable and sometimes substantial, varying according to the proximity of the reversion.

12. (*a*) That it is not possible (nor, if possible, expedient) to distinguish between rates for permanent improvements and those for other purposes; or to say that this part of the rate is for a permanent, and that for a temporary object; that this part should be paid by the owner, and that by the occupier.—(*b*) That these so-called "improvements" may, by opening up new thoroughfares and diverting traffic, &c., actually diminish the value of the land in certain districts.—(*c*) That it is the total amount of the rate in the pound, and not the distribution of the rate among particular objects, that affects the occupier.

13. That the occupier does not pay twice over for public improvements, &c.—once in rates and again in increased rent. During the currency of the lease the lessee bears the burden and enjoys the benefit which exactly cancel one another.* At the expiration of the lease both burden and benefit will be taken into account in renewing the agreement.

14. (*a*) That, if it be true, that the builder or occupier has been called upon to bear an unforeseen and unexpectedly large increase of rates, he has, on the other hand, enjoyed the benefits of an equally unforeseen and unexpectedly large increase in the value of the property, of which benefit the owner is altogether deprived during the term of the lease. —(*b*) That, in most cases, the appreciated value of the

* But this does not take into account the sinking fund, under which the public improvement may be paid for before its benefits are exhausted.

property which he has enjoyed, has by far exceeded any loss caused by increased rates.

15. (*a*) That the leaseholder has deliberately taken a risk (of an increase or decrease of rates), and cannot justly complain if the bargain has gone against him.—(*b*) That it would be unjust to allow the builder or leaseholder to reopen the contract as regards his loss, and allow it to stand as regards his gain.

16. That, in the case of a long lease, the owner cannot benefit from the expenditure for a long period of time; the ground rent is a fixed sum. There are prospective risks as well as prospective profits, and the latter often outweigh the former; yet it is proposed to throw additional immediate taxation on the owner whether he ultimately benefits or not.

17. That the incidence of rates is determined by economic causes, which cannot be altered by legislation. That, therefore, whether the occupier or the owner actually pays the rates in the long run, there is no injustice in a system which, for the sake of convenience of collection, throws the rates in the first instance on the occupier.

18. (*a*) That a change of system would not in the end in any way advantage him.—(*b*) That, whatever their nominal incidence, as a matter of fact, the owner in the long run does pay the rates; for the amount of annual rent paid is governed by the amount of annual rates to which the property is liable.—(*c*) That, in building leases especially, this is so. The amount of the occupation rent that can be obtained determines the amount of the ground rent, for the builder must make his profit. That which tends to increase or to diminish the occupation rent, tends to increase or diminish the ground rent. Rates tend to diminish occupation rent, for they are taken into account in fixing the rent, and they therefore tend to diminish in the same degree the

ground rent. The owner, therefore, already pays indirectly all the rates and taxes.

19. That, as regards the reversion—the "unearned increment" so called,—the owner and the builder (or leaseholder) carefully consider the matter when the bargain is made; and the owner is content to let his land for a number of years at a rent far below the annual value of the land, in consideration of its development by others, and the reversion to him of the whole property at the end of the term.

20. (*a*) That during the term of the contract, the variations of the rates will no doubt advantage or disadvantage the occupier; but an adjustment would be made when the contract comes to an end, and the rates would then be thrown on the owner.—(*b*) That the rent represents the amount the landlord can obtain for the property free of taxes. If he is called upon compulsorily to pay a portion of the rates, he will compensate himself by raising the rent by a like amount.

21. (*a*) That it is immaterial to the tenant—who is prepared to pay a certain total sum for the property—whether he pays it in the shape of rent or of rates.—(*b*) That the tenant, in taking a house, always considers, in estimating its worth to him, not only what is the rent, but what are the actual and the probable rates. He is quite capable of making his own bargain, and does not require the law to step in to his aid.

22. That, no doubt, if a rise in rates is foreseen, the tenant obtains his house at a lower rent than he otherwise would; but this would happen as much under the existing system as under the new one. If the lease be a short one, the question of increased rates would soon come up, and would be settled in connection with the new bargain. If the lease be a long one, the occupier and not the owner

obtains the full benefit of the communal advantages obtained for the rates, and should therefore pay them.

23. (*a*) That urban land being practically a monopoly, the owner will, at the end of the contract, raise the occupation rent by the amount of the rates statutorily shifted to him from the occupier, and thereby appropriate to himself the whole benefit intended for the occupier.—(*b*) That, thus, the occupier would obtain no relief from the change; and the alleged grievance would remain unredressed.

24. That the only way in which the occupier could gain, would be if, during the period of his existing contract, he were allowed to relieve himself of a part of his rates, contrary to his contract, and to put them on to his immediate landlord—a flagrant injustice.

25. (*a*) That, if any benefit did accrue at the expense of the reversionist, it would go, not to the occupiers on short tenures (these would have their rents proportionately raised to cover the rates from which they had been relieved) but almost entirely to the building owner or middleman.—(*b*) That the working classes, for the most part, have no leases and pay no rates (which are "compounded" and paid by the landlord); the change would therefore not affect them one way or the other.

26. (*a*) That, though the pecuniary position of the owner as regards the rates would, in the end, probably be unaltered, to allow the change to be carried through would encourage further attacks on property.—(*b*) That, in any case, the property of the owner would be depreciated. The change would cause a feeling of unsettlement, and a fear that additional burdens would be cast on the land. Further, a part of the value of land values lies in the fact that they represent a fixed and not a variablo income; this advantage would be lost if they were saddled with variable rates.—(*c*) That the different interests in the property have, as a

rule, already been sold over and over again, the price being based on the existing rating system. To upset this basis would involve grave injustice.

27. (*a*) That the change would constitute a gross and unnecessary interference with the ordinary dealings in property.—(*b*) That it would be a gross violation of the terms of existing contracts.

28. That, taking into account the burden of rates and of taxes placed upon it, land does already fully bear its share of local and imperial taxation.

29. That the occupier is the person who has the plenary voice in, and the control over the local expenditure. The owner of the land value, as such, has no such voice or control over it. It would be grossly unfair therefore to tax him by rates in which he has no voice, and from which he does not directly or indirectly benefit; and it would not be practicable to give him local representation.

THE SEPARATE ASSESSMENT AND TAXATION OF SITE VALUES AND BUILDING VALUES

Various schemes have from time to time been promulgated with a view to distinguish between the site value and the building, value of a particular property and to place a special rate on the site value.*

These ideas have gradually crystallized into the proposal

* For particulars of these schemes, see Report of the Town Holding Committee, P.P. 214 of 1892, and Reports of Royal Commission on Local Taxation, Cd. 638 of 1901; and the various private members Bills of the last few sessions.

that the value of the premises, land and buildings together—at present assessed and rated as one—should be divided into two distinct portions, and separately assessed on the building value, and the site value; and that while the general rate should continue to be levied on the occupier as before, a new and special rate should be placed, for purposes of local taxation, on the capital value of the site.*

It is generally proposed that the ordinary rent-payer, usually the occupier, will be entitled to deduct from his rent the amount of the rate levied on the site value of the premises; and that each intermediate person who pays rent to another, shall be entitled similarly to deduct the same amount from his rent.†

The "Site value" may be defined as the annual rent, or its capitalised value, which at the time of valuation might be reasonably expected to be obtained for the land as a cleared site if let for building.

The "Owner" may be defined as the person (or persons)

* The Minority of the Royal Commission in their Report, while condemning the various schemes put before them for the taxation of site values according to individual interest, proposed that the site value of the premises should be ascertained by valuation, and that a moderate but special and direct rate should be levied on this value in respect of the local expenditure in public improvements. All existing contracts to be respected.

The rate to be a special site value rate—half to be charged on owners and half on occupiers—to be levied alongside the existing rate, and to be collected in like manner from the occupier, who will be entitled to deduct the owner's share from his rent. The amount in the pound to be limited by statute (p. 166). The Majority condemn all proposals to tax land values.

† A more ingenious plan found favour at one time. Under it, the whole land value rate would, in the first instance, be collected from the occupier. But, in so far as he had no beneficial interest in the value, he would pass on the rate to his immediate landlord by deduction from his rent. This latter would likewise do the same by the next interest; and so on through each interest in the property; the amount of site value to be deducted diminishing as the respective beneficial interests of the parties came into play. Both the Town Holdings Committee and the Royal Commission con demned the scheme as too complicated, and consequently unworkable.

who derive a revenue, or use, or value equivalent to revenue, from the value of the site.*

Most of the arguments already given in the previous section apply equally to this proposal. But it is more specifically supported on the following grounds:—

1. (*a*) That, at present, rates are levied indiscriminately on landed property in proportion to its supposed rental value, without regard to the nature or origin of that value.—(*b*) That site value and building value are essentially different, and even opposite, in character; and it is unfair and unwise to treat them as exactly alike for rating purposes.

2. That there can be no objection in equity to the taxation of capitalised value, equally with rental value. Capitalised value is a convenient mode of ascertaining real as against fictitious value.

3. (*a*) That the present system is faulty, inasmuch as it does not distinguish between the value of the building which is a wasting value of limited life, and that of the land which is permanent; and which neither originally, nor subsequently, necessitated any direct outlay on the part of the owner. —(*b*) That there are two distinct values in urban land: the ground value, and that of the structure erected upon it; the latter is solely due to the capital expended upon it by the builder, whilst the value of the land is entirely created, as well as maintained, by the presence of the town in which it is situated, and by the improvements (public or private) introduced at the expense of the community.—(*c*) That the communal expenditure, while increasing the site value, might actually diminish the value of the building by rendering it

* *Ground rents* are, of course, quite a different matter. A particular ground rent is a purely arbitrary sum, usually arranged between the owner and the builder, and which, as a rule, has no necessary relation to the real value of the particular part of land. And even if so fixed at the beginning of the lease, it ceases to represent the true value as time goes on. The so-called ground rent is merely an annuity forming a first charge on the property. It is secured equally on the whole property, site and structure together, and the ground landlord comes into the reversion of the whole property at the end of the lease.

unsuitable to the locality; or in other ways it may be diminished to a vanishing point, yet the occupier and not the owner pays the rates.

4. That, in regard to permanent improvements, the occupier pays twice over, once in current rates and again in the increased rent exacted at the end of his lease based on the public improvement. This is more especially the case, when (through the sinking fund) the capital expenditure for the improvement has been paid off during the currency of the lease, though much of the benefit of the improvement remains unconsumed.

5. That the increase in local expenditure accentuates the disparity of burden borne by the land and the buildings; and greatly hampers the local authority in undertaking necessary or advantageous expenditure.

6. (*a*) That the general principle, apart from details, on which the proposal is founded is just and inconvertible, namely, that each interest in the property should bear a burden proportionate to the benefit which it enjoys from the expenditure of the locality.—(*b*) That this is the ideal; and, so far as practicable, should be attained.—(*c*) The whole question, therefore, is not one of justice but of feasibility; not should it be done, but can it be done?—(*d*) That the present system of charging all rates in the first instance, whatever their final incidence, on the occupier, obscures the actual diffusion and the shifting of the burden; and unduly narrows the reservoir of taxable capacity.

7. (*a*) That the object of the reform is not so much to benefit one individual at the expense of another, as to benefit the whole community, by obtaining a new source of local revenue from the taxation of a description of property which is not taxed, or is insufficiently taxed, for local purposes. —(*b*) That the object is to get at, and tax, the full annual profit accruing from the mere possession of a piece of ground; and thus, the burden of the rates would be justly apportioned to the benefit received; and the incidence of local taxation would be fairly adjusted.

8. (*a*) That the separate valuation and assessment of the site would enable the rating to keep up with the increase of

value; and those occupiers who hold an improving property at a fixed rent would not continue to escape their share of the rates.—(*b*) That the system provides for worsement (depreciation in value) equally as for betterment (appreciation in value). If the site value falls, the assessment, and therefore the burden of rates, diminishes proportionately.

9. That even if it be a fallacy to suppose that there is a huge untapped source of revenue in connection with urban land, it is no fallacy to think that urban site value is a form of property which, from its nature, is peculiarly fit to bear a direct and special burden.

10. (*a*) That when the bulk of the existing leasehold bargains were made, it was not, and could not be foreseen, that the rates would be increased so rapidly and for so many new objects.*—(*b*) That the result has been far more burdensome on the occupier, and far more advantageous to the owner, than was intended or anticipated by either party to the original bargain.†—(*c*) That, to whatever extent the rates then existing were considered at the time the bargain was made, every addition to the rates, whether foreseen or no, and certainly if not foreseen, has fallen exclusively on the occupier.

11. (*a*) That however the burden of the rates may be subsequently manipulated, it is the duty of Parliament to decide what is just in regard to the ultimate incidence of taxation, and to fix the first incidence accordingly.—(*b*) That if the occupier does pay more than he ought, it is right that the law should come to his relief.—(*c*) That, taking into account the variety of intermediate interests and the complications of the leasehold system, it may be impossible absolutely fairly to adjust

* "We are higher taxed. Within the last eighteen months there has been added to the Lighting, Pavement and Improvement Rate 10s. yearly, to the Poor Rate £1, to the Sewer Rate 10s.," and this on Rates that before amounted in all to some £6 to £7.—Mrs Carlyle's "Budget of a Femme Incomprise," 12th Feb. 1858.

† From an interesting Return of the Vestry of St George's, Hanover Square, published by the London County Council in their "Local Government and Taxation Committee's Report" (May 1891), we find that in that parish the total rate has increased pretty steadily from 2s. 5d. in 1858 (lowest 5s. 4d. in 1860), to 4s. 6d. in 1889: the assessment from £755,000 to £1,760,000; the amount of rate levied from £88,400 to £381,000.

the incidence of the burden; but any inequalities that might arise, would be far less than those that exist at present.

12. That there must be something radically wrong with the incidence of a tax when it bears the obloquy of being paid by two sets of persons. In regard to the rates, as at present levied, the owner believes that he really pays them, the occupier knows that he pays them directly.

13. That though there may be many intermediate owners, and complications of interest in the whole value of the premises, the premises themselves can be clearly divided into the two values: site value and structural value.

14. (*a*) That at present the occupier has no direct and legal means of passing on to the owner that portion of the taxation which should legitimately be borne by the other interests in the property.—(*b*) That in large towns the land is practically a monopoly, and the occupier is at the mercy of the owner. Even if the alleged "higgling of the market" enables the occupier, through a reduced rent, to pass back a portion of the rates on to the owner, it would be better and simpler that the latter should be directly charged in the first instance.—(*c*) That, as a matter of fact, the amount of rent charged does not depend to any great extent on the amount of rates. Few tenants enter into nice calculations as to the rates they will have to pay (and the amount cannot indeed be altogether foreseen). They look chiefly to the rent asked, and roughly estimate rates and taxes at so much more in proportion. They are ready to pay a certain definite sum in rent, and no more, and will not willingly pay an increased rent even though relieved of a portion of the rates.—(*d*) That the owner of the ground value, being practically a monopolist, has already exacted the greatest rent that can be got for the land, and he would not easily, or to any large extent, be able to pass on to the occupier, by an increased rent, the new charge thus directly laid upon him.—(*e*) That, doubtless, where the value of land had risen, and there was an increasing demand for accommodation, the owner (at the expiration of the lease) would be able to raise the rent; but this would be wholly apart from the question of rates.

15. (*a*) That direct taxes tend to stick where they are imposed; and the owner, if directly rated, would not be able long

to shift his share of the burden on to the occupier.—(*b*) That the burden of the income tax, imposed on the owner, but collected in the first instance from the occupier, remains on the owner.

16. (*a*) That, if it be true, as argued, that the landowner pays all the rates in the end, there would be no hardship in placing them on him at the beginning. If he can shift them all off on to the tenant, it would do him no harm or injustice to put them on him at first.—(*b*) That, if it be true, that the ultimate incidence of the rates would still fall on the occupier, the change should be welcomed by the owners; as, without loss to themselves, an apparent grievance on the part of the occupiers would be removed, and the invidious imputation of exceptional immunity from taxation under which owners now rest would disappear.—(*c*) That the state of public sentiment on the matter, constitutes a serious danger to property. It would be to the advantage and the safety of the landowner, that he should appear visibly and directly to pay his fair share of the rates.

17. That the opposition of the owners to the proposed change, shows that they do *not* believe that it is they, rather than the occupier, who really bear the burden of the rates.

18. That the owner of the site value would not be taxed twice over for the same purpose; so far as the ordinary rate is a burden on him, the special rate would relieve the ordinary rate to a like extent. The total rates would be the same, but would be more equitably apportioned to benefit.

19. That the existing system of valuation, viz., the rent at which a property might reasonably be expected to let, is hypothetical and arbitrary. Yet this hypothetical valuation is the recognised basis on which rates and rents are fixed.

20. (*a*) That the site has a distinct value if clear of holdings, and surveyors habitually distinguish the two when valuing.—(*b*) That in many cases already, such as railway stations, banks, clubs, and public buildings, the basis of rating consists of a separate valuation of site and of building, the two being then together. —(*c*) That the evidence afforded by sales and leases of sites would constitute an adequate basis for the expert valuation.—(*d*) That, "a valuation of sites sufficiently accurate for the purpose, and not inferior to the present valuation of heredita-

ments, could be made without undue labour and expense." * And even if the first cost was considerable, the future annual cost would be slight.

21. That a separate valuation of site and building has been carried out lately in Paris.

22. That, in future, the deductions for repairs, insurance, &c., in order to arrive at rateable value, would be on the structure only, to which alone they legitimately apply; and thus would disappear the inequality which exists under this head, between one property and another, and between districts which contribute to a common charge.

23. That the present incidence of the rates by placing the whole burden of the rate on the occupier and on the building, tends to discourage building and to make houses fewer, worse, and dearer. If more of the burden were thrown on the site value, by means of a special rate, the portion left to be borne by the building would be diminished, and this would weigh with the builder who is hesitating to embark on the erection of new structures.

On the other hand, besides the general arguments already given, the particular scheme for the taxation of Site Values is opposed on the grounds:—

1. That it is an entirely novel principle of rating to tax on the capital value of a property, and not on the income derived from it.

2. (*a*) That it is not just to select one particular class of property, and to put upon it special and exceptional burdens, in addition to the burdens which it bears equally at present with all other classes of rateable property.—(*b*) That the special taxation of site values is not justified upon either of the two grounds which have hitherto formed the basis of the system of local taxation, since neither in respect of their ability to pay, nor of the benefits which they receive, does it appear that the owners of land values contribute inequitably to local expenditure at the present time, as compared with the owners of other classes of rateable property. That it would be

* Minority, R. C., page 169.

difficult to maintain any effective distinction between sites which have increased and sites which have diminished in value; but, even if it were possible, land is not the only class of rateable property, the value of which may be enhanced by circumstances beyond the influence or control of its owners, and there is no reason why, by reason of such enhancement of value, land should be placed in a new and separate category so far as rating is concerned.

3. (*a*) That in any case, if a special burden is to be imposed on land, on the ground of any increase of its value, the object could not be equitably met by the imposition of a new rate on site value from year to year. The extent of such increase varies not only as between district and district, but as between different parts of the same district, and in some cases there is either no increase at all, or a diminution of value.—(*b*) That the imposition of a new rate of a given amount upon the annual value of all property in land would, therefore, bring into existence new inequalities of liability, unless measures were taken to differentiate not only between district and district, but between property and property.—(*c*) That no possible modification of the existing rating machinery could satisfy this objection.

4. (*a*) That the site value, and any enhanced value, is already fully included in the value of the whole property on which rates are at present assessed; and thus the owner of the site value, whoever he may be, bears his fair proportion of the burden.—(*b*) That, as the site value is already included, and would remain included in the rateable value, the owner of the site value would be taxed twice over, he would pay both the ordinary rate and the special rate.

5. That while public expenditure doubtless improves the value of some sites, it diminishes that of others; and yet all sites would have to bear this additional taxation, even though they had been worsened by the very expenditure which necessitated the rate.—(*a*) That, whatever the incidence, site values are already fully rated, for the full rateable value of each property is assessed for rates. The change proposed would therefore tap no new source, nor produce additional revenue. Certain persons would be relieved at the expense of others, but the community at large would in no way benefit.—(*b*) That there is much misconception and exaggeration in regard to the

revenue that could possibly be derived from the taxation of land values.—(*c*) That the supposed existence of a new source of revenue would tend to still greater local expenditure and increase of local burdens.

6. (*a*) That the proposal does not strike the real dividing line between the owner and occupier; for there is no such dividing line.—(*b*) That, in the great majority of cases, urban rateable property is not owned and occupied by the same person; but rights and interests in it, of different kinds and for varying periods of time, are distributed between several persons. These rights are so complicated, antagonistic, and intermingled, that no useful purpose would be served, no essential improvement would be gained by a separate valuation of the site apart from the building.—(*c*) That it would be impossible, by any process of valuation, levy, or deduction, fairly to apportion and tax the different interests. An apparent interest in the building alone, may, and probably does, derive part of its value from the site.

7. That it would perpetuate a source of unfairness that is now much felt. An occupier, by improving his house, increases his rating, and the whole of this increased rating falls on him; yet, when the lease terminates, the improved value is absorbed by the reversionist. Conversely, if he allows the house to deteriorate, he is less highly rated, and the owner comes into a less valuable reversion. If the rate on the building were to be distinguished from that on the land, this injustice would be greatly accentuated.

8. That so great are the complications of ownership, that there are no means whereby site values can be equitably taxed; and none of the various schemes put forward (ingenious, but unworkable), have shown how to determine the question of who is the owner of the site value.*

9. (*a*) That it would be almost impossible to distinguish between, and separately to assess, the value of the land apart from the value of the building.—(*b*) That the ultimate basis of valuation is "market value"; and it is by market value that the Local Assessment Committees work.—(*c*) That the only check on the estimate of value made by professional valuers and the only test of their correctness, is market value.—

* For the analysis, see Minority Report of Royal Commission.

(*d*) That the only ultimate basis of a valuer's knowledge is his experience of actual market values; and as the land and the houses upon it are sold and let together, and the only market value existing is made up of the value of the whole property, no such basis can exist for a separate valuation of the two things.—(*e*) That, valuers will value anything; and, no doubt, at great cost, a professional "valuation" could be made. But it would be arbitrary, unjust, and lead to great uncertainty, complication, litigation, and friction.

10. (*a*) That the system would involve a fresh, complicated, and enormously costly valuation of the whole of the 600,000 houses in the Metropolis; and in each case it would involve a valuation of two interests instead of one.—(*b*) That, as the relative values of land and building varies year by year, there would, instead of the quinquennial, have to be a yearly valuation and assessment, with a corresponding variation in the amount of the rate charged on the building and the land respectively.—(*c*) That the valuation to be just, would have to take into account, not only the actual use to which the site was put, but the use to which it might be put; and this is impossible.

11. (*a*) That the proposed plan of levy and of deduction is far too complicated for a system of rating, the essence of which should be simplicity.—(*b*) That the present rough-and-ready system of rating, which throws the first incidence on the occupier, fairly distributes the ultimate incidence of taxation among the various beneficiaries; no new system would be so simple or so equitable.

12. (*a*) That, as far as possible, the existing administrative machinery should be utilised, and the change that is made should be in consonance with tradition and habit. The proposal made would involve the creation of an entirely new system of valuation, assessment, rating, and collection.—(*b*) That, instead of the Rating Authority dealing simply, as is done now, with the occupier, whose position is known, it would have to deal also with the owner, whose identity it is often difficult to discover.—(*c*) That the complicated assessment would give rise to endless disputes.

13. That the system would in no way prevent the owner from re-transferring to the occupier, by means of an increased rent, the burden thus compulsorily thrown on him; and thus nothing in the end would have been gained.

14. That it would be the thin end of the wedge in the spoliation of property. The special rate levied might, at first, be light and fair, but the burden would soon be increased and graduated until it amounted to confiscation.

15. That the area of rating requires broadening, but this should be done by bringing personalty under contribution, and not by putting fresh burdens on realty.

EXISTING CONTRACTS

The question arises whether, if fresh taxation, in the form of a special rate, is placed on land values, the new charge should apply to Existing Contracts.

On the one hand it is contended :—

1. That in London, at all events, the bulk of the premises are held on long leases, or under agreements which run for many years. Unless, therefore, the new taxation is imposed on land values as a whole, in spite of existing agreements, the benefit to be derived from it will be for years hardly appreciable.

2. That those who would gain from the exemption of existing contracts would be chiefly the wealthy freeholders, whose land is held on long leases.

3. That the question must be looked at more from the point of view of the ratepayers as a whole, than from that of the individual lessee or owner.

4. (*a*) That the new charge being intended to discount the inequalities of the existing charges, and to proportion the local burdens more equally to the benefit received, there would be no injustice in imposing it, in spite of existing contracts.—(*b*) That (if existing contracts were respected) the occupying tenant would simply be burdened with a new rate which he would be unable to pass on to the owner of the site value. Thus the inequality of rating would be aggravated, and not relieved.

5. (*a*) That, owing to the monopoly of land, the two parties have not contracted on equal terms.—(*b*) That if the special rate only comes into force at the end of the lease, the owner will, in nearly every case, be then able to throw back his burden on the lease-holder in the shape of increased rent.

6. (*a*) That Parliament is perfectly entitled—especially by way of a new tax—to interfere freely with existing custom or contracts.—(*b*) That, especially is this the case, when the condition of things, under which the arrangement was originally made, has been radically altered; and, more especially, if the alteration be due to increased statutory obligations involving additional local expenditure.—(*c*) That the imposition of the Education rate was an interference with the equities as between parties to existing contracts, to the detriment of the occupier. —(*d*) That, similarly, the equalisation of Rates Act (and other Acts) has over-ridden existing contracts, and relieved one set of ratepayers at the expense of others.—(*e*) That the principle of Imperial taxation is that no person shall be allowed to contract himself out of his liabilities; that no private arrangement shall be allowed to narrow the area of taxation. A precedent for interference, founded on this principle, exists in the case of the income-tax; which, though in the first instance, collected from the occupier, is recovered by him from the owner, any contract to the contrary notwithstanding.

7. (*a*) That the owners are not deserving of much consideration. Without any cost to themselves, they have profited enormously and unexpectedly from the increased rates, and from the "unearned increment." *—(*b*) That, in no other instance, has property risen so continuously and so greatly in value, without exertion on the part of the owner.

8. That where the contract contained no specific stipulation

* "Suppose there is a kind of income which constantly tends to increase without any exertion or sacrifice on the part of the owners, those owners constituting a class in the community whom the natural course of things progressively enriches, consistently with complete passiveness on their own part. In such a case it would be no violation of the principles on which private property is grounded, if the State should appropriate this increase of wealth, or the part of it, as it arises. This would not, properly, be taking anything from anybody; it would merely be applying an accession of wealth, created by circumstances, to the benefit of society, instead of allowing it to become an unearned appendage to the riches of a particular class. Now this is actually the case with rent." (Mill, Bk. V., chap. ii. sect. 5.)

that the occupier should pay the rates, it need not be regarded; in the case of contracts where such a specific stipulation exists, it is generally agreed that some fair compromise would have to be arrived at to prevent injustice and spoliation.*

On the other hand it is contended:—

1. That legislation enabling occupiers to violate the contracts they have deliberately made, and to escape the obligations which they have solemnly undertaken, is indefensible, and spells confiscation.

2. (*a*) That it would be a gross injustice to impose a special burden on one party to the contract, without allowing the agreement to be reconsidered.—(*b*) That as the payment of rates are considered in the rent, the rent must be allowed to be re-considered if a special rate is put on the party who, under the agreement, was not to pay any rates.

3. (*a*) That, after all, the lessees of town property have not made by any means a bad bargain, nor one of which they should be relieved.—(*b*) That in dealings with urban real estate the bargain made is sometimes the payment of a lump sum down,

* The Committee of 1870 (Mr Goschen's) recommended that the case of existing contracts would be equitably met, by exempting the owners of property held under lease from the proposed division of rates for a period of three years; and, by providing, that while the deduction of rates should then take effect, the owner should be entitled, at the same time, to add to the rent an annual sum equivalent to the proportionate annual average sum paid in rates by the occupier during the above three years. By others it is suggested that the three years' average should date from some fixed year (1870 is proposed, as the year in which the Committee reported) before the great rise in rates took place. The occupier would pay an addition to his rent equal to half the rates then in force, less half the present rates. For instance, if the rates in 1870 had been 3s., and those of 1892 were 4s. in the pound, the occupier would deduct 6d. in the pound from his rent. Others suggest that the actual date of the contract should be taken as the starting-point. That the amount of rate existing at that time should continue to be paid by the occupier, but that he should be entitled to deduct half of any increase of rate that might have subsequently taken place. For instance, if the rate was 2s. 6d. in the pound when the bargain was made, and has since risen to 4s., the occupier would be entitled to deduct 9d. in the pound from his rent.

and sometimes the payment of a rent, and often partly in one form and partly in another. Thus (if existing contracts are broken), A., who has bought the leasehold of his house, will have to pay the site value rate, while B., who has a lease and pays an equivalent annual rent, will escape.

4. (*a*) That the immense mass of occupation tenancies are of short currency. The vast majority of leases, other than those at large rents, are for under twelve months. There is no occasion, therefore, to violate the sanctity of contracts, which would destroy confidence and discourage building enterprise.*—(*b*) That the holders of long leases are substantially a section of investors, and have no claim to legal interference with their contracts.

5. (*a*) That the freeholders who more immediately benefit most from the increase in land values, are those whose leases are short, or about to fall in, and who would soon therefore be subjected to the special taxation.—(*b*) That the freeholder of property under long leases obtains no present benefit from increased ground values, and should not be additionally taxed until he obtains the benefit of the enhanced value, *i.e.* until the termination of existing contracts.

6. (By some.) That (with existing contracts respected) the existing occupying tenant would not be burdened with a new and additional burden. The vast bulk of the tenancies are of very limited duration; while the extension of the system of the taxation of site values to vacant land, would so relieve the local rates, that the tenant would be paying less and not more.

THE RATING OF VACANT LAND

Uncovered land, in England and Wales, is not liable to rates except at its agricultural value. It is proposed that Vacant Land should be assessed for all local rates at a

* See Royal Commission, p. 164.

compounded annual value on its selling value, or be liable for the site value rate.

In addition to the argument already given, this proposal is specially supported on the grounds:—

1. (*a*) That, "at present, land available for building in the neighbourhood of our populous centres, though its capital value is very great, is probably producing but a small yearly return until it is let for building."*—(*b*) That, "the owners of this land are rated not in relation to the real value, but to the actual annual income."*—(*c*) That, "they can thus afford to keep their land out of the market, and to part with only small quantities, so as to raise the price beyond the natural monopoly price which the land would command by its advantages of position."*—(*d*) That, "meantime, the general expenditure of the town on improvements is increasing the value of their property."*

2. That, "if this land were rated at say, 4 per cent. on its selling value, the owners would have a more direct incentive to part with it to those who are desirous of building, and a two-fold advantage would result to the community. First, all the valuable property would contribute to the rates, and thus the burden on the occupiers would be diminished by the increase in the rateable property. Secondly, the owners of the building land would be forced to offer their land for sale, and thus their competition with one another would bring down the price of building land, and so diminish the tax in the shape of ground rent, or price paid for land, which is now levied on urban enterprise by the adjacent landowners; a tax which is no recompense for any industry or expenditure on their part, but is the natural result of the industry and activity of the townspeople themselves."*

3. (*a*) That the expenditure from the rates does largely increase the capital value of vacant building land.—(*b*) That the owner of the land is expending nothing on it himself, and all the burdens of the district in the benefits of which

* Report of Royal Commission on the Housing of the Working Classes, 1885.

he shares—are cast by law on his neighbours.—(*c*) That it is not just that this substantial and increasing "unearned increment" of land value should escape its fair share of taxation.*

4. That whatever may be the case in regard to the other proposals, the taxation of vacant land, on the basis of the site value, would bring in a large revenue, to the substantial relief of local taxation.†

5. That, in some cases, large amounts of ground rents are received by the owner for vacant land already let for building, but not yet built upon, and this income entirely escapes all rates.

6. That the present system offers a direct incentive to keep land out of the market; the capital value is ever growing, without the owner having to pay outgoings on it in the shape of rates.

7. That the evil is not a diminishing one; inasmuch as, while existing "vacant land" may be gradually built over, the growth of urban districts is always creating fresh "vacant land."

8. (*a*) That this tendency deliberately to keep land out of the market, and its consequent dearness, helps to accentuate the evils of overcrowding.—(*b*) While the fact that the exemption from rates enjoyed by the vacant land throws a heavier burden of rating on the other rateable property, discourages building.

9. (*a*) That, in rating vacant land, a distinction would of course be made between land advantageous as open spaces,

* In Edinburgh there is land unbuilt on which is rated on a value of £2,570 per annum, and which brings to the town £344 a year. If it were rated at 4 per cent. on its actual value, it would give a rateable value of about £27,000 or £28,000 a year. The total rate income of Edinburgh is about £300,000 a year.

† The Land Valuation Committee of the London County Council (June, 1889), "have reason to believe that in Kensington the value of the vacant land is not less than £1,700,000 . . . certain fields in Kensington of a selling value of £400,000 are now rated only at £62 a year." In Paddington "the vacant land amounts to about 100 to 150 acres. The selling value of the land is about £3,000 per acre, and it now escapes rating altogether," &c., p. 10.

and land merely kept back for a larger profit. (*b*) That the taxation of vacant land intended for building purposes would provide a fund that might be used for securing more open spaces; and open spaces could be acquired more cheaply if the land were rated, while still in private hands.

On the other hand, it is argued:—

1. That to attempt to proportion the annual contribution to saleable value and not to annual receipts, would be contrary to habit and usage, and to the general principle of taxation prevailing in this country.

2. That rating is based on profitable use or occupation, and vacant land is producing nothing.

3. That it would be unjust, first to lay rates on the capital value, when little or no income was being derived from the land, and afterwards to rate the property on the income that is actually earned. The ultimate income could thus be rated twice over, once in anticipation and again in possession.

4. (*a*) That to tax vacant land would necessitate the creation of new administrative machinery.—(*b*) That the difficulty of defining what was, or was not, "vacant building land," and the difficulty of fairly assessing it when defined, would be almost insuperable.

5. That as agricultural land gradually ripens into building land, the value of vacant land would be ever changing with the changing circumstances of the neighbourhood; an annual valuation and assessment would be necessary.

6. That the assessment would give rise to endless disputes and difficulties.

7. (*a*) That rates do not benefit vacant land; while as soon as the land is built over, and the rates begin to benefit it, the land comes under rating.—(*b*) That the great bulk of the rates are incurred for services that solely benefit the land that is already built on, and in no way benefit the vacant land. Public improvements are not, as a rule, undertaken in those districts in which much land still remains vacant.

8. (*a*) That the ordinary operations of trade in land should not be artificially interfered with by special taxation.—(*b*) That

it would tend to crush out the small holders—who could not afford to hold unproductive land and also to pay rates—and would concentrate land in the hands of a few.

9. (*a*) That building land is not in any way unduly kept off the market at present; it is to the interest of the landowner to bring his land into profitable occupation as quickly as he can.—(*b*) That land may be legitimately withheld for a time from building, because the owner desires to develop the estate as a high-class residential property, and not to let it to the first comer.

10. That the taxation of the site value of vacant land would delay development and hinder building. Building on any scale is usually carried out by speculative syndicates, who buy up the land, map it out, and prepare it for building by making roads, &c. This they can now afford to do in anticipation, and wait until the land is ripe for building. But if it was heavily rated, they could not afford to, and would not undertake the operation, for all their perspective profit would be swallowed up in immediate rates.

11. (*a*) That the taxation of vacant lands would have the effect of forcing land into use, but not to the best advantage of the neighbourhood or of the rating authority.—(*b*) That it would lead to jerry-building, and to the setting up of a poor class of houses, at a low rateable value; whereas, if the owner is allowed to follow his own interest, a much superior rateable value is created, and the whole community of ratepayers will profit.

12. (*a*) That by unduly forcing building land into the market, the proper development of estate, the accommodation of good roads, and open spaces, &c., would be prevented. The neighbourhood would be injured, and the rates would not be benefited.—(*b*) That it would act as a penalty on open spaces; for it would tend to drive into the building market open spaces, private parks, gardens, &c., which, greatly to the advantage of the neighbourhood, are now free of buildings, and would so remain much longer, or for ever, if not rated.

13. (*a*) That it would lead to the collusive alienation of portions of the frontage, &c., in order nominally to destroy the value of the land, for rating purposes.—(*b*) That, unless empty houses, at present exempt from rates, were also rated, the law

would be evaded by the provision of temporary structures, left uninhabited. But to rate empty houses would act as a discouragement to that development of building which the rating of vacant lands is intended to promote.

14. (*a*) That the quantity of land still left vacant, where land is of high rateable value, is very small, and the relief to the rates from taxing it would be infinitesimal.—(*b*) That the evil, as far as it exists at all, is of a temporary nature, and is rapidly diminishing as the vacant lands come into the market.

GRADUATION OF THE INCOME TAX

In the last two editions of this Book, the question of the "Income Tax" was discussed from the point of view of Direct or Indirect Taxation.*

It is, however, now generally conceded that in order that every class of citizens bear a share of taxation, and in view of the enormous expenditure of the country, that Indirect as well as Direct Taxation must each form a part of the National Revenues.

Moreover, the proportionate part of the whole taxation borne by direct or indirect taxation respectively have, of late years, steadily altered to the advantage of Indirect Taxation.†

* In the earliest editions of this Book, this section stood under the heading of "Direct *v.* Indirect Taxation," and the question of the retention or non-retention of the Income Tax was argued out. But since the book first appeared, the question of the retention of the Income Tax is no longer open to question.

† No precise distinction can be drawn between taxes which are indirect and taxes which are direct. But for purposes of comparison, *Direct Taxation* is usually held to include Income Tax, Death Duties, Stamps, Land Tax, House Duty, Licenses, &c.; while *Indirect Taxation* implies taxes on consumable articles (Customs, and Excise exclusive of Licences, &c.).

On this basis, the proportions between Direct and Indirect Taxation have altered as follows:—

	1841	**1851**	**1861**	**1871**	**1881**	**1891**	**1901**
Direct	27	33	38	39	40	44	50
Indirect	73	67	62	61	60	56	49

See P. P. 163, of 1896, and Budget speeches.

Each particular Indirect Tax has its disadvantages and its opponents; but its special remission is argued more on the demerits of the particular Tax in question, than from the point of view of the general relations between Direct and Indirect Taxation.

In reference however to *Direct* Taxation, there is a strong feeling in favour of its graduation where possible. The *Death Duties* are already fully graduated;* and it is proposed that the Income Tax also should be graduated.

Under the existing state of the law, all incomes below £160 a year are exempt from *Income Tax.* On all incomes between £160 and £400, there is an abatement of £160 (*i.e* on an income of £300, Income Tax is charged on £140 only); on incomes between £400 and £500, an abatement of £150 is given; on incomes between £500 and £600, the abatement is £120; on incomes between £600 and

* (57 & 58 Vict. chap. 30)

The rates of Estate Duty are according to the following scale:—

Where the Principal Value of the Estate					Estate Duty shall be payable at the Rate per cent. of
Exceeds	£100	and does not	exceed	£500	One pound.
,,	500	,,	,,	1,000	Two pounds.
,,	1,000	,,	,,	10,000	Three pounds.
,,	10,000	,,	,,	25,000	Four pounds.
,,	25,000	,,	,,	50,000	Four pounds ten shillings.
,,	50,000	,,	,,	75,000	Five pounds.
,,	75,000	,,	,,	100,000	Five pounds ten shillings.
,,	100,000	,,	,,	150,000	Six pounds.
,,	150,000	,,	,,	250,000	Six pounds ten shillings.
,,	250,000	,,	,,	500,000	Seven pounds.
,,	500,000	,,	,,	1,000,000	Seven pounds ten shillings.
,,	1,000,000				Eight pounds.

£700, the abatement is £70. The full Income Tax is charged on all incomes exceeding £700.

These abatements work out as follows—taking the Income Tax at a shilling in the pound.

An income of £200 pays 2.40d. in the pound; an income of £300 pays 5.60d.; an income of £400 pays 7.20d.; an income of £600 pays 9.60d.; an income of £701 pays 12d.*

The Income Tax has been progressively productive. At its imposition in 1842 it produced £772,000 per penny; in 1860, £1,122,000 per penny; in 1880, £1,850,000; in 1890, £2,140,000; and in spite of the alleviations subsequently granted, it now produces two and a half millions per penny. In 1902-3, the total receipt was £38,700,000 with the tax at 15d. in the pound.†

The further and full graduation of the Income Tax is advocated on the grounds:—

1. (*a*) That, as Adam Smith has laid down, "The subjects of every State ought to contribute towards the support of the government as nearly as possible in proportion to their respective abilities; that is, in proportion to the revenue which they respectively enjoy under the protection of the State." And, this being so, "It is not very unreasonable that the rich should contribute to the public expenses, not only in proportion to their revenue,

* For further figures and tables, and for the further detailed History of the Income Tax, the reader is referred to *Finance and Politics* and to *Mr Gladstone as Chancellor of the Exchequer*.

† For tables and information concerning the Income Tax, see Annual Reports of the Commissioners of Inland Revenue.

but something more than in that proportion."—(*b*) That each man ought to pay in proportion to the protection and security he enjoys. At present the poor man, who has little to preserve, pays far more in proportion, in taxes, than the rich man.

2. That something ought to be done to reduce the inequalities of wealth, and this can be most conveniently accomplished, and without hardship to individuals or injury to property, by an alteration in the incidence of taxation, in the direction of graduation.

3. That "equality of contribution" is not "equality of sacrifice." The latter is the true groundwork of taxation, and the burden of taxation ought to be distributed according to the ability of the taxpayer to bear it.

4. (*a*) That under present conditions, the larger incomes, taking all taxation into account, pay less in proportion in taxation than the smaller incomes. It is the poor man who pays for his poverty, not the rich man who pays for his wealth.—(*b*) That the inequality of the burden of indirect taxation on the poorer man, who pays in a larger proportion to his income and expenditure, can only be redressed by the imposition of direct taxation on a basis which will reverse this position, *i.e.* by means of graduation.

5. That the bulk of the Income Tax is contributed by those of small means, rather than by the wealthy, and these are just the incomes that specially require relief.*

6. That the Income Tax forms the foundation of National

* Out of 350,000 "persons" assessed, under Schedules D. and E., 318,000 are assessed at incomes not exceeding £400 a year, and of those, 211,000 have incomes under £200 a year.

"There is no class in the community," said M Lowe in 1872 (then Chancellor of the Exchequer), "who are so severely pinched by taxation as the lower class of the Income Tax payers."

finance, is easily collected, and little oppressive; and should therefore rest on the most equitable and stable, and consequently productive basis.

7. (*a*) That in early days, when the Income Tax, originally imposed for a temporary purpose, was looked upon as an emergency tax, it was neither worth while nor expedient to graduate it. But it is now a permanent tax, levied at a high rate, and it should therefore be overhauled, and placed on a juster basis.—(*b*) That the poundage of the Income Tax having of late years been largely increased,* and this without readjustment, its severity should be further mitigated at the lower end of the scale.†

8. (*a*) That the principle of the graduation of direct taxation is already fully admitted in regard to the Death Duties, and also in regard to the Inhabited House Duties.—(*b*) That the principle of a graduated Income Tax is already practically conceded. Under the exemptions and abatements which exist in the assessment of the Income Tax, the tax is already graduated up to a certain point.

9. (*a*) That the abrupt line at which graduation ceases, at £700 a year, is a purely artificial limit; and from time to time has been arbitrarily altered and extended.—(*b*) Income should be taxed in arithmetical proportions. Graduation, if introduced, should in justice extend throughout. There

* Peel's Income Tax of 1842 was a sevenpenny income tax, and was charged on all incomes above £150, without deduction. In 1853 the tax was changed to 5d. on incomes between £100 and £150, and 7d. above that limit. The first abatement was given in 1863, when incomes between £100 and £200 received an abatement of £60. Since then the exemption has been raised to £160, and the abatement to £160, as explained above.

† The Income Tax, when reimposed in 1846, was fixed at 7d., at which figure it remained until the Crimean War. During the Crimean War it rose to16d., from which figure, with fluctuations, it went down to 2d. in 1874. From this figure it gradually rose again, and in 1894 it was raised to 8d., at which figure it stood until 1900, when it was raised to a shilling, and the following year to 14d., and in 1902 to 15d. In 1903 it was reduced to 11d.

is no reason why the tax on an income of £600 should be graduated, while an income of £800 is placed on the same footing as one of £8000.—(*c*) That if it is right and just to discriminate between incomes of under £700 a year, it is right and just to discriminate between those of greater amount.

10. That the difficulties of collection are greatly exaggerated. Already, where the income is derived from a profession or business or trade, the person has to make a return of his whole income. That under the system of abatement no less than 600,000 persons annually return their whole income in order to obtain the rebate.

11. That Pitt's original Income Tax of 1799 was levied on the individual income from all sources; with the obligation of a return of the whole income.

12. (*a*) That there would be but little administrative difficulty in insisting on a return of the whole income, and not much opportunity for evasion.—(*b*) That every year evasion is becoming less popular and less possible.

13. That, unlike the Death Duties, graduation would not tempt to evasion by grants of property during life; while, if it were to do so, it would diffuse wealth, which would be an advantage.

14. That the system of a graduated Income Tax has been adopted, and successfully worked in Prussia, in Victoria, and elsewhere.

[Some, while not thinking it possible satisfactorily to graduate the Income Tax, or to levy it except at its source, would desire to see a considerable extension of the present system of abatements (though not in exemption), and would consider that abatement might well be given up to £1000 or more a year.]

On the other hand, some few would argue against the principles of graduation, on the ground :—

1. (*a*) That taxation should be so arranged as to take from every person an amount strictly proportionate to the benefit he receives under the protection of the State, and ought therefore to be arranged in a strictly arithmetical proportion to the income of each man.—(*b*) That no line, for purposes of taxation, can be drawn between wants primary, immediate, or necessary, and those which are not; discrimination between incomes is neither possible nor just.

2. That in a system of graduation there are no stages, no landmarks, no limits. There is no principle of justice, no principle of prudence, no guide as to where a halt should be made.

3. That all estimates of the taxation of individuals or of classes are fallacious, and worthless for purposes of comparison. It is impossible to say what proportion of taxation is borne by any one class, and what by another it is impossible indeed to draw the line between classes themselves.

4. That the income of every one, rich or poor, is either spent or saved. If spent, it gives employment; if saved, it increases the wage fund. It cannot be made to do double duty; and though a greater amount of taxation might, in the first instance, be obtained from the rich by taxation, to that extent would their powers of employment be diminished. The whole question is one of incidence, not of increased means.

5. That any system of graduated taxation, of taxation on wealth, instead of merely shifting a burden, would cripple industry, would diminish the incentive to thrift, would drive capital out of the country and thus, in the end, would

impoverish the nation, diminish the revenue, and injure, primarily, the working classes.

It would be, however, usually contended:—

That there is no matter of principle involved—the graduation of the Death Duties having decided that question—and that the matter is simply one of expediency and practicability.

Full graduation of the Income Tax is opposed on the grounds:—

1. (*a*) That the proportions between the burden of direct and indirect taxation, have steadily altered to the advantage of indirect taxation,* and it would be unfair and inexpedient, by graduation, greatly to raise the contribution from the Income Tax.—(*b*) That the compensatory taxation of 1894, namely the imposition of heavier and graduated death duties, which is a tax on accumulated income, has more fairly equalised the taxation of the richer and poorer Income-Tax payers.

2. (*a*) That the Income Tax on its present basis is a great engine of finance, necessary in peace, and a powerful reserve in time of emergency, and no steps should be taken which could possibly interfere with its productiveness and efficiency.—(*b*) That the power of increasing the Income Tax on a sudden emergency would be largely discounted if it were already a graduated tax levied at a high rate.

3. That the simplicity of the tax, the facility of its levy, the ease with which it can be adapted to the requirements of the year, or of the time, is a proof that its present basis of levy is just, satisfactory, and popular.

4. (*a*) That, at present, the Income Tax is collected *at its*

* See note, p. 303.

source; and no return of the *whole* individual income has to be disclosed or given, unless it incidentally happens to be derived from one source only.*—(*b*) That a return of the whole income is only required in the case of those desiring to avail themselves of the advantage of the abatements.

5. (*a*) That, at present, two-thirds of the Income Tax is automatic and practically self-collecting, that is to say, by deduction from the income before it reaches the hands of the taxpayer.†—(*b*) That this is the case practically in regard to Schedules A, B, and C, as well as largely the case under Schedule D.‡

* Even here it does not follow that any return or disclosure is necessary. For instance, the income may be entirely derived from an investment, the Income Tax on which is paid before the dividends or interest reaches the holder. It is only in the case of a business or profession or office, from which the whole income of the individual is derived, that a return of the *whole* income is necessarily made.

† For instance, no uncommon case, a man may have an income of say £3000 a year, entirely derived from investments, the dividends of which are paid to him after the Income Tax has been deducted by the Companies or concerns in which his money is invested. Thus he himself makes no return of Income Tax, for he himself pays none directly; the State stops it at its source.

Or, again, a man in business makes a return of his profits (under Schedule D), and is assessed for Income Tax on them; but, in addition to this, he may, and probably has, money invested in other concerns or investments, which are not included in his return, and on which the Income Tax is stopped before the dividends reach him.

Thus in neither case does the man make a return of his individual income.

‡ The following are the Schedules under which the Income Tax was levied in 1900-1901.

	Gross Income.
Schedule (A)—Profits from the ownership of land and houses	£233,000,000
Schedule (B)—Profits from the occupation of lands, &c.	17,600,000
Schedule (C)—In respect of annuities, dividends, &c.	41,400,000
Schedule (D)—Profits from professions, trades, employments, railways, mines, iron-works, &c.	466,000,000
Schedule (E)—In respect of salaries, public offices, &c.	75,400,000
	£833,400,000

6. (*a*) That any attempt to graduate the tax would necessarily involve a radical change in the system of assessment, levy, and collection.—(*b*) That under a system of graduation, every individual would have to be required to declare the *whole* of his income from whatever source derived, and this in minute detail.—(*c*) That such inquisitorial proceedings would be repugnant to the public feeling; universal self-assessment would be much resented by the ordinary Englishman, and would render the Income Tax very unpopular.

7. (*a*) That universal self-assessment would open the door wide to evasion, whether dictated by fraud, ignorance, or negligence.*—(*b*) That the ordinary and natural inclination of the individual in returning his income, is to put it below, not above, its full amount, and to give himself the benefit of any doubt. And this would be still more the case if he considered himself unduly or unfairly taxed.

8. (*a*) That most wealthy persons spread their investments over all kinds of securities; and the wealthier the person, the more confirmed the habit. Each of these investments is taxed at its source, and the individual cannot escape the tax; while self-assessment would enable him largely to evade the tax.—(*b*) That, on the other hand, the large landowner, or the individual with one investment, which is not taxed before it reaches him, would continue to be taxed to the fullest extent, for evasion would not be possible.

9. (*a*) That the evasions, or attempted evasions, under Schedule D, are already considerable, and it would be a grave mistake to enlarge that possible area.—(*b*) That while

* Pitt's original Income Tax of 1799 was assessed on the *individual income*, and a return of income *from all sources* was required. The obligation of making a return of the whole income was very unpopular, and led to much evasion; and, in 1803, Addington, in reviving the Income Tax after the rupture, substituted *particular returns of income from particular sources* in lieu of a return of the whole individual income. This system still prevails.

the return of income received from a business or profession can be partially checked at Somerset House, and is open to correction, no such check would be possible in reference to the whole of a man's income.

10. That one of the chief reasons for the greater productiveness of the tax, is that in consequence of the supersession of private firms by Limited Liability Co. (which have to publish their accounts), the opportunity for evasion of the tax has been much diminished. This advantage and others, would disappear with graduation, for the Income Tax would cease to be collected from the Companies, and would have to be collected from the individuals.

11. That the higher the Income Tax and the heavier the graduation, the greater the temptation to fraud and evasion.

12. That thus, in every way the object of graduation would be defeated, the revenue would suffer, and the graduated tax would be less profitable than the simple poundage.

13. (*a*) That though the existing system of exemption and abatement may be said to contain the germ of graduation, they were not introduced with that purpose, and need not logically be carried any further.—(*b*) The exemption given on the Income Tax was given in order to cover all those incomes which are derived from manual labour, from wages as distinct from salary or earnings.—(*c*) That the abatements given under the Income Tax were introduced, not with a view to place an increased burden on the more wealthy, but as a relief to the poorer classes of Income-Tax payers, who suffer most from taxation, and they were so arranged as to render the burden less abrupt.—(*d*) The various steps in the system of exemption and abatement has relieved and eased the burden where it

galled the most; there is no reason to extend the system further.

14. That to graduate the Income Tax would be still further to accentuate its unfairness, as between incomes derived from earnings and those derived from invested capital.

15. That the attempts formerly made (in 1377, 1641, 1698, and partially, in 1798) to impose a form of graduated income or poll-tax were eminently unsuccessful in their results.

16. (*a*) (By some.) That the great ease with which the Income Tax is levied, and can be raised, tends adversely to National economy; and graduation, by increasing the yield, would accentuate this evil.—(*b*) That, as under graduation, a small minority would pay the greater share of the tax, the majority would be inclined still further to enter on extravagant expenditure, of which they would bear no adequate proportion; and to meet this expenditure they would be inclined still further to graduate taxation.

17. (By some.) That the system of abatement and of exemption (and especially of exemptions) has already been carried too far and has dangerously narrowed the basis of the tax, by restricting the number of persons liable for the tax or for their proper share of the tax.

18. That the case of Prussia (with its officialdom) and of Victoria (a tiny community), are not on all fours with the case of England.

[Some argue that the whole question of the incidence of the Income Tax should be the subject of enquiry, in order that its incidence and assessment and levy should be placed on a fairer basis.]

OLD AGE PENSIONS.

IT is proposed that a system of "Old Age Pensions" for the aged deserving poor should be instituted :—

There have, of late, been several inquiries into the question.* The first, the Royal Commission of 1893, was appointed to enquire "whether any alterations in the system of Poor Law relief are desirable in the case of persons whose destitution is occasioned by incapacity for work resulting from old age, or whether assistance could otherwise be afforded in those cases."

The Royal Commission did not, however, see their way to make any recommendation in favour of Old Age Pensions.

In 1896, a Committee was appointed "to consider any schemes that may be submitted to them for encouraging the industrial population, by State aid or otherwise, to make provision for old age; and to report whether they can recommend the adoption of any proposals of the kind, either based upon, or independent of, such schemes; with special regard, in the case of any proposals of which they may approve, to their cost and probable financial results to the Exchequer and local rates; their effect in promoting habits of thrift and self-reliance; their influence on the prosperity of the Friendly Societies; the possibility of securing the co-operation of these institutions in their practical working."

* See P. P., C. 7684, C. 8911, No. 296 of 1899, and 276 of 1903.

This Committee came reluctantly to the conclusion that none of the schemes submitted to them would attain the objects which the Government had in view; and they were themselves unable, after repeated attempts, to devise any proposals free from grave inherent disadvantages.

In 1898 a Parliamentary Committee was appointed to "consider and report upon the best means of improving the condition of the Aged Deserving Poor, and for providing for those of them who are helpless and infirm; and to enquire whether any of the Bills dealing with Old Age Pensions, and submitted to Parliament during the present Session, can with advantage be adopted, either with or without amendment."

This Committee made specific recommendations, alluded to further down.

In 1903, a Select Committee of the House of Commons was appointed to consider and report on a Bill drawn more or less on the lines of the recommendations of the Committee of 1898.

The different schemes of Old Age Pensions that have been from time to time proposed may be classified as follows :—

1. Schemes involving compulsory contribution towards a Pension fund, (i.) either by way of the German method of deduction by employers from wages paid by them, assisted by a contribution levied from the employers; or (ii.) by way of an annual, or a lump payment made by all young persons before a certain age, and accumulated at compound interest until the Pension age.

Practically no one now advocates "compulsion," so that this proposal need not be argued.

2. Schemes providing a universal grant of Pensions to all persons upon attaining a certain age, without requiring from

them any direct contribution, and without any examination into their merits or their needs.

This is Mr Charles Booth's scheme. Elaborated, the proposal was that every person, male or female, without regard either to merit or to thrift, should, on attaining the age of 65, be entitled to claim a pension of 5s. a week from public funds.

The estimated cost of this scheme was £24,500,000 a year, less two millions a year to be saved on Poor Law expenditure.

3. Schemes providing State aid towards Old Age Pensions for members of Friendly Societies only. Under some of these schemes members of Friendly Societies, as such, should, on arriving at a certain age, receive Pensions from the public funds. Under others the pensioners would receive part of their Pension from their Society, and the rest from public funds.

These proposals have dropped out of favour, as it is admitted that they would be very unequal in their operation; and that, in some way or other, they would necessitate interference with, and a guarantee of the solvency of, the Friendly Societies.

4. Schemes providing special facilities and encouragement to voluntary insurance against old age, with material assistance from the State.

The name of these schemes is Legion.

To these must now be added the specific proposal made by the House of Commons Committee in 1899, as follows:—

(i.) A Pension Authority to be appointed by the Poor

Law Guardians from their own number, to be established in each Union; (ii.) an independent Pension Authority to be established in each Union; (iii.) to consist partly of persons appointed by the Poor Law Guardians from among themselves, and to be partly representative of the public bodies within the area; (iv.) the amount of the Pension to be not less than 5s., or more than 7s. a week. The Pension to be for three years, when it may be either renewed or withdrawn; (v.) the qualification for a Pension to be—age 65; residence within the district; income not exceeding 10s. a week; recipient not previously a convicted criminal, nor received Poor Relief, other than medical relief, for twenty years past; has endeavoured to the best of his ability, by his industry or by the exercise of reasonable providence, to make provision for himself and those immediately dependent on him; (vi.) the cost of the Pensions to be borne by the Common Fund of the Union. A contribution from Imperial sources to be made to that fund in aid of the general cost of the Poor Law administration, such contribution to be allocated, not in proportion to the amount distributed in each Union in respect of Pensions, but on the basis of population, not to exceed one-half of the estimated cost of the Pensions.

The total immediate annual cost of this scheme is estimated at, for Great Britain, £10,000,000 sterling; rising to £15,000,000 a year in twenty years.*

The total expenditure on Poor Relief and its contingent expenses amount (for England and Scotland) to about £9,000,000 a year.

The total number of persons in the United Kingdom of 65 and over, in 1899, was estimated at 2,000,000. How many of these would be pensionable would depend on the terms and conditions of the Pension. The number estimated to be qualified

* See P. P., Cd. 67.

for Pensions under the proposals of the Parliamentary Committee is 655,000.*

The general principle of Old Age Pensions is supported on the grounds :—

1.—That whatever improvements have of late taken place in the condition of the working class, and of the aged poor, there are still a large and appalling number of the latter in a state of destitution or in receipt of Poor Law relief.

2. That, throughout the United Kingdom, no less than some 40,000 persons have no better provision for their old age than the workhouse or the scanty dole of outdoor relief; both coupled with the stigma of pauperism.

3. (*a*) That, in spite of the praiseworthy efforts of Friendly Societies and Trades' Unions, one out of every three of the whole population who reach the age of 65 become paupers.—(*b*) That, deducting the well-to-do classes, nearly one in two of the wage-earning class who attain the age of 65, become paupers.—(*c*) That in the case of the agricultural labourers, the unskilled workers, the lower wage-earners, two out of three of those over 65 receive, at some time or other, aid from the rates.

4. That the need for assistance is not limited to those who are actually receiving relief. There are many others who are kept off the rates by the assistance of relatives or friends, or by charity. These persons are as fully deserving, and more deserving, of assistance by way of pension; and assistance in their case would be more practically effective.

5. That pauperism rapidly increases with age.

6. (*a*) That there are large numbers of the working classes whose career has been industrious and deserving, but who find themselves, from no fault of their own, at the end

* The Committee of 1903 criticised some of the above proposals and their Report should be studied. P. P. 276 of 1903.

of a long life without means.—(*b*) That they have either to live on their relations, to starve on inadequate outdoor relief, or to seek the distasteful shelter of the workhouse.—(*c*) That as they have played their part in the industrial system, they have a claim in their old age to support under decent conditions, and without any taint of pauperism or loss of civil right.

7. (*a*) That a proper system of Old Age Pensions would not diminish, but would tend further to develop the habits of thrift and providence.—(*b*) That at present it is practically impossible for a working man to save enough to provide himself with an annuity for his old age; and *any* saving for old age is thereby discouraged.—(*c*) But if he could depend on his savings being supplemented by an adequate Old Age Pension, he would know that the more he could save the more comfortable he would be in his old age. He would have every inducement to save.

8. That, under existing conditions, there is no inducement to save, but a positive discouragement to saving, inasmuch as the working man is unable to receive poor relief so long as he possesses any savings unexpended.

9. That if a State Pension were assured at a certain age, it would give a great impetus to the provision, through Friendly Societies, Trades Unions, the Post-Office, &c., of small annuities to supplement the pension.

10. That, at present, while there is widespread saving, by subscription to Friendly Societies, Trades' Unions, &c., for sickness or "out-of-work," there is practically no saving for old age.

11. (*a*) That it is impossible for the Friendly Societies to carry out any large system of Old Age Pensions. The rate of contribution necessary to provide for this, as well as for sick pay, would be prohibitory.—(*b*) That, even now, Old Age Pensions being largely given in the form of con-

tinuous sick pay, have constituted a heavy drag on the funds of the Societies, and rendered many of them actuarially unsound.

12. (*a*) That even where Friendly Societies have instituted a separate old age provision, it has been seldom utilised.—(*b*) That the Post-Office Deferred Annuities are not popular.

13. That the contingency is too remote, the inducement to save too slight, to encourage saving for old age.

14. (*a*) That while wages are what they are, it is impossible for the working man to make any adequate provision for old age.—(*b*) That even where saving may have taken place, "out of work," sickness, accident, failure of a Society, &c., may absorb or destroy the savings.

15. (*a*) That whatever may be the case with the men, the women of the wage-earning class cannot save for old age. A vast number do not earn wages at all; where they do earn wages, the wages are on a low scale.—(*b*) That, on the average, women live longer than men, and therefore there are a larger proportion living after 65.

16. That though the totals of expenditure involved in any Old Age Pension scheme may appear formidable, the charge involved will be economical in the end.

17. (*a*) That the aged poor are already maintained in some form or another by the labour of those who are at work. —(*b*) That, therefore, their maintenance at the public charge would involve little, if any, increase in expense to the community as a whole. It would be merely the readjustment of an existing burden.

18. That the total sum required would be reached only by degrees; and the taxation of the country could be adapted accordingly.

19. That the introduction of a system of Old Age Pensions would greatly relieve the burden of the Poor Rate.

20. That the working classes have a healthy and satis-

factory distaste of "The House"; yet the necessity of taking advantage of the workhouse in old age, tends to diminish their dislike to Poor Relief.

21. That the rate of wages could not be affected by the grant of a pension at 65. The amount of effective labour involved is infinitesimal.

22. That sharper competition, higher wages, liability on employers under the Compensation Act, &c., are tending to squeeze out the elderly worker. The necessity for Old Age Pensions becomes more urgent every day.

23. That though the term "Pension" may be something of a misnomer, the proposal implies a natural right on the part of the recipient to relief in old age, in consideration of a life spent in work for the benefit of the community.

24. (*a*) That any system of contributory Pension would greatly increase the motive for thrift and saving.—(*b*) That such a system would encourage thrift, and not be in substitution of individual effort.

25. That Old Age Pensions schemes are in force, and work satisfactorily, in Germany, Denmark, New Zealand, and Victoria.

On the other hand, it is contended :—

1. That the term "Old Age Pension" is an entire misnomer. A "Pension" implies something of the nature of deferred pay for special services duly rendered. The proposals now made are essentially of the nature of Poor Law Relief. It is an eleemosynary grant resting on no foundation of natural right.

2. That any system of Old Age Pensions would produce greater evils than it would cure.

3. That nothing would do more to sap the robuster qualities of the English people than that the working-classes

should look to the State and not to their own exertions to support them in their old age.

4. (*a*) That there has, of late, been a remarkable development towards habits of thrift and providence among the working classes; and anything which tended to arrest these efforts would be disastrous.—(*b*) That there is some danger that those who are in a position to save money might be discouraged from saving, by the reflection that the more they had saved the less they would receive in the form of a pension.

5. (*a*) That any scheme of State-provided Old Age Pensions would distinctly tend to discourage thrift and providence.—(*b*) That all inducement to provide for the contingency of old age would disappear.

6. (*a*) That it is not true to say that the aged labourer has, in general, only the workhouse before him in which to end his days.—(*b*) The number of aged poor who seek public relief has much lessened in proportion to population in the last thirty years.—(*c*) That the aged poor who receive in-door relief are accommodated in the workhouse because of bodily or mental deficiencies; and would be there anyhow, pensions or no pensions.

7. (*a*) That a large number of the industrial population do already, by prudence, self-reliance, and self-denial, make their old age independent and respected.—(*b*) That it is in this direction, rather than in that of State aid, that we must look for the solution of the problems of old age poverty.

8. That, year by year, the financial and moral conditions of labour are improving, enabling more and more saving to take place.

9. That, by means of Benefit Societies, Trades' Unions, and in other ways, the working-classes have increasing opportunities of saving, of which they increasingly avail themselves.

10. (*a*) That most of the saving of the working-classes is done through Friendly and other Societies, managed by themselves, and wonderfully successful.—(*b*) That any action tending to discount the services of those Societies, and to diminish the inducement to utilise them, would be a misfortune.

11. (*a*) That the cost of any effective system of Old Age Pensions is prohibitive.—(*b*) That it would involve the State in an enormous and unknown liability which it cannot afford.

12. That the great increase which has taken place in national and local expenditure of late years, and the consequent increase in taxation and rating, has rendered it impossible to provide the funds requisite for any scheme of pensions.

13. That the relief in the burden of the Poor Rate would be very slight, compared to the great addition to the general cost, for the bulk of the aged at present receiving In-door Relief are cases of bodily or mental infirmity, requiring special care, and which, under any circumstances, would require asylum.

14. (*a*) That to impose on the State generally, and therefore on the industrial classes, a heavy charge that would benefit a portion only of those classes, would be unfair.—(*b*) That the enormous increase in taxation which would be involved, would seriously cripple trade and industry, and thus would react on the working-classes.—(*c*) That such taxation ultimately comes out of the wage fund, and the general result would leave the working-classes, as a whole, no better off than before.

15. (*a*) That the handling of the enormous sums involved is fraught with danger of maladministration and corruption. —(*b*) That it would lead to political corruption. There would be continual pressure on candidates to extend the range and the amount of the Pensions.—(*c*) That it would be neither fair nor expedient to leave to a locally-elected

body the duty of deciding upon the merits of large numbers of its constituents.

16. (*a*) That the administration of the fund would be a task of enormous difficulty.—(*b*) That it will be almost impossible—in view of the migratory habits of much of the population—justly to assess the share of liability to each district.—(*c*) That the difficulty of ascertaining the age, income, character, and past history of the applicants would be enormous; and would give rise to much fraud and abuse. —(*d*) That especially would this be the case in those parts of the country where there is a vast migratory or sea-faring population.—(*e*) That that which is comparatively easy in a small country could not be carried out here.*

17. That any attempt (and it would be necessary) to make a minute inquisitorial enquiry into the means and circumstances of the masses of the population, would be utterly repugnant to the English character.

18. That all this administration would necessitate a costly staff.

19. (*a*) That if the State provides the funds, it must administer; but the State cannot administer that which must be essentially a local matter.—(*b*) That if the fund be administered locally, and the State contributes towards it, there would, of necessity, be lax and varying administration. —(*c*) That there will be a manifest temptation on the part of the locality to throw as much as possible of the Poor Law Relief into the Pension Fund.

20. That the fund must be administered locally; and it can only be properly administered by the members of the Board of Guardians; the taint of pauperism will therefore extend to the Pension Fund.

* In Denmark, where there is a system of Old Age Pensions, the qualification of a fixed residence in the country of ten years is required. In New Zealand an annual enquiry is required into the means of the Pensioners.

21. That unless pensions were universal and received by every one—and such a system would be enormously extravagant and costly—the taint of pauperism must attach more or less to the Pension. It is not the *form* of relief but the *causes* which have led to it, that constitutes the disease or taint.

22. That, at whatever age the Pension line is drawn, it will work unequally. One man is hale and hearty at 65, and capable of working and of earning wages, and requires no Pension; another man has broken down long before 65 and requires a Pension before that age.

23. That the necessity of providing for old age is one factor which goes to fix the rate of wages. If the industrial classes are relieved of any such obligation, the rate of wages would tend to fall.

24. (*a*) That, as the recipient of a Pension could afford to take a wage below the current rate, a system of Old Age Pensions will have an adverse effect on the rate of wages.—(*b*) That thus, while the individual will be little better off than before, the wage-earners, as a whole, will be injured—(*c*) That to prohibit a pensioner from working, as far as he is able, would be economically wasteful, and humanely injurious.

25. That no scheme yet proposed is feasible or workable.

[Many believe that the best way of dealing with the question of the Aged Poor is to introduce improved and more humane methods of administration into the Poor Law relief.]

Special objection is taken to proposals which involve, as antecedent to the grant of a Pension, some contribution or certified saving on the part of the pensioner. On the ground:—

1. (*a*) That any system of contributory Pension would benefit

those only who could afford to make the required contribution; and would leave unaffected the great majority of the working-classes.—(*b*) That it would leave out of account those equally deserving whose (i.) rate of wages had been insufficient to enable them to save: (ii.) who had suffered from want of work, sickness, accident, &c.: (iii.) whose savings, through no fault of their own, had been lost: (iv.) who had saved or spent in other ways equally provident.

2. That such a scheme would necessarily be confined to the higher strata of the working classes: and that little benefit would therefore result to those most likely to become destitute in old age.

3. (*a*) That there is no particular virtue in saving by way of the purchase of an annuity. There are many other forms of provident investment—cottage, furniture, little business, &c.—which could not, however, be taken into account.—(*b*) That, indeed, in many cases, the most provident form of "saving" is expenditure on education, tools, starting the family in life, &c.—(*c*) That an annuity may be the worst form of saving, seeing that it ends with the life of the annuitant, and leaves his wife and children unprovided for.

4. That in the varying and various conditions of a workman's life, thrift will take many forms; and an attempt to prescribe a fixed form would be eminently injurious.

5. (*a*) That any contributory scheme, depending on membership of a Friendly or other Society, would necessarily involve the State with the supervision over, and the guarantee of the solvency of, these Societies.—(*b*) That such an interference would be much resented by the Societies, and would destroy the whole idea and system on which they are based.—(*c*) That it would involve the ruin of many of the Societies, which, while practically solvent, are not actuarially so.

6. That to make the pension dependent on a contribution would necessarily defer practical operations for many years. But few aged poor are at present in a position to produce the requisite sum.

THE IMMIGRATION OF UNDESIRABLE ALIENS

It is proposed to check the free flow of foreign poverty-stricken and low-class immigrants into the United Kingdom, by legislation directed against such Immigration.

It is not easy to arrive, with any accuracy, at the number of foreign immigrants that annually settle in this country; nor at the number of foreigners actually resident in the country. The Census returns of 1871, 1881, 1891, and 1901, show respectively a foreign population in the United Kingdom of 114,000, 136,000, 219,000, and 287,000. Of these 60,000 were living in London in 1881, a number that had risen to 135,000 in 1901; of whom 53,500 were Russians and Poles. Manchester comes next with 11,700 aliens.

But these figures only include those who return themselves as born out of Great Britain, and do not include the naturalised foreign element; while the figures are untrustworthy, inasmuch as the tendency, on the part of the foreign working-class element, would be to return themselves as British subjects.

There are no returns of foreign immigration on which any real estimate of the annual influx (apart from the outflow) of foreign immigration can be based. Under the Alien Act of William IV. (6 Will. 4, c. 11) it is the duty of the master of a vessel arriving from a foreign port, to make a return of the aliens brought over in his ship. This Act had, until 1890, become practically a dead letter. The Board of Trade have, however, of late years, practically revived it; and now issue monthly returns. These returns give the number of aliens arriving from the Continent at ports in the United Kingdom, dividing them into "aliens *en route* to America," and "aliens not stated to be *en route* to America," "but it is not thereby implied that the latter come to this country for settlement." These returns, which are not even professedly accurate or complete, show that in the twelve months ending December 1891, 98,400 aliens "*en route* to America," and 38,150 others "not stated to be *en route* to America," arrived in this country; total 136,550. In 1901 the respective figures were 79,100 and 70,000; total 149,700. In 1902 the figures were 118,500, 81,400, and 199,900 respectively.

Out of the aliens "not *en route*, etc.," who came to this country in 1900, 25,600 were Russians and Poles; of these 18,000 came to London.*

The total annual number of British and Irish emigrants in 1891 was about 250,000, the number of British and Irish immigrants about 100,000, a net emigration of British subjects of some 150,000. In 1900 the figures were—emigrants 146,000; immigrants 100,000; net emigration of British subjects about 50,000.

Legislative restriction on Foreign Immigration is supported on the grounds:—

1. (*a*) That the unrestricted influx of foreigners—whether actually destitute or no—is very injurious to the country;

* See Parliamentary Papers, Report of Select Committee, 1888-9, P. 305 of 1888 and 311 of 1889, and also 112 of 1887, 333 and 167 of 1891, 176 of 1901, C. 7222, and the monthly returns of aliens. See also Report of Royal Commission, which has been issued since the above was in type.

inasmuch as they overcrowd the labour market, displace English labour, and lower the wages and the standard of living of the British working man.—(*b*) That on arrival many of the aliens are in an impoverished and destitute condition, deficient in cleanliness and sanitary habits; and being subject to no medical examination on embarkation or arrival, are liable to introduce infectious diseases.—(*c*) That amongst them are a considerable number of criminals, anarchists, prostitutes, lunatics, idiots, and persons of bad character.

2. That the Census figures of "foreign residents" are totally fallacious, as representing the real foreign element in the country; a large proportion of the immigrants either have actually become, or return themselves as, British subjects, and yet to all intents and purposes remain aliens.* The alien does not assimilate or intermarry with the native rate.

3. (*a*) That the exact amount of immigration is not very material. The effect on the condition of our own work-people, both as regards localities and trades, is out of all proportion to the actual numbers of the immigrants.†—(*b*) That the foreign element is not spread over the country generally, and thus rendered innocuous by its relative insignificance. It is almost entirely congregated in the towns, and to a few special towns only.—(*c*) That in these special towns themselves, the foreign element is accumulated in particular districts, and thus produces great pressure in certain localities.‡—(*d*) That, moreover, the pressure is

* The bulk of the professed aliens live in Stepney—which harbours no less than 54,300 out of the 135,000 inhabiting London; and of these 42,000 are Russians or Poles. (Report, Royal Commission, 1903).

† The towns in which the foreign element chiefly congregate are London, Manchester, Liverpool, Leeds, and Hull.

‡ In 1861, in the Whitechapel district of London, the foreign element (according to the Census) formed 7·7 per cent. of the whole; in 1871 it had risen to 10·6; in 1881 to 13 per cent. (Report, Select Committee, p. vii.)

especially felt in certain trades — the shoemaking and tailoring trades,* the baking, cabinet-making, and hawking trades, &c.

4. (*a*) That the influx of foreign immigrants intending to settle in England, and especially in London, is ever increasing in volume; and the proportion of alien to native population has been for many years, and is, on the increase.—(*b*) That the position has been aggravated, on the one hand, by the increasing ease and cheapness of travelling; on the other, by the Continental persecution of the Jews and Socialists, and by the increasing burden and dislike of conscription. — (*c*) That each newcomer, by inviting his friends, and relations to come over, and by assisting them with passages, forms a nucleus for further immigration.

5. That each year the aggregate total is larger and the position is aggravated. Each year sees, in certain districts, especially in the East of London, new localities and fresh streets invaded by the foreigner and deserted by the English working classes.

6. (*a*) That England is already overcrowded; and yet emigration can be no relief to the congestion of population at home, if the place of those who emigrate is taken, or partly taken, by a foreign population.—(*b*) That the last state is worse than the first. Able-bodied British subjects, mostly with some little capital and enterprise, leave the country, and their places are taken by Continental poverty-stricken trash.

7. That the better class of immigrants arrive in transit only, and go on at once, or as soon as they have earned the

* It is estimated that in St George's-in-the East, no less than 80 per cent. of those engaged in the tailoring trade are foreigners (p. viii.). See also Mr Burnett's Report (P. P. 112 of 1887, p. 11) and Report of Sweating Committee. According to the Census returns of 1891 one third of the (unnaturalised) Russians and Poles in England were working as tailors and shoemakers.

passage money, to the United States. The worst class, the least efficient, the most destitute, the most criminal, remain behind. Thus we retain only the refuse of the Continental labour markets.

8. (*a*) That the immigrant, arriving destitute, ignorant of the language and the laws, accustomed to poor wages, long hours, and a low standard of living, is absolutely at the mercy of the "sweater," and is forced to accept such terms and conditions as the latter chooses to impose.—(*b*) That even when he has become a skilled worker he is willing to accept a low wage.—(*c*) That a few workers, willing and able to accept lower wages, and to work longer hours than those usually prevailing in a particular trade, soon lower the standard rate of wages and lengthen the hours of work.—(*d*) That the acceptance by the foreigner of a lower wage and worse conditions, seriously depreciates the value of labour in the home market.—(*e*) That the supply of foreign cheap labour is practically inexhaustible; a cloud ever hanging over and depressing the home labour market.

9. (*a*) That the influx of the foreign element makes difficult or impossible effective combination for the improvement of their condition among the workers in the trades especially affected. The aliens do not form, and will not join, Trades Unions.—(*b*) That, practically, the bulk of them never rise in the industrial scale, and are always at the mercy of the sweater.

10. That a reduction in the rate of wages means a diminution in the general standard of comfort and well-being of the working classes.

11. (*a*) That, not only do the aliens accept a rate of wages, work a length of hours, and labour under conditions to which no English workman ought to submit, and under which he could not with decency exist; but their habits,

their mode of living, their low ideal of life, constitute a moral and physical evil, and react injuriously on the well-being of the working classes.—(*b*) That it is useless to strive to improve the status of our own working classes so long as the free influx of cheap competing Continental labour is allowed.—(*c*) That their presence amongst us is the principal cause of the existence of the so-called "Sweating System," with all its appalling evils.

12. (*a*) That the "Housing" question is very much aggravated, especially in London, by the influx of these aliens, who overcrowd still more the congested areas, and drive out the English working men from the dwellings erected for their benefit.—(*b*) That we are providing housing for the unhoused population of the East of Europe, to the great detriment of our own population.

13. That it may be that the foreign immigrants do not actually, to any large extent, come on the rates themselves; but, by displacing home labour, and by reducing the rate of wages, they do that which is worse, pauperise British working men and make the poor still poorer.

14. (*a*) That, though the foreign immigrants have almost monopolised certain trades, these trades would still exist, and be carried on, under better conditions, if confined to Englishmen.—(*b*) That the inferior quality of the articles produced by cheap foreign labour tends to lower the general standard of production, and to discredit English workmanship and goods.—(*c*) That even the destruction of these special trades—and they would not disappear—would be a lesser evil than their continuance under present conditions.*

15. That the foreign immigrants add neither to the strength, wealth, nor welfare of the country; and, both on social and on economic grounds they should be excluded.

16. (*a*) That no racial or sectarian question is involved.

* See note, p. 337.

The immigrants are not objected to because they are foreigners, because they are Jew or Gentile, but purely on social and economic grounds.—(*b*) That, indeed, there is grave risk of an anti-Semitic crusade in England itself, if no restrictions are placed on the influx of foreign Jews.—(*c*) That the English Jews themselves try to discourage the influx of their compatriots.

17. That the question of the right of asylum to political refugees does not arise. The principle of the right of asylum is this: that those who seek the refuge of British shores, to escape prosecution for their political convictions, shall not be surrendered to the authorities of the country from which they have fled. This principle, applying to individuals, would be in no way invalidated by the general exclusion of undesirable aliens.

18. (*a*) That charity begins at home. We may deeply sympathise with those who, on account of their religious opinions, are persecuted abroad; but we must not allow our pity to get the better of our judgment, or to indulge in sentimental feelings at the expense of our own people.—(*b*) That we have our own serious social problems to solve, and we ought not to aggravate them by allowing other nations to shoot their rubbish on our shores.—(*c*) That our Australian Colonies have, and rightly so, excluded the Chinese, on the ground that socially and economically they are disadvantageous immigrants.

19. That the difficulties in the way of carrying out any excluding law are great, but not insuperable.

20. That the United States of America strictly carry out such a law,* and we could adapt it to our own peculiar conditions.

* By Acts of Congress of 1882 and 1891, it is provided that 50 cents per head be collected from the owner for every foreign immigrant brought over in his vessel, to constitute an "Immigration Fund" to defray the expenses of regulating immigration. Officers are appointed to examine

21. (*a*) That our insular position gives us exceptional advantages in dealing with the matter, without the necessity of re-introducing a system of passports.—(*b*) That, by our custom-house system, we can trace (and if necessary prevent) the entry of foreign goods of all descriptions; similarly, we could prevent the free influx of undesirable aliens.

22. That, already, we have an alien law, by which, under penalty for neglect or falsity of declaration, it is the duty of the master of a vessel, arriving from a foreign port, to hand to the Customs' officer a list of aliens on board his ship, containing the name, rank, and occupation of each. This law, if properly enforced, would constitute a valuable record of, and a check on, the immigration.

23. That seven-eighths of the immigrants come to four ports only—London, Hull, Grimsby, and Newhaven; and seven-eighths from Hamburg, Bremen, Rotterdam, and Libau.* The regulations affecting immigrants could be easily enforced at the four British ports by means of receiving places, &c.

into the condition of the passengers arriving, and if, on such examination, there shall be found among such passengers any convict, lunatic, idiot, or polygamist, persons suffering from disease, or contract labour, or any person unable to take care of himself or herself without becoming, or likely to become, a public charge, such persons shall not be permitted to land, and the expense of returning them is to be borne by the owners of the vessels in which they came.

In commenting on the Act of Congress of 1882 to our Minister at Washington, Mr Bayard, on behalf of the United States Government, states that "The economic and political conditions of the United States have always led the Government to favour immigration, and all persons seeking a new field of effort, and coming hither with a view to the improvement of their condition by the free exercise of their faculties, have been cordially received. The same conditions have caused other kinds of immigration to be regarded as undesirable, and led to the adoption by Congress of Laws to prevent the coming of paupers, contract labourers, criminals, and certain other enumerated classes. Such immigration the economic and political conditions of the United States render peculiarly unacceptable."—P. P. C. 5109, 1887, pp. 5-16. (See also Appendix 6 to Report of Select Committee on Foreign Immigration, 1888-9.)

* See P. P. 176 of 1901.

24. (*a*) That—as is proved in the case of the United States,*—the knowledge of the existence of laws directed against unsuitable immigrants would be sufficient, without any wide enforcement, to keep away the bulk of the unsuitable immigrants who are now enabled and encouraged to flock to our shores.—(*b*) That the steamship companies, and the charitable societies would cease to encourage immigration to England, and friends, already settled here, would eease to send tickets to friends to bring them over.

25. That if, as in the States, the responsibility and cost of returning unsuitable immigrants were cast on the steamship companies bringing them over, they would be much more careful in the class of passengers they accepted.

26. (*a*) That the question of "Free Trade" or "Protection" is altogether beside the mark. The question is not one of merchandise but of flesh and blood, not one of commodities but of the social condition of our own people.—(*b*) That the import of cheap foreign goods must be ultimately paid for by exports; that of cheap foreign labour simply displaces home labour.

27. That there would be no real loss on, or diminution of, the transit trade; the emigrant *en route* to America would not be affected by any immigration laws.

28. (*a*) That, as there is practically no British working-class emigration to the Continent, no reprisals would be possible.—(*b*) That, as there is no American emigration to England of the class that would be affected by the law, and as, moreover, the law would apply to foreign-speaking immigrants only, no reprisals on the parts of the States need be feared.—(*c*) That, as a matter of fact, both on the Continent and in the States, strict laws against the entry of unsuitable foreign immigrants already prevail.

* The annual number of immigrants debarred from landing, and returned from the States, now average about 4,570.

On the other hand, it is contended :—

1. That the question is one of very limited dimensions; the alleged evils are infinitesimal.

2. (*a*) That the dimensions of foreign immigration are grossly exaggerated; and, as compared to the population of English, the resident foreign element is most minute, and quite negligable.—(*b*) That the bulk of the immigrants do not intend to and do not settle in the country; but are either directly *en route* to the States or elsewhere, or are intending, and do, proceed there after a short stay in England.—(*c*) That, hence, the argued effects of the immigration on the social and economic condition of the British working man are illusory.

3. (*a*) That to carry out a policy of exclusion would be to adopt a peculiarly narrow and insular view of national interests.—(*b*) That the question should be discussed from a national not from a local point of view.

4. (*a*) That, as a matter of fact, the immigrants who remain are not, for the most part, "paupers," but bring some little capital or possessions with them.—(*b*) That very few of them come on the rates; they find at once work sufficient to support themselves.

5. (*a*) That, though they usually begin at the bottom, they are frugal and diligent, and gradually work themselves up in the industrial scale.—(*b*) That, while at first, they may be forced to accept a rate of wages and to work a length of hours out of proportion to the remuneration they receive, they soon improve their position, and insist on receiving a fair rate of wages.

6. That the actual competition of the immigrant with native labour is very slight. The foreigners have largely created special trades which in no way compete with the regular home trade. These special trades are unsuited to the native labour, and would not have existed

without the cheap labour and enterprise of the alien, and would disappear with their exclusion.*

7. That, in the trades especially affected, the consumer obtains the benefit arising from the cheapness of production, while the creation of these trades has stimulated other trades employing native labour.

8. That, thus, the foreign element does not constitute a burden on, but is rather a profit to the country.

9. (*a*) That, while it is true that the immigrants, for the most part, live on rough fare and are content with poor accommodation, they are quick at learning and industrious, are capable of very hard work, and are altogether efficient workmen.—(*b*) That they are, as a whole, moral, sober, thrifty, and inoffensive; and in these respects set a good example to their English brethren.

10. (*a*) That there are below the average criminal or "undesirable."—(*b*) That crime is best dealt with under the ordinary operations of the law.

11. That any insanitary conditions or social evils that may arise from overcrowding, &c., should be (and are being) met, not by excluding the foreigner, but by sanitary and factory laws.

12. (*a*) That the principle of free trade—namely, that labour (as well as goods) should be allowed free access to its best market wherever it may be—would be infringed, and the policy of protection would be introduced.—(*b*) That it would be the first step towards a policy of prohibition and protection.

13. That it would be an abrogation of that right of

* Value of "apparel and slops" exported from United Kingdom in 1887, £4,000,000, of which from London £2,500,000; "Boots and shoes," £1,750,000, of which from London £1,100,000.—First Report Select Committee of 1888-9, p. 249. In 1900 the total value of "apparel and slops" exported was £5,280,000, and of "boots and shoes" £1,960,000.—Statistical Abstract, 1901.

asylum to political and religious refugees, which England, alone among European nations, has always freely offered, and of which Englishmen are justly proud.

14. That the Jews, who constitute the bulk of the immigrants, are suffering (in Russia and elsewhere) under intolerable oppression, and it would be inhuman to refuse to give them asylum.

15. That racial and sectarian dislikes are at the bottom of the demand for legislation—it is an anti-Semitic crusade.

16. That, in former days at least—as the time of the Huguenots, for instance—the unrestricted influx of foreign immigrants was as beneficial to England, receiving, as it was injurious to the country expelling them.

17. That the profitable transit trade that now exists would be destroyed; the through immigrants, and they constitute the vast bulk of the immigration, would be deterred from passing through England.

18. (*a*) That, inasmuch as the emigration of British subjects to other countries exceeds the immigration of foreigners, England has more to lose than to gain by the application of the principle of restriction on the free circulation of labour.—(*b*) That any action taken would provoke retaliatory measures.

19. (*a*) That the conditions under which immigration into the United States is and can be restricted, are totally different from those that prevail in England.—(*b*) That, in the case of the States, the immigrants practically all arrive at two ports only, Boston and New York; are landed after a long sea voyage, and can, without difficulty, be temporarily detained and examined on landing.—(*c*) That in the case of England the immigrants enter at no less than twenty-seven ports. The very short sea voyage, and the necessarily brief interval at landing, would make it impossible to obtain adequate

information as to destination and condition, as to whether suitable, or unsuitable, as to whether in transit, tourists, travellers, or intended settlers.—(*d*) That any attempt, as in the States, temporarily to intern the immigrants at receiving places at the port of arrival, would constitute an intolerable restriction on the freedom of communication, and the ordinary passenger traffic. The game certainly would not be worth the candle.

20. (*a*) That the difficulty of distinguishing between suitable and unsuitable settlers would be insuperable.—(*b*) That no practical test of "suitability" exists. Simple destitution would not necessarily be a sign of unsuitability, if the immigrant were otherwise able-bodied and efficient; while the possession of certain means, in the case of a "weak" family for instance, would not render the immigrants really suitable.

21. That the United States exclusion laws are directed only against immigrants likely to become a public charge; exclusion is not based on the ground of poverty.*

22. (*a*) That our insular, yet easily accessible position, plus free trade, renders any proper check impossible.—(*b*) That, without the revival of a passport system—which the country, and rightly, would never stand—no real supervision, or distinction between immigrant and emigrant is possible.

23. (*a*) That it would not be practicable to insist that the steamship companies should take back the unsuitable immigrants they had brought.—(*b*) That, even if it were possible to return a cargo of unsuitable immigrants to the port from whence they had come, they probably would not be allowed to re-land; for, in the vast majority of instances they would not be citizens of the country to which the port belonged.—(*c*) That international complications would

* See note, p. 333.

speedily arise between England and the Northern seaboard Continental nations.

24. That the Select Committee of the House of Commons, appointed in 1888 to enquire into the question, came to the conclusion that the number of immigrants was not sufficiently large to create alarm, and reported that they were not prepared to recommend any immediate restrictive legislation.*

Since the above was in type, a Royal Commission, appointed to enquire into the question of Alien Immigration, has reported (Cd. 1741):—

The Commission suggest (1) That the immigration of certain classes of aliens should be subjected to State control and regulation. (2) The appointment of a Department of Immigration. (3) Improved methods of securing correct returns relating to aliens. (4) That the Immigration Department have the power to make, and to impose orders and regulations. (5) That their officers should have power to "make such enquiry as may be possible from the immigrants on their arrival, as to their character and condition." If the officer considers that any immigrant comes under the class of "undesirables," *i.e.* criminals, prostitutes, lunatics, bad characters, etc., or likely to become a charge upon public funds, he is to report the case to the Department, and it shall be their duty to act upon the information. (6) That immediate proceedings shall be taken before a Court of Summary Jurisdiction, pending which the immigrant may be placed in charge. (7) That any alien immigrant who within two years of his arrival "is ascertained, or is reasonably supposed," to be a criminal, a prostitute, a notoriously bad character, etc., or who shall become a charge upon public funds, or have no visible means of support, may be ordered (by a Court of Summary Jurisdiction) to leave the country; and the owner of the vessel who brought him over may be ordered to reconvey him back to the port of embarkation. (8) That when any immigrant is found, on arrival, to be suffering from an infectious or

* Report, p. xi.

loathsome disease or mental incapacity, or gives false information, the shipowner shall be compelled to convey him back to port of embarkation. (9) When an alien is convicted of any felony or misdemeanour, he may, as part of his sentence, be directed to leave the country. (10) That to prevent overcrowding, the Department may schedule an overcrowded area as a prohibited area for aliens. Notice of the prohibition shall be given to aliens on arrival. (11) That all aliens coming from, or arriving at certain ports, should be registered. On registration, if he has already decided on, or as soon as he has obtained a residence, the alien is to state where he intends to live. Any change of residence during the first two years to be notified.

ELEMENTARY EDUCATION

THE Education Acts of 1902 and 1903 * radically altered the basis on which the Elementary Education of England and Wales previously rested.

Under these Acts (1) the School Boards, originally created in 1870, ceased to exist, and (2) their places have been taken by the County Council in Counties (and in London), by the Borough Councils in County Boroughs and in Municipal Boroughs of over 10,000 inhabitants, and by the District Council in Urban Districts of over 20,000 inhabitants.

These Education Authorities are responsible for, and have the control of all secular instruction in all public elementary schools. The Education Authority has to establish an Education Committee, consisting, as to a majority of its members, of its own members; and as to the rest, of other persons whom the Council consider suitable. For the "provided schools" (*i.e.* the Board Schools), a body of managers are to be appointed, to work under the control of the Education Authority.†

* 2nd Edw. VII. chap. 42, and 3rd Edw. VII. chap. 24.

† In the case of London the Borough Councils are to appoint two-thirds, and the London County Council (the Education Authority) are to appoint only one-third of the local managers.

As regards the "non-provided schools" (*i.e.* the Voluntary Schools) they are managed by a body of managers, of whom four, the foundation managers, are appointed under the provisions of the trust-deed of the school, and the other two are appointed by the Local Authorities.

The Education Authority is bound to maintain and to keep efficient all public elementary schools within its area, and has the control of all the expenditure necessary for that purpose; and the whole educational grant voted from the taxes will pass through its hands.

The managers, in the case of the non-provided schools, are bound to keep the school-house in good repair (except wear and tear, due to the use of the rooms for educational purposes), and must make such alterations and improvements in the building as are required. The managers are to carry out any directions of the Local Education Authority as to the secular instruction to be given in the school, including any directions with respect to the number and educational qualificatious of the teachers to be employed for such instruction. But the managers have the right of appointment or dismissal of teachers, subject to the consent of the Educational Authority.

The educational grants from the taxes were increased, but any balance of the cost of the schools, whether provided, or non-provided, is to be made good out of the Rates.

In other words, practically the entire cost and maintenance of elementary education, of Board and Voluntary Schools alike, will in future be borne by the taxpayer or the ratepayer.

POPULAR CONTROL OF STATE-AIDED SCHOOLS

The passing of these Acts, and the provision in regard to the management of the non-provided ("voluntary") schools now maintained from the rates, has brought into greater prominence the question of the public control of State-aided schools.

On the one hand, it is contended—

1. (*a*) That taxation and representation should go together. Public money should not be given without public control, the spending authority should be the controlling authority.—(*b*) That if the denominational schools are to be entirely supported from public funds, they must be brought under direct and effective public control.—(*c*) That, otherwise, the ratepayer who has contributed to their support is deprived of one of the primary rights of citizenship.

2. (*a*) That when the voluntary schools were receiving aid solely from the taxes, they were under the direct control of the Education Department, as representing the taxpayer. —(*b*) That now that the Local Authority has taken the place of the Education Department, and now that denomina-

tional schools are to receive aid also from the rates, the control should be in the hands of the Body representing the ratepayers. It should have effective control; whereas it has been expressly excluded.

3. That when the promoters of the voluntary schools were making considerable sacrifice, by voluntary subscriptions, for the maintenance of these schools, they had a claim to retain the control. But voluntary subscriptions are no longer compulsory nor necessary.

4. That it was the cardinal basis of the Educational settlement of 1870, that whilst Imperial taxes might go to denominational schools, wherever the local rates went, there the religious instruction should be undenominational.

5. That to force a man to pay rates to a denominational school of which he disapproves, is a violation of conscience.

6. (*a*) That the provided and non-provided schools are not on the same footing. The Denominationalist who is compelled to contribute to the former, has a citizen's full share of the management and administration of the provided schools; the Nonconformist who is compelled to contribute to the non-provided schools, has little or no voice in their management.—(*b*) That if a man is not content with a school that is really national, he should provide the education he requires mainly at his own expense.

7. (*a*) That one of the chief grievances of the existing system of national education is, that the management of the voluntary school is, in the majority of cases, in the hands of one man, the clergyman of the Church of England.—(*b*) That this grievance is accentuated in the case of the 8000 parishes where but one school exists; and in which, therefore, there is no choice of schools for the parent.

8. (*a*) That the full control will still remain in the hands of the clergy, who will command the majority vote in all matters, secular as well as religious. The existence

of the so-called "representative managers" is but an irritating and deceptive fraud, giving an appearance of popular control without the reality.—(*b*) That the management will still be clerical. The clergyman will now be independent of subscribers, will himself be a manager, and will nominate the others.—(*c*) That these managers will select the teachers, and create the "atmosphere" of the school; and thus they will have the complete control of the school, secular as well as religious.

9. (*a*) That if control is to be effective, the representative element must, at least, be a majority.—(*b*) That to give the Local Authority two representatives out of six managers, is a travesty of representation.

10. (*a*) That the one-man management, though nominally modified by the introduction of the foundation managers, will, in the bulk of the cases, still continue. The foundation managers will be denominationalists, appointed by the clergyman, and under his influence and control.—(*b*) That more especially will this be the case where the principal Local Authority only nominates one manager, and the minor Local Authority nominates the other. There will thus be no homogeneity nor common interest between the two so-called representative managers.—(*c*) That even if there were homogeneity between them, they will be in a hopeless minority, totally unable to exercise control.—(*d*) That the foundation managers are on the spot; the representative managers will often be non-residents, and also responsible for several schools.

11. (*a*) That there is not the least reason nor likelihood why the two "representative" managers should be undenominational.—(*b*) That most of the County Councils, who have the appointments, are essentially Church of England.

12. (*a*) That, thus, the conscientious grievance of the Nonconformist, that his children are compulsorily obliged to

attend a school, of the religious teaching of which he disapproves, and in the control of which he has no voice, will be accentuated, and not diminished.—(*b*) That this grievance is especially acute in the thousands of parishes in which there is only one school, and that a denominational school.

13. (*a*) That the purely clerical manager, looking upon the school as his own, considers it an appanage of the Church of England; and the interests of the Church, rather than of education, are often paramount. The door into the school leads to the door into the Church. The State-endowed Church will now have a rate-endowed branch added.—(*b*) That the conscience clause is inoperative; and in many cases the school is used as a proselytizing agency.—(*c*) That simple creeds and Church catechisms are not now in question, but far-reaching doctrine and new and strange practices.

14. (*a*) That, as regards the teacher, a religious test practically exists. The ordinary rule in denominational schools is, that "no Nonconformist need apply."—(*b*) That the teacher is placed entirely at the mercy of the clerical manager.—(*c*) That the teachers are constantly selected for reasons other than their educational fitness. They are chosen rather for their willingness to do parish or personal duties than for their capacity to teach the children.

15. (*a*) That these evils will continue unabated, seeing that the managers retain the power of appointment and dismissal of the teachers.—(*b*) That the matter is aggravated by the specific exclusion of the head teacher from section 7 of the Act.*

16. That teachers in these schools, who will now practically become civil servants, should be free of all sectarian tests, and subject only to the Local Authority.

17. (*a*) That even if there is (as alleged) much exaggera-

* See note, p. 352.

tion in regard to all these matters, the suspicion of undue clerical influence exists, and can only be dispelled by the introduction of effective public management over denominational schools.

18. (*a*) That where the clergy had previously, and wisely, associated themselves with a body of Representative Managers, the process had worked well, and to the advantage of all.—(*b*) That public management would lead to greater educational efficiency. The lesser efficiency of the Voluntary School as compared to the Board School, is due largely to the want of a proper Managing Body on the former.

19. That there is no desire to deprive, nor intention of depriving, the Voluntary School of its distinctive denominational character. With proper popular control, the religious teaching would be left in accord with the Trust or Foundation deeds of the school; the control would be chiefly over the secular instruction.

20. That to show fear of representative management is a great sign of weakness on the part of the Church. The position of the Church would be strengthened, not weakened.

21. That with effective popular control, greater public and parental confidence in the schools would be engendered, and the popularity of education would be increased. Without it a dislike and resistance to education will be created.

On the other hand it is contended :—

1. (*a*) That the alleged grievance is imaginary; the State, through the Local Authority, will have full control over all public elementary schools.—(*b*) That, for the first time, purely representative bodies are made responsible for the secular instruction in the "Voluntary" schools;

and will have a voice in the religious instruction as well.

2. (*a*) That the whole system of school management provided by the Act must be taken into account, and of this the local management is only a fragment, and, from the point of view of secular instruction, the least important fragment. The dominant element is the popularly-elected Education Authority.—(*b*) That the managers will not have the independent management of the school; they will take their orders from, and be under the control of, the superior authority.

3. (*a*) That the Local (undenominational) Authority, as representing the ratepayers, has the full power of the purse; and the paymaster is necessarily master. It controls the expenditure, not only of the money provided by itself, but of all the money provided by the State as well.—(*b*) That the Education Authority has "the control of all secular instruction in public elementary schools throughout their area," and the managers are to "carry out any directions it may give as to the secular instruction given in the school."—(*c*) That this Authority can determine (so far as secular education is concerned) *what* is to be taught; *how* it is to be taught; *when* it is to be taught.—(*d*) That it can decide on the number of teachers, and on their salary. It can veto their appointment, and dismiss them or veto their dismissal.—(*e*) That it can insist on such structural alterations and improvements as it considers essential.

4. That, thus, for all educational purposes in which the public are interested, or for which they pay, there is ample and efficient public control.

5. (*a*) That the two representative managers will have far more influence than is indicated by their numerical position. They will have a powerful voice in the delibera-

tions, and a real control over the actions of the body of managers, inasmuch as they will have the Local Authority behind them.—(*b*) That the management of the school (apart from ultimate control) will no longer be in the hands of the clergy, inasmuch as a third of the managers will represent undenominational bodies; and of the remaining two-thirds, the majority will always be laymen.—(*c*) That, thus, in any case, the "one-man power," the undue clerical influence, that existed in some schools, and which caused suspicion, friction, and ill-feeling, has necessarily ceased to exist.

6. That as long as the Anglican Church is the Established Church of the country, the clergy are, at all events in some degree, responsible for the religion of their parishioners, and have some special claim to consideration in the matter.

7. (*a*) That the whole essence of a "Voluntary" School is that it should be under the control of those who have founded it, and who maintain it. Place the whole management in the hands of elected, or representative managers, and the school ceases to be a Voluntary School. Give full popular control, and the denominational character vanishes. —(*b*) That if the school is to continue as a denominational school, the denominational element must have a dominant voice in the appointment and dismissal of the teachers, especially of the head teacher.

8. That the alternative system would accentuate religious differences; and would import the religious question into the working of the school, with disastrous results.

9. (*a*) Without State-aid the voluntary system, in these days of essentially heavy educational expenditure, could not continue.—(*b*) That the bulk of the Voluntary Schools would rather cease to exist than come under complete public control.—(*c*) That thus their places would have to be taken by Board Schools at enormous expense; and to the great loss of educational competition, variety, and efficiency.

10. That the result would speedily be a system of secular education, disastrous both to religion and to education.

11. That what is really desired is to obtain public control over the religious part of the teaching; and to destroy the denominational character of the Voluntary Schools.

12. (*a*) That, in any case, any system of full public management applied to Roman Catholic schools would be entirely incompatible with the whole of their system of life, of custom and of education.—(*b*) That the difficulty could not be met by discriminative treatment. It would be intolerable that a distinction should be drawn between Roman Catholic and Church of England schools, to the disadvantage of the latter.

13. (*a*) That there is no real hardship on the Nonconformist parent.—(*b*) If they desire schools of their own, they can erect and maintain them themselves.—(*c*) That the children and the parents are completely protected against any religious injustice by the conscience clause.—(*d*) That as regards the secular teaching, no distinction is made between the children.

14. (*a*) That, in any case, there is no greater injustice or violation of conscience in compelling Nonconformists to contribute to the cost of denominational non-provided schools, than there is in compelling Denominationalists to contribute to the support of the non-denominational provided schools of which they disapprove.—(*b*) That the Denominationalist has not the citizen's full share in the control of the provided schools; his liberty of action is fundamentally restricted by the Cowper-Temple clause.*

15. That voluntary schools are the property of their respective Churches. The Denominations (apart from maintenance) have provided a capital sum, in the shape of buildings,

* Under which denominational teaching cannot be given in Provided (Board School) schools.

of some £20,000,000; and therefore, as the cost of denominational schools is still in part provided by the denominations, they have a claim to a full share in the management of the schools.

16. That "the religious test" grievance in regard to the appointment of teachers, will be greatly mitigated by the presence of the representative managers, and by the provisions of the Act itself.*

17. That the working-class element will be represented by working-men managers, and also through the representatives of the parents, who will be put on the management of many schools.

18. That it is an illogical position to have acquiesced in the payment of a large annual amount of taxes to the voluntary schools without demanding any public control, and now to insist on full control as an accompaniment of a small contribution for the rates.

* In "Non-provided elementary schools assistant teachers and pupil teachers may be appointed, if it is thought fit, without reference to religious creed and denomination; and in any case in which there are more candidates for the post of pupil teacher than there are places to be filled, the appointment shall be made by the Local Education Authority, and they shall determine the respective qualifications of the candidates, by examination or otherwise."—*Education Act* 1902, sec. 7 (4).

TARIFF CHANGES

THE question of fundamental Tariff Changes has suddenly sprung into prominence. The three questions that are most to the fore, are the re-adoption of Protection, the imposition of Retaliatory Duties, and the grant of Preferential Tariff advantages to the Colonies.

These three questions can be supported as a whole, or taken in twos, or advocated separately, according to the view taken by the particular person.

As the arguments for or against Protection are generally applicable to the other two questions, they are put first, and are supplemented, in the later sections, by further arguments especially applicable to Retaliation or to Preference.

The Tables in the Appendix, which have been compiled with some care, may be found useful. Other facts and figures can be found in the official returns, and in the "literature" (not always so accurate as could be wished) with which the country is inundated.

Fiscal Free Trade is founded on the principle of non-interference with producer and consumer, and on the complete freedom from taxation of all imports and exports. To the extent that taxation has to be imposed on imports, the necessary Customs tariff is imposed for revenue purposes only, and with no ulterior motives; and the necessary Customs and Excise duties are confined to a minimum number of articles, and levied on those articles alone which produce substantial sums. Further, whenever an article taxed is produced at home as well as imported from abroad, the Excise duty on the former is equivalent to the Customs duty on the latter. Thus the indirect taxation of a free trade country would neither prohibit, protect, advantage, discriminate, nor differentiate.*

It is proposed to subvert this principle, and to levy on certain foreign imports a heavy Customs duty, without any equivalent Excise duty. This with the object (i.) of either excluding foreign goods which compete in the home market with the home manufacturers or producers, or so to handicap these goods by heavy taxation that the home industry would be better able to compete with them; (ii.) of utilising the duties as a weapon against protective nations; (iii.) of enabling us by their means to give a preference to the import of Colonial produce.

* An account of the adoption of the principle of Free Trade and Fiscal Reform, and how it was carried out, will be found in *Finance and Politics* and in *Mr Gladstone as Chancellor of the Exchequer*.

PROTECTION

The advocates of the imposition of Protective import duties on foreign goods base their proposals on the grounds:—

1. (*a*) That the prophecies confidently made by Peel and Cobden, that if we adopted free trade the other nations would follow suit, and that trade would follow its natural course, have been totally falsified. No other nation has followed our example; all other nations are increasingly protective.—(*b*) That Great Britain alone has adopted free trade; and it is presumptuous to assume that we are necessarily in the right, and all other nations necessarily in the wrong.—(*c*) That whatever may have been the position fifty years ago, all the circumstances and conditions have so altered, that a reconsideration of our fiscal position has become essential.

2. (*a*) That at the time that free trade was adopted, England (then protectionist, and in consequence of protection) was in the van; was indeed the only great manufacturing nation. At first, therefore, free trade, combined with her natural, physical, material and commercial advantages, led to a great expansion of her trade.—(*b*) That the great revival of industry which followed free trade was due primarily to other causes which synchronised with the adoption of free trade; namely, improvements in machinery, the extension of railways, the invention of the telegraph, the greater production of gold, &c.—(*c*) That if it were true that commercial prosperity were primarily due to fiscal freedom, the trade of the other great nations would have remained undeveloped, instead of becoming more prosperous than ours.

3. (*a*) That free trade was intended to create a free interchange of all commodities between all nations, and this might have been beneficial. Such a result has not, however, ensued. We have not got "free trade," but only free imports. That is, we have opened our markets free to the world, and every one is at liberty to sell us what they like; whilst other countries have not in return opened their markets to us, and by their import duties they have hindered us from selling our goods to them.—(*b*) That while universal free trade might benefit the world, partial free trade injures the country which adopts it.

4. That while it is true, generally, that the prosperity of other nations is an advantage to us, it is not so when their prosperity is based on our decadence.

5. (*a*) That Germany and the United States have acquired their wealth, not in spite of, but in consequence of their system of protection.—(*b*) That it is clear, therefore, that it is protection that stimulates and strengthens, and free trade that enfeebles and injures, an industry.—(*c*) That clearly also protection tends to develop industrial methods, character, aptitude, economy, and industry.

6. (*a*) That protection encourages diversity of trades and occupations, prevents the weaker industries from going to the wall, and protects the stronger from unfair competition; while it enables the nation to take advantage of any new opening for trade.—(*b*) Then a great variety of occupations in a country minimises the loss and distress which is caused by trade depression, for all trades are not equally depressed at the same time.—(*c*) That free exchange tends to over-specialisation of industries; and any derangement of these specialised industries involves disaster to the country.

7. That a country (or Empire) should, as far as possible, be independent of other countries, both industrially and as regards its food supplies; and this can only be attained by

protection. Free trade tends to make the country more and more dependent on other countries for its necessities and its comforts.

8. (*a*) That one of the chief objects of the tariffs of protective countries is to make themselves as far as possible self-sufficient. This has been the result, and thus we are less and less able to find in civilised countries a market for our manufactured goods.—(*b*) That in consequence of their protective import duties, our trade to most of the chief protective countries has of late years shown a continual decline. It becomes increasingly difficult to dispose of our exports—necessary to pay for our imports—on advantageous terms, or on any terms at all.

9. (*a*) That until a few years ago, our commercial and industrial supremacy was unchallenged. It is now not only challenged, but has disappeared. Of late years, fostered by protection, Germany and the United States have been rapidly out-distancing and superseding England in commerce and trade.*—(*b*) That, thanks to protection, they not only succeed in keeping their home markets, but in increasing their exports; we neither guard our home markets nor increase our exports.*—(*c*) That we are no longer the workshop of the world. Nations which used to receive our goods are now our rivals, not only in neutral, but in our own markets. Instead of their buying manufactured goods of us, we buy of them.

10. (*a*) That while the export trade of the chief protectionist countries is on the up-grade, our export trade is on the down-grade.†—(*b*) That with the extension of the trade of the world our trade ought to have largely expanded, while at the best it has remained stationary.

11. (*a*) That our staple industries especially are waning.‡

* See *Retaliation*. † See Appendix III., Nos. 5 and 7.
‡ See Appendix III., No. 5.

(i.) Looking to the vastly increased world demand for Iron and Steel—for ships, railways, bridges, buildings, &c.—our steel and iron industries should be making rapid headway. But, on the contrary, the exports of these goods show an almost continuous decline, while the imports of these articles of foreign manufacture show a steady increase;* (ii.) That it is notorious that Public Bodies, Railway Companies, &c., are increasingly induced to obtain their electric plant, bridge work, rails, etc., from abroad, where they obtain them better and cheaper than at home; (iii.) That, as regards Textiles, here again the English trade does not obtain its share in the increasing consumption, while the chief falling off in export has been in the most highly-finished goods; (iv.) That the Silk trade has been almost entirely destroyed by the competition of foreign protected silks.*

12. That the highly protective America tariff has literally killed some of our trades—such as the tin-plate trade—which depended on the American market.

13. (*a*) That, thanks to free trade, the state of agriculture—still our largest industry—is disastrous to the country economically, morally, and physically.—(*b*) That our dependence on foreign food supplies would be a serious national danger in time of war.

14. (*a*) That the Home Trade is the really important trade, and any displacement of home products by foreign products constitutes a dead loss to the country, in profit and employment. — (*b*) That under our system of free imports, manufactured goods, which could be satisfactorily produced in England, are allowed to flood the home market, in constantly increasing quantities,† thus ousting our home industries, ruining our manufactures, and depriving the working-men of work and wages.‡—(*c*) That,

* See Appendix III., No. 5. † See Appendix III., Nos. 5 and 7.
‡ See *Retaliation*.

with very few exceptions (some "fancy" wares), all these imported goods could be produced, and equally well made, at home.—(*d*) That in many trades the import of semi-manufactured articles is superseding that of the raw material, and thus less employment and less profit ensues.

15. (*a*) That the occupation of the working-man is going, and with it his income.—(*b*) That not only is labour displaced, but the community has cast upon it the burden of the maintenance of the men thus thrown out of employment.—(*c*) That it would be better for the working-men (as well as for the community) to have to pay something more for his articles of consumption, and to receive compensation in increased wages and employment, and protection against the competition of cheap foreign labour.—(*d*) That wages in Germany have increased under protection, and in the United States are very high.*

16. (*a*) That, under free trade, one-fourth of the whole population are always on the verge of starvation; a number that is continually being recruited in consequence of the gradual disappearance of profitable industries.—(*b*) That if it be true that the physique of the population be deteriorated, it must be in consequence of free trade, under which the existing population has grown up.

17. That the greatest boon that could be conferred upon the working people of this country would be such a fiscal reform as would ensure to every industrious man full and constant employment at fair wages; and this can only be obtained under protection.

18. (*a*) That the displacement of British manufactured goods by foreign goods in the home market has made rapid and disquieting progress of late years.†—(*b*) That much of this is due to the "dumping" of goods below cost price,

* For the Wages question, see Cd. 1761, pp. 259-293, etc.

† See Section on *Retaliation*, and Appendix III., Nos. 5 and 7.

with which it is impossible for the home producer to compete.—(*c*) That, up to now, the United States manufacturer has been chiefly occupied in driving the foreign manufacturer out of the American market. This accomplished, he will be in a position, and intends to flood our unprotected market with his goods.

19. (*a*) That, on all hands, our industries are gradually and surely being undersold and destroyed; when once destroyed, they can never be revived.—(*b*) That under our policy of free trade, such industries as remain to us are impoverished, unprofitable, out of date, or are becoming extinguished.—(*c*) That, at the same time, no new trade or industry has been started or developed in England during the last twenty years; and no new inventions introduced.

20. That the state of trade competition makes it clear that protectionist nations can manufacture at a lower rate for exportation than a free trade nation.

21. (*a*) That commercial energy, enterprise, and invention must be founded on some likelihood of an extended market and an adequate return. The system of free trade discourages the investment of capital, destroys enterprise, prevents energy, checks invention, and offers no incentive to improvement.—(*b*) That the protected manufacturer can produce his goods at a cheaper rate than his free trade rival, and is therefore underselling him, not only in neutral, but in his home market; and not only in special articles, but in articles of every class.—(*c*) That it is not merely a few individuals who are crushed out, but whole trades are extinguished.

22. (*a*) That the cost of production, which formerly depended on the cost of the material, the cost of labour, and the working expenses, now depends, in most trades, chiefly on the quantity produced. The larger the out-put,

the cheaper the cost of production of the article produced.*—(*b*) That therefore cheapness depends on quantity, quantity depends on demand, and demand depends on the markets open to the producer. The protected manufacturer, with two markets at his disposal, can manufacture larger quantities at cheaper rates than his free trade competitor, who has only one available market.

23. (*a*) That a manufacturer, in a protected country, desiring to enlarge his business or to create a new industry, is assured of the home market against foreign competition, while he also has at his disposal the English market, free of any taxation. His English rival has no reasonable certainty or security of his own home market (which is open equally to his protected competitor), and he is excluded from, or handicapped in, the foreign market.—(*b*) That thus the protected manufacturer is able, first, by a large out-put, which reduces the cost of production, and secondly, by selling in his home market at non-competitive prices,† to dispose of the balance of his stock in the English market at a price at which his free trade competitor cannot make a profit.

24. (*a*) That thus the insecurity due to the existence of free trade fatally handicaps the home manufacturer, and necessarily destroys confidence and security, energy and enterprise.—(*b*) That protection, on the other hand, gives security, reduces the risks of manufacturing, en-

* *I.e.* an article manufactured by the hundred might cost 2d. apiece to produce; if manufactured by the hundred gross, it might be produced at a cost of only a halfpenny.

† This, it is also argued, is no hardship to his compatriot, the home consumer, who has to pay dear for the article in order that it may be sold cheaply abroad. If there were not the free trade market for the manufacturer to fall back upon for his surplus stock, he would not be able to produce the article so cheaply; the home consumer would therefore have, in any case, to pay as much, or even more than he does now for it, while less capital would be used and employment given in the country itself.

courages new industries and inventions, promotes enterprise, and evokes energy, and offers advantageous conditions to the producer which enable him to cheapen the cost of production.

25. That in consequence of the constant changes (usually for the worse) in the protective tariffs of other nations, and the unfair competition which cannot be anticipated due to "dumping," British trade has no stability nor certainty, but is subject to unforeseen and disastrous disturbances.

26. That it is a total fallacy to suppose that a manufacturer, driven by undue competition out of one trade, can turn his knowledge, industry, and capital into a new channel. On the contrary, the particular trade is destroyed, and with it the capital and the employment it gave, and there is nothing to take its place.*

27. That as regards our Colonies and Dependencies, we are losing our commercial connection and hold over them. Instead of trade following the flag, the flag is followed by foreign trade; we make the sacrifice, the foreigner reaps the benefit.†

28. That the only way to resist foreign competition is by Protection—there is no half-way house.

29. (*a*) That it is the duty of the State to foster and develop the prosperity of its citizens, commercially as well as otherwise.—(*b*) That it is the business of the State to find out which industries, either existing or nascent, are injured by foreign competition, and then to give them protection.—(*c*) That, under a system of reciprocity, only

* The particular case of Coventry is often instanced by the free trader as a case in which one industry (silk and ribbon) which gradually ceased to be profitably worked, has been superseded by another, the manufacture of bicycles. The Protectionist argues that the destruction of the one trade was not necessary to the growth of the other, and that there is no reason why *both* trades should not have flourished together, if the silk trade had been protected from foreign competition.

† See *Preference.*

those industries would be assisted which were indigenous to the soil, and which had shown that with fair treatment they could hold their own.

30. (*a*) That in consequence of our free trade policy, the manufacturer and producer are disappearing, and we are becoming simply a nation of middlemen and consumers. Such a state of things cannot last. We cannot continue to buy or to handle if we do not continue to produce and to sell.—(*b*) That, as regards the consumer, free trade means, in the end, not cheapness but dearness. The foreign protected producer may undersell at first (perhaps at even a loss to himself), with a view of killing his free trade rivals and monopolising the trade. This accomplished, prices are raised.—(*c*) That the welfare of the consumer is bound up with that of the producer; the purchasing power of the former depends entirely on the continuance of profitable industries at home. The disappearance of the producer would ruin the country. Most men are actual producers as well as consumers, while those alone who are consumers and not producers would suffer without compensating gain from protective duties; and such persons are of little value to the country.

31. That the import duties are only paid for by the consumer when there is no competing home industry; where such exists, the duty cannot be added to the price, but is paid by the foreign importer.*

32. (*a*) That if protection raised prices, and increased the cost of living (which is denied), profits, wages and salaries would be proportionately increased, for the country would be more prosperous.—(*b*) That with protection all round, all industries would be benefited alike.

33. (*a*) That a large revenue (paid by the foreign im-

* For instance, it is argued that the corn duty of 1902 did not raise the price of corn or of bread. But, see for this, Cd. 1761, pp. 124-126.

porter) could be derived for the taxation of foreign imported manufactures, now amounting to £100,000,000 a year; * and this sum could go to the relief of taxation elsewhere.—(*b*) That the protective duties would either diminish the imports of foreign goods, and so advantage the home industries; or if foreign goods still come in, the taxpayer would benefit by the revenue derived from them.

34. (*a*) That there would be no difficulty in drawing a clear distinction between the fully manufactured imports ready for immediate use, and the partly manufactured articles which are subsequently worked up here.—(*b*) That the former, as giving no employment to English capital and labour, should be subjected to the highest duty.—(*c*) That, even as regards the latter, as it would be better for the country that all the stages of manufacture should be done here, the partly manufactured articles should also be subjected to a duty.

35. (*a*) That while it is admitted that an excess of imports (the goods we buy) over exports (the goods we sell) is not unsatisfactory, the enormous and increasing discrepancy between them has increased alarmingly of late years.† The adverse balance is so large, and so increasingly large, that, making every allowance for shipping, profits, interest on investments, &c., it is clear that we are now selling less than we are buying, and that we must be living on our capital.—(*b*) That to the extent of our exports of coal (£27,000,000 in 1902) we are consuming our natural capital.—(*c*) That continued consumption of capital implies ultimate bankruptcy.

36. (*a*) That a great distinction should be drawn between competitive and non-competitive imports.—(*b*) That the first, and non-competitive, phase of imports, that of raw material, was wholly and universally beneficial. In the second phase, when some imports, those of foodstuffs, began to be com-

* See Appendix III., No. 4. † See Appendix, III. No. 2.

petitive, they were still mainly beneficial, by cheapening food, though, by depressing agriculture, partly destructive. In the third and most dangerous phase, competitive imports in the form of finished goods have become mainly destructive, and are only partly beneficial.

37. (*a*) That it is a delusion to suppose that the purchase of the goods of a particular nation must necessarily lead to a corresponding purchase by it of our goods. The trade returns show that there is no relation between the two.—(*b*) That in the case of the United States, the disproportion, and the increasing disproportion, between our purchases from her, and her sales to us, is so great that we must be rapidly becoming her debtor.*

38. That there need be no fear of retaliation on the part of the foreigner. Everything that could be done to cripple our export trade has already been done; while our imposition of protective duties could be used as a lever wherewith to obtain better terms from the foreign protective country.†

39. That a policy of taxation of manufactured goods is not inconsistent with a policy of free imports—namely, the free entry of food and raw material, neither of which (under Protection) it is proposed to tax.

40. That as our manufacturers are hampered by Factory Acts, Mines Acts, Merchant Shipping Acts, &c., burdened by heavy rates and taxes, &c., they cannot, without the help of partial protection, successfully compete with those of other nations; and as these restrictive laws have been imposed upon them by the legislature, they may fairly ask for compensating protective assistance.

41. That improved technical, commercial, or other educa-

* The value of our total exports to the United States in 1890 was £46,300,000; in 1901, £37,600,000; in 1902, £43,000,000. The imports from the States were £97,300 000 in 1890, £141,000,000 in 1901, and £127,000,000 in 1902.

† See *Retaliation*.

tion is no advantage to the community, if there are no trades left to learn nor to conduct: the question is economic, not educational.

On the other hand, the imposition of Protective Duties is opposed on the grounds :—

1. That protectionist England, fifty years ago, was in the last throes of industrial and agricultural depression. Trade was declining, profits dwindling, the people were in distress, pauperism and crime were increasing, discontent was rampant, the country was on the verge of bankruptcy.

2. That though, no doubt, invention, railways, gold discoveries, &c., stimulated our trade, it was the adoption of free trade which initiated our prosperity; and each successive repeal of import duties has been followed by a further expansion of commerce.

3. (*a*) That there are no signs of incipient decay in our industries, commerce, or shipping. No reason exists for resorting to drastic remedies. The trade of the country must be taken as a whole, and not merely inevitable fluctuations in particular industries. The British external trade of last year was the largest volume of trade ever transacted by any country in the world,—namely, £877,000,000, or £20, 18s. 5d. per head of the population.*—(*b*) That our export trade of manufactured goods is twice as great per head as that of Germany, and six times as great per head as that of the United States.†

4. That too much stress is laid on the question of our external trade, which probably represents not more than ten per cent. of the whole volume of our home trade. The home trade is in a flourishing condition.

5. That all returns, whether of income-tax, death duties, Savings Bank deposits, railway receipts, relative pauperism,

* See Appendix III., No. 2. † See Appendix III., No. 7.

&c., show a progressive increase in the wealth and prosperity of the country.*—(*c*) That the shipping trade of the country, both actually and relatively to that of other nations, shows an increase of tonnage and clearings.*—(*d*) That there is no diminution, but a continuous increase, in the imports of the raw materials of manufactures †—a proof that there is no falling off in the total amount of manufactures; and that the home consumption more than makes up for any slackening in the foreign demand.

6. (*a*) That, deplorable as is the poverty that still exists among us, the poverty in protectionist countries is far greater. We are, on the whole, the best fed, the best employed, and the most highly paid people in Europe.‡—(*b*) That the rate of wages is lower, the hours longer, and the conditions of labour worse in protectionist Germany than in free trade England.‡—(*c*) That in the United States, while wages are, on the whole, higher, the strain of work is greater, and the cost of living much higher.

7. That twenty years ago, when the last protectionist epidemic occurred, similar doleful apprehensions prevailed. Our trade, it was alleged, was going from bad to worse, and the excess of imports spelt speedy ruin. These predictions have been entirely falsified; trade, incomes, wages, have all expanded, and instead of living on our capital, we have been increasing it.§

8. (*a*) That while, no doubt, in aggregate value our foreign trade has not greatly progressed of late years, this is due to the great fall in prices all the world over, in the last thirty years.‖ Our out-put and consequent employment have largely and progressively increased; and if prices and profits have been lower, trade has been steadier and less fluctuating.

* See Appendix III., No. 1. † See Appendix III., No. 6.

‡ For the Food and Wages question, see especially Cd. 1761, pp. 209-258, and 259-293.

§ See Appendix III., No. 1. ‖ See Appendix III., No. 3.

9. (*a*) That whether the adoption of free trade was right or not, this country, highly organised and densely populated, has grown up under commercial and social conditions founded on a system of free imports, and any tampering with these conditions would be disastrous.—(*b*) That, desirable as was a free trade system fifty years ago, to-day it is essential. Not to have chosen the path of free trade fifty years ago would have been a pity; to abandon it to-day would be a calamity and a disaster.

10. That it was not to be expected that, as time went on, and other nations developed, we should be able to retain our relative commercial supremacy. Foreign production and international competition was bound to increase. But this competition is due to many causes other than fiscal. Our free trade system enabled us the longer to maintain the lead, and now best enables us to profit from the prosperity of other nations.

11. (*a*) That our two greatest commercial rivals, Germany and the United States, while in a sense protectionist, are largely free trade countries. They have partial protection applicable to comparatively small parts of their total industries, but the rule is free trade.—(*b*) That Germany, by its Zollverein, has established complete free trade among its 58,000,000 of inhabitants, while only a certain number of its industries are "protected."—(*c*) That the commercial prosperity of America is largely due to the fact that she has within her borders complete free trade. Her inter-State commerce to-day, among a community of 80,000,000 of people, is the largest trade carried on anywhere under conditions of absolute free trade; while, moreover, the protected industries do not employ more than a fraction of the occupied population.—(*d*) That it is this, and her great natural and commercial advantages,* which, in spite of her

* The area of the United States is as great as that of Europe proper. New York State alone has an area equal to that of the United Kingdom.

protective system, has made the United States so prosperous. The most fatally false fiscal system would do no more than delay her progress.

12. That the limits of a Kingdom are equally artificial with those of an internal State. If the principle of protection be advantageous, the United States and Germany would have each been more prosperous if they had enjoyed protection between the various States that go to make up their respective Zollvereins. But admittedly their internal free trade has been enormously to their economic advantage.

13. (*a*) That the commercial expansion of Germany and of the United States is mainly due to their system of scientific and technical education, to superior trade and economic methods, to adaptability, energy, and perseverance.—(*b*) That British manufacturers should "wake up." They are too much inclined to rest on the success of past years when international competition was far less, instead of adapting themselves, like their rivals in trade, to the requirements of the day and the needs of their customers.

14. (*a*) That protectionist countries complain greatly of our competition; are more afraid of us than we are of them, and endeavour to protect themselves still further against us.—(*b*) That, in spite of protection, we are able, thanks to our free trade, to send to protectionist countries in every instance, and in the aggregate, a far greater amount of manufactures than they send to us.

15. (*a*) That free trade is founded on the principle of non-interference with producer and consumer, taxation for revenue purposes only, and simplification of the tariff.—(*b*) That free trade, by allowing each country to produce that which it can most easily produce or manufacture, promotes division of labour and economy, in their best and most extended sense.—(*c*) That the fewer the obstacles in the way of trade, the better will it flourish; capital and labour,

if let alone and unfettered, will find out the most profitable fields for investment.—(*d*) That some industries can no doubt be fostered and developed by protection, but only at the expense of all other industries.

16. That Free Trade widens the circle of exchange; and the possibilities of economic advantage increases as it widens. Mutual wants are developed that can only be satisfied by exchange of goods. A "self-contained" country must forego many of the necessities and the comforts of life.

17. (*a*) That the extension of the area and sources of supply and of exchange are the best preventive to any far-reaching collapse of trade and industry.—(*b*) That, thanks to free trade, there are a greater variety of trades and industries in England than in any other country.

18. That free trade gives stability and certainty to a trade. Protective tariffs can be and are continually being altered, giving rise to disturbance and uncertainty.

19. That protection tends either to over-production or to the creation of a monopoly—both economically an evil.

20. (*a*) That free trade is in itself a good thing, even if rejected by other nations. Though, undoubtedly, the protective system adopted by other nations injures our international trade, it would be still more injured and curtailed if we also adopted a system of protective tariffs, and erected barriers at the other end of the bridge as well.—(*b*) That we admit the goods of other nations free, for our benefit, and not for theirs. The act of trading is a purely voluntary one, and would not take place if it did not suit both parties. Each side expects to make a profit; and if we make our profit, it cannot injure us if the other side also makes a profit.—(*c*) That the imposition of protective duties would seriously diminish the volume of the trade of the world; and we, more than any other nation, are interested in its expansion; the increasing wealth of other

nations is to our advantage. Our principal rivals are our best customers.—(*d*) That free trade enables us to purchase in the cheapest, and sell in the dearest market; and any restrictions must alter this for the worse.

21. (*a*) That the imposition by us of protective duties would reduce our imports—*i.e.* our purchases—and by the amount of that reduction would the power of other nations to take our exports—*i.e.* our sales—be diminished. If they cannot sell to us, they will not have the where-with-all to buy from us.—(*b*) That our introduction of protective duties would be met by the imposition of still higher duties abroad; and trade on both sides would be still further dislocated and diminished.

22. (*a*) That, under free trade, London has become the banking, the financial centre, and the clearing-house of the world.—(*b*) That a large trade of imports as well as exports has enormously developed the shipping and carrying trade, by enabling it to be conducted cheaply and profitably; the shipowner is certain of obtaining a return cargo. We have become the carriers of the world.—(*c*) That, owing to the system of free imports, Britain has become an important centre for the distribution of the produce of other countries, which she sells along with her own.

23. (*a*) That the tariff could, no doubt, be made to "protect" in the home markets. But it would not avail us in the neutral or protective markets. On the contrary, free trade, by enabling us to produce cheaply, enables us to compete better. Protection, by increasing the cost of production, and by raising all round the price at which goods could be profitably sold, would diminish our powers of competition, and therefore our trade in all foreign markets, whether protective or neutral.—(*b*) That the chief falling off in our exports is to the United States, consequent on its heavy Protective duties, and they have unquestionably injured

various branches of our trade. But the grant of protective duties to these industries would not help them to compete better in the American market.*

24. That if we have a difficulty now in maintaining our commercial position, we should maintain it with still greater difficulty if we threw further obstacles in the way of the extension of trade, or further handicapped our powers of competition. If we are badly off under free trade, we should be much worse off under protection.

25. (*a*) That protection does not create capital, nor trade, nor markets, nor add to the sum-total of production; all it can do is to displace and divert capital and labour from one industry to another.—(*b*) That it is a fallacy to suppose that there is an unlimited supply of labour, and especially of skilled labour, in the country, or that we can do everything at once.—(*c*) That, therefore, a new trade is not worth creating unless it is a more profitable trade than the one it displaces.

26. (*a*) That it would be impossible justly to decide which particular industry should be selected for protection; and pressure, wire-pulling, and corruption would be rampant.—(*b*) That, under protection, the general interest is left out of account. In the United States, the capitalists and protected manufacturers spend millions at the elections, dictate to a considerable extent the nomination of members of Congress, control its actions, own the great newspapers, purchase favourable legislation, and debauch the people.—(*c*) That free trade has done much to maintain a high standard and absolute purity in the British Government, House of Commons, and Civil Service.

27. (*a*) That only a limited number of trades and industries could possibly benefit from protection, nor, indeed, be protected. The great export trades in cotton, woollens,

* See *Retaliation*, and Appendix III., No. 13.

steel, iron, &c., would not be assisted by protection.—(*b*) That a vast number of home industries are unassailable by foreign competition, and do not therefore require to be protected.—(*c*) That the most that could be done would be to protect some home industries at the expense of all the other industries; for the cost of production of all industries would be increased.

28. That it would be impossible, however, to protect one branch of manufacture or industry without assisting all. Each has as good a claim to protection as another, and would not rest content to see others protected at its expense, whilst obtaining no advantage itself.

29. That though, at the moment of imposition, protective duties might benefit the particular manufacturer, the inevitable rise in the price of all commodities would soon make them worse off than before.

30. That the artificial fiscal assistance given to one class of the community would be given at the expense of all other classes. As the object of protection is to enable the particular home producer to obtain a higher price, the consumer would have to pay more for his purchases, inasmuch as the price of imported goods would be enhanced by the duty, and more than the duty; while the price of similar goods produced at home would be correspondingly raised.*

31. (*a*) That protective import duties are paid by the importing consumer, not by the exporting producer.†—(*b*) That the more the consumer has to pay for his goods, the less he has to spend on other things, and therefore the less the demand for commodities as a whole.

32. (*a*) That all the classes in the community dependent on non-competitive trades—building trade, railways, &c.—or receiving fixed incomes or salaries—professional men,

* See *Preference*, against, No. 35.

† See as to a corn duty Cd. 1761, pp. 124-126.

clerks, servants, employees, &c.—while suffering from the increased cost of living, could gain no corresponding benefit.—(b) That even if working-men obtained more employment (which is denied) and higher wages (which is also denied) in consequence of protection, they would be none the better off—the price of commodities would rise in a still greater ratio, and the purchasing power of their wages would be diminished.*

33. (a) That the most vigorous, healthy, and profitable trades do not require protection, and would be injured by it. State assistance (at the expense of the community and of other trades) would be chiefly invoked to bolster up the least efficient and worst equipped branches of trade; industries which would not naturally flourish, and the capital invested in which could be better employed in some other way.—(b) That trade that cannot maintain its existence without State assistance is not sufficiently advantageous to the country to be worth protecting.

34. (a) That a free market and open competition is stimulating, invigorating, and productive; while State protection is enervating and deteriorating.—(b) That in the old days of protection, it was the most protected trades, such as the silk trade and the woollen trade, &c., which suffered most from vicissitudes and from depression.—(c) That freedom of enterprise and cheapness of production has induced and enabled many of the trades most injured by protective duties to seek and to find better markets elsewhere.—(d) That some trades, the iron trade especially, are continually passing through natural crises owing to the replacement of old processes for new. These improvements and developments would be hampered and delayed under protection, and the British manufacturer would be less able to compete with his foreign rival.

* See *Preference*, against, Nos. 37-42.

35. (*a*) That protective duties, once imposed, could never be repealed; and, however moderate at first, would infallibly be increased. The industry, enervated by protection, would be less able to stand against foreign competition; and (as seen abroad) would be ever clamouring for, and receiving, greater protection at the expense of the community; while vested interests would be created, and grow stronger every year.—(*b*) That the producer would depend on Parliament for his profits rather than on his own industry.

36. (*a*) That in Germany protection has created Syndicates and Cartels, and has increased Socialism to an alarming extent. In America it has produced and fostered Trusts, Rings, and multi-millionaires.—(*b*) That Trusts, Syndicates, and Combines are only possible, on a large scale, when they are free from foreign competition. They flourish under protection and retaliation, not under free trade.—(*c*) That if the foreign competitors were withdrawn or reduced in consequence of protection, Rings and Trusts would be formed, which would force up the home price of articles used in manufacture or in shipbuilding, &c., greatly to the detriment of these industries, and to trade generally.

37. (*a*) That the excess in the value of our imports (the goods that we buy) over our exports (the goods that we sell), indexes our accumulated wealth and our profitable foreign trade.* It does not in any way show that our expenditure exceeds our income.†—(*b*) That the excess balance is due (i.) to the interest on our foreign investments, and (ii.) to the

* See Appendix III., No. 2, and Cd. 1761, p. 102.

† A sample imaginary case will illustrate the point. Woollen goods to the value of £1000 are exported to the Argentina, and appear as £1000 in the export tables. The freight (paid to an English shipowner) is, say, £50, and the goods are sold in Buenos Ayres at a profit of £100. With the £1150 he has thus received, the merchant buys £1150 of wheat, and brings it to England. The freight is, say, £60, and this is added to the value of the wheat when declared an importation here. Thus, declared exports, £1000, declared imports, £1210, excess of imports, £210, and this on a transaction that is clearly advantageous to this country.

profits on our trading, shipping, insurance, etc.*—(*c*) That trade is in essence merely barter, the exchange of goods against goods; imports are paid for by exports. Money is merely a go-between; a useful common denominator, but goods are not paid for in gold.—(*d*) That our exports are the sacrifice we make (the goods we give), the imports the rewards (the goods) we receive; and on balance there is a large gain; unless this were so, we should be impoverished instead of being enriched by our foreign trade. That the greater the amount of exchange, the greater the gain. It is the *volume* of trade, not specially the amount of the exports, that is the true test of trade prosperity.

38. (*a*) That clearly we are not living on our capital. The whole income-tax returns, and the estimated income derived from foreign investments, prove that both our home and foreign investments are increasing, and not diminishing.†—(*b*) That the export of coal is no more the export of capital than is the export of articles which consume coal in their manufacture. Further, coal is of no value unless worked and sold; operations which imply employment, conveyance, handling, and which increase the wealth and capital of the country.

39. (*a*) That the practical difficulties in the way of imposing protective duties are very great; such imposition would be fiscally, financially, and commercially inexpedient.—(*b*) That the imposition of manifold protective duties would necessitate a complicated and elaborated tariff, which would involve great expense and loss of time, harassing fiscal regulations, and impediments to trade, in declaration, examination, and handling of goods; would involve an army of officials and custom-house officers, and would lead to the recrudescence of smuggling.

* See Appendix III., No. 1. In Cd. 1761, pp. 101-103, (i.) is officially estimated at 60 to 70 millions, and (ii.) at 90 millions.

† See Appendix III., No. 1.

40. (*a*) That it is not proposed, for purely protective purposes, to levy a duty on *Articles of Food* (including articles of consumption already highly taxed, like tea, tobacco, sugar, wines, spirits, etc.), amounting in all to £230,000,000.—(*b*) That it is generally agreed that the *Raw Material of Manufacture*, amounting to £180,000,000, must not be subjected to a duty; for such a tax would greatly injure our own manufacturers.—(*c*) That these two items (taking the total imports at £530,000,000) make up four-fifths of the whole imports.*

41. (*a*) That the balance of about £120,000,000 consists of *Manufactured* articles and *Semi-manufactured* articles. But these last, amounting to £30,000,000, are the raw material of finished manufacture, which it would be inexpedient to tax. Thus is left a total trade in "manufactured" articles of some £90,000,000 at the most against which protective duties might be levied.—(*b*) That much of this total consists, however, of "fancy goods," which do not really compete with home industries,† or which would only be bought if of foreign make. Of the balance, few articles are of such a character, or imported to such an amount, as would either repay the imposition of a duty, or give protection.‡ (*c*) That, further, much of the so-called "manufactured articles" really constitute the raw material for divers home industries; and its importation enables the British manufacturer to produce

* See Appendix III., No. 4.

† Such as china, artificial flowers, pigments, marbles, toys, drugs, musical instruments, embroidery, pictures, &c. Taxation on these or similar articles would only bring in a few thousand pounds to the Exchequer.

‡ The only finished manufactures imported to any substantial amount are as follows:—Silk goods, thirteen millions; woollen goods, nine millions; iron and steel goods (including machinery), nine millions; cotton goods, four and three-quarter millions; glass, three millions and a half; gloves, one and three-quarter millions; and lace, two millions. Considerably under fifty millions sterling in all. Of these, moreover, silk, gloves, and lace are foreign specialities. See Appendix III., No. 4.

at a cheaper rate, and therefore to compete better abroad. No real dividing line can be drawn between the raw material and the finished manufacture.* The finished article of one branch of trade forms the raw material of another, and gives rise to the further employment of capital and labour.

42. That the ramifications of trade are so diverse and complicated, that the protective taxation of a particular article, at a particular stage, while possibly benefiting (by protection) one branch of trade, might, and probably would, seriously injure another, and even more important branch of trade.

43. That it would be madness to reverse our whole commercial and fiscal system, and to disorganise our external trade of between £800,000,000 and £900,000,000 for the sake of attempting to tax, at the most, some £50,000,000 of foreign manufactures.

44. That it is a fallacy to suppose that, with protection, the home manufacturer, instead of the foreigner, would supply the demand for the manufactured goods, now imported, and that by that amount the home trade would be increased. As the price of all manufactured articles would be raised, less goods would be consumed at home; while as less goods would be bought from the foreigner, by that much his demand for our goods would be reduced, and our export trade would be diminished. Moreover, a large portion of the manufactured imports are articles of luxury or fancy make, such as could not be made in England, or if of English make would not be bought.

45. (*a*) That our imposition of protective duties on foreign goods would lead to retaliation on their part; they could injure us much more than we could injure them;

* "What is raw material? Take the iron industry for instance. Pig iron is raw material to the bloom-makers. Blooms, again, are raw material to the bar-rollers, and bars, again, are raw material to sheet-rollers and wire-drawers; and, again, wire is raw material to the screw-makers, etc."

while the mutual retaliation would seriously affect the volume of trade.—(*b*) That our exports of manufactured goods on which protective duties could be placed vastly exceed the imports of manufactured goods against which we could impose protective duties. Thus our powers of attack, as compared to the power of retaliation, are out of all proportion, making it practically impossible for us successfully to retaliate on foreign countries.*—(*c*) That, with the single exception of France, we export to every protectionist country a greater amount of manufactured goods than we import from them.

46. (*a*) That protective duties, as a means of raising revenue, are hurtful and unsatisfactory. The cost to the consumer of the whole supply of the article taxed, whether home, colonial, or foreign, is raised by the amount of the tax, while revenue is received only from that portion of the article which is imported from abroad.†—(*b*) That so far as the system of protective duties was effective, we should get neither goods nor revenue; both tax-payer and consumer would lose.

47. That it is perfectly compatible with real free trade to impose import duties for revenue purposes only—(i.) By levying import duties on certain articles not produced at home, and therefore not competing with home produce or manufactures; (ii.) by levying a custom duty equal to the excise duty imposed on articles of domestic production, or *vice versâ*.

48. (By some.) That the present system of partial free trade is, on the whole, beneficial to England, especially in regard to the United States of America. If America were not handicapped by her protective system, she would constitute a most formidable commercial rival to England

* See *Retaliation*, against, Nos. 10, 14, and 15.
† See *Preference*, against, No. 35.

"RETALIATION"

It is proposed that we reassert our right, in carrying out fiscal arrangements, or in negotiating Commercial Treaties with other nations, to impose on the import of their goods "retaliatory" duties, if they on their part—

(i.) Penalise the imports of Colonial produce because the Colonies, or a particular Colony, has granted to the Mother country, or has received from her, preferential treatment.

(ii.) Will not give reciprocal or "fair" treatment to the goods we export to them.

And (iii.) that such retaliatory action should be more especially directed against the import of foreign goods that are "dumped" here, *i.e.* that are imported and sold here at a price below the commercial cost of production.

The retaliatory duties would be maintained until the foreign protective country agreed to our terms, when they would be relinquished, and only held in reserve.

The arguments already given in favour of Protection for the most part apply equally to the question of Retaliation.

But the proposal is also upheld on the grounds :—

1. (*a*) That free trade means the unrestricted interchange of commodities at their natural price.—(*b*) That this principle

is entirely abrogated as regards our exports to protective countries, in consequence of the hostile, protective, or prohibitory duties that they levy against our goods.—(c) That the position has become generally worse, especially in the last twenty years. Tariff walls have shut out our competition in protectionist countries, while free imports facilitate the sale of their goods in this country.

2. (a) That the form which protection has taken has sensibly altered during recent years. Foreign countries no longer restrict their activity to the protection of their own market. They give a kind of protection which assumes an offensive shape, and which leads to the invasion of the markets of other countries by their highly-protected produce.—(b) That, sheltered by the constantly-increasing tariffs, there have grown up in Europe and America huge trade combinations, or huge trusts, which not only monopolise the home market of their own country, but which stimulates the production of vast quantities of goods which the home market cannot absorb, and which are sold at very low rates, in some cases below the cost price, in the markets of other countries.—(c) That these transactions are rendered possible by bounties, subsidies, relief from taxation, low charges on freights, &c., given sometimes by the Government itself, sometimes by trading associations.—(d) That the foreign producer, having the monopoly of the protected market, as well as free access to the English market here, is able to produce on a large scale, and to keep his machinery running full time, and thus to produce at a low price.*—(e) That thus, in all these ways, the foreign producer is able to export goods to this country at a price with which it is hopeless for the home producer to attempt to compete.

3. (a) That, besides this, there is the unfair and illegitimate competition of the foreign sweated industries, against

* See *Protection*, for, Nos. 22 and 23.

which the British manufacturer and the British workman should be protected.—(b) That the British workman is protected against insanitary conditions and against sweating, by Factory Acts; and, by the operation of Trade Unions, the "Fair Wages' Clause,"* &c., enjoys good wages and short hours. This very protection tends to destroy British industries, unless it is supplemented by protection against underpaid industry abroad.

4. (a) That in all these instances there should be retaliation, either by prohibition or by means of retaliatory import duties, to counteract the illegitimate advantages enjoyed by the foreign producer and importer; and sufficient to place the British producer and exporter on a fair competitive footing. —(b) That each particular case must be judged by its merits, and a decision come to as to how far, by means of cheap labour, by actually maintaining a high price in the home market, by bounties, subsidies, or trade combinations, &c., the articles in question can be brought over here and sold at a price below the fair cost of production. The retaliatory tariff would be based on these considerations.

5. That, more especially, should retaliation be directed against the Syndicates, Trusts, Cartels, and Combines that have sprung up so rapidly of late years, and which are becoming increasingly formidable, by artificially and unduly inflating or depressing prices, and by dislocating and disorganising the course of trade.†

* See Appendix II.

† For instance, "The syndicate of rail manufacturers sells rails in Germany at 115 marks the ton and at 85 marks abroad; sheet iron is sold at 125 marks a ton in the home market and at 100 marks a ton on the foreign market; the Union of Nail Manufacturers sells its products at 250 marks a ton in Germany and at 140 marks a ton abroad. The absurdity of the system in respect of the home market was very well shown last year during the period of the so-called 'coal famine,' when the price of pit coal in Germany rose to 18·50 marks the ton, while it was being at the same moment exported to Austria at 8·80 marks a ton."—*Lord Lansdowne, quoting Dr Raffalovich*, H. of L., 15th June 1903.

6. (*a*) That we are entitled to demand reciprocity, *i.e.* equal treatment on both sides, and this can only be obtained by means of retaliation.—(*b*) That "Retaliation" in no way implies "Protection." Reciprocity is the keystone to free trade, and without it the latter cannot exist. The object of retaliation is to extend the freedom of trade and of commerce, by forcing other nations to adopt the principle, or at least to move in that direction.

7. (*a*) That the way to encourage freedom of trade is to discourage high tariffs. This can only be done by negotiation, and negotiation can only be effective if both sides have something to give and something to withhold. Without liberty to negotiate, and something to negotiate with, a good bargain cannot be made.—(*b*) That the weapon of retaliation is necessary in order to bring protectionist nations to their senses, and to force them to come to terms.—(*c*) That England, in the process of adopting free trade, has gradually stripped herself of the fiscal weapons by which alone the war of tariffs can be fought. These she must resume, and place at the disposal of the Government, in order to retain freedom of negotiation, which means freedom of trade.

8. (*a*) That it is idle to expect other nations to modify their policy, or adopt the principle of low duties, unless we retain in our hands the power, by retaliation, of forcing them to adopt it, at least as regards our goods.—(*b*) That, if they refused to come to terms, we should be able to continue to tax or prohibit their goods so long as they taxed or penalised ours.

9. (*a*) That though nominally we enjoy "most-favoured-nation treatment," as a matter of fact, in consequence of our being unable to negotiate on equal terms, the heaviest duties are imposed on the goods imported from us, the lightest duties are on the goods principally imported from other protective (and retaliatory) countries.—(*b*) That this is more

especially the case in regard to the more highly refined or finished goods, which are the really profitable part of manufacturing.

10. (*a*) That the imposition of reciprocal duties would give us a leverage whereby we should be enabled to negotiate fair Commercial Treaties with other countries; be saved from their hostile interference or caprice; be less dependent on them for our supplies of goods and food; and, in the long run, we should be buying in the cheapest market and selling in the dearest.

11. (*a*) That, being as we are the one open market of the world, we are the one "dumping" ground of the world; our isolated free trade position greatly aggravates the situation. — (*b*) That, thus, our one-side fiscal system greatly handicaps our produce and manufactures, and renders fair competition wholly impossible, both in the home as well as in foreign and neutral markets.

12. (*a*) That, British trade and commerce, which, if given a fair field, is perfectly able to hold its own, is gradually being ruined by illegitimate competition.—(*b*) That this is more especially the case in regard to the oldest and most important trades—the textile trade, and the iron and steel trades—which are not only suffering in the matter of exports, but which are severely hit by the foreign competitive imports.*—(*c*) That "dumping" is especially prevalent in the case of the iron and steel trades.*

13. (*a*) That the chief object of "dumping" is to capture the British market by ruining the British producer. Once captured, the prices would be put up to monopoly level.—(*b*) That, therefore, while the consumer, or some producers, may for the time being gain from "dumping," by being able to buy their commodities artificially cheap, the result in the end, when the competition is destroyed, will be that they will

* See Appendix, No. III., Nos. 5 and 7.

have to pay inflated prices.—(*c*) That any present gain to one home industry, due to "dumping," is more than counterbalanced by loss and ruin to other home trades. And by the time the "dumping" has served its purpose and prices are again put up, the latter trades will have disappeared, while the former trade, over-dependent on artificially cheap material will find itself crippled.

14. That it is not an advantage that one particular home industry, or one section of the community, should benefit at the expense of others; or that the workers in one trade should work short time, in order that the workers in another should earn higher wages.

15. That as the object of retaliation is to obtain a reduction in the protective duties, and fairer terms of competition, a temporary loss (in consequence of the imposition of retaliatory duties) to a trade or to the consumer (even if it occurred) would be more than offset by the future advantages to trade. In such a matter as this, we may fairly do temporary damage for permanent gain.

16. (*a*) That no war of tariffs or reprisals need be feared. Ours is the "biggest revolver," and the foreign nations would "come down" if we made it clear that we should not hesitate to shoot.—(*b*) That the protective duties of other countries are already so high that they could not well be increased. The war of tariffs exists, but at present it is all on one side.

17. (*a*) That if the Executive were entrusted with a general power to retaliate where it was thought necessary, or to negotiate on reciprocal terms, no action on their part would probably be necessary; the power and the threat would be sufficient to ensure success.—(*b*) That even if it came to a war of tariffs, we, possessing the largest trade, and being in the strongest financial position, would come off victors.

18. (*a*) That, already, the first step in retaliation has been taken, and taken successfully, in regard to sugar. Our mere threat to prohibit bounty-fed sugar was sufficient to bring about a general International agreement to abolish the bounties.—(*b*) That the principle can easily be extended to coal, iron, textiles, and any other of our productions where unfairly treated.

19. (*a*) That if action became necessary, it would not be difficult to decide what foreign import should be penalised, and in what way, and how far this should be done, in order to bring the foreign nation to its senses, and to place the British competitor on equal terms.—(*b*) That the particular home competitive industry would be benefited while the protection lasted; and would be permanently placed in a satisfactory position when retaliation ceased, in consequence of the protective country agreeing to our terms.

20. (*a*) That the United States are the greatest offenders, and we could easily retaliate on her by heavily taxing her imports, which amount to £127,000,000 a year, while our imports to her only amount to £43,000,000 a year.—(*b*) That, moreover, our exports to the States consist largely of articles of the nature of luxuries, which are so heavily taxed that the duties could not easily be increased; or, even if they were, the demand would not be much affected.

21. That, as regards Germany, our greatest trade rival, we import £34,000,000 from her, and export £33,000,000 to her. She is therefore as vulnerable as we are.

22. (*a*) That more especially must we retain in our hands the power of retaliation against any foreign nation that seeks to prevent the free exercise of the right of a British self-governing Colony to enter into closer trade relations with the mother country. The fiscal relations between the mother country and the Colonies must be absolutely protected from

foreign interference, direct or indirect.*—(*b*) That we cannot allow our Colonies to be treated by foreign nations as separate entities, and not as integral parts of the Empire, simply because we have given them self-government and fiscal freedom.

23. (*a*) That unless we come effectually to the rescue of the Colonies, and assert ourselves, there is an end to all hope of closer fiscal union within the Empire.—(*b*) That, under present conditions, we are in the humiliating position of being absolutely helpless to protect Canada or the other Colonies from hostile or discriminating attack.—(*c*) That the German Government has penalised Canada's imports, on the avowed ground of the preference she has given to goods from the United Kingdom. In spite of repeated expostulations, the German Government have maintained their hostile reprisals, and also threaten further discrimination, not only against Canada, but against every other Colony that follows her example, and even against Great Britain herself if she accepts these advantages to the detriment of German trade.

The arguments already given against Protection mostly apply also to the question of Retaliation. But the imposition of Retaliatory duties is also opposed on the grounds:—

1. (*a*) That trade is not warfare, for which retaliating "weapons" are required. Mutual trade is an advantage, not an evil. It is a benefit to obtain goods as well as to sell them; and indeed, in the long run, the one cannot be done without the other.—(*b*) That greatly to our own

* See *Preference.*

advantage, England has been, till now, the peaceful mart for all goods from all the world. By entering into a war of tariffs we should become a hostile and disturbing factor in international trade.

2. (*a*) That the imposition of Retaliatory duties would result, not in greater freedom of trade and of commerce, but in greater restrictions all round. Experience shows that retaliation does not lead to agreement and reduction of duties, but to further retaliation; not to the breaking down of tariff walls, but to the erection on both sides of still more insuperable barriers to trade.—(*b*) That, indeed, as the object of protective duties is to protect, and as the object of bounties, &c., is to foster trade, it is highly improbable that other nations would give way to our demands; and certainly not without a severe fiscal struggle, and a disastrous war of tariffs.—(*c*) That the competition that the foreign producer most fears is that of British goods, and retaliation is more likely to be answered by prohibition than by reduction of duties.

3. That we, being the greatest trading nation, and the greatest exporting nation, stand to lose most from any further restrictions on trade and dislocation of commerce.*

4. (*a*) That, though we are a free trade nation, and therefore have no "weapon" of offence for use in our commercial negotiations, we nevertheless enjoy the "most-favoured-nation treatment" in every country (*i.e.* any fiscal benefit or relaxation given to another country is granted also to us). In no case (with the exception of Portugal and Haiti) are products worse treated, and in some cases we enjoy considerably better treatment than other nations who negotiate Commercial Treaties by means of threats

* See Appendix III., No. 7.

and retaliation. Our valuable custom and our open mart are our best "weapons."—(*b*) That the benefits we thus derive would be lost if we discriminated between country and country, or between goods and goods; and especially if we plunged into a war of retaliatory tariffs.

5. (*a*) That to base our tariff on, and to vary it according to, the conditions under which production takes place abroad would be pure protection.—(*b*) That Retaliation is simply Protection in disguise; and, whatever the ultimate object, it would inevitably and rapidly lead to a system of protection all round.

6. (*a*) That even if originally imposed for the somewhat harmless purpose of negotiation, the retaliating duties would soon be looked on, and become purely protective.—(*b*) That experience conclusively proves that a protective duty, under whatever guise, once imposed, becomes subsequently difficult or impossible of relinquishment.

7. (*a*) That the object of a retaliatory duty is to protect a particular industry from a particular form of competition, legitimate or illegitimate, by placing heavy or prohibitive duties on the foreign article of import. No one trade has a greater claim to protection than another, and nearly every industry could show "unfair" treatment also in its own case, and would be equally justified in claiming reciprocal protection.—(*b*) That, as the protection of one trade leads directly or indirectly to the disadvantage or injury of others, each industry could claim some compensating assistance or protection.—(*c*) That, thus, protection under the name of retaliation imposed in one case, would inevitably lead to a claim for protection in all cases.

8. That under free trade the fiscal interests of the various industries do not conflict. But retaliation would benefit one industry, and injure another, and by giving rise to conflict-

ing claims for assistance, would lead to sharp and direct antagonism and conflict between trade and trade.

9. (*a*) That it would be absolutely impossible for any Government, or any Department, to work out the equity of a particular reciprocal duty; to say which industry was especially entitled to receive protection, and in what way; and to decide to what extent it was unfairly treated, and in what way and to what extent it should be protected.—(*b*) That none of the factors which go to make up the alleged "illegitimate advantage" can be reduced to figures, and so be accurately countervailed. The adverse effect of trusts, of cheap labour, of indirect bounties or subsidies cannot be estimated; nor the advantage obtained by the competing producer from protection.

10. (*a*) That in most cases, the retaliatory duties could not be effectively applied against the import of goods similar to those of the industry that was suffering most from protective duties. Retaliation would have to be carried out by the taxation of a foreign import of a different nature to the home trade that it was desired to protect.*—(*b*) That, thus, for the time being, so long as the retaliatory duties remained in force, the particular trade for whose benefit they were imposed, would receive no benefit, and indeed might suffer from further retaliation; while another industry altogether, that was not suffering from undue foreign competition

* For instance, Russia, the most protective nation, heavily taxes our imports, especially our manufactures. But we import practically no manufactures from her. Thus Retaliation on Russia must take the form of taxation of food-stuffs or raw material, for there are no manufactures to penalise. Similarly, the United States, only second to Russia in the severity of its protection tariff, hits our woollen manufactures very hard, but we import no woollen stuffs from America, and so some other American industry, other than the woollen industry, must be singled out for attack. This would have to be food-stuffs, or raw materials, for we import only a small amount of manufactured articles from the United States. See Appendix III., No. 13.

(or it could itself have claimed to have retaliatory duties imposed), would be protected and subsidised.—(*c*) That, if the retaliatory policy were unsuccessful, this trade (that required no assistance) would continue to benefit, while the other trade (that required assistance) would continue to suffer.—(*d*) That if the policy were successful, and the retaliatory duties thereupon relinquished, the latter trade would at last benefit; but the former, by losing its protection, would now itself be injured.

11. (*a*) That the industries that, in the long run, would suffer most, if the policy of retaliation were successful, would be just those which had been picked out for experimental protection. The imposition of heavy import duties would protect the particular home trade, and by so doing, would foster an increased output at home.—(*b*) That sooner or later, the retaliatory policy would be successful in inducing the foreign nation to come to terms, and to reduce her duties. The retaliatory duty must then be taken off, and the foreign goods are again freely imported, in competition with the home industry. The artificial inflation in prices and production in the home industries, created and stimulated by the retaliatory-protective duties, would disappear; the industry would be adversely affected, and capital and labour would suffer. It cannot be a sound fiscal policy to foster or to create by the imposition of a duty, only to destroy when the duty, having played its part, has to be repealed.

12. That the probable alternative would be that the powerful vested interest that would spring up under the retaliatory duties, would be strong enough to resist their abolition. The policy of retaliation would have therefore failed to lower the foreign duties, and would have saddled us with protective duties of our own.

13. That it is not sufficient to assert that the mere threat

of retaliation would bring a particular protective nation to its senses. If we threaten, we must be prepared to act, and the method of action must be thought out beforehand.

14. (*a*) That we are not in a position to retaliate without injuring ourselves more than we should injure the foreigner. In every case—and especially from the most protective nations—our exports of manufactured goods, which are most hit by the tariff, are greatly in excess of the imports to us of their manufactured goods on which we could retaliate.—(*b*) That the United States injures us most in the matter of protective duties and of "dumping"; yet, except by taxing the food of our own people, or the raw materials of industry, we are powerless to retaliate on her.*

15. That Retaliation (equally with "Preference") would inevitably lead to a tax on food. By the taxation of food-stuffs alone (the taxation of raw materials being barred) could successful retaliatory pressure be brought to bear on the more protective nations.†

16. That retaliation on our part would diminish and not increase the export of our goods to protective countries; for retaliation would be met by the imposition of higher duties on our goods.

17. (*a*) That while the Customs difficulties in the way of carrying out a system of protection are great, the difficulties of carrying out a retaliatory policy are far greater, for it would necessitate discrimination between countries as well as between goods.—(*b*) That universal examinations of all imports, with the attendant evils of cost, friction, and delay, would be necessitated. Moreover, certificates of origin would be essential; and certificates of origin are vexatious, open to

* *Vide ante*, p. 390, and Appendix III., No. 13.

† See Appendix III., No. 13.

great abuse and easy evasion.—(c) That selective taxation is moreover impracticable, for there is no criterion by which Customs officers could decide on importation whether goods were going to be "dumped" or not. The declared value of the goods might be satisfactory, and yet the goods might be ultimately sold below cost. The goods cannot be followed into the market.

18. That there is a great exaggeration in regard to the amount of "dumping." How little the iron trade, the alleged chief sufferer, has been really injured by dumping, is shown by the figures of trade, and by the gross income assessed to income-tax under the head of ironworks.*

19. That much of the underselling by foreign goods is due to the very prosperity of our own industries of late years. The English manufacturer, working to his full capacity, either cannot take further urgent orders, or will not quote a low price, and the goods are obtained from abroad.

20. That "dumping" can only be a temporary matter and due to temporary causes, such as miscalculation, over-production, or compulsory sale under commercial pressure. No producer can afford indefinitely to continue to sell at a loss.

21. (a) That while there may be cases of goods sold here at unduly low prices, the vast bulk of the imported goods, which compete with home production, are produced legitimately and sold at a fair profit. To tax such goods would be pure protection to the British producer.—(b) That retaliation would be directed against the free import of the

* The profits (as assessed to income-tax) of the iron trade were £3,000,000 in 1898-99, £3,211,000 in 1899-1900, and £5,380,000, in 1900-1. Between 1896 and 1900 the value of steel and iron manufactures imported from Germany was £891,000; our total similar exports during the same period were £49,000,000.

best and cheapest goods—for if not cheap and good they would not find a market here—to the disadvantage of the consumer, and of the manufacturer who largely utilises such goods.

22. That it cannot be to our disadvantage to be able to buy cheaply, or at even below cost price. We benefit entirely at the expense of the foreigner.

23. (*a*) That goods are "dumped" elsewhere than in England, and the foreign producer, who is thus enabled to buy cheap, would be advantaged in his competition with the English producer if the latter were prevented from buying cheaply also.—(*b*) That if "dumping" is prevented here, the goods would be diverted to the neutral or Colonial markets, increasing the present severity of the competition in those markets.

24. That any system of preference, retaliation, or protection that checked foreign imports, and competition in raw materials, would be far more disastrous than any possible "dumping."

25. That the Colonies are strongly protectionist, and also "dump" goods here as well as foreign nations. If foreign protection and cheap goods are an injury, Colonial protection and cheap goods equally injure us, and would equally necessitate retaliation.

26. (*a*) That in any case the consumer benefits from the low price at which he can buy.—(*b*) That, in most cases, these cheap goods form the basis of some further process, and the fact of being able to buy them cheap, enables the British manufacturer to sell cheaper to the consumer, and to compete better with his foreign rival.*—(*c*) That what the

* For instance, Spanish iron ore is imported into England in English ships. It is worked into iron bars here. These are sold at a fair price to Germany, and are made by them into steel forgings. The steel forgings are

maker of semi-manufactured goods loses from "dumping," the maker of finished goods gains, and the community as a whole benefits, for the manufacture of finished goods gives the most profitable employment.

27. (*a*) That Trusts, Rings, Combines, Syndicates, &c., are best dealt with by the operation of the unrestricted competition which goes with free trade. Any limitation of free interchange would assist the operations of existing foreign Trusts, &c., and would encourage their creation here. Tariffs breed Trusts.—(*b*) That the German syndicates, &c., constitute a greater evil to their own home industries, by artificial interference on the operations of trade, than they do to the British competitor, and great complaints are made against them in Germany.

28. (*a*) That it might be conceivably necessary to take action against another country, or against the action of Trusts or Combines, if commercial treatment were meted out to us, that was specifically hostile and unfair. But, before resorting to retaliation, it should be shown that there was no other way of achieving the desired result, that commercial reprisals would be effective, and that they would not injure us more than our adversary.—(*b*) That a new fiscal policy should not be inaugurated in order to deal with an emergency that may seldom, perhaps never occur; and which, if it did occur, could and should be dealt with by special legislation.—(*c*) That the case of the sugar bounties forms a precedent for exceptional treatment when a particular case arises.

29. (*a*) That it is not necessary to arm the Executive

sent to England, again in English ships, and sold here at a low price, much lower than the price prevailing in the German market; and they are then used in building ships, etc. The consequence is that the ships can be built at a much cheaper rate here than in Germany, which enables us to retain the supremacy in our shipping trade.

with any fresh fiscal powers. Under the existing state of things, the Government can, if they wish, at any time, ask Parliament for power to deal, by way of retaliation or otherwise, with any special fiscal question that may arise.—(*b*) That the only alternative to this, is to give the Executive Government a general power to impose retaliatory duties on their own initiative, and without asking the assent of Parliament. Such a power, arbitrarily to interfere with any trade at any time, would be a dangerous power to place in the hands of any Government.

30. That if the Government possessed a general power of imposing retaliatory duties at their will, the Executive would be perpetually exposed to undue pressure or corrupt influences on the part of different trades.

31. (*a*) That the question of the fiscal treatment of the self-governing Colonies does not really arise in connection with Retaliatory duties.—(*b*) That the British Government has already declared that the self-governing Colonies are fiscal units, with entire fiscal independence; and this absolute fiscal freedom the Colonies desire to retain. If they are treated as fiscal units in one matter, they must be treated as fiscal units in all matters.—(*c*) That, as the exports from foreign countries to the Colonies consist mainly of manufactured articles, while Colonial exports to them consist almost exclusively of articles of food, it is recognised that, if discrimination did take place, "the Colonies have an effective remedy in their own hands." *

* Report of Colonial Conference, 1902, p. 38.

COLONIAL PREFERENCE

IT is proposed that fiscal arrangements should be negotiated within the Empire which would give a material commercial advantage to all its parts. Under this scheme, the Colonies and Dependencies would give preferential advantages to the Mother country, in the nature of lower duties on the import of the goods of Great Britain over those charged on the goods of other countries; while, reciprocally, the Mother country would admit Colonial produce free, or at a lower rate than that charged on competing Foreign imports, either already taxed, or to be taxed if the scheme came into operation.

This proposal is supported on the grounds :—

1. That Imperial Federation can only be founded on a system of fiscal union. Imperial unity involves commercial solidarity. Political Union is no use without commercial ties.

2. (*a*) That if the different portions of the Empire are not to drift apart, they must be knit together more closely by commercial ties. The realisation or abandonment of the idea of Imperial Federation is involved.—(*b*) That "a system of preferential tariffs is the only system by which this Empire can be kept together." * In other words, "No Preference, no Empire."

* Mr Chamberlain at Constitutional Club, 26th June 1903.

3. (*a*) That the Empire can alone rest upon community of interest, and community of sacrifice.—(*b*) That the Colonies, both in respect of the assistance they gave us in the South African war, and in the desire they have evinced to contribute to the naval and war expenditure of the Empire, have shown a practical loyalty, which we should reciprocate.—(*c*) That the Colonies strongly desire a preferential fiscal system, and it is worth some sacrifice on our part (if sacrifice is involved) to bring about this consummation.

4. (*a*) That the Colonies are anxious to meet us in the matter. Canada is prepared to give further preferential advantages to our goods; Australia and New Zealand have declared that they will place our imports in a better position than foreign imports; the Cape has already granted a preliminary preference.—(*b*) That it will be deeply disappointing and discouraging to the Colonies if we decline to meet their advances.

5. That especially will they feel resentment, if we leave them open to the retaliatory attacks of protectionist countries, because they grant advantages to British goods.*

6. That it would be the refusal to meet the laudable desire of the Colonies, not its acceptance, that would lead to friction and ill-feeling.

7. (*a*) That it depends on us whether the preferential advantages already given or promised by the Colonies shall be developed in the future, or withdrawn as non-acceptable to those whom it was sought to benefit.—(*b*) That if the opportunity of fiscal union be neglected, it may never recur; the Colonies, if repelled by the Mother country, must seek commercial reciprocity elsewhere.—(*c*) That, already, in the case of Canada, it is a question of a reciprocal commercial treaty with us, or with the United States. If we can offer Canada

* See *Retaliation*.

no advantages, and she is forced to negotiate with the States, she will gradually drift away from us and towards America.

8. (*a*) That, as regards India, there would be no practical difficulty in giving her preferential advantages (for instance on tea) without interfering with her free trade system.—(*b*) That similarly, in the case of the Crown Colonies, some advantage could be given to each of them.

9. That the arrangement would not lead to any interference with the political independence or fiscal freedom of the Colonies. Each part of the Empire would still retain its entire fiscal freedom, subject only to a voluntary arrangement for the mutual benefit.

10. (*a*) That the scheme involves no real question of free trade or protection. The question is Imperial and Colonial more than fiscal or financial.—(*b*) That the justice and expediency of a policy must be judged by the needs of the day, not by the musty formulas of fifty years ago.

11. That Preference is not Protection. While Tariffs restrain the field of commerce, Preference enlarges it.

12. (*a*) That in the case of Germany, the introduction of the Zollverein system (*i.e.* fiscal freedom within the Empire) has politically and commercially knit together its various parts in a strong bond.—(*b*) That the fiscal freedom which exists between the States that make up the United States of America has been of enormous advantage to the trade of that country.

13. (*a*) That complete free trade is not as yet feasible between the different parts of the British Empire. But preference is the first necessary step towards free trade within and throughout the Empire, and the greatest commercial prosperity

of the future is for the nation with the largest free trade area. —(*b*) That if the British Empire were knit together by fiscal ties, she would have a great industrial and political future before her; otherwise she must remain a conglomerate of isolated economic units.

14. (*a*) That British trade is becoming ever more and more dependent on inter-Empire trade. Foreign protective nations are increasingly building up their tariff walls, and are developing their own industries. Neutral markets are diminishing, and our trade there is open to ever severer competition.* —(*b*) That our only hope for the future lies in the Colonial markets, and unless we speedily obtain command of them, they will be captured by the foreign competitor, or become themselves self-sufficient.

15. That it would be to the advantage of the Colonies themselves to make some sacrifice of protection and of revenue for the common object. They would gain by the greater demand for their produce; by shipping it by the trade route protected by the Imperial navy; by exporting it to the country that provides the best and cheapest means of transport, and the greatest and most stable market.

16. (*a*) That our trade with the Colonies is expanding, our trade with foreign countries is contracting.†—(*b*) That the British Possessions already take two-fifths of our total exports;† and at the present rate of development the Colonial will soon exceed the Foreign trade. Trade follows the flag. That preferential duties would therefore encourage the most valuable and the most hopeful part of our external trade.

17. (*a*) That the Colonies buy far more from us in pro-

* See *Protection* and *Retaliation*.

† See Appendix III., Nos. 2, 9 and 10.

portion to population than foreign countries.*—(b) That their population is growing rapidly, and its prosperity and increase would be accelerated by the preference given to Colonial agriculture.

18. That it is "best to cultivate trade with our own kinsmen and fellow-subjects, who take from us at the present time more than £100,000,000 in manufactured goods. Shall we lose the opportunity for the sake of an attempt to conciliate 300,000,000 of foreigners, who take from us only a few shillings a head?" *

19. (a) That the value of trade is not to be measured only by its volume. The comparative character of the foreign and the colonial trade must also be taken into account. The Colonies take far more in proportion of our manufactured goods, and especially of the most highly manufactured goods. Exports to foreign countries consist, in a larger proportion, of coal and other irreplaceable raw material. Our exports to these protected countries are decreasing in quantity, and deteriorating in their profitable character.—(b) That our exports of manufactures to foreign countries are rapidly diminishing under the development of their own manufactures, aided by their tariffs. Compensation for the loss of foreign trade must be found in larger Colonial trade.—(c) That "the exports of our manufactured goods to our own Colonies, including India, equal the total exports of our manufactured goods to all the protected states in Europe and the United States of America."

20. (a) That it is better to cultivate the trade with our own people than to let it go in order to keep the trade of those who are our competitors and rivals.—(b) That the more we buy from British possessions the more they will buy in

* Total white population of the self-governing Colonies eleven million; or about £5, 10s. per head of our imports to them, amounting to about £60,000,000.

return, whereas the gold we pour into foreign countries helps to foster and develop the very industries which are competing with ours more successfully every day.

21. (*a*) That any loss of foreign trade involved by the change would be very much more than made up by increased Colonial trade.—(*b*) That there would be no reason why our export foreign trade need be adversely affected.

22. (*a*) That while our foreign trade is stationary, there are infinite possibilities in our Colonial trade.—(*b*) That every article that we now obtain from abroad could be produced within the Empire, which might be made self-supporting and self-sufficient. The Empire is so wide in area, its products are so various, its climates so different, that there is absolutely nothing which is necessary to our existence, hardly anything which is desired as a luxury, which cannot be produced within the borders of the Empire itself.—(*c*) That the Mother country, at least, through the development of the Colonies, could be made entirely independent of foreign food or foreign raw material.

23. That preferential treatment of the Colonies would greatly develop their national resources, by giving them a larger and preferential market for their producers. Thus, not only would their prosperity be increased, but they would become far better customers for our goods.

24. (*a*) That the scheme involves not the mere exchange of a definite quantity of one trade for a definite quantity of another, but a scheme for the stimulation of every industry within the Empire. A preference given to Canadian corn, for instance, would mean an enormous influx of settlers into Canada. These settlers will want furniture of every kind for their houses, tools and machines of every sort for their farms, tram lines and electric light for their new towns, railways to bring them in touch with their markets.—(*b*) That these wants would far exceed the power or the capacity of

the Colonial manufacturer to supply, and would be supplied by the United Kingdom.

25. That the whole of the Colonial trade in articles which we can supply, and which are at present supplied by the foreigner, amounting to many millions a year, would, in consequence of the preference, be absorbed by the British producer.*

26. That experience shows that a preference does advantage trade. The Canadian preference given to British goods since 1897 has not only stopped the decline in British imports, but has largely increased them. A similar system applied to other parts of the Empire would lead to similar or even more satisfactory results.†

27. That neither the English manufacturer nor the English consumer would suffer from a system of preferential tariffs. It is not proposed to tax raw materials; and the necessary taxation on food stuffs would be compensated for by reduction in the existing taxation on other articles of consumption.

28. (*a*) That the English manufacturer would greatly benefit, for he would have a larger and ever-increasing market for his goods consequent on the increased prosperity of the export trade to the Colonies.—(*b*) That the working man would likewise benefit from the increased trade and consequent employment that would ensue.

29. That "even if the price of food is raised, the rate of wages will certainly be raised in greater proportions." ‡

30. (*a*) That the cheaper the staple food the lower is the minimum of wages that the poorest class of labour will accept, and *vice versâ.*—(*b*) That wages in Germany have

* See Appendix III., No. 11.

† The rebate is now one of 33⅓ per cent. on goods from the United Kingdom. The imports from the United Kingdom in 1897 were £6,000,000; in 1902 they were £10,100,000. See note, p. 43; also P.P. 310 of 1903.

‡ Mr Chamberlain, letter, 3rd June 1903.

increased under protection, and in the United States are very high.—(*c*) (By some) That the taxation derived from the foreign imports of food could be applied to the benefit of working men in the form of old age pensions, or in some other way.

31. (*a*) That the preference need not involve any very heavy duty on food-stuffs; a small preference would be sufficient to stimulate Colonial production and gradually to substitute for foreign imports.—(*b*) That there is no proposal to restore the old corn law; half the supply of corn (Colonial and home) would be free, and an abundant food-supply would be secured.—(*c*) That the proposal is not to raise the price of wheat, but to stimulate the production of wheat within the Empire, on areas most peculiarly adapted to its cheap production on a large scale. The development and organisation of the wheat industry in Canada would probably lead to a fall rather than a rise in the price of wheat.

32. That, while it cannot be stated with certainty on whom falls the burden of a particular indirect tax, it is certain that the main portion of an import duty (such as this) falls not on the consumer, but to a large extent is distributed between the foreign producer, the foreign importer, and the various middlemen.*

33. (*a*) That, while it is true that "if we are to give a preference to the Colonies we must put a tax on food," † the taxation levied from corn and from meat could be counterbalanced by the remission of taxation on other articles of consumption which are already taxed (tea, coffee, cocoa, sugar, currants, etc., as well as tobacco), to the extent of £25,000,000 a year.—(*b*) That thus, for instance, "if a working-man were called upon to pay 3d. a week additional on the cost of his

* This, it is argued, was the case in regard to the Corn Duty of 1902. See, however, Cd. 1761, pp. 124-26.

† Mr Chamberlain, House of Commons, 29th May 1903.

bread, he might be relieved by a reduction of a similar amount in the cost of his tea, his sugar, or his tobacco. What was taken out of one pocket would be put into another." *

34. That by a duty upon corn, we should be making the foreigner contribute to the revenue; and by simultaneous relief on other articles of consumption, we should be benefiting the producers of tea and other commodities in the British Colonies and Dependencies.

35. (*a*) That even if the scheme involved an actual net tax on food, it would be worth the doing, with a view to knit the Empire together, to extend trade, and to enlarge commerce.—(*b*) That by encouraging the interchange of British manufactured products for Colonial agricultural products, it would stimulate Colonial farming, direct the stream of emigration to our own Colonies, and so hasten the time when the Empire would be competent to feed itself, and it would be no longer necessary to maintain the tax on food.

36. That dependence on foreign sources for our own food supplies is inexpedient; and would be very dangerous in time of war, when corn might be declared a contraband of war and could not be imported in neutral bottoms.

37. (*a*) That the home agricultural interest, which has admittedly been most injured by the policy of free imports, would be greatly stimulated and benefited by the taxation

* Taxation of Food (not including intoxicants). (Ann St.)

	Gross Amount of Duty received.	Taxation per head of population.
	£	s. d.
Coffee and Chicory	229,427	0 1¼
Cocoa	258,030	0 1½
Tea	6,361,016	3 0¼
Sugar	5,974,068	2 10
Dried Fruits	445,217	0 2½
Total Food	13,267,758	6 3½
Tobacco	12,398,168	5 10¾
Total Food and Tobacco	25,665,926	12 2¼

of foreign food stuffs.—(*b*) That thousands of acres would be brought back into cultivation.—(*c*) That the continuing immigration of the population from the country into the towns, with all its attendant evils—social, economic, moral, and physical—would be stayed.

38. That the old system of Colonial preference was founded on a totally different basis to the scheme now proposed, and forms no precedent nor analogy.

On the other hand, it is contended :—

1. That all are in favour of knitting together more closely the Colonies and the Mother country, and are prepared to make sacrifices with that object in view.

2. (*a*) That fiscal union is not necessarily a part of Imperial Federation.—(*b*) That the best links are those based on the consciousness of kinship, of common blood, of pride of race, and of history; links that unite without galling.—(*c*) That, under this system, the Empire has become stronger, wealthier, more united, has grown and flourished prodigiously. There is nothing in the present conditions to warrant the belief that the Empire is on the verge of dissolution, or that it requires the adoption of a new fiscal system to keep it together.

3. (*a*) That instead of making for Imperial unity, a system of preferential duties would embitter and strain the harmonious relations now happily subsisting between the different parts of the Empire.—(*b*) That, at present, each self-governing Colony, as well as the Mother country, enjoys complete independence and freedom of action in fiscal, financial, commercial, and industrial legislation. Once make the fiscal system of the Empire inter-dependent, this freedom would disappear, and the interests of the different parts of the Empire would come into collision.

4. That an arrangement which would bind us to admit Colonial goods into our markets on equal terms with our own producers, while English goods were refused admission to the Colonial markets on equal terms with their own producers, would be manifestly unfair. The scheme would be unworkable; an Imperial fiscal system cannot be based at the same time on free trade and on protection.

5. That to associate the Colonies with a tax on food, to connect them with hardship, privation, and discontent, would render them a grievous burden in the eyes of the English people; and thus the Imperial sentiment, and even the unity of the Empire, would be greatly endangered.

6. (*a*) That the proposal of preferential rates is mainly based on business grounds, and must be judged from that point of view; namely, whether the price that would have to be paid is greater than the mutual benefits which would accrue.—(*b*) That the Colonies are asking of us infinitely more than they are prepared to grant to us. A change in our free import policy is of far greater consequence to us than any fiscal change can be to the Colonies. Their grant of preference does not touch their supplies of food or raw material. Our grant of preference would directly affect the whole of our population in the matter of food. The interests of 40,000,000 of people would be sacrificed to the interests of 11,000,000.

7. (*a*) That the object, and the result of the adoption by Germany of a "Zollverein" was the abolition of all internal barriers to trade. Germany is a free trade nation as regards its 58,000,000 of inhabitants, and over its whole area, which is twice the size of the United Kingdom.—(*b*) That, similarly, the United States is the greatest free trade nation in the world; there is absolute free trade between its 80,000,000 of people, and over an area of the size of Europe.

8. (*a*) That the German Zollverein has been of immense

political, fiscal, and financial advantage to Germany, by freeing and increasing internal trade, and by consolidating and unifying the interests of the different parts of the German Empire. It has done much to counteract the disadvantages of protection.—(*b*) That, similarly, the internal free trade of the United States, combined with her natural advantages of climate, soil, minerals, and water, has enabled her trade to develop enormously in spite of her protective system.

9. That a real Zollverein, *i.e.* the adoption of absolute free trade within the Empire itself, and the abolition of all internal custom-houses (which might be advantageous), is impracticable. The self-governing Colonies being protectionist, and desiring to foster their own industries, would not consent to the free entry of British goods. Depending also, as they do, on customs duties (chiefly on British goods) for their revenue, they could not afford to relinquish these duties.

10. (*a*) That while a Zollverein, or Customs Union, would constitute a great step in the direction of free trade, preferential and discriminating duties would be essentially protective; and would involve separate bargains of a protective nature with each Colony.—(*b*) That a system of preferential duties, instead of freeing trade, would necessitate the erection of new and additional fiscal barriers to free intercourse.—(*c*) That it would involve great complication of tariff, universal examination of goods, extreme vexation and great loss of time; all of which would tend to the disturbance, dislocation, and injury of trade.—(*d*) That it would be necessary to enquire in each case into the source of origin—a fruitful source of worry, delay, irritation, and fraud.

11. That, at the best, it would merely divert our trade from foreign countries to the Colonies. To divert trade is to diminish trade.

12. (*a*) That not only is the United Kingdom a free trade country, but India and the Crown Colonies, and to a

large extent the South African Colonies also, are on a free trade basis—*i.e.* the taxation is imposed for revenue purposes. The other self-governing Colonies, Canada, Australia, New Zealand, alone are protectionists.—(*b*) That, thus, under a system of preferential tariffs, free trade England and the free trade Colonies would cease to be free trade, while the protectionist Colonies would remain protectionist.

13. That the Empire would cease to be an Empire at fiscal peace with all the world, and would become an Empire bristling with tariffs at every point, brimful of retaliation on the slightest pretext, and an object of hostile attack all over the world.

14. (*a*) That our trade with the Colonies and India represents but a small portion of the whole trade of the country—£220,000,000 out of £870,000,000.*—(*b*) That India takes one-third of our whole Colonial export trade; and being on a free trade basis, has little to gain and much to lose from the introduction of any system of preferential duties.†—(*c*) That the various Crown Colonies have little or nothing to gain from a system of preferential duties.—(*d*) That the protectionist self-governing Colonies (for whose benefit the preferential rates are proposed) represent a total trade with us of about £120,000,000, of which only £60,000,000 represent our exports.—(*e*) That thus our enormous trade of over £870,000,000 is to be disturbed and risked for a problematical advantage to us on a trade of only £60,000,000.‡

15. (*a*) That our trade with Europe is not falling off; and is more progressive than our trade with the Colonies.§ Comparing 1899-1901 with 1896-98, while our exports to continental nations increased 18 per cent., our exports to British possessions only increased 15½ per cent.—(*b*) That

* See Appendix III., Nos. 9 and 10.

† See Debate, House of Lords, 10th January 1903.

‡ See Nos. 21-26.

§ See Appendix III., Nos. 2, 8, 9 and 10.

our foreign trade is of greater importance to us than our Colonial trade. Our exports to Germany, Holland and Belgium alone are double our exports to Australia and Canada.*

16. (*a*) That as is admitted by the preferentialists †—our whole trade would be injured and jeopardised by any alteration in our fiscal system. Trade would be forced out of its natural channels into others, from which less economic advantage would be derived; as we should buy less from foreign countries they would be able to buy less from us; protectionist nations would retaliate and injure us; while the cost of production would be increased.—(*b*) That our foreign trade, our Colonial trade, and our trade with neutral markets, and even our powers of meeting competition in our own markets, would be severely handicapped by the increased cost of production consequent on the increased cost of living, due to the preferential rates.

17. That the taxation of food products would (with the exception of the United States) hit hardest the least protectionist countries—Denmark, Holland, Argentina, etc.,—and injure our considerable trade with them; while our greatest trade rivals, Germany and France, would escape altogether.

18. (*a*) That there would be great danger of reprisals on the part of foreign countries, especially in the case of the United States, who could, if they wished, seriously injure our trade by imposing (for instance) an export duty on cotton, or by prohibiting the export passage of Canadian wheat over her territory.—(*b*) That, in any case, we should lose the immense advantage we at present possess of "most-favoured-nation treatment" applied to our foreign exports, which constitute two-thirds of the whole.

* Exports (1901) to Germany, Belgium, and Holland, £60,600,000; to Canada (9) and Australia (24), £33,000,000.

† "You must promote Colonial Trade with the Mother country by means of Preferential Tariff . . . even, if by doing so, we lessen somewhat the trade with our Foreign Competitors."—*Mr Chamberlain.*

19. That if we place a duty on foreign food-stuffs for the benefit of the Colonies, we shall have relinquished all power of utilising, in our commercial negotiations, or for purpose of Retaliation, the most effective (in some cases the only) weapon in our armoury—the taxation of food stuffs.* A food-tax cannot be utilised both for Preference and for Retaliation. For Preference it is necessarily permanent, for successful Retaliation it is necessarily temporary.

20. (*a*) That the home trade is more important to the prosperity of the country than its external trade. To raise the food bill of the whole population of 40,000,000 must diminish their purchasing power on every other article, and exercise an injurious effect on the vast internal trade of the country.—(*b*) That the social system of the country has grown up under the policy of free imports of food and raw material. Any radical alteration would injuriously affect many classes, and especially the poorest and most struggling.

21. (*a*) That the great bulk of the internal trade of the Empire is already done with the mother country;† and being carried on largely on a free trade basis, while it might possibly be diminished, it would not be increased by any protectionist device.—(*b*) That our exports to our self-governing Colonies are increasing rapidly and satisfactorily under the present system. It is best to leave well alone.

22. (*a*) That neither the present capabilities, nor the possible future development of the self-governing Colonies of Australia and Canada, give promise of greatly enlarged capacity for the purchase of British goods.—(*b*) That Canada, great though her fertility, is ice-bound for a considerable portion of the year, and is not capable of indefinite development.—(*c*) That Australia, through lack of water, and in

* See Appendix III., No. 13.

† See Appendix III., Nos. 9 and 10.

consequence of droughts, can never be more than a populated fringe of a great continent.

23. (*a*) That the foreign trade of the self-governing Colonies is comparatively small, and the bulk of it is in articles which we do not, and cannot produce, such as wine, tobacco, oil, or raw materials and food stuffs. These deducted, the amount left of foreign imports which could be replaced by English goods is not great; * and is infinitesimal compared to our whole trade.—(*b*) That, therefore, even if English goods were admitted free into the Colonies, the amount of additional Colonial trade that could be won is small.

24. (*a*) That both workmen and employers in Canada and Australia are strongly protectionist, and there is not the least intention on their part to admit British goods free, or other than at duties sufficiently heavy effectually to protect their own manufactures.—(*b*) That under the so-called "Canadian preference," Canadian manufactures still enjoy a protection of 24 per cent. over English goods; and Canada is not prepared to give any further substantial concessions.—(*c*) That Australia and New Zealand have specifically declared that they cannot reduce their very high protective tariff directed against British goods, and that all they can do is still further to penalise foreign competitive goods.—(*d*) That, indeed, all these Colonies depend so largely on their Customs for their revenue, that they could not afford appreciably to lower their tariff.†

25. (*a*) That "preference" such as this is of little practical advantage to the English producer. Our competition in Colonial markets is not so much with the foreign importer as with the Colonial producer. The displaced foreign trade would be absorbed by the Colonial, and not by the English manufacturer.—(*b*) That, indeed, as a result of the increased cost of production, here consequent on the

* See Appendix III., No. 11. † See P.P. 299 of 1903.

tax on food, and probably on raw materials, the home manufacturer would be in a worse position than before to compete in Colonial markets, either with the foreign or Colonial competitor.—(*c*) That, further, the object of each protectionist Colony in fostering its own industries, is to become in time self sufficient, or even to become exporters. Even if at first, therefore, the British manufacturer were able to increase his Colonial trade, he would eventually be driven out of the Colonial market; and, meanwhile, he would have jeopardised or lost his foreign market.

26. That the one concrete case—namely the preference given by Canada to British goods—has not produced any material effect in increasing our Colonial trade, though it has been in force for five years, and has been carried out under favourable auspices, and without any disturbing influences.*

27. That it is not therefore probable that our export trade to the Colonies would be greatly promoted; while the whole foreign trade of the country would be disturbed and proportionately diminished; and, at the same time, we should be called upon to pay a heavy tax on our food (and probably raw materials) for the benefit of the Colonies.

28. (*a*) That it would pass the wit of man to devise a scheme of preferential treatment that would be equitable and workable as between ourselves and the Colonies, and between the Colonies themselves.—(*b*) That the interests of all the different parties to the arrangement, and of their respective industries, are diverse, conflicting, and often antagonistic. A preference given on one article from one Colony might be disadvantageous to another Colony or to

* While the total amount of the exports from the United Kingdom to Canada have somewhat increased since the grant of preference, their proportionate amount to the whole Canadian imports has fallen from 27.58 per cent. in 1897 to 24.95 in 1902. There was a greater increase of trade with foreign countries than with Great Britain. "The substantial results have been altogether disappointing."—*Mr Chamberlain*, Colonial Conference, 1902, and see P.P. 310 of 1903.

another trade, a duty imposed on some other article (raw material, for instance) might be disastrous to the mother country.—(*c*) That the basis of preferential treatment is equality of gains and losses; a fiscal bargain impossible to make between a country which was seeking to increase its exports of manufactures, and a country which was chiefly concerned to protect its industries from competition.

29. (*a*) That any scheme or preferential treatment would involve a series of bargains with the Colonies, a process of haggling and wrangling in which each party would be trying to get the most from, and to give the least to, each other.—(*b*) That not only would there be disputes in each case whether the equivalent either party received was sufficient, but each colony would question whether what it was to receive were equal in value to that granted to the others. Friction, discontent, ill-will, and disunion would ensue.—(*c*) That there would be no central authority to whom appeals could be made, and who could, in the last resort, authoritatively decide the rights of the case and the points of issue.

30. That if a particular Colony refused to grant a preference, or only gave a preference less advantageous than that granted to the Mother country by some other Colony, it would be necessary, in order to give equality of treatment, to have a different and less favourable scale of preference applied to her goods. The tariff would become absolutely unworkable.

31. (*a*) That the divers and conflicting interests of the various home trades affected (and in the Colonies the interest of their home trades) would be almost impossible of adjustment.—(*b*) That by adhering to free trade, the Executive have been able to avoid having to deal with extremely difficult and irritating problems concerning the interests of competing industries in this country, and concerning the conflicting interests of the different Colonies.

32. That the introduction of a preferential system would in the end inevitably lead to a system of "protection." Each trade, in which the cost of production, consequent on the preferential duties, had been increased without any corresponding benefit, would claim, and justly claim, beneficial treatment also. Thus first one, and then another trade, would receive a preference, and finally all trades would be protected.*

33. (*a*) That the preference once given, the step, as far as this country is concerned, is irrevocable, and would only be reversed at the risk of disruption. Vested Colonial and home interests would have been encouraged to grow up, and whatever the circumstances, and the necessity and urgency of repeal, they would command the situation.—(*b*) That yet there could be no security nor permanency in the arrangement. A change of view, or a change of Government, in Australia or Canada, might withdraw them from the arrangement, with but little disturbance to their trade. But England would have ceased to be a free trade country, would have lost much foreign trade, and would remain saddled with a tax on food.

34. (*a*) That it is admitted, that "if you are to give a preference to the Colonies, you must put a tax on food."† For in order to give an effective preference to Colonial food imports, and in order to obtain the revenue necessary for other fiscal purposes, or dependent social reforms (and certainly if the scheme is to bring land back under cultivation), a "considerable duty" must be imposed on foreign corn, meat and dairy produce, etc.—(*b*) That however low the duties might be fixed at first, they (like all protective duties) would be certain to be gradually raised on the ground that they were not sufficiently effective.

35. (*a*) That as foreign food stuffs represent 75 per cent.

* See sections, *Protection* and *Retaliation*.

† Mr Chamberlain, House of Commons, 29th May 1903.

of our food supplies, a tax on their import would raise their price, and correspondingly the price of all Colonial imports and home-grown food.*—(*b*) That, thus, the amount taken out of the pockets of the consumer would be far greater than the benefit accruing to the Colonies, or than the amount received by the Exchequer.† Further, the more the plan were successful, the less would be the proportionate receipt from the duty, though the aggregate burden on the community would remain the same.

36. (*a*) That the rise in the price of food consequent on the duty, would increase the cost of living, and wages, salaries, or income, would purchase less than they did before. Thus all classes would be worse off, and the increased cost of living would fall severely upon the working and lower middle classes.—(*b*) That those millions who now just manage to subsist on a living wage would be put to much hardship and suffering; the margin which exists between them and absolute want would be broken down.

37. (*a*) That there is no reason why dearer food should be followed, either immediately, or at any time, by a general rise in wages or salaries—they are indeed more likely to fall.—(*b*) Why, when, where, at what point, and to what extent, and how, would wages rise because of the increase in the cost of living? Where is the fund to come from, which would enable the increased wages to be paid?—(*c*) That, in any case, no immediate rise of wages, even in

* See Appendix III., No. 4.

† A charge of 5s. a cwt. on foreign wheat would produce £5,100,000, in taxation; besides this, the price of Colonial wheat consumed here would be enhanced by £1,229,000, and that of home-grown wheat by about £2,000,000. Thus the English consumer would pay £8,320,000 additional for his bread, while the Exchequer would only gain £5,100,000, and the Colonial grower only £1,220,000.

Further, if a moderate duty were placed on foreign meat and dairy stuff, it would cost the people of the United Kingdom some £11,000,000, a year, of which the Exchequer would only receive £4,200,000, while the gain to the Colonial importers would be but £850,000, a year.

the benefited trades, could take place. Development of trade is a slow process.

38. (*a*) That even if the prosperity of a few trades, especially interested in Colonial commerce, were promoted, the other export industries (representing an infinitely larger trade), would not be in any way benefited; but would, by the general dislocation of trade, and by the increased cost of production, be materially injured.—(*b*) That the home trade could not be benefited by the preferential tariffs; while its general prosperity would be checked by the diminished power of purchase, and the increased cost of production.—(*c*) That the prosperity of the shipping trade, and these directly or indirectly interested in it, is absolutely dependent on the low cost at which ships can be built, combined with free access and free exchange, free imports and free exports. Any diversion of or obstruction to trade would seriously cripple this great industry.

39. (*a*) That none of the working classes, men or women, employed in the various home trades—builders, miners, stevedores, dock labourers, carriers, busmen, gas-workers, &c., &c.—could hope to receive increased wages; these trades would be unaffected by the preferential duties.—(*b*) That the lower middle class—the clerks, men and women, those employed by business firms, &c., &c.—where wages and salaries are kept down by acute competition, could not hope to obtain any general or individual increase.—(*c*) That there would be no valid reason why the wages or salaries of those employed by Government, by municipalities, by public bodies, by the railways, by public companies, &c., should rise. Or if they were to rise, the taxpayer, the ratepayer, the shareholder would suffer doubly.—(*d*) That the tradesman, the middleman, &c., would not be able to increase their profits to cover the increased cost of living; or if they did, the customer would doubly suffer.

40. (*a*) That the wages would either remain the same, go up or go down. If they went down, the workmen would be in a sorry plight. If wages remained the same, the employer would be paying the same wage for an inferior article of labour; for corn and meat are the raw material of labour, and labour less well nurtured is less efficient and economical labour. On the other hand, if wages were to go up correspondingly to the increased cost of living, the employer would be paying more for an article of labour equal only to that which he was receiving before.—(*b*) That thus, unless wages go down, the cost of production must go up.—(*c*) That, already, competition, abroad, at home, and in the Colonies, in protected and in neutral markets, is very severe, and any increase in the cost of production would greatly handicap the British manufacturer and producer, and seriously injure trade all round.—(*d*) The employer therefore would not be in a position to increase wages, and in most cases he would be obliged to reduce them.

41. That it is doubtful, therefore, whether, in *any* trade, wages would rise in consequence of preferential rates, while it is certain that in the overwhelming majority of cases they would not rise; and that in very many cases they would fall; * while in every case the cost of living would be increased.

42. (*a*) That wages in Germany (where the cost of food is higher than in England) are lower than in England, while the hours are longer; of late, too, wages have fallen there.—(*b*) That wages in the United States are higher than here, but the cost of food is even lower there than in England.

43. That the demand for increased wages on the part of the men to enable them to bear the increased cost of living,

* "A tax on food would mean a decline in wages. It would certainly involve a reduction in their productive value."—*Mr Chamberlain*, House of Commons, 12th August 1881. See Cd. 1761, pp. 259–293.

or their resistance to a demand on the part of their employers for a reduction of wages in order to enable them to reduce the cost of production, would give rise to far-reaching industrial disputes and injury to trade.

44. (*a*) That no relief of taxation on tea, sugar and tobacco would be an equivalent offset to the hardships involved by the taxation of bread or meat. Bread and meat are indispensable and primary commodities of universal consumption, and form the staple and essential articles of food of the great mass of the people.—(*b*) The poorer the family, the more the food tax would affect them. Their expenditure on bread constitutes a irreducible minimum that should not be touched by taxation; and the suffering that would be caused to them by an increase in the cost of the necessities of life could not be relieved by any reduction in the cost of their luxuries.

45. (*a*) That as the tax on food-stuffs would raise their cost to the consumer to a far greater extent than it would benefit the revenue, the relief that would possibly be given by corresponding remission of other taxation, could not represent more than a portion of the whole burden involved.* —(*b*) That if the preferential policy were successful, the Colonies would ultimately provide all the food-stuffs we require, and the revenue derived from the tax on foreign imports, which is to be utilised for the remission of the tea, sugar and tobacco duties, would disappear. The tea, sugar and tobacco duties would have again to be imposed; while the cost of food-stuffs would continue to be enhanced by the preferential duty which would have still to be maintained in order to continue to protect the Colonies.

46. That, in any case, the country was entitled to look to the remission of the tea and sugar duties at some future time, in the ordinary course, without any offset.

* See No. 35, and note.

47. (*a*) That any system of preferential tariff would not only involve a duty on food-stuffs, but, whatever the original intention, would inevitably lead to a duty also on the raw material of manufacture—wool, cotton, iron, timber, &c. —(*b*) That each Colony produces some considerable article of commerce distinct from the other Colonies. A preference given on one particular article (for instance, corn), while advantageous to Canada, would be no advantage to the Cape. Yet each Colony can justly claim equal consideration, and some particular article that she produces in abundance must receive preferential treatment. Preferential treatment cannot therefore be confined to food-stuffs.*

48. (*a*) That when once the principle of preferential treatment is agreed to, each particular Colony and the dominant interests in it, would have the controlling voice in deciding which of her products should be favoured; we could not dictate to her in the matter.—(*b*) That Australia and South Africa would claim, and justly claim, preference on their wool and their hides; India and some of the Crown Colonies, a preference on their cotton or their sugar; some of the other Colonies a preference on their wood, etc.* —(*c*) That each industry would expect to be equally advantaged. The Australian wool-merchant is as much entitled to preference as the Canadian wheat-grower.—(*d*) That thus, in order to carry out the policy of equitable preference, a tax on the raw material of manufacture of our staple industries would be absolutely inevitable; and it is generally admitted that to impose duties on the raw materials of manufacture would be disastrous to our trade, and especially to the cotton, woollen and iron industries.

49. That the agricultural interest which has been most severely injured by the policy of free imports, would have nothing to gain from preferential duties, the object of which

* See Appendix III. No. 12.

is merely to transpose free Colonial for free foreign food-stuffs.

50. That the introduction of a preferential system would necessitate a policy of retaliation on foreign countries.*

51. That the system of Colonial preference that formerly prevailed was admittedly injurious to the Colonies as well as to the Mother country.

51. That it is very questionable whether it would not constitute a grave danger in time of war to have our food supplies concentrated in British hands. A large foreign importer (say the United States) would be less inclined to admit that food-stuffs were "contraband of war" if she were largely interested in supplying Great Britain.

52. That (to sum up) a system of trade preference would be disastrous. On political grounds—for it would lead to friction and misunderstandings and disputes between various parts of the Empire, tending to disintegration rather than to consolidation. On economic grounds—the possible trade to be won is infinitesimal, while the rest of the trade of the Empire would be dislocated and diminished. On social grounds—inasmuch as the cost of living would be increased, and the position of the working and struggling classes would be worsened.

[Some would argue that the Colonies might of themselves well grant certain preferences to British goods, as a contribution to the cost of the Empire, now almost entirely borne by Great Britain, without asking for any equivalent from the Mother country.]

* See *Retaliation*.

APPENDICES

APPENDIX I.

PRIME MINISTERS SINCE 1783.

DATE.	
Dec. 1783	WILLIAM PITT
March 1801	HENRY ADDINGTON (LORD SIDMOUTH)
May 1804	WILLIAM PITT
Feb. 1806	LORD GRENVILLE (*W.*)
March 1807	DUKE OF PORTLAND (*T.*)
Nov. Dec. 1809	SPENCER PERCIVAL (*T.*)
May June 1812	EARL OF LIVERPOOL (*T.*)
April 1827	GEORGE CANNING
Aug. 1827	VISCOUNT GODERICH (EARL OF RIPON) (*W.*)
Jan. 1828	DUKE OF WELLINGTON (*T.*)
Nov. 1830	EARL GREY (*W.*)
May 1832	* ,,
July 1834	VISCOUNT MELBOURNE (*W.*)
Dec. 1834	SIR ROBERT PEEL (*T.*)
April 1835	VISCOUNT MELBOURNE (*W.*)
Aug. 1839	* ,, ,,
Sept. 1841	SIR ROBERT PEEL (*T.*)
Dec. 1845	* ,, ,,
July 1846	LORD JOHN RUSSELL (EARL RUSSELL) (*W.*)
March 1851	,, ,,
Feb. 1852	EARL OF DERBY (*T.*)
Dec. 1852	EARL OF ABERDEEN (Coalition, *W.* and Peelite)
March 1855	VISCOUNT PALMERSTON (*W.*)
Oct. 1865	EARL RUSSELL (*W.*)
July 1866	EARL OF DERBY (*C.*)
Feb. 1868	BENJAMIN DISRAELI (*C.*)
Dec. 1868	W. E. GLADSTONE (*L.*)
Aug. 1873	* ,, ,,
Feb. 1874	B. DISRAELI (EARL OF BEACONSFIELD) (*C.*)
April 1880	W. E. GLADSTONE (*L.*)
July 1885	MARQUESS OF SALISBURY (*C.*)
Jan. 1886	W. E. GLADSTONE (*L.*)
July 1886	MARQUESS OF SALISBURY (*C.*)
Aug. 1892	W. E. GLADSTONE (*L.*)
March 1894	EARL OF ROSEBERY (*L.*)
June 1895	MARQUESS OF SALISBURY (*U.*)
Aug. 1902	ARTHUR BALFOUR (*U.*)

T=Tory. *W*=Whig. *C*=Conservative. *L*=Liberal. *U*=Unionist.

* Resigned, but again took Office.

APPENDIX II.

WORKMAN'S COMPENSATION ACT.

THE Workman's Compensation for Accidents Act was passed in 1897; and it may be of use to many for their own information, or to enable them to advise working men in regard to its provisions, if they are shortly summarised.

The benefits of the Act were, in 1900, extented to agricultural labourers; and in 1901 to those employed in loading and unloading ships in midstream. These two additions are included in the following summary.

I.—PERSONS ENTITLED TO ITS BENEFITS.

All persons, male or female, who receive injuries by accident; whether employed by the Government, or private persons, or Companies in any of the employments mentioned below.

It does not matter upon what terms they have been engaged, or how long they are engaged for, or have been engaged, or whether they are employed for wage, or are apprentices. Not only persons, male or female (adult or child), generally called "workmen," who are engaged in hand labour, are entitled to the benefits of the Act, but also clerks, overlookers, managers, &c.

The persons and employments included in the Act are the following:

1. Railway servants.
2. Workers employed in factories, and in all places which come under the provisions of the Factory Act. But workshops are not included.
3. Workers employed in mines, quarries, or engineering work.

4. Those employed (other than the crew) in docks, wharfs, quays, or warehouses; and (other than the crew) in loading and unloading ships.

5. Workers constructing, altering, or repairing railroads, harbours, docks, canals, or sewers, or any other work of the same kind, if steam, water, or other mechanical power is used in doing the work.

6. Workers on, in, or about a building of any kind which is more than thirty feet high, and in which scaffolding is used in constructing, repairing, or demolishing it.

7. Those employed in agriculture.

II.—The Kind of Accidents Compensated.

Every kind of personal injury by accident (serious enough to incapacitate him for more than two weeks) met with in the course of the workman's employment, entitles the workman injured to compensation. The injured man has merely to prove that he was working at one of the employments named, and that somehow, no matter how, whether any one was to blame for it or not, he was injured. The only exception is if the accident was caused by the injured man's own wilful misconduct, such action abrogates his own claim to compensation; but the claim to compensation of any other persons injured by his misconduct is not affected.

Moreover, the employer is liable, although the injury may be caused by the fault of a fellow-workman of the man who is injured. What is known in the law of Master and Servant and under the Employers' Liability Act as the rule of "common employment," disappears. When a workman is injured in the course of his employment by a workman of another employer, he can either obtain the Compensation this Act gives him from his own employer, or he can sue the other employer to recover any damages for which he may be liable at law. He must choose between these two courses.

Any accident for which compensation is claimed must be of a sufficiently serious nature to prevent the injured man working at full wages for two weeks; and the right to compensation does not begin until two weeks after the accident.

III.—The Amount of Compensation Secured.

1. In case of *death*.

Where the workman leaves any members of his family *wholly* dependent upon him, £150 is the lowest, and 156 times his weekly average wage up to £300, is the highest sum he can claim in compensation, whichever of the two, £150 or 156 times the weekly wage, is the larger.*

Dependants mean the wife, husband, parent, or child of the deceased. If only a wife or husband is left, all the compensation would go to that one. If the deceased left a parent and a child as well, the money would be divided between them either by agreement or as the arbitrator might decide; and he may order it to be invested according to circumstances for the benefit of any infant or child of the deceased. If the members of the family of the deceased were only partly dependant on his earnings, or if he had no dependants, the arbitrator (in case of dispute) is to decide the amount that should be given.

2. In case of an *injury* preventing work, either totally or partially.

The injured workman is secured in a weekly payment (after the first two weeks) up to half his average weekly earnings. But the amount must not exceed £1 per week.†

This payment is to be continued so long as his partial or total incapacity for work lasts.

These weekly payments may be altered by mutual agreement, or under arbitration, upon good reason being shown by either employer or workman. After twelve months, upon the application of either the employer or the workman, a lump sum may be fixed instead of the weekly payment, either by agreement, or by the arbitrator, and when this sum is paid to the workman the weekly payments cease.

All compensation money must be paid to the workman or to

* For instance, if the wages were 30s., a claim for £234 (156 × 30s.) could be made, but if the wages were 50s. only £300, and not £390 (156 × 50s.) could be claimed.

† For instance, if his wages had been 20s. a week he would receive 10s. a week during incapacity; if 40s. he would receive 20s., but if the wages had been over 40s., he would still receive only 20s.

his dependants; no one else can be given the right to receive the money, and it cannot be seized for debts. Under any and all circumstances it is the workman's own. In the case of the bankruptcy of an employer who has insured against his liabilities under this Act, the Insurance Company is made responsible to the injured workman, and the employer's creditors have on claim on the sum.

After notice has been given of the accident, the employer may require the workman to allow himself to be examined by a medical man employed and paid for by the employer.

The same rule applies during the period of weekly payments.

IV.—How to Proceed to Obtain Compensation.

Notice.—Notice of the accident must be given as soon as possible to the employer, whether he knows of it or not, and must be given before the workman has left his employment of his own accord. The notice must be sent, and sent promptly.

The notice must state (1) the name and address of the person injured; (2) the date when the accident happened; (3) what caused the accident.

By Agreement.—When the employer receives the notice, he may offer a certain sum, and it is for the workman, or for his dependants if the workman has been killed, to decide whether they will accept this offer or not.

Where there is no agreement, the matter must be decided by an *Arbitrator*, who is usually the County Court Judge.

In any event, it is not necessary to employ a lawyer; a workman can act for himself, or can appoint any one else to act as his agent, and whoever so acts, even though it be a solicitor, can only claim fees according to a fixed scale and at the discretion of the arbitrator.

If the workman himself claims (1) if he is unable to work at all owing to his injuries, he must state that, while he so continues unable to work, he requires to be paid half the amount of the weekly wages he was earning before the accident; or, (2) if he has returned to work, a sum equal to the amount of half his weekly wages for the number of weeks during which he was unable to work. If he has been earning partial wages during the time he was suffering from the injury, he must deduct their amount from the full wages he earned at the time when he was injured, and claim half of the balance.

When it is the dependants who are claiming, they must say whether it is the £150 they claim, or whether it is 156 times the weekly wage, or if it is £300.

V.—Contracting out of the Act.

An employer cannot say, "If you wish to be employed by me, or to continue being employed, you must agree that you will give up your right to be compensated under the Act." An employer, whether it be the Government, a Company, or a private employer, must, if desirous that their men should contract out of the Act, provide some other scheme of compensation or benefit not less favourable to the workmen and their dependants than the benefits under the Compensation Act. No contracting-out scheme is legal which requires a workman to join it as a condition of his employment. The judge as to the benefits of the scheme is the Registrar of Friendly Societies, who is accustomed to decide on similar matters; and there can be no contracting out before he has given a certificate that the workmen will be at least as well off under the voluntary scheme as they would have been under the Act.

The certificate lasts for five years.

It is proposed that the provisions of the Compensation Act should be extended generally to all trades and industries, and to all classes of workmen, on the ground that each workman in any trade is as much entitled as his brother workmen in another trade, to receive compensation for injury; and that it is equally to the public weal that he should so receive compensation.

On the other hand, it is conceded that no principle is now involved; and that the provisions of the Act must ultimately (with perhaps some necessary modifications) be extended to all trades and industries. The extension of the operation of the Act is merely a question of time and of opportunity.

"FAIR WAGES" RESOLUTION *

As the above Resolution is often referred to, it may be useful to give its text. On 13th February 1891, the House unanimously resolved :—

"That in the opinion of this House, it is the duty of the Government in all Government contracts to make provision against the evils recently disclosed before the Sweating Committee, to insert such conditions as may prevent the abuse arising from sub-letting, and to make every effort to secure the payment of such wages as are generally accepted as current in each trade for competent workmen."

* I may, perhaps, be permitted to recall the fact that the Resolution was adopted by the House, on a motion moved by myself.

APPENDIX III.

No. 1.

INCOME TAX.

(*From Report of Commissioners of Inland Revenue. Cd.* 1717.)

Gross Income Assessed.		Increase.	Gross Income Schedule D. (Trades and Professions).
1868–69 ...	£398,794,000	£145,500,000*	£173,054,000*
1875–76 ...	544,376,000		271,973,000*
1894–95 ...	657,097,000	210,000,000	340,559,000
1901–02 ...	866,993,000		487,731,000

* "Periods of the greatest prosperity."

Estimated Income from certain Investments Abroad.

1881–82, £30,600,000 1891–92, £54,700,000 1901–02, £62,000,000.

("A minimum figure which is probably largely exceeded."—*Board of Trade. Cd.* 1761, p. 103.)

POST OFFICE SAVINGS BANKS.

	1887	1897	1901
No. of Depositors ...	3,952,000	7,240,000	8,788,000
Due to Depositors ...	£54,000,000	£116,000,000	£140,000,000

MERCHANT SHIPPING.

(*From Parliamentary Paper* 290 *of* 1903.)

The total net tonnage of British ships is 11,120,000 tons, against 12,500,000 tons of the Shipping of the principal foreign countries.

The annual tonnage built in the United Kingdom was (in tons) 394,000 in 1870; 473,000 in 1880; 813,000 in 1890; 944,000 in 1900; and 950,500 in 1902.

The tonnage of vessels entered and cleared at Ports in the United Kingdom, was—

	1870	1890	1902
British ...	25,000,000	54,000,000	65,000,000
Foreign ...	11,600,000	20,300,000	35,000,000

No. 2.

TOTAL TRADE UNITED KINGDOM.

(*From Statistical Abstract.*)

	In *Million* £			Per head of Population.	In *Million* £ Excess of Imports over Exports.
	Exports.	Imports.	Total Trade.	£ s. d.	
1860	164	210	374	12 18 0	46
1870	244	303	547	17 10 10	59
1880	286	411	697	20 3 0	125
1887	281	362	643	17 11 8	81
1890	328	420	748	19 19 7	92
1895	286	416	702	17 17 10	130
1897	294	451	745	18 12 4	157
1899	330	485	815	19 19 4	155
1900	354	523	877	21 6 4	169
1901	348	522	870	20 18 9	174
1902	349	528	877	20 18 5	179

Other years will be found in the *Statistical Abstract*, p. 49.

No. 3.

THE YEAR 1873.

The year 1873 is often taken by Protectionists for comparison with other years. But 1873 was a year of enormously inflated prices, higher than any year since 1826, consequent on the ending of the Franco-Prussian War, and on a sudden bubble revival of industry.

If the Imports and Exports of other years are calculated on the basis of the values prevailing in 1873, the following results (the Exports are of domestic produce only) would appear (in *Million* £) :—

	Declared Values of			On approximate basis of Value of 1873.		
	I.	E.	Total.	I.	E.	Total.
1873	371	255	626	371	255	626
1883	426	240	666	526	295	821
1893	405	218	623	611	329	940
1902	528	283	811	797	418	1,215

(From answer, President, Board of Trade, Aug. 12, 1903.)

In other words, the trade of 1892 was double that of 1873; and if the value of the Exports (our sales) has fallen, the value of the Imports (our purchases) has fallen in a still greater proportion.

No. 4.

IMPORTS CLASSIFIED (1902).

1. *Food-stuffs* (Food and Drink)—

From Foreign Countries . .	£179,500,000
,, British Possessions	43,800,000
	£223,300,000
Tobacco . .	5,800,000

2. *Raw Materials*—

From Foreign Countries .	£124,800,000
,, British Possessions . .	51,800,000
	£176,600,000

(Such as cotton, wool, flax, jute, hemp, hides, petroleum, gutta-percha, wood, seeds, iron and metal ores, oil manure, tallow, etc.)

3. *Semi-Manufactured Articles*—

From Foreign Countries .	£19,200,000
,, British Possessions . . .	8,300,000
	£27,500,000

(Such as yarns, unwrought iron and steel, iron pig and puddled, lead pig and sheet, tin blocks, copper wrought and unwrought, leather, etc.)

4. "*Manufactures*"—

	Foreign.	Colonial.	Total.
(i.) *Wholly manufactured material and plant* .	£59,800,000	£3,100,000	£62,900,000

(Such as manufactures of wood, iron and steel, machinery, glass, linen, cotton, woollen and jute goods, leather, chemicals, soap, matches, hats, paper, glue, drugs, cement, etc.)

	Foreign.	Colonial.	Total.
(ii.) *Luxuries*	£28,500,000	£105,000	£28,600,000

(Such as silk, motors, pictures, musical instruments, watches, pipes, books, embroidery, toys, furs, playing cards, lace, beads, curios, etc.)

5. *Miscellaneous*—£3,500,000 (such as horses, ice, cut flowers, plants, and parcels post).

Total Imports, £528,000,000.

EXPORTS CLASSIFIED (1902).

(*From Trade and Navigation Returns, December* 1902.)

I.	Animals, Living	£824,361
II.	Articles of Food and Drink	*16,439,603
III.	Raw Materials	31,171,616
IV.	Articles Manufactured and partly manufactured, viz.:—	
	A. Yarns and Textile Fabrics	103,336,862
	B. Metals and Articles manufactured therefrom (except Machinery and Ships)	42,612,141
	C. Machinery and Mill Work	18,751,812
	D. Ships new (not registered as British)	5,891,775
	E. Apparel and Articles of Personal Use	12,150,371
	F. Chemicals and Chemical and Medicinal Preparations	9,586,728
	G. All other Articles, either Manufactured or partly Manufactured	39,296,233
	H. Parcel Post	3,478,478
	Total Value	£283,539,980

Total Value (as below)	£283,540,000
Foreign and Colonial Merchandise	65,810,000
Total Exports	£349,350,000

* A large proportion of these are manufactured articles.

No. 5.

EXPORTS AND IMPORTS OF SOME SPECIAL MANUFACTURES.

(*From Statistical Abstract.*)

	1887	1901
Woollen Manufactures—		
E.	£20,600,000	£14,200,000
I.	7,700,000	9,580,000
Cotton Manufactures—		
E.	59,600,000	65,700,000
I.	2,280,000	4,780,000
Silk Manufactures—		
E.	2,330,000	1,430,000
I.	10,380,000	13,030,000

EXPORTS AND IMPORTS—*continued.*

	1887	1901
Glass Manufactures—		
E.	£1,020,000	£1,060,000
I.	1,670,000	3,530,000
Furniture, Frame and Woodwork—		
E.	574,000	634,000
I.	488,000	2,280,000
Iron and Steel (wrought and unwrought)—		
E.	25,000,000	25,300,000
I.	3,650,000	11,500,000
Machinery—		
E.	10,600,000	16,300,000
I. . . .	— *	3,600,000
Cutlery—		
E. . .	2,920,000	3,540,000
I.	— *	1,152,000
Leather Manufactures—		
E.	2,470,000	2,770,000
I.	2,245,000	2,237,000
Clocks, Watches and Parts—		
E.	154,000	104,000
I.	1,150,000	2,030,000

* Not separately distinguished in 1887.

No. 6.

IMPORTS OF RAW MATERIALS.

(From Statistical Abstract.)

	1887	1901
Iron Ore (tons) . .	3,760,000	5,550,000
Raw Cotton (lbs.)	*1,500,000,000	*1,623,000,000
Wool (lbs.) . . .	*258,000,000	*398,200,000
Leather (cwt.) . . .	754,000	1,315,000
Indiarubber (cwt.) . .	237,000	466,000
Wood (loads)	5,650,000	9,200,000
Silk (lbs.)	3,010,000	2,000,000
Copper (tons)	200,000	264,000

* Actual amount retained for home consumption.

No. 7.

TOTAL EXPORTS OF DOMESTIC PRODUCE (including Food stuffs, Raw Material, and Manufactures) of CERTAIN COUNTRIES.

(*From Board of Trade Returns. Cd.* 1199 *and* 1761.)

In *Million* £

	U.K.	France	Germany	U.S.A.
1883 .	240 (213)	138 (74)	164 (98)	168 (28)
1885 .	213 (188)	124 (65)	143 (90)	151 (31)
1890 .	263 (228)	150 (80)	166 (107)	176 (31)
1895 .	226 (195)	135 (76)	166 (109)	165 (38)
1900 .	283 (224)	164 (90)	230 (149)	286 (90)
1901 .	271 (221)	160 (90)	222 (144)	304 (86)

(The numbers in brackets represent the respective exports of articles, wholly or partly *manufactured*, of each country.)

EXPORTS AND IMPORTS OF MANUFACTURED ARTICLES FROM AND TO THE U.K.

In *Million* £

	1883	1885	1890	1895	1900	1901	1902
E.	213	188	228	195	224	221	229
I.	53	54	63	76	93	94	99

(The exports, in both the above tables, are exclusive of the value of ships.)

No. 8.

TRADE WITH CERTAIN FOREIGN COUNTRIES, 1902.

(*From Statistical Abstract.*)

In *Million* £

	Imports from	Exports to	Total Trade
Germany ...	34	33	67
Holland ...	35	13	48
Belgium ...	26	13	39
France ...	51	22	73
Russia ...	26	14	40
Denmark ...	16	4	20
United States	127	43	170

(Tables showing our Trade with France, Germany, Holland, and U.S.A., for the last twenty years, will be found in the Board of Trade Return. Cd. 1191, p. 11, etc.)

No. 9.

TOTAL TRADE OF U.K., distinguishing between FOREIGN COUNTRIES AND BRITISH POSSESSIONS.

(*Extracted from Parliamentary Paper* 214 *of* 1903.)

IMPORTS.

In *Million* £

	From Foreign Countries	From British Possessions				Grand Total
		Self-Governing Colonies	India	Others	Total	
Average 1881-85	305	43	36	16	95	400
,, 1886-90	300	42	32	15	89	389
1891	336	50	32	17	99	435
1895	321	52	26	17	95	416
1900	413	62	27	21	110	523
1901	416	60	27	18	106	522
1902	421	60	29	18	107	528

(Bullion and specie excluded from these tables.)

EXPORTS OF BRITISH AND IRISH PRODUCE.

In *Million* £

	To Foreign Countries	To British Possessions				Grand Total
		Self-Governing Colonies	India	Others	Total	
Average 1881-85	151	38	30	13	81	232
,, 1886-90	155	37	32	12	81	236
1891	161	41	31	14	86	247
1895	156	33	25	12	70	226
1900	197	48	30	16	94	291
1901	175	52	35	18	105	280
1902	174	60	33	16	109	283

TOTAL EXPORTS (including Foreign and Colonial Produce).

In *Million* £

	To Foreign Countries	To British Possessions				Grand Total
		Self-Governing Colonies	India	Others	Total	
Average 1881-85	207	42	31	15	88	295
,, 1886-90	210	41	33	14	88	298
1891	216	45	32	16	93	309
1895	210	37	26	13	76	286
1900	252	53	31	18	102	354
1901	235	58	36	19	113	348
1902	232	67	33	17	117	349

No. 10.

TOTAL COLONIAL TRADE.

(*From Parliamentary Paper* 262 *of* 1903.)

The total aggregate Colonial Trade in 1900 was 482 million £—imports 244, and exports 238. Of this (1) imports 117, exports 108—total 225, was with the U.K.; (2) imports 46, exports 43—total 89, was with other British Possessions; and (3) imports 81, exports 87—total, 168, was with Foreign Countries.

(NOTE.—The above figures include bullion and specie, excluded in the previous tables.)

No. 11

TRADE TO BE WON.

(1).

Foreign imports into Self-Governing Colonies, 1901 :—

Canada and Newfoundland . .	£29,300,000
Australia and New Zealand . .	14,500,000
Cape and Natal	5,900,000
	£49,700,000

Of this (roughly) :—

United States sends	£31,000,000
(Mostly raw materials, coal, cotton, metals, etc., food-stuffs, oil, etc.)	
European Countries send . . .	12,000,000
(Largely sugar, oil, wine, etc.)	
Other Countries send	6,700,000
(Chiefly tea and tropical produce.)	
	£49,700,000

(2).

Imports from Foreign Countries into certain Colonies and Dependencies.

(*From Board of Trade Return. No.* 322 *of* 1903.)

	1901. Food and Drink.	Raw Materials.	Manufactures and Semi-Manufactures.
Australia .	£2,315,000	£910,000	£9,211,000
New Zealand .	313,000	58,000	1,647,000
Natal . .	605,000	193,000	756,000
Cape . .	1,930,000	334,000	2,103,000
Canada . .	7,253,000	7,503,000	14,065,000
Newfoundland	268,000	20,000	185,000
Total . .	£12,700,000	£9,000,000	£28,000,000
India . .	3,270,000	1,310,000	9,850,000
Crown Colonies	6,600,000	4,700,000	4,300,000

No. 12.

THE TAXATION OF RAW MATERIALS.

(*From Custom House Return. Cd.* 1617.)

Imports, 1901, from—

	Australia	New Zealand
Wool . . .	£11,500,000	£3,900,000
Skins and Tallow .	1,500,000	880,000
Meat . .	1,900,000	3,500,000
Corn, Butter, Cheese, Fish, etc. .	3,300,000	1,550,000

Imports from—

	Food	Other products
Canada . . .	£13,000,000	£6,800,000
Australia and N.Z.	10,200,000	25,600,000
Cape . . .	...	10,000,000

If preference be limited to food stuffs, Canada would gain on two-thirds of her whole imports to the United Kingdom; New

Zealand would gain on one-half; Australia would gain on a fifth only; and the Cape would not gain at all.

The imports from the Cape (exclusive of gold), are, roughly, £10,000,000, of which about half are diamonds. Of the balance, £3,000,000 is wool, £900,000 feathers, £500,000 skins, and £340,000 copper.

No. 13.

RETALIATION.

(From Custom House Return. Cd. 1617, *and Cd.* 1761.)

(1) Imports from Russia (1902)—

Food-stuffs	£13,500,000
Raw materials	10,000,000
Manufactures (chiefly paper)	290,000
Semi-manufactures	110,000
All other articles	1,770,000
	£25,670,000

(2) Imports from U.S.A (1902)—

Food-stuffs	£62,500,000
Raw materials (chiefly cotton)	45,500,000
Manufactures	9,300,000
Semi-manufactures (chiefly leather)	3,900,000
All other articles	5,800,000
	£127,000,000

Estimated average *ad valorem* equivalent import duties levied by the undermentioned countries on the principal articles of British export from the United Kingdom :—Russia, 131 per cent.; United States, 73; Austria-Hungary, 35; France, 34; Italy, 27; Germany, 25; Belgium, 13.

INDEX